MW00395855

JOSEPH EJERCITO "ERAP" ESTRADA

# The Centennial President

To Judy, John & Family,

Here is hoping you have as much fun reading this book as we had researching and writing it –

Rod & Eleanor

24 August 1998

JOSEPH EJERCITO "ERAP" ESTRADA

# The Centennial President

By Aprodicio and
Eleanor Laquian

Institute of Asian Research
University of British Columbia
Vancouver, B.C., Canada

College of Public Administration
University of the Philippines
Diliman, Quezon City, Philippines

1998

**Canadian Cataloguing in Publication Data**

Laquian, Aprodicio A., 1935-
Joseph Ejercito "Erap" Estrada

ISBN 0-88865-171-6 (bound) -- ISBN 0-88865-173-2 (pbk.)

1. Estrada, Erap. 2. Philippines--Politics and government--1986- 3. Elections--Philippines. 4. Democracy--Philippines. I. Laquian, Eleanor R., 1939- II. University of British Columbia. Institute of Asian Research. III. Title.
DS686.616.E87L36 1998 959.904'8 C98-910634-9

*Para sa mga masang mulat*
(To the empowered Filipino masses)

# CONTENTS

*Opponent's "dirty" tricks on election day saying Erap had backed out of presidential race. Standing L-R, Marita Ejercito, Erap's youngest sister, the Presidential candidate, Pat de Guzman, elder sister and youngest brother Jesse Ejercito. Seated, Mama Mary Ejercito and sister Dr. Pilarica Ejercito*

# ACKNOWLEDGMENT


Early in 1998 , the *Manila Times* and the Ateneo Center for Social Policy and Public Affairs published *Showdown '98 : The Search for the Centennial President.* On 11 May 1998, the Filipino people ended that search by electing Joseph Ejercito "Erap" Estrada as the Centennial President.

But how do you write about the Erap phenomenon? To us, writing this book meant following Erap about the country, joining noisy motorcades, mixing with the crowds in jam-packed rallies and handing out Erap stickers and wristbands. It meant leaning out of moving vans to distribute posters and our arms being bruised black and blue by eager Erap fans grabbing campaign materials. It also meant closed-door strategy sessions with Erap and his advisers until the wee hours of the morning. It meant ten-hour bus rides along the full length of Luzon where happiness was a Petron gas station with clean rest rooms or a Jollibee open at all hours for hamburgers and *barako* coffee.

We are grateful for this experience of a life time to Joseph Ejercito "Erap" Estrada who gave us the opportunity to write this book.

We are deeply grateful to the Ejercito family for having adopted us for six months while we actively participated and closely observed the hectic and exciting campaign. Mama Mary Ejercito, Erap's irrepressible 93 year-old mother, welcomed us as her "Canadian *balikbayan* children who have come home." "Supremo" Raul and "Prayer Dept. Head" Pat de Guzman, who were our original links to Erap, found us a home in Greenhills and supplied all our earthly needs. Dr. Loi Ejercito, Erap's "one and only," did not only share with us the early years of the Erap-Loi courtship, she kept us so well fed during Sunday *pochero* lunches that we had to have new clothes made by the time the SWS exit polls heralded an Erap victory.

It was a joy and a privilege to have experienced the campaign with the Greenhills Group headed by our "Commander Ica" (Dr. Pilarica Ejercito) and Chief Campaigner Marita, Erap's youngest sister. We acknowledge with thanks the joyous company of the "Spice Girls" Monette and Dolly, the quiet presence of "The Silent Types"—Ejercito brothers Paul and Jesse, and the warm friendship of Nenita and Caline Montilla, Sonia Co, Anching Martinez, Melly Lee and her brother "Brigadier" Brigido and his wife Conchita. We were blessed with new friends from the Mare group of Justa K. Tantoco, the indefatigable Ging Cruz and the Mare van "stewardess"Annabelle Cordon, plus all the praying partners in our Holy Rosary Circle.

Our work at LAMMP campaign headquarters was made fruitful by the full support of Manny Zamora, Orly Mercado, Susy Pineda Mercado, Rod Reyes, Ding Gageloña, Lito Banayo, Jesse Ejercito, Tonette Velasco and Manny de Guzman. We appreciate the efficient trio of Norio, Joy and Tess who agonized with us in preparing our policy briefs. We thank SWS Chief pollster Mahar Mangahas and PSRC President R.J. Esteban for access to their poll data and archives as well as for in-depth briefings in secure back rooms. We are grateful to the members of the Policy Studies Group of Raul de Guzman, especially to Ben Diokno, Liling Briones, Cris Collado, Elisa Areza, Mar Guillermo, Cris Abanes, Leo Lazatin and Paeng Esmundo for their contributions to the Transition Teams Report submitted to Ronnie Zamora.

The College of Public Administration and the School of Urban and Regional Planning, University of the Philippines, became our intellectual homes while doing research for this book. We thank U.P. President Emil Javier, Dean Jose Endriga and Dean Benjamin Cariño for all their help. Grateful thanks also go to Mila Reforma, Danny Reyes, Dodong Nemenzo, Belinda Aquino, Romy Ocampo, Chit Tapales, Norman Ramos, Asteya Santiago, Luz Tancangco and other faculty members who shared their data and insights with us.

The hardworking professionals around Erap Estrada shared much valuable information with us despite their heavy work loads. We were enthralled by Ronnie Puno's briefing on the Byron Hotel operation and we thank Jun Veron Cruz for enlightening us further on the *Halalan '98* project. Our appointments with Erap were facilitated by Cheryl Jimenea and Malou Florendo who kept us informed of our candidate's daily schedule. Without the able guidance of Jimmie Policarpio, scheduling master, we would have wasted many hours getting lost in provincial sorties. We are grateful to the ever-loyal Erap spokesman Ike Gutierrez for his insights. Our thanks too for the security provided by "The Quiet Ones"—Tony Gana, Colonel Rodolfo Diaz, Jet Villadolid, Jeff Tamayo and the many strong silent men who made up our candidate's security detail especially the man who carried the yellow bullet-proof security blanket.

Domestic arrangements are always big problems on missions like ours. Thus we are grateful to Dr. Fe Pastorfide, Marianne and Archie for giving us a home away from home and to Fely Villareal for lending us supplemental comfort-furnishings. We thank Ricky and Bobby de Guzman as well as Bobby's wife, Flora, for giving us access to cars and vans on request, e-mail, fax and cell phones, and thanks to Jean Zapanta and Tess Mendoza for making all the arrangements. We were fortunate to renew old friendships with Ricky and Paloming Papa, Efren and Perla Segovia, Nancy Laureta, Baby and Perfecto Padilla, Tacing Jimenez, Ed and Jo Bago— avid Erap supporters all.

We are grateful to Ernie Pernia for his helpful Q&A and for explaining to us the inescapable economic problems Erap will inherit . We were impressed by the dedication of NGOs working for peaceful and honest elections—LEAD, Samahang LAMMP, Inaanak ni Erap, Kaibigan ni Erap and JEEP among others. We thank the JEEP "operators"—Robert Aventajado, Boy Morales, Father Ed de la Torre, Fely Villareal, Jose (Oying) Rimon and Buddy Garbanzos—for the chance to work on the Erap Program of Governance earlier on. Thanks are also due to Senator Edgardo Angara's Chief of Staff Sally Zaldivar Perez and the Zaldivar family (Ike, Nona and Lorna) for all their insights, hospitality and joyful company. And to our *Inaanak sa Kasal* and "No. 3 Son" Jaime Flor Cruz, married to Ana Zaldivar Segovia, for his thoughtfulness and advice on media strategies.

We owe the opportunity for our six months leave in the Philippines to colleagues at the University of British Columbia—Dean Frieda Granot of Graduate Studies, Director Terry McGee of the Institute of Asian Research and Director Bill Rees of the School of Community and Regional Planning

We are grateful for the study leave given to us by UBC and the temporary relief from teaching and administrative duties. We also thank Lisa Kwan of the IAR for her patience and late nights in helping us with the design and format of this book.

To our son George and his "PITA" Brenda Jamer go our thanks for looking after our Vancouver home and houseplants while we were away,and for many hours spent proofreading this manuscript. We also thank our daughter Helen and her husband Dan Flagg in Boston for their concern over our safety and their regular e-mails. We look forward to their gift of our first *apo* so thoughtfully scheduled to arrive after the Erap presidential campaign.

When we thanked Erap for giving us the opportunity to be with him up close during the campaign so we could gather materials for the book, his reply was typical Erap. With a disarming smile, he said he was the one who should be grateful for our support during the campaign and for faithfully recording the events that culminated in his victory.

This is the record of those events and our own analysis of what happened. We wrote this book "on the run" banging away on a battered laptop in airport lounges and lonely hotel rooms. Readers will notice a few typos and redundancies— we sometimes sacrificed style for timeliness. For these and other lapses, we take full responsibility, especially for errors of fact and interpretation.

To us, the 1998 elections, an important milestone in Philippine history, marked the convergence of many social elements and political forces that somehow focused on one man—Joseph Ejercito "Erap" Estrada. We are honored and deeply grateful for the opportunity of having witnessed, from ringside seats, the election of the Philippine Centennial President. Finally, our thanks go to the Filipino voters, especially the empowered masses, for making all this happen in a relatively peaceful, honest and democratic process.

Prod and Eleanor Laquian

Vancouver, B.C., Canada
30 June 1998

# PART I

## THE SETTING

# Chapter 1

# Electing the Centennial President

No. 1 Polk Street in North Greenhills, San Juan, the Estrada family residence, is at the center of three residential compounds. All three compounds are linked to Erap's yard with private back gates. East of the yard is the home of Erap's elder brother Paul and his wife Margie, the north side lot is occupied by Erap's brother-in-law, Raul de Guzman and his wife Pat. When Erap was still in the movie business, what is now the large courtyard used to be a swimming pool where the Ejercito clan, especially the young ones, frolicked on weekends. The pool area also doubled as a movie lot, where many Erap movies were shot.

The swimming pool has now been filled up, replaced by a manicured lawn bordered by lush tropical shrubs, coconut palms and a landscaped garden. A large enclosed *lanai* has been constructed at one end of the yard. The western side of the compound is the boundary wall of the exclusive North Greenhills subdivision and the southern sector is a heavily guarded security gate. Adjacent to the gate is Erap's old house, now converted into an office, where the Vice President's personal staff provides full communication and secretarial support. Rolly Ramirez, Cheryl Jimenea and Malou Florendo are kept busy all day responding to the thousand and one calls—all seemingly urgent—that require the Vice President's attention. Among his staff, Erap was simply referred to as "Vice."

When Erap and his wife Loi bought this house on Polk Street, they probably never considered it auspicious that all the streets in this subdivision are named after American presidents. President Polk is next to Buchanan, which in turn intersects with Kennedy, Roosevelt, Madison, Hayes and Arthur. Now, as election day drew nearer, the No. 1 on the Polk Street address seemed like an excellent omen for someone who would be "*Numero Uno*."

Like other Filipinos, Erap is not ostentatiously religious. However, he also does not believe in tempting Fate. He gladly observes spiritual and religious rituals.

Before every important event in his political life, Erap had attended a special Holy Mass just for him, often at midnight to start the eventful day right. He also consults fortune tellers and enjoys having his horoscope read. On the advice of his many Chinese friends, he occasionally consults a *feng shui* master. Months before, he had inked one eye of a *Daruma* doll, a gift from a Japanese friend, for good luck.

Although Erap is not openly religious (he once said he hates to be seen praying in public) he is not averse to religious rituals. Thus, Erap agreed to Loi's suggestion that Masses be celebrated at their home at 6:00 A.M., 12:00 noon and 6:00 P.M. daily from 10 to 12 May. He also agreed to turn their lanai into a private chapel where a novena was held and prayers were offered for honest, orderly and peaceful elections during the three-day vigil of the Blessed Sacrament.

Sunday, 10 May 1998 was Mother's Day. It was the day before elections and the Erap Greenhills home was jammed with supporters and well-wishers. White canvas tents had been set up in the courtyard where caterers were serving meals non-stop. The narrow dead-end street in front of No. 1 Polk was impassable with cars and vans double-parked even on the sidewalks. Men bringing in flowers, cakes, fruits, trays of food and cases of drinks had to walk two blocks to deliver their offerings to the man who would be President of the Philippines, God willing.

A noon day Mass was being held to pray for Erap's electoral victory in a clean election. The young priest celebrating the Mass was openly partisan to LAMMP (*Laban ng Makakabayang Masang Pilipino*—Erap's political party) in asking his flock to join him in offering the Prayers to the Faithful:

> Lord, we hold up to your love, Joseph Estrada. Bless his decision to seek the highest office of the country: the Presidency. Give him victory over his enemies, triumph over his opponents. Cover him with your most precious blood, from the crown of his head to the soles of his feet. And by the power of your most precious blood, keep him safe from all harm, all injury, dangers, sickness and hidden disease. Shield him from all attacks of evil ones. Save him from all harassment, malice, treachery, betrayal and deceit. Surround him with your light. Walk beside him, behind him, in front of him. Watch over him always, day by day, moment by moment…
>
> Bless the coming elections with peace and integrity, with victory for Joseph Estrada, Edgardo Angara and the twelve Senators. Purify the hearts of their opponents, that they may be delivered from any evil plans to cheat or terrorize. Melt the envy and greed from

> their hearts, that they will do only what is your will. We pray for the mighty anointing of your Holy Spirit upon Joseph Estrada, just as you have chosen David to be king. Seal Joseph Estrada now with the blood of Jesus, and anoint him to be your servant, to be the President of our beloved country, the Philippines.
>
> Dear Mama Mary, our mother of our salvation, embrace Joseph Estrada with your love. Walk with him every step of the way. Listen to the cries of his heart and draw him closer to the heart of Jesus, your son. We ask all of these in the mighty name of Jesus, our Lord. Amen.

The priest intoning the prayer did not quite go to the extent of anointing Erap with holy oil, as Brother Eddie Villanueva had done to Speaker Jose de Venecia at a Jesus is Lord rally the previous week. However, he was very explicit about what "dirty tricks" Erap should be protected against from his opponents. Indeed, even if the priest had wanted to put his hand on Erap's head, the"anointed one" would have been safely out of reach. Like any normal Filipino man at Mass, Erap was standing at the edge of the congregation, partly hidden behind a coconut frond, ready to slip away as soon as the priest started giving Holy Communion. In this Holy Mass where he was the one being honored, Erap had decided not to take center stage.

After Mass, Erap did not slink away. This being Mother's Day, he came in with a huge bouquet of flowers for his mother, Mama Mary, the 93 year-old matriarch of the Ejercito clan. For Mother's Day, the young priest blessed all mothers at the end of the Mass and moved by a romantic impulse, he asked all fathers in the congregation to kiss their wives "lips to lips." There was much cheering when Erap sought out his wife, Loi, and kissed her fully on the lips. This was a repeat of "the kiss" after the Thanksgiving Mass at Pinaglabanan Shrine that had been splashed on page one of a major newspaper the previous day and it drew much teasing and loud applause.

A sumptuous lunch was served, with guests queuing up before two long tables loaded with appetizers, main dishes and desserts. Now and then, Erap relaxed and gracious, joined the festive throng. Guests and friends vied with each other to have their pictures taken with him. There was much joyful bantering as persons who had been involved in the campaign exchanged anecdotes and traded taxi-driver stories on why the *masa* were so fanatically behind Erap. Someone was heard repeating an old Erap joke that if there was no cheating, the Vice President would win "by a landscape." The latest version of this joke goes to win "by a LAMMPscape." It still draws laughs.

Now and then, Erap would slip back inside the house and confer with his advisers. Spokesman Ike Gutierrez, doing his real life imitation of a disheveled Lieutenant Colombo, was constantly at Erap's side, cat-alert to respond to his every bidding. Lito Banayo, trusted aide and ever-ready speech writer, was on standby for any last minute statements. Robert Aventajado's imposing frame hovered nearby—as national president of JEEP (Justice, Economy, Environment and Peace), he was in constant touch with efforts to safeguard the polls and respond to any reported dirty tricks. Ronnie Zamora, Rod Reyes, Orly Mercado, Jimmie Policarpio and Erap's youngest brother Jesse—the hard core of the Erap campaign staff—flitted in and out of the inner sanctum intent on carrying out their respective tasks. They had no time to join the festivities, knowing that they were facing a dangerous and potentially lethal opponent—*dagdag-bawas* (cheating by adding or shaving votes).

The seriousness of the threat from the "dirty tricks" department of the administration party became suddenly apparent with the distribution of an alleged special issue of the *People's Journal,* a sequestered paper now owned by the government, with the headline, ERAP BACKS OUT. The news item said that Erap had suffered a heart attack and was confined at the Makati Medical Center. It also reported that Erap, upon withdrawing, had endorsed the candidacy of Mayor Fred Lim. Around noon, a flurry of queries went online in the computer room.

The "damage control" crew of Rod Reyes and Ike Gutierrez immediately swung into action. An impromptu media conference was called, denying the news of Erap's withdrawal. A TV spot interview showed Erap hale and healthy, surrounded by party workers having a good time. George Kintanar, a LAMMP computer consultant, rushed to the computer room and relayed the information by e-mail to about 40 contact points all over the Philippines that the *Journal* article was a hoax and that Erap was at home enjoying himself at a party. A picture was taken of Erap, smiling broadly and obviously very much alive, with his family. He was holding forth a copy of the bad-news *Journal.*

The merry-making continued despite the concern about the *Journal* article. The release of the SWS (Social Weather Stations) poll the previous day showing Erap ahead with 33% of the votes gave the Erap partisans great confidence. Around midnight, Erap left with his security detail to spend the night at a safe house. Because of a number of rumored assassination plots against him, Erap decided to end his presidential campaign at noon on Friday, 8 May, with a Mass at Pinaglabanan Shrine in San Juan. For other candidates, the campaign did not officially end until midnight Sunday, 10 May. A few die-hard partisans stayed in the yard until the wee hours of the morning, waiting for the opening of polling places.

## Election Day

Monday, 11 May, was one of the hottest El Niño days on record, a blistering 38ºC. Erap had awakened early to prepare for the day—the end of three months of grueling rallies and motorcades, the culmination, at last, of a decade of preparation to attain the Presidency of the Philippines.

On this election day, the astrologers agreed that "the stars favor Estrada." Madame Zenaida Seva, who writes an astrology column in the *Manila Standard*, indicated that "the planet Neptune—the planet of enchantment, illusions, fantasies and dreams—was in exact contact with the country's psyche (the Moon)." Basing her chart reading on Erap's birth at 8:00 P.M. on 19 April 1937, Madame Seva said that Neptune was associated with films and the glamour of romance. In her view, this "allows the Filipino masses to project or decode upon Erap their hopes and wishes, their deepest longings, their idealized version of life." The astrologer concluded that: "Estrada has this solid grip on the psyche of the Filipino people which no logical analysis by political pundits or pollsters can unravel."

At 6:00 A.M., Erap attended Holy Mass, celebrated beneath white tents in the courtyard of his home. Then, he had breakfast with Max Soliven, publisher of the *Philippine Star,* and Mike Gonzales, the deputy editor of the Editorial page of the *Asian Wall Street Journal.* Soliven said that Erap was in good form—relaxed and very confident that he was going to win the elections. Gonzales surprised Loi with a question—where will you live "when" (not "if") Erap becomes president. The question caught Loi by surprise and she admitted that she and Erap had not discussed this possibility at all—they had been so completely focused on just winning the election.

Soliven reported that Gonzales was very much taken by Erap's graciousness and hospitality. Upon leaving the Erap home, Gonzales whispered to Soliven—"Why, he speaks good English!"

Soliven, who had declared openly the previous week that he was voting for Erap could only ask—"What could I retort to that?"

While Erap was having breakfast, the first shift of 1.1 million poll watchers (six each for every one of 185,000 precincts) and 3,500 lawyers and paralegals recruited by LAMMP, JEEP, and LEAD (Lawyers for Estrada, Angara and Democracy) were trooping to polling places all over the country. They had been alerted by party leaders that, unlike in previous years, when electoral officials reported to their respective precincts by 6:30 A.M., the time had been advanced by 30 minutes on this particular election day. Not taking any chances (LAMMP trainers had warned that "a lot of cheating can happen in 30 minutes"), the Erap troops were at the precincts before the crack of dawn.

Soon, it was time for Erap to go to the polling place. The *feng shui* master had said that the most auspicious time for Erap to vote was at 10:15 in the morning. Accompanied by his son, Jinggoy, Erap timed his arrival at the Pedro Cruz Elementary School in San Juan so that he could vote at the precise lucky hour.

The election day headlines were not very comforting. The *Philippine Daily Inquirer* headlined: BISHOPS TELL VOTERS, ANYBODY BUT ERAP. A side bar in the *Inquirer* had the lead: EL SHADDAI FLIP-FLOPS ANEW, indicating that the leader of the El Shaddai Catholic charismatic group, Brother Mike Velarde, who had earlier been rumored to support Erap, had decided to play it safe and not endorse him. The only consolation was that Velarde did not endorse any other candidate despite the fact that Gina de Venecia was said to have hounded him in a comic chase through Ayala Alabang the previous day.

More troubling were other headlines: RISING WAVE OF VIOLENCE ALARMS PNP, CANDIDATES bannered the *Manila Times.* Under a sub-head indicating POLITICAL VIOLENCE, the *Manila Standard* reported BARANGAY CHIEFS SEIZED, CHOPPERS STRAFED. The *Times* was also running a special news feature entitled PAROXYSMS OF PASSION AND VIOLENCE: WHY MAYHEM MARS PHILIPPINE ELECTIONS. There were fears that as in previous years, blood would be spilled on this election day.

When Erap and Jinggoy arrived at the Pedro Cruz Elementary School, they could barely get through the crush of cheering supporters and media people who had staked out the polling precinct where Erap was going to vote. Erap's casting of his ballot had to be moved to the school yard to accommodate the media. Nattily dressed in a cream-colored *barong tagalog,* Erap had to stage casting his ballot several times so the media could take their photo op shots.

About ten kilometers from Erap's Greenhills home, at the Byron Hotel near Edsa, the real nerve center of the Erap campaign activities was also excitedly hopeful. Ronnie Puno, head honcho of the Byron operations, had projected a 40% Erap share of the votes and he was carefully scrutinizing reports coming in from more than 3,500 operatives from all over the country. The numbers looked good—a few hours after the polls closed at 3:00 P.M., the Comelec announced a very heavy turnout of around 80% of the 34.5 million registered voters. This was good—Erap's support came mostly from the rural and urban poor, which had a reputation for not voting. A heavy turnout would be very good for Erap.

In a small back room of Erap's office, a computer was hooked up to the Byron Hotel and the Namfrel- ABS-CBN- *Philippine Star* "quick count" tabulations. George Kintanar, who with his brother Chito, had set up the system, was at the terminal. He was all set to rush the results of the vote count to Erap as soon as they came up on the screen.

Nearby, the e-mail messages cascaded on the monitor from all over the country. Malou Florendo, Erap's secretary, was taking notes.

Tagig reported that leaders of administration candidates were paying P1,000 per vote—with fake peso bills. Tuguegarao, Cagayan said that voting was delayed because election paraphernalia had not arrived. From Marikina, Pasay and Pateros came reports that the so-called "indelible ink" issued by Comelec to prevent people from voting more than once could be washed away easily by soap and water. Hundreds of reports came in about voters not finding their names on the computerized list of voters. San Fernando, Pampanga, reported that poll watchers hired by LAMMP were not showing up. From Pasig City came a report that LAMMP poll watchers had been bought out by the administration candidates. Many Central Luzon networks reported simultaneous electrical brownouts in their towns—this had been anticipated so LAMMP poll watchers had all been issued with flashlights, aside from their radios, cameras, pagers and cell phones.

Cheryl Jimenea, Erap's assistant,was by the fax machines scooping up messages coming out in an endless stream. Outside, two mega screens under the tents, one on each end of the lawn, were showing the ABS-CBN coverage of the elections, watched by a knot of anxious supporters quietly talking among themselves.

After the hectic three months of campaigning, election day itself turned out to be quite uneventful. When the polling places closed at 3:00 P.M., no major disaster had been reported. There were reports of men in ski masks hijacking ballot boxes in Isabela and of a man stabbed at the Makati city hall. Voters in about 22 precincts in Mindanao were not able to vote because armed terrorists had threatened to shoot anyone going to the polls. A failure of election was declared in that area and special election would have to be scheduled. However, the feared nationwide No-El (No Elections) scenario never materialized. The Commission on Elections (Comelec) declared the elections "generally peaceful."

At 2:30 A.M. on 12 May, the sleepy crowd under the tent suddenly came alive when SWS Chief pollster Mahar Mangahas announced over ABS-CBN the results of an SWS conducted exit poll showing Erap leading with 39%of all voters polled saying they voted for him. The report was received with applause by Erap supporters. Later, the Filipino people heaved a deep sigh of relief as reports came in that the elections had been orderly and peaceful. The Comelec and Philippine National Police said that compared to other elections, 1998 had more cases of reported "incidents" (151 cases as of 6:00 A.M. of 12 May as against 121 in 1995 and 87 in 1992). However, "only" 51 people were killed and 80 were wounded in election-related incidents. These were much lower than the 83 persons killed and 91 wounded in 1995 and the 60 killed and 144 wounded in 1992. General Clemente Mariano, Philippine Armed Forces Chief of Staff, called the election process "positively boring."

### The Long Count

In Philippine elections the transfer of power does not occur overnight. This is because the counting of ballots from about 34.5 million registered voters is done manually. In a national election, election tabulators usually expect that a significant trend in voting can be established only after about five days. As the polls closed at 3:00 P.M. on Monday, LAMMP and other groups hunkered down for the long count.

The election vigil at No. 1 Polk Street had a fiesta atmosphere. It was as though everybody sensed a LAMMP victory in the offing and they had all come to Erap's house in droves, ostensibly to attend the 6:00 P.M. Mass. People who did not participate in the campaign, even Erap relatives he had not seen in years, suddenly appeared at the gate bearing gifts. Everybody wanted to be with the winner and the winner was gracious enough to welcome everyone to his party.

The first tabulation numbers started coming in around 7:15 P.M. By some fluke, the first numbers came in from Batac, Ilocos Norte. They promised a good omen—coming in from one of the smallest precincts from the so-called "solid north" which was expected to go for De Venecia, the tallies were: Erap Estrada, 4; Jose de Venecia, 2 and Raul Roco, 2. The report was quickly superceded by another one from Ramon Magsaysay High School in suburban Quezon City: Roco, 28; Erap 21; De Venecia, 9. Very early reports from Cebu were encouraging: Erap, 69; Roco, 52; Lito Osmeña, 33; Lim, 18; De Venecia, 9. Davao City from Mindanao checked in with another report: Erap, 13; De Venecia, 9; Osmeña, 6; De Villa, 3 and Lim, 3. The vote counts were coming in trickles but they were all for Estrada.

The morning papers headlined the good news: ESTRADA JUMPS TO AN EARLY LEAD (*Philippine Daily Inquirer)*; The *Manila Times* headline was: HEAVY TURNOUT IN POLLS; ERAP TAKES EARLY LEAD. The *Times* also reported vote tallies as of midnight after election day showing Erap way ahead with 15,193 votes; Osmeña, 6,457; De Venecia, 6,366; and Lim, 5,596. For the vice presidential contest, Macapagal had 15,810 votes, Angara 9,110, Osmeña III, 6,799, Orbos, 4889, and Tatad, 655. The senatorial contest was reported at 7-5 with LAMMP having Pimentel, Osmeña, Ople, Biazon, Sotto, Aquino and Bagatsing and Lakas-NUCD with Legarda, Cayetano, Barbers, Guingona and Revilla.

By 10:00 A.M. of 12 May, the early lead of Erap continued. Erap was polling 145,101 votes against De Venecia's 75,666. Gloria Macapagal was tops at 165,191 for vice president against Angara's 98,127. The senatorial pattern was still stuck at 7 LAMMP and 5 Lakas-NUCD.

President Ramos held an impromptu press conference in Malacanang at 10:30 A.M. Looking tanned and relaxed but quite subdued, the President reminded the people that Tuesday was a regular working day. Behind his presidential seat in Malacanang was a large banner saying: LET US GET BACK TO WORK!!! The President congratulated the police and the army for a relatively peaceful election. Ever one for statistics, the President indicated that while there were more incidents of trouble in 1998 compared to 1995 and 1992, there were less people killed or wounded. He appealed to political contenders and the people at large to protect the ballot and not allow cheating and violence to happen.

Asked what he thought of the elections and Erap Estrada's early lead, the President said that it was too early to tell what the final results would be. He called on all the candidates to start the process of healing. He said that he was happy that the Philippines had an orderly and peaceful election, which was a good sign that democracy was alive and well in the country. He immediately ordered the department of public works and other government offices to start cleaning up the election posters and mountains of debris created by the campaign.

At home, a very relaxed Erap was receiving greetings and congratulations from his family, friends and supporters. On election day, he had predicted he would win by a landslide. Reiterating what he said earlier, Erap said that he would give "the greatest performance of his life" as the next president. He also pledged that he would prove his critics wrong, especially Cardinal Sin and the bishops, who had campaigned vehemently against him. He would forgive his enemies and unite the country as it enters the next millennium.

**Sore Loser, Generous Winner**

For the first time in Philippine history, a party in power that was losing badly, openly accused the opposition of cheating at the polls. An agitated Speaker de Venecia chided ABS-CBN on television for broadcasting the results of "partial and incomplete" counts from field reporters. Specially harsh words were aimed by the Speaker at the release of exit poll results by SWS—De Venecia charged that SWS had been paid by the opposition, at which, an equally irritated newscaster, Noli de Castro, responded that ABS-CBN had commissioned the polls. In a memorable exchange of accusations and corrections repeatedly aired by the TV company, de Castro corrected De Venecia's allegation that the AMA computer network, which was openly identified with the LAMMP camp, had been used by the TV company—Noli said Speaker de Venecia was wrong; they had depended on STI for their data gathering.

The blow that knocked the winds from De Venecia's sails was the release of the SWS exit poll 24 hours after the close of voting. Acccording to SWS president Mahar Mangahas, his contract with ABS-CBN was that the Metro Manila exit poll results would be aired by 2:30 A.M. on 12 May and the full national results by 3:00 P.M. Mangahas confirmed that by 10:00 A.M. of 12 May, he had received poll reports covering 8,490 homes. About 4,842 respondents indicated their choice for president, 4,570 their choices for vice president and 4,452 wrote at least one choice for senator. Within an error margin of plus or minus 1.5%, SWS disclosed the initial report on the people's verdict: Erap had won 38.7% of the votes; De Venecia, 16.4%; Roco, 13.6%; Osmeña, 11.6%; Lim, 9.3%; De Villa, 4.7%; Santiago, 2.9%; Enrile and Imelda, 1% each; Morato, 0.3%; Dumlao, 0.2%.

It was not quite a landslide but the Erap victory had exceeded even the best expectations of every one—including LAMMP itself. Erap apparently had been elected the Philippines' Centennial President.

The official proclamation of Joseph Ejercito "Erap" Estrada as 13th President of the Philippines, by the joint session of Congress on 29 May, was almost anti-climactic. Erap got 10,722,250 of the 26.9 million votes cast or 40%. His closest rival, Jose de Venecia got 6.45 million votes or 23.9%. Gloria Macapagal Arroyo was elected vice president with 12.66 million votes (47.1%) trailed by Edgardo Angara with 5.6 million votes (20.8%). LAMMP senators won 7-5 against the Lakas-NUCD ticket. Estrada's victory was hailed as the triumph of democracy in the Philippines. Actually the biggest winner in the 1998 elections were the pollsters. SWS was barely 1% off the mark. The Ronnie Puno *Bantay Halalan* '98 polls that predicted a 40% Estrada margin hit it right on the nose.

# Chapter 2

# The Philippines in 1998

It was a Sunday in late January 1998. We had just finished eating the traditional *pochero* lunch that reunites all members of the Ejercito clan every Sunday at No. 1 Polk Street, North Greenhills. The weekly gathering of the clan revolves around Maria Marcelo Ejercito, "Mama Mary," to everyone, Erap's doting 93 year-old mother. At these lunches, held in the *lanai* of his home, Erap the "black sheep" and only college drop-out in this family of professionals becomes the dutiful son, making *mano* (respectful kissing of older person's hand) to Mama Mary, carefully managing minute details of what food to serve, even ordering special dishes from restaurants himself, and entertaining everyone with his anecdotes and Erap jokes.

"Can a person really plan his life in politics?"

Erap, as he often does, was answering a question with another question. We had just asked him when he first decided to run for President of the Philippines.

The previous Sunday, 18 January, Erap had been officially proclaimed the presidential candidate of the *Laban ng Makabayang Masang Pilipino* (LAMMP). It was more of a coronation than a convention. There was no contested nomination—what transpired was a presentation of the chosen candidates by the leaders to the party faithful. A couple of weeks before, LAMMP stalwarts had decided in caucus that Erap would be the candidate for President and Edgardo "Edong" Angara would slide down to Vice President. Senator Ernesto Maceda, president of NPC (the other party in the LAMMP coalition) who had aspired to be the vice presidential candidate, had been left out in the cold. He bitterly complained about the "secret deal" between Erap and Edong and threatened to pull NPC out of the coalition.

"Maceda was really upset," Erap said, "he had been warned by his *manghuhula* (fortune teller) that misfortune was going to hit him but he kept hoping things would turn out all right."

Apparently, the day before the convention, Maceda had gone to his usual fortune teller for advice. The fortune teller laid out the cards and said "From here on, all I can see is darkness—there is no other way for you but down."

"Maceda even tried to influence the fortune teller," Erap laughed, "he wanted a better prediction. However, the fortune teller said, sorry, that is what the cards are saying. I do not have the power to change what Fate has destined for you."

Erap was in a relaxed bantering mood. He kept talking to his mother in broken Spanish. Mama Mary was proud of her Spanish heritage but prouder still of her son, whom she hope would be President of the Philippines in a matter of months.

We reminded Erap that we were writing a book about the campaign. He said he was happy that we were recording all the events. He welcomed any questions from us and offered us a car and driver for our personal use.

Eleanor asked Erap again "when did the idea first strike you that you wanted to be President of the Philippines?

Erap lighted his ubiquitous Lucky Strike cigarette and became pensive.

"Actually, I had never thought of a career in politics," he said. "I was doing very well in the movies, winning awards, making a lot of money. Becoming Mayor of San Juan was farthest from my mind."

However, a friend of Erap, a well known movie actor, decided to venture into politics in the '60s. Old political pros laughed at him. "They told him that movie actors were only *pang bakya*" (for masses) he said. Erap got mad. "They said that all movie actors were stupid. I wanted to show them who was stupid."

Another individual responsible for Erap's getting into politics was the parish priest in San Juan at that time, an old Erap friend. He thought that Erap would be able to reform the municipal government—he particularly saw a special need to do something about the town's corrupt and abusive police force. Erap said he did not know anything about politics—all he was good at was being a movie actor. However, the Pinaglabanan parish priest was very persistent so Erap finally agreed to run for Mayor

Erap ran for Mayor of San Juan in 1967. His friend, Fernando Poe, Jr., agreed to be his campaign manager. Erap's motorcades and rallies drew huge crowds because aside from Ronnie Poe, Jr., such movie stars as Susan Roces, Nora Aunor, Jess Lapid, Eddie Rodriguez, June Aristorenas, Barbara Perez, Lou Salvador, Jr., Helen Gamboa and Zeny Zabala joined the campaign.

Erap found out, very quickly, how dirty local politics could be. There were charges and counter-charges of cheating, vote buying and physical intimidation. His opponent, Dr. Braulio Sto. Domingo, was proclaimed by the Comelec as the elected Mayor. There was trouble with the counting of ballots and the courts ordered a recount. The case went all the way up to the Supreme Court which in 1969 ruled that Erap had actually won, with a pencil-thin margin of 192 votes. Years later, the daughter of Justice Calixto Zaldivar, Sally Zaldivar Perez, revealed that it was her father, together with Chief Justice Roberto Concepcion, who had penned the decision favorable to Estrada. Sally was Chief of Staff of Angara's vice presidential campaign, in tandem with Erap.

Sally recalled that the first time she saw Erap, she couldn't take her eyes off him. Erap looked so much like her late husband. Afraid that Erap would notice her staring, she approached him to explain, adding "I hope you won't mind if I look at you" to which Erap had replied, "Not at all; please help yourself."

But when did Erap start seriously thinking of becoming President? Eleanor persisted.

"It must have been when I was a Senator," he said. "The debates on Subic and Clark were very heated. I sincerely thought that for as long as American bases were here, we would continue to be mendicants in our own country. I became completely committed to a truly independent Philippines. That slogan—*Walang tutulong sa Pilipino kundi kapwa Pilipino* (No one can help the Filipino except fellow Filipinos)—I honestly believed that. I thought I could be a leader of a nationalist movement."

The way Erap told it, he never consciously chose politics as a career. He did not set out in life wanting to be President. Things just kept happening that encouraged him to stay in public life even as he continued to star in Tagalog movies. The strong support of the Philippine masses—first for his movies, then for his political career—truly inspired him. Although he was born to a middle class family, Erap's feelings for the *masa* were genuine. He felt he owed them—*isang malaking utang na loob*—(a strong debt of gratitude). He sincerely wanted to repay them for their support. He often said that without the support of the masses, his movie fans, he wouldn't be what he was today.

"I believe in destiny," Erap confessed, "it just seemed that some force out there was guiding my life and making good things happen."

Since he entered politics in 1967, Erap had been a Mayor for 16 years, a Senator for six years, and a Vice President for six years. For most of those years, he had continued to make movies, invested in real estate, dabbled in a number of business ventures (a restaurant, a nightclub). He proudly said that politics, for him, was not a way to get rich. As Mayor of San Juan, his salary was P5,000 per month—he could net P300,000 per movie. In fact, Erap revealed that his total salary, since he became Mayor, had all been donated to the *Erap sa Mahirap Scholarship Foundation*, run by his elder sister, Pilarica and his brother-in-law, Raul. They had used the money to support almost 2,000 Erap scholars all over the country.

"I have never been obsessed with becoming President of the Philippines," Erap said. "Even now, my attitude is—if it happens, it happens. God has a plan for each one of us. I can tell you, honestly, that I have never lusted for the presidency."

**The Philippines, 1998**

The Philippines that Erap did not consciously aspire to lead is a country of 72 million people inhabiting over 300,000 square kilometers of land and ocean. In 1998, it was celebrating 100 years of its proclamation of political independence against Spain (the first Philippine republic was proclaimed in Kawit, Cavite on 12 June 1898, after a brief rebellion against Spanish colonial domination). The 1998 elections, therefore, were considered most important by Filipinos—they would be electing a centennial president and the chosen leader would lead them into the next millennium.

Despite its pride of being the first democratic polity in Asia, the Philippines is beset with many serious problems. Among these are: (a) a rapidly growing population; (b) unstable economic development; (c) environmental degradation; (d) crime; (e) graft and corruption; and (f) social polarization and potential class-based conflict. This last problem, however, can become a positive force in Philippine nation-building if the class differentiation is seen not in the Marxist sense of class conflict but in terms of the evolution of a sense of identity and empowerment among the Filipino masses.

Politically, the Philippines is a republic, with its constitutional structure patterned after that of the United States. There are three co-ordinate and co-equal branches of government (executive, legislative, judicial) supposedly following the doctrines of separation of powers and checks and balances. In point of fact, the Philippine presidency is one of the most powerful institutions in the world.

The tradition of a strong Philippine presidency was established early during the dictatorial rule of General Emilio Aguinaldo in 1898. Even then, factionalism plagued the Philippine fight for independence and Aguinaldo had to impose his will over other leaders such as the proletarian Andres Bonifacio and the intellectual *ilustrados* such as Jose Pardo de Tavera and Pedro A. Paterno. Some of Aguinaldo's competitors were killed—Bonifacio included. Unfortunately, American intervention interrupted Asia's first experiment with popular democracy—the Philippines became an American colony from 1900 to 1946.

A strong presidency also arose from the authoritarian dominance of Manuel L. Quezon as he fought for independence from the United States during the Commonwealth period and struggled for unity in a government in exile during World War II. Quezon, lined up against the formal and placid Sergio Osmeña, had no problem arrogating unto himself massive legislative and executive powers. Even when he was critically ill and near death, Quezon continued to dominate Philippine political life.

The paramount presidency, of course, was consolidated during the 20 years of unchallenged rule by Ferdinand E. Marcos who imposed martial law in 1972 to strengthen his hold over the reins of government. Marcos had politicized the military and drew unto his camp bright but politically naive technocrats who heeded his personal bidding. He also set up a strong network of crony capitalists who amassed wealth and corrupted legislators and judges—though much of the booty, he kept for himself.

President Corazon Aquino fought hard to exert the powers of the Presidency but she was faced with at least nine coup attempts, natural disasters and corruption by some of her relatives. Any erosion of presidential power under Cory was restored under her "anointed successor"—President Fidel V. Ramos. Ramos consolidated power by pacifying the generals (most of whom were his friends), forming strategic alliances (Jose de Venecia's Rainbow Coalition in the House of Representatives supported his legislative program), crony capitalism and widespread graft such as the PEA-Amari deal, psychological war operations (led by his National Security Adviser, Jose "JoAl" Almonte), manipulation of public opinion and media hype. Even Ramos' political strength, however, was not enough to change the Constitution (the so-called Cha-cha efforts) to allow Ramos to stay in power.

**The Population Problem**

One of the most important issues in Philippine development is one that no presidential candidate has been willing to discuss openly--population. Growing at 2.3% per year, the Philippine population, set at 72 million in 1998, could reach 111.5 million by the year 2025 and 137 million by 2050. As the only predominantly Catholic country in Asia, the Philippines is in a state of denial on the population issue. The Church does not accept any method of birth control other than natural family planning. Although there are governmental and non-governmental family planning programs, access to modern methods, especially on the part of the rural and urban poor, is severely limited.

Early in 1996, we had an occasion to discuss with Erap the population problem. On 29 May 1996, the United Nations Population Fund (UNFPA) invited Erap to be a guest speaker at the launching of the "*State of World Population Report*" at a conference held at the Pandanggo Room of the Manila Hotel. Also appearing as speakers were Senator Leticia Ramos Shahani, the President's sister, who had been a UN Assistant Secretary General, Congresswoman Teresita Aquino-Oreta, the youngest sister of the martyred Ninoy Aquino, Secretary Cielito Habito of the National Economic and Development Authority, Secretary Carmencita Reodica of the Department of Health and Cecille Yasay, head of the Population Commission (Popcom).

Erap believed then, as he does now that each couple has the right to decide whether they will have children or not and how many children they want to have. Pressed on the issue, Erap says he is "pro-choice"—if they so choose, people should be entitled to population information and access to family planning services. Basically, Erap will leave the issue of population to the conscience of each individual. On the issue of abortion, Erap is strongly "pro-life"—he feels that abortion is not an acceptable family planning method and that human life is sacred.

"I'm the 8th in a family of 10 children," Erap explains. "If my parents practised family planning, I wouldn't be here today."

To most analysts of Philippine development, the taboo topic of population is the key to Philippine socio-economic development. Although the Philippines is an agricultural country, it is not able to feed its rapidly growing population. In 1997, the Philippines imported 960,000 metric tons of rice. It was expected to import 1.2 million tons in 1998, mainly due to a 13 to 16% decline in rice yields because of drought caused by El Niño.

The Philippines has a very young population—median age is 25 years. A full 40.2% of Filipinos are of school age (between 6 and 23). However, more than 10.2 million children of school age are not in school. The Department of Education, Culture and Sports admits that 12,000 out of 43,000 *barangays* (village and neighborhood units) do not have an elementary school.

The quality of education in the villages and neighborhoods that do have schools is woefully low. A 1993 National Elementary Achievement Test (NEAT) found that pupils had an overall score of 42.2 %against a target of 75 %. Of 131 competency skills tested, only 38 (29%) were satisfactorily learned. In an international test of students in 16 countries, Filipinos scored lowest in the areas of language, reading, comprehension, science and mathematics.

More than half of all Filipinos now live in urban areas—still, cities and towns continue to grow at 3.4% per year. On the outskirts of large metropolitan areas such as Manila and Cebu, annual population growth rates can exceed 6%. Filipinos are extremely migratory—it is estimated that more than 8 million Filipinos are working or living abroad, most of them as temporary contract workers.

Cities and towns are the economic engines that create economic and social development. In the Philippines, however, such cities and towns are clogged with rural-urban migrants living in dense shantytowns. Traffic jams, air pollution, rotting garbage, criminality, drug addiction and lack of affordable housing plague almost all urban areas, especially mega-cities like Manila and Cebu. Unless something is done about population, Philippine development will remain problematical.

Most important of all, rapid population growth is tending to gobble up most of the economic development gains of the country. Artificial family planning methods are banned by the Church. Even liberal Filipinos argue that "development is the best contraceptive"—all that is needed, according to them, is for the Philippines to progress economically and people will automatically reduce their fertility.

The Philippines, however, defies the given wisdom that socio-economic progress will spontaneously reduce fertility. Most Filipino couples are aware of family planning information. Filipino women have one of the highest literacy rates in Asia (85.9% of them can read and write). The labor participation rate of women is also very high—most Filipino women have high education, work outside the home, have access to the mass media, and know about at least one family planning method. Theoretically, all these factors are supposed to correlate highly with reduced fertility but fertility continues to be high. It is obvious that high fertility among Filipino women is not being influenced by socio-economic development but by other factors such as resistance due to strict admonitions from the Church.

## The Philippine Economy

Economically, the Philippines was still convalescing from the Asian economic contagion in the early months of 1998. The Philippine peso had lost almost half its value—trading at P26 to US$1.00 before July 1997, the peso plunged to P46 to $1.00 in early 1998. A month before the May elections, the peso was holding steady at around P38 to $1.00. The Ramos administration was claiming that the worst was over. Much was made of the fact that the Philippines had "graduated" from the IMF structural adjustment tutelage in March and that the Philippine economy had escaped the Asian economic crisis relatively unscathed.

The Department of Finance, in its 1997 annual report, said the Gross Domestic Product (GDP) had grown at 5.1% and that a worst case scenario would see a GDP growth of 6.5% in 1998. Secretary of Finance, Salvador Enriquez claimed that in 1997, inflation had been kept at a low 5.1% because of wage restraints in both the public and private sectors, the effective price monitoring efforts of the government, reduced government borrowing, an across-the-board cut of 25% in non-personnel government expenditures, and the sale of government assets. DOF revealed that total revenues in 1997 were P471.8 billion, expenditures were P470.4 billion and that government surplus was P1.4 billion.

On the same day that DOF released these good economic indicators, however, the Asian Development Bank published its assessment of the Philippine economy. The ADB predicted that GNP in the Philippines would grow at 2.9% in 1998 and that the inflation rate would be 10%. The reasons given by ADB for this grim scenario were as follows:

- Agricultural productivity will grow at only 2.4% because of the effects of El Niño (drought) and La Niña (floods).
- There will be a number of corporate defaults (especially banks) because of the devaluation of the peso and the high interest rates.
- High liquidity due to monetary expansion, especially because of continued high levels of government spending and massive expenditures for the 1998 elections.

- Lower collections by the Bureau of Internal Revenue and the Bureau of Customs that will encourage more public borrowings and continued deficit financing.

- Increased fund allotments to local government units to pay for both economic services and social services.

- Snags in the privatization of government agencies and sale of assets because of corruption and other charges.

One of the main claims of the Ramos administration was that compared to its Asian neighbors, the Philippines had been hurt less by the Asian economic crisis because its economic fundamentals were right. Professor Jose Diokno of the School of Economics, University of the Philippines, questioned this assertion.

"The Philippines was hurt less by the Asian contagion because it was at a much lower level of development," said Diokno, "not because its economic fundamentals were right." Diokno likened the situation in Asia to two vehicles. The Philippines, with a GDP growth rate of 5% is like a car travelling at 50 kph while another country, say Thailand with a double-digit GDP growth rate, is like a car travelling at 100 kph. If both cars meet an accident, the slower car will naturally sustain less damage. However, this does not mean that the slower car is inherently better than the faster one.

Professor Leonor Briones of the U.P. College of Public Administration estimated that if Erap is proclaimed president on 30 June 1998, he would inherit from the Ramos government a national budget of P565.3 billion. However, annual payments for the interest on the Philippine public debt alone costs P112.7 billion, amortization of government loans costs another P49.9 billion, assumed liabilities total P16.7 billion and other automatic appropriations cost P20.6 billion. Thus, the effective budget available to the new president is only about P342.9 billion. However, about half of that would have been spent by mid-year so that, in fact, the new administration taking over from President Ramos will have a budget of only P175 billion.

The economic slowdown, coupled with the government's precarious financial position, will probably have negative consequences for employment. The Department of Labor has estimated that around 44,000 workers had been laid off in the first quarter of 1998 alone. The Philippine Chamber of Industries, on the other hand, has estimated that at least 500,000 workers would lose their jobs in 1998.

The Ramos administration has declared that the level of absolute poverty in the Philippines had been reduced to 35.5% since 1994. However, in net terms, poverty reduction in the Philippines had averaged only 1.0% per year between 1985 and 1994. Poverty in the Philippines is also very unbalanced—in Mindanao, for example, because of the El Niño phenomenon, some 97,460 families needed urgent food assistance as of April 1998. In fact, some Mindanao lumads (indigenous ethnic groups) have been dying of poisoning because of eating improperly prepared wild yams.

The external debt of the Philippines was US $46.2 billion in September 1997. This was divided into $27.6 billion for the public sector debt and $18.6 billion for the private sector debt. The estimated external debt of the Philippines in 1998 was $51.9 billion, according to the Central Bank of the Philippines.

## Environmental Degradation

In its headlong pursuit of economic development, the Philippines has despoiled its environment. Less than 15% of formerly lush Philippine forests remain, rapacious logging has transformed them into crop lands or eroded clearings. Trawl fishing, destruction of fish habitat such as tidal basins and mangrove swamps, and the use of dynamite and poison have reduced fisheries yields to an extent that artisanal fisherfolk with traditional gear are not able to catch enough fish to feed themselves.

Each year, thousands of hectares of rich crop lands are converted to urban uses. In 1997, 54,836 hectares of land were converted to factory sites, subdivisions, roads and golf courses. The cementing over of land surfaces has created run-offs in a number of urban areas, adding to the devastation created by annual floods.

An island archipelago, the Philippines has 27,000 hectares of coral reefs. However, a 1997 survey of 742 sites had revealed that 30.5% of these sites have been badly destroyed—coral cover has been reduced to 0 to 24% of the ocean bottom. Only 3.9% of the sites were in excellent condition—25.2% were good, 39.0% were fair and the rest were poor to very poor.

Rivers, lakes and coastal zones have been destroyed by the indiscriminate pumping of manufacturing and industrial waste into bodies of water. The Pasig River, Manila's main tributary, remains biologically dead despite valiant efforts of the First Lady and her "Save the Pasig" campaign to restore it to health. The Pampanga River, with its rich prawn and shellfish resources has been heavily polluted by an alcohol distillery which continues to operate despite armed attacks by radicals. Even Laguna de Bay, a potential source of water for Metro Manila, is so badly silted and polluted that experts believe it will be more expensive to tap it for water than far off rivers in the Sierra Madre range.

In urban areas, water supply has become one of the most serious environmental problems. The destruction of watershed areas in Cebu, Davao, General Santos and Cagayan de Oro threatens the area's water supply. In Metro Manila, a 1996 study showed that about 40% of total water consumption comes from private wells instead of the regional waterworks system. Among industrial users of water, 80% rely on private wells for water. For the period 1990 to 1996, another study estimated that private wells extract about 840,000 cubic meters of water per day. The same study found, however, that the amount of water recharged into the ground is only 523,000 cubic meters. In some areas of Metro Manila, therefore, the water table has been getting lower and lower, resulting in soil subsidence and sink holes. Groundwater is in danger of being contaminated.

It is in urban areas, of course, that environmental degradation has been most serious. Metro Manila, for example, generates more than 6,335 metric tons of garbage per day (each Manila resident produces 0.65 kg per day). More than half of that garbage is wet or organic (food and kitchen waste, yard and field waste, wood) while the rest is inert (paper, plastic, sand, metals, glass). At the rate the metropolitan population is growing, the metropolitan will be producing about 11,706 million tons of garbage per day by the year 2014.

In 1998, Metro Manila has practically run out of dumping facilities and there were controversial proposals to install a P14 billion incinerator in San Mateo, Rizal. Suspicions of corrupt dealings involving the incinerator, however, stopped the project. Unfortunately, this action has also prevented the passage of the Clean Air Act, a much needed legislation for environmental regulation.

Despite the passage of many environmental control laws, Philippine economic development remains unsustainable. Corruption makes implementation of those laws ineffective. Lack of awareness of the environmental consequences of developmental action exacerbates the problem. Among the poor and marginalized sectors (forest products gatherers, slash and burn farmers, dynamite fishers), the need to simply survive forces them to commit what is tantamount to ecological suicide. Many of them are aware of the environmental consequences of their acts. However, it is a case of dying now from hunger or dying later without leaving any more resources for coming generations.

## Criminality

Most Filipinos agree that criminality is directly related to poverty. Where most people are poor, their children find it hard to get a good education that can help them find jobs and get out of their misery. Low salaried employees, like policemen, firemen and others in positions of authority augment their income by cuddling criminals or becoming criminals themselves. Studies in Metro Manila found that a high proportion of policemen live in slum and squatter areas where they become friendly with criminals. A mutually beneficial relationship gets established, therefore, between those who violate the law and those who enforce he law.

"A farmer can sell his carabao to send his children to college," Erap explains. "But a policeman has only his gun so he becomes a gun-for-hire."

The price of common criminality for the Philippines is extremely high. For example, many crimes are related to the drug trade. The number of addicts is a heavy cost to the medical system. More seriously, many addicts turn to theft and other criminal activities to earn enough money to feed their habits.

Many foreign investors have been reluctant to come to the Philippines for fear that their families or they might be kidnapped for ransom. The losses from this situation are enormous but the jobs and income foregone due to fear are hard to calculate. Serious crimes such as hold-ups and bank robberies also have high economic costs. For one, the money that goes into the security industry could have been invested in more directly productive endeavors.

Due to the concerted efforts of police and military forces, kidnappings declined in the first quarter of 1998. However, the Citizens Action Against Crimes (CAAC) noted that petty crimes such as hold-ups and robberies have increased. Rape cases are also rising according to General Santiago Aliño of the Philippine National Police.

Organized crime and white collar crime are also serious deterrents to economic development. Syndicates in charge of gambling, prostitution, drugs, and the protection racket exact a heavy toll on the society. Their criminal actions become even more serious when they are able to strike alliances with politicians who protect them from prosecution. White collar crimes such as *estafa*, confidence games, pyramid schemes, theft and other types of scams are common in the Philippines. Cleaning them up will go a long way toward helping the country progress more rapidly.

## Graft and Corruption

To be listed by *Fortune Magazine* as the second most corrupt country in Asia (next to Indonesia) is enough to make any Filipino bow his head in shame. Graft and corruption has serious costs to the society. For one, government revenue is reduced considerably by kickbacks, commissions, fees and "transactional costs." A study by the U.P. College of Public Administration estimated that about 20% of government funds are lost through graft and corruption. The former Secretary of the Budget in the Ramos Government has admitted that the losses through corruption in the execution of pork barrel funds could be as high as 40%.

Graft and corruption adds to bureaucratic delays and red tape because the very act of instituting checks also encourages corruption—each point of transaction and discretionary authority provides an opportunity for bribes. A number of studies in agencies such as the Bureau of Customs and the Bureau of Internal Revenue have shown that additional procedures involving checks and counter checks may actually increase corruption. Streamlining processes and procedures, provided officials are honest and trustworthy, might lead to efficiency and higher outputs.

One of the worst hindrances to attracting foreign direct investments in a country like the Philippines is the fear that crony capitalism and other manifestations of graft result in unjust and inequitable decisions. Transactions such as those involving privatization of government assets become opportunities for making money. The infamous Public Estates Authority-Amari deal is said to have involved P300 million in commissions. During the Marcos regime, it was widely known that cronies of the President amassed great wealth from kickbacks and commissions on transactions involving public funds.

Private investors, domestic and international, require transparency in government deals to make public decisions more predictable. They ask for a "level playing field" in order to give each investor an equal opportunity to come up with the best offer. Without these assurances, honest investors will be reluctant to come to the Philippines. If collusion between public officials and corrupt business people become the norm, then only unscrupulous fly-by-night operators will be attracted to this country.

One of the most serious problems in the Philippines is graft and corruption in the judiciary. The Philippine court system used to be a model of uprightness—now, "hoodlums in robes" have tainted the reputation of that system. It is widely known that many fiscals are really "fixcals," willing to arrange deals for a price. Many judges and even justices are for sale. In a country with a disproportionate ratio of lawyers to the total population, the sordid knowledge that justice is for sale creates a great deal of cynicism and mistrust among the citizentry.

A serious implication of corruption in the justice system is the widely shared feeling that justice is only for the rich—the poor, who cannot afford to pay for the services of lawyers, invariably are the ones who go to jail. Even when some rich people are found guilty, they are able to arrange comfortable accommodations with the connivance of prison officials. A strong argument has been advanced against the restoration of the death penalty in the Philippines—it has been found that a great majority of prisoners on death row are poor folks. This does not mean that poor people are more likely to be criminals—it is just that the corrupt justice system is stacked against them.

**Social Fragmentation and Class-based Politics**

Philippine society is characterized by physical and social fragmentation. A country of more than 7,000 islands finds it hard to develop a common identity. Historically, social integration has been hampered by transportation and communication difficulties. The Philippines boasts no less than 76 distinct languages and dialects—to this day, visitors find it difficult to communicate with people in rural areas, although Tagalog and English are inceasingly understood by many.

The main cleavage in Philippine society, however, is socio-economic: the richest 20% of Filipinos owns 50% of the wealth while the bottom 40% have only 17%. Officially, the government claims that "only" 35.5% of Filipinos live below the poverty line. The World Bank, however, says that 60% of Filipinos earn less than $100 per month, the usual indicator for being poor.

More than three-fourths of poor people in the Philippines live in rural areas. Government policy has traditionally neglected agriculture, despite the fact that most people depend on it for their livelihood. Agriculture productivity is a low 1.4% per year. The crops sub-sector, which accounts for 60% of total agricultural output, has been growing at about 1%.

There are indication that the May 1998 election may signal a populist revolt against elite domination. Ironically, the person responsible for this basic social change is a bourgeois individual name Erap Estrada. In launching his presidential campaign, Erap has repeatedly sounded populist messages that endear him to the masses.

Erap has taken off from the nationalist emotions of the centennial year to drive home his message that the westernized Philippine elite has not looked after the welfare of the great majority of poor people. His alleged inability to speak the English language has become an endearing quality of Erap to his mass admirers. The thinly veiled insults from the elite that Erap is not bright have been taken by many poor people who also do not speak English well as a direct questioning of their abilities. The more that members of the elite attack Erap's persona, the more he becomes endeared to his admirers.

Many social analysts point to a number of basic social changes within the past three decades that may explain the desire of the Filipino masses to be heard. First, there is the process of globalization. The information revolution has linked most Filipinos to the outside world through print, radio, TV, movies, video, karaoke, cell phones, fax and e-mail. Even in the most remote villages, people can now link up to the global knowledge network.

The globalization of labor has also wrought great changes even in Philipine rural areas. In most villages, remittances from the eight million or so Filipinos working abroad are changing the local economy and people's lifestyles. Returning Overseas Filipino Workers (OFWs) bring back with them not just dollars, TV sets, blue-seal cigarettes, ghetto blasters and tacky souvenirs—they also have technical skills, entrepreneurial drive, and a new sense of empowerment. The money they bring home goes into education of family members, luxury goods, land purchases and enterpreneurial enterprises. International migration has broken the elite's monopoly over travel, foreign exchange, and business opportunities.

A notable change in Philippine society has been the great boom in the entertainment industry that has resulted in what has been called the"starization" of social life. Perhaps, as a function of the media explosion and the impact of Hollywood-style stardom, well known persons in the movies, TV, and sports have ventured into politics. Erap Estrada was one of the earliest of these stars turned politicos and he has been, certainly, the most successful. In the 1998 elections, at least seven senatorial candidates were TV, movies or sports stars. Many more such stars were running for congressmen, governors, mayors and city council positions.

As a result of the "starization" of politics, campaigning styles have also changed. President Fidel Ramos, supporting De Venecia, does his Edsa jump. Speaker de Venecia does the sha-la-la and a mean boogie. Senator Gloria Macapagal sings, dances and does her best to imitate Nora Aunor. Former Finance secretary Bobby de Ocampo sings and plays the guitar as well as demonstrates flying karate kicks.

In all these, of course, the professional entertainers and genuine performers outdo their rivals. Tito Sotto clowns and sings, Jaworski tosses basketballs, Loren Legarda smiles, Rene Cayetano speaks legalese, and Ramon Revilla scowls—the *masa* audiences lap it up. In making their future leaders perform during the electoral silly season, the Filipino masses are exacting their psychological revenge in advance.

Ideologically, the collapse of Communism and weakening of local leftist groups have also changed Philippine society. With the New People's Army down to a small fighting force and the Communist leadership divided between a leadership in exile and fractured local pockets, the revolutionary elements are in disarray. In their place has sprouted a mass-based civil society movement dominated by NGO's, environmentalists, feminists and social justice activists. The "party list" provision in the Constitution allowing marginalized groups to nominate congressional candidates has made "parliamentary struggle" rather than armed violence the chosen strategy for most progressively minded Filipinos. Almost all of these cause-oriented groups have taken the cudgels for the poor, the handicapped, the underprivileged and the downtrodden despite the fact that most of their leaders and key organizers are academics, intellectuals, members of the literati, artists and other middle class individuals.

Even changes in Philippine religious life are adding to the evolution of class-based politics in the country. Were the Iglesia ni Cristo used to be the only sect endorsing candidates and instructing their followers to support those candidates, born-again groups like the Jesus is Lord movement or the charismatic El Shaddai have also decided to get involved in partisan politics. The emergence of these "command votes" blocks, many of the members of which are drawn from the poor and underpriviledged, lend an element of class conflict to current political life. The big question, of course, is whether the activism of these religious groups will translate into programs that are pro-poor, or will they only serve to consolidate the power positions of their founders and organizers?

Up to now, many social analysts have bewailed the failure of the two-party system in the Philippines. Unlike in the United States, England and Canada, they say, Philippine parties do not represent qualitatively different policies and programs that the voters can choose from. The many political parties in the Philippines are mere temporary alliances for political gain. They do not represent different ideas or ideologies. In a SWS survey, 90% of respondents said they did not identify with any political party. Philippines elections are about individuals, not parties. This is the reason why personal popularity, charisma, name recall and even notoriety have become the basis for choosing candidates.

As Filipinos trooped to the polls on 11 May 1998, there were signs that some kind of social polarization was happening in Philippine society. The elite *versus masa* appeal of Erap Estrada and his partymates in LAMMP was not just rhetorical—people sensed that Erap is sincerely committed to genuine social reforms that respond to their most basic needs—food on the table, jobs, decent wages, prices even the poor can afford, children's education, health, social housing, and above all, people's participation in public decision making.

Erap's call for an end to traditional politics that made the poor mere followers of elite politicians intent on delivering their "command votes" to the highest bidders hit a corresponding nerve among the people. His exhortations on the excesses of the elite were echoed by the masses who were fed up with old line *trapo* politics. Erap's populist stand that every person is important (*Bawat isa, mahalaga*) found support. Emboldened by Erap's call for reform, the people rejected political parties, local machines, elite families and dynasties, ward heelers—even Church leaders and civic NGOs and influentials. Even when they sold their votes to local leaders, they still voted for candidates of their choice.

To the masses who flocked to LAMMP rallies, the anti-elite emotions stoked by Erap and his partymates in their campaign speeches were visibly palpable. Erap's nationalistic appeals, reflected in his references to local heroes and historic events in his speeches (Aguinaldo in Cavite, Diego Silang's revolt in the Ilocos) were applauded by the masses.

Erap's use of Tagalog was welcomed, even by those whose mother tongue was Visayan, Capampangan or Ilocano, and his "murdering" of the English language evoked loud laughter but appreciative applause. Since 1998 is the Philppine centennial year, these nationalistic appeals played beautifully in provincial campaign rallies.

The 1998 centennial year celebrations generated debates among Filipino intellectuals on elite-mass relationship, especially during the period leading up to the 1898 Philippine revolution. Ambeth Ocampo's popularization of the Bonifacio-Aguinaldo rivalry serialized in a leading Manila daily triggered off heated discussion on whether the original "revolt of the masses" led by Bonifacio had actually been co-opted by the western-educated Filipino elites led by Aguinaldo, who used treachery in killing the founder of the revolution.

Erap Estrada himself added fire to this debate when he said, during his official proclamation as president-elect by the joint session of the House of

Representatives and the Senate on 29 May that his election victory could be regarded as "history repeating itself."

"Bonifacio was condemned by the *illustrados* (ruling elite), by the Church, by the bourgeois society. That's how I was also condemned—and still the masses supported me," Erap said. "So this is the revolt of the masses, the new modern Bonifacio."

When reporters reminded Erap that Bonifacio was executed by his rivals after a serios rift developed between his faction and that of General Emilio Aguinaldo, Erap quickly retorted, "That is why I said 'modern day' Bonifacio."

Erap's witticisms aside, did the 1998 election really signal the coming about of class-based cleavage in Philippine society along classical Marxist-Leninist lines of violent class struggle rooted in historical determinism? To believe in this is probably gross exaggeration. The consciousness of *masa*-ness on the part of the great majority of poor Filipinos in 1998 is probably more of identification and differentiation (we the masses against you, the elites ) rather than a manifestation of true class conflict. It arises from a sense of unfairness and injustice—a rejection of the victimization of the poor because of the elite's monopoly over authority and power and the use of corrupt means for perpetuating hegemony.

At its core, this new sense of class among the Philippine masses is probably not based on a desire for violent struggle—it arises more from a sense of empowerment that, now that the masses have found their voice and can now be heard in the formulation of party policies, the poor would finally find their basic concerns included in the goverment's agenda. The 1998 election does not signal a revolt but a coming of age—the empowered masses have, at last, become, an integral part of Philippine politics, and , through Erap and LAMMP, they intend to have their proper role in the decision making process.

# Chapter 3

# Cha-cha, Pirma and No-El

It was not an auspicious day to campaign for the Centennial President of the Philippines in the place where it all began a hundred years ago. Confusion gripped preparations for the Joseph "Erap" Estrada motorcade and rally in Cavite that hot humid day in February 1998. The Scheduling Team kept changing its mind. First, it was announced there would be a motorcade through the small towns of this historic province. This being the Philippine centennial year, a rally was scheduled for Kawit, where Philippine Independence from Spain was first proclaimed on 12 June 1898 by a band of revolutionaries led by General Emilio Aguinaldo. Then, the schedule was changed—no more rally in Kawit. No more motorcade either—all campaigners should proceed directly to Dasmarinas for lunch. The main rally would be held in Cavite City that evening.

For the motorcade, we were supposed to rendezvous at the Puerto Azul exit of the South Diversion Road at one in the afternoon. What faced us, when we got there, was a monstrous traffic jam. Hundreds of cars and vans, jeepneys with *JEEP ni Erap* streamers, buses with balloons and buntings, and the candidates' support vans blaring a cacophony of jingles that competed with honking vehicles that jammed the highway exit. Campaign volunteers in bright orange vests were busy handing out Erap-Edong stickers to passengers in stalled buses. A handful of harassed policemen tried to unsnarl the traffic, their whistles shrill in the sweltering summer heat. Instead of the joyous gaiety of a campaign rally, the atmosphere was tense and testy, tempers flaring at the obvious lack of organization.

Informed that the motorcade was canceled, we drove past the choked exit and proceeded towards Dasmarinas. Traffic was heavy. The acrid smoke of diesel buses poisoned the air. Jeepneys with their unmistakable clatter and whine labored through the winding roads. Not even the tips of exuberant pink *kakawati* blossoms moved in the blistering noonday sun. The air conditioner in our *Pregio* van was laboring with semi-cold air.

As we reached Cavite's hilly terrain, however, the scenery turned lush and verdant—we passed green coffee plantations, groves of graceful coconut palms, thick hedges of flowering bouganvilles, towering cascades of golden shower trees and the torrid red of flame trees in full bloom. We did not notice too many Erap-Edong posters—not a very good sign. To the strongly partisan campaigners in our van who had been in the wildly successful Laguna motorcade the previous week to kick off the campaign, the passive faces of the people along the road who rarely waved back to our exuberant greetings, were a big disappointment. We wondered where the advance teams in charge of "Operation Dikit" (those who stuck posters and hung streamers along the motorcade route) were. There were also some mutterings among the partisans in our group that former Governor Johnny Remulla's people did not seem to be as prepared as the operatives of Governor Joey Lina of Laguna were—in the previous week, the LAMMP workers in Laguna had plastered practically every empty space with posters from San Pedro just outside Manila to Sta. Cruz town.

On paper, plans for the Cavite rally had all looked so organized and orderly. There was an "Orange Guide" issued to all candidates and key campaign officers that had a detailed minute-by-minute schedule of campaign activities, a sketch map of the province, a neat drawing of the rally site, even an indication of the order in which the various vehicles would travel and how far each car in the motorcade should be from the lead escort car (dubbed by the Security Detail as "Baker One"). The guide also had a two-page "Policy and Issue Brief" that provided background information on the province.

As LAMMP Campaign Officers for Public Policies and Issues, it was our job to prepare this "Policy and Issue Brief" for every place the candidates would visit. This "situationer" (a peculiar Filipino neologism meaning "the situation") was issued a week in advance and was a key part of the "Orange Guide." Writing the brief involved a lot of research as we also attempted to find out key issues people were concerned with in the places to be visited. Problem was, we were not even sure if our candidate, who was notorious for not wanting to read anything beyond one page, was actually reading our daily briefs. The press releases of the other candidates showed, however, that, at least, they were using our materials.

Our policy brief for the Cavite rally on 20 February 1998 suggested the centennial theme:

> Caviteños are very proud of their cultural heritage and the historical role of the province in our national history. This pride is

> particularly strong this year, with the celebration of the Philippine centennial. Many Cavite natives are strong Erap supporters, arguing that the first Filipino President, Emilio Aguinaldo, was Tagalog and that after 100 years, it was time another Tagalog was elected President.

The note was a blatant appeal to the twin factors that had bedeviled Filipinos since the beginning of their history. First, there was the nationalistic theme—at a time when the Filipino nation is celebrating the 100th anniversary of the revolution against Spanish colonial domination, the Erap-Edong campaign would be wise to wrap itself in the flag and proclaim its patriotism. Almost in the same breath, however, the briefing note appealed to the regionalism and "tribal politics" that also characterize Philippine society. Tagalogs vote for Tagalog candidates, Ilocanos for Ilocanos, Bicolanos for Bicolanos.

The Ejercito family is pure Tagalog stock. Erap's grandparents on his father's side were from Kawit, Cavite, while the Marcelos, on his mother's side, were from Binan, Laguna. Don Emilio Ejercito and Doña Maria Marcelo, however, met, married and raised their family in Manila. As if to complete Erap's patriotic ancestry, he was actually born in the proletarian district of Tondo, Manila—also the birthplace of the great revolutionary hero, Andres Bonifacio.

At that evening's rally in Cavite City, we listened to Erap's set campaign speech when his turn finally came at around midnight. We laughed at his ice-breaker jokes even if we had heard them all before. His timing, cadence, pregnant pauses, and odd mixture of Tagalog and English were perfect. He had the audience of more than 5,000—people who had been waiting for him from eight in the evening until midnight—in the palm of his hand.

Then, he deviated from the set speech and touched on the centennial theme. He noted that 1998 was the 100th anniversary of the Philippine proclamation of independence against Spain and that this had happened in the historic province of Cavite. Loud applause and cheers.

Erap then noted that the first President of the Philippines was a Tagalog—a Caviteno, in fact—General Emilio Aguinaldo. He then started tracing the ethnic origins of the other Presidents—Quezon was Tagalog, Osmena a Cebuano, Laurel was from Batangas, Roxas from Capiz, Quirino an Ilocano, Garcia was Boholano, Magsaysay was from Zambales, Macapagal was Capampangan, Marcos was Ilocano, Cory Aquino was Capampangan and Ramos was a Pangasinense. Erap paused and raised the crucial question: "Isn't it time that after 100 years, the next President of the Philippines should be Tagalog again?" (*Wild cheers and applause*).

To our pleasant surprise our candidate did read his briefing notes that day.

**Many Candidates, Few Choices**

The year 1998 is doubly significant to most Filipinos—the 1998 elections will choose the country's centennial president and the winner will lead the country into the next millennium. Yet, according to a number of opinion makers—especially cynical columnists, the eleven or so individuals seeking the presidency were positively "underwhelming."

In their book *Showdown '98: the Search for the Centennial President,* the *Manila Times* and the Ateneo Center for Social Policy and Public Affairs, drew portraits of the "presidentiables" as follows:

- Jose de Venecia, Jr.—Lord of the pork, the most promising pol
- Renato de Villa—The clone on his own, a firebrand too late
- Juan Ponce Enrile—Been there, done-that yeoman
- Joseph Estrada—Made in the movies, next attraction in Malacanang?
- Alfredo Lim—Cory's choice, Robocop for president
- Imelda Marcos—A widow's swan song for the strongman
- Emilio Osmena—The Promdi has coño roots, no common touch
- Raul Roco—The honorary ma'am is a sure-footed survivor
- Miriam Santiago—Genius unbound, the perennial pain

The Ateneo and *Times* book did not include two other candidates—Manuel Morato, the former Lotto King who ran purposely to thwart the presidential ambitions of Estrada and Santiago, and Santiago Dumlao, a born-again Christian who campaigned on a platform of godliness in government. Dumlao, the Harvard-educated candidate, promised to give every Filipino a P500 allowance every month and abolish income tax, prompting newspaper commentators to wonder if he took any economics courses at Harvard. The book also ignored more than 70 other nuisance candidates, including one who claimed to be "God, the Father of Jesus Christ," another running to be "King of the Philippine Solar System," and a third who styled himself as an international playboy. It is disturbing that 81 Filipinos filed their certificates of candidacy for president.While participatory democracy may be laudable, clowns aspiring to be president trivialize the highest position in the land.

It is one of the ironies of the year that, in spite of the large number of people applying for the job, the presidential candidates thrust forward to contest the election prompted many voters to want to write "None of the above." One columnist noted, in fact, that the candidates for vice president seemed more competent than their presidential team-mates.

**Cha-cha, Pirma & No-El**

It is hard to believe that the campaign for the 11 May 1998 elections had actually begun on schedule—90 days before election day. In May 1996, when we volunteered to work for Erap's presidential campaign, we were not even sure there would be elections in 1998. Although Erap had openly launched his candidacy much earlier, uncertainty was in the air as Manila filled with rumors about military operational plans similar to the infamous Oplan Sagittarius that launched martial law in 1972.

If Manila scuttlebutt was to be believed, the administration party's plans for the 1998 elections played like a madman's game of scrabble.

First step was No-El or "No Elections"—President Ramos and the thousands of officials whose terms were ending on 30 June 1998 would simply extend their official status to the year 2000 supposedly to save money and to provide continuity to Ramos' successful economic and social development policies.

If No-El failed, then, the strategy would shift to Fa-El or "Failure of Elections"—there will be so much cheating and violence, especially in the island of Mindanao and other areas controlled by the government party, that the election results would be declared null and void. The army would come in to quell the violence—much of it of their own doing—and President Ramos would come in as the general on horseback, declare martial law, save the country from rebellion and restore peace and order.

Should Fa-El fail, the next step would be No-Proc or "No Proclamation"—the election results would be met with so many protests and interminable litigation that Erap, even if he won, would not be proclaimed. There would be a constitutional crisis and, perhaps, Gloria Macapagal, who seemed certain to be elected as Vice President, would assume the duties of President. Of course, if No-Proc results in widespread unrest and violence, Ramos would save democracy by declaring martial law as well to suppress the revolt of the masses who would not quietly accept an Estrada defeat.

As 1996 drew to a close, the first of these threats, a campaign appropriately called Pirma was launched in Manila. Pirma was short for "People's Initiative for Reform, Modernization and Action" which was an attempt to obtain more than six million signatures for a petition to allow President Ramos to remain in power beyond 30 June 1998. Pirma paid P99,000 for a full-page ad in the *Philippine Daily Inquirer* enjoining people to "assert their rights and power" to sustain the economic reforms of President Ramos. Pirma supported Charter changes to lift constitutional constraints limiting President Ramos to a term of six years. It also proposed synchronizing the terms of office of national and local elective officials so elections would be held after the year 2000 instead of May 1998.

The persons behind Pirma were Ambassador Alberto Pedrosa and his wife Carmen, aka "Chit." Alberto was appointed by President Ramos as Ambassador to the European Community from 1992 to 1995 and Chit was a journalist who wrote an unauthorized biography of Imelda Marcos. After retirement from the diplomatic service, the Pedrosas returned to the Philippines to organize Pirma. Since they were old Ramos friends, it was assumed by many cynical Filipinos that their efforts enjoyed the full backing of the President. The fact that there were very few visible funding sources for the campaign meant, to most people, that it was being supported by the Presidential palace or the Lakas-NUCD party in power.

President Ramos, of course, denied that he was behind the activities of Pirma and the Pedrosas. He said he had no intention of staying in office beyond his constitutionally mandated term. On the oft-quoted statement of the President indicating "This is my last term in office, period, period, period," a sharp-eyed columnist observed that a series of dots after a statement means continuity rather than stop. Few people believed that the President had no intention of remaining in his position after the expiration of his term because it was obvious that he immensely enjoyed the authority, status, power and prestige of the presidency.

On the same day that Pirma was launched, it was joined by another pro-Cha-cha group, the Movement for People's Initiative (MPI) led by lawyer Delfin Lazaro. On 6 December 1996, Lazaro of MPI, accompanied by the Pedrosas, went to the Commission on Elections (Comelec) to submit a petition asking the poll body to help it in setting up signature stations nationwide. Opponents of people's initiative challenged this request right away, saying that public funds (of Comelec) should not be used to support a private initiative. They filed a petition for a temporary restraining order which was granted by the Supreme Court on 19 December. This set back the Pedrosas, Pirma and the Movement for People's Initiative a little but they remained undaunted.

If the paranoid fears of the political opposition had become reality, the 1998 elections would not have happened. Indeed, in the early months of 1997, there were signs everywhere that President Fidel Ramos and his supporters were expanding plans for him to remain in power beyond his Constitutionally determined term. These plans looked into three options: (a) Charter change or Cha-cha, which called for revising the Philippine Constitution to allow Ramos through a Constitutional Convention or the convening of a joint session of the Senate and the House of Representatives to remain in power or be allowed to run again in the 1998 elections; (b) changing the Constitution through a people's initiative brought about by a nation-wide signature campaign (Pirma) already started by the Pedrosas; and (c) not holding any elections in 1998 at all. These options occupied the attention of Philippine politicians for much of the latter years of the Ramos administration.

On 19 March 1997, the Pirma and MPI suffered a serious setback when the Supreme Court ruled that Republic Act 6735, the people's initiative and referendum law, was "inadequate" to lend legality to the Pirma signature campaign. Pirma filed a motion for reconsideration with the Supreme Court to overturn this move. On 10 June, the Supreme Court ruled with finality that RA 6735 was inadequate and the signature campaign was ordered stopped.

For much of 1997, President Ramos kept Filipinos guessing whether he really wanted to "graduate" from the presidency in June 1998 or do a Marcos and continue as president despite constitutional limitations on his term of office. He kept denying he was interested in another term but he also insisted that the launching of a people's initiative was a "legitimate aspiration" of a group like Pirma as it was guaranteed by the Constitution. Some of the President's supporters, whom he did not restrain, even issued thinly veiled threats that stopping the President from extending his term might just encourage him to resort to authoritarianism and even declare martial law. Reacting to statements of Cardinal Jaime Sin urging people to rise against moves to amend the Constitution, National Security Adviser, Jose "JoAl" Almonte told the vocal prelate to "stick to the spreading of the Gospel and quit engaging in politics."

Pirma predictably met with vehement opposition not only from Cardinal Sin but from former President Corazon Aquino, former Ramos officials Ramon del Rosario, Jr., and Peter Garrucho, and even Ramos' sister, Senator Leticia Shahani. Cory said the time was not right to amend the Constitution because the issue would be too divisive. She reminded people about what happened when Ferdinand Marcos tried to amend the Constitution and martial law was declared.

"We lost our rights and freedoms," Mrs. Aquino said, "Many of us sacrificed a lot to regain our rights. So, it is best to leave the Constitution alone at this time. I'm sure the changes can wait."

Erap Estrada, of course, joined in the opposition to Pirma, especially since Chit Pedrosa had openly admitted that the initiative was primarily designed to stop him from becoming president. The lady journalist who had authored an unflattering best-seller about Imelda Marcos spent her venom on Erap, whom she called "totally incompetent to become president." In her newspaper columns, Pedrosa referred to Erap as "Asiong Salonga," a notorious outlaw figure Erap had portrayed in an award-winning movie and to the Filipino masses as *masang tanga* (stupid masses).

Erap urged Ramos to follow the example of Cory Aquino who voluntarily refused to seek a second term despite the prodding of her advisers. He added that "The Constitution is the bible of government. Amendments should not be done in haste but after a thorough study on the possible provisions to be affected."

Informed of accusations that he was determined to stay in power beyond 1998, President Ramos lashed back at his critics. He repeated his statement that he would step down after his term. However, Executive Secretary Ruben Torres revealed in February 1997 that the ruling Lakas-NUCD party would like the President's term extended through a constitutional amendment. Furthermore, President Ramos had endorsed a proposal to amend the Constitution in order to limit the powers of the Supreme Court. Critics observed that if the amendment clipping the powers of the Supreme Court was going to be passed, what was to prevent anyone from changing the charter's limitation on term limits as well?

**Cha-cha and Other Tunes**

Amending constitutional provisions on presidential term limits was only one of the tunes the advocates of Cha-cha or Charter change were playing in early 1997. Actually, a number of proposals were being advanced. These included proposed changes on the Charter provisions governing the national economy and patrimony, amendments to the Bill of Rights, the passage of an anti-terrorism law, and the introduction of a national identification card system. Various groups were pushing and lobbying for these specific changes.

In Muslim Mindanao, Governor Nur Misuari strongly advocated Charter changes to achieve what he called his Mindanao Agenda. The core elements in this agenda were: (a) the election of one Vice President each for Mindanao, Luzon and the Visayas; (b) the regionalization of elections for senators; and (c ) the appointment of more persons from Mindanao to the Supreme Court, the Cabinet, the police forces, and the military.

Aside from the substantive changes mentioned above, there were also a number of recommendations on how the Constitution could be revised. The idea of holding a Constitutional Convention was rejected early because it would have been extremely complicated and expensive. However, there were quite a few advocates of Charter change who favored a constituent assembly made up of the House of Representatives and the Senate that could then tackle the amendment of the Constitution. The recommendations of the assembly, in turn, would be confirmed through a national referendum.

One approach greatly favored by many advocates of Cha-cha was the people's initiative. This was provided for in Section 2 of Article XVII of the Constitution which indicated that: "Amendments to this Constitution may ... be directly proposed by the people through initiative upon a petition of at least 12 per centum of the total number of registered voters, of which every legislative district must be represented by at least three per centum of the registered voters therein."

To implement this constitutional provision, the Congress passed Republic Act 6735. Pirma, in pushing for people's initiative, argued that RA 6735 was an adequate basis to amend the Constitution. However, the Supreme Court of the Philippines, in a 9-5 decision on 19 March 1997, declared that the present statute was an inadequate basis for a people's action to amend the Constitution.

Disappointed by the High Court's decision, Malacanang immediately launched a legislative program to have an alternative law passed during the opening of Congress on 28 July 1997. A bill was proposed in the House by a Lakas congressman. However, another bill was filed in the Senate by Senator Miriam Santiago, a staunch opponent of Cha-cha.

As the Congress opened its session on 28 July, there was great anticipation on whether the administration would push for passage of a bill proposing a new people's initiative or not. Pirma was lobbying for a bill that would give it enough time to get the Comelec and the Supreme Court to permit a signature campaign that would allow the lifting of term limits for elected officials, including the President. It was also interested in passing legislation that would allow the holding of a referendum on term limits before the May 1998 elections.

With Speaker De Venecia's "Rainbow Coalition" controlling the House of Representatives, Pirma and its allies would not have encountered any problem in getting their legislative agenda passed. The problem was in the Senate, where opposition to Cha-cha was strong. Opposition senators, especially those interested in running for president in 1998, were not in favor of Cha-cha because they argued that it would lead to a political crisis. Some even argued that when President Ramos agreed to run for President in 1992, he entered into a contract with the people that he would abide by the constitutional limitation on term limits. He should, therefore, observe that limit.

Blocked in the Senate, the people advocating Cha-cha decided to put pressure on the Supreme Court. The Pedrosas and Comelec filed a motion for reconsideration intended to convince some Supreme court magistrates to change their decision on RA 6735. Specific targets for the pressures were identified: Justices Jose Vitug, Regino Hermosisima, Jr., Justo Torres and Artemio Panganiban were some of those mentioned as being lobbied by the Pirma activists. The pressures got so intense that there were talks of a "white paper" detailing some of the "dark secrets" of some of the justices—with implied threats that these would be divulged if the targets refused to cooperate. To the credit of the justices, they acted independently and refused to be pressured. Not even the involvement of a close relative of Chief Justice Andres Narvasa who joined Pirma could sway the court from its position that there was no legal basis for the proposed initiative.

Even as the Supreme Court was considering the petition of Pirma and Comelec, Pirma advocates already started getting their signature campaign going. They claimed to have succeeded in getting six million signatures favoring Cha-cha. However, it was pointed out that the Comelec would face extreme difficulties in verifying the signatures. To begin with, the computerized list of registered voters was not going to be ready until early 1998 so it would have been impossible to determine whether Pirma was able to gather 12% of the votes or not. People pointed out, also that because of the pressure of time, even if the Supreme Court decided in favor of the motion for reconsideration by the Comelec and the Pedrosas, it would have been impossible to verify all six million signatures before the 11 May elections.

In July 1997, the Supreme Court, voted 7–0, rejecting the Pirma motion for reconsideration. Undeterred, the advocates of initiative decided to establish the Philippine People Power Foundation, Inc, (PPPFI) in order to pursue the campaign for Charter change. About 120 local government officials led by Governor Roberto "Obet" Pagdanganan of Bulacan launched what the newspapers called Pirma II, another well-financed effort to push for lifting of term limits. An 11 July news item asked: "People Power or is it Pirma All Over Again?" The news item reported that PPPFI was going to gather volunteers nationwide to conduct consultations about Charter change. Jun Tupas, PPPFI president said their volunteers would conduct public fora where people would be asked to sign their names, indicate their precinct numbers and pass resolutions in support of a second term for President Ramos.

The President, in turn, continued to play coy on the issue of Cha-cha. He reiterated his oft-quoted pledge that he would "retire on June 30, 1998 when my term ends, my one and only term." Then, in almost the same breath, the President would say one of his problems was that he found it very difficult to say no. "Six years is good enough for me even if a good number of the citizenry may wish for me to try again and to continue," the President said. "That's the problem, saying no against such a widespread clamor."

President Ramos firmly believed that under the Constitution, "our people have the right to mount an initiative to amend the basic law and other laws of the land." While others may question the wisdom of the extension of the President's term, President Ramos argued that the principle of using initiative to change the Constitution was unassailable and was proof of democratic decision making in the country. This line of argument was picked up by National Security Adviser JoAl Almonte who nevertheless warned that halting people's initiative efforts to Charter change would destabilize Philippine society and frustrate genuine democratic aspirations.

The pro- and anti- positions on Cha-cha came to a head on 21 September 1997 when Cory Aquino, Cardinal Sin and hundreds of prominent Filipino leaders held a gigantic rally against Cha-cha on the 25$^{th}$ anniversary of the declaration of martial law by President Marcos. There were controversies on how many people actually attended the Sin-Aquino-led rally—the police estimated half a million, organizers claimed many times more than that. What was obvious, however, was the widespread opposition to efforts to amend the Constitution to allow President Ramos to continue in office. While there was widespread agreement that the Ramos presidency had been good for the country, the cynical and manipulative means used by the Ramos supporters to carry out Cha-cha were roundly criticized.

**No Way and Never Again!**

The voice most loudly heard at the Luneta rally on 21 September was that of former President Corazon Aquino. She warned persons who wanted to be President of the Philippines:

> "Power intoxicates; too much power is addictive. And there will always be power drug dealers who will feed your habit as President."

Turning to the literary hyperbole that characterized her speeches when she was still President, Mrs. Aquino said:

> "Today, there is a dark wind blowing across our country again—the wind of ambition, a gathering storm of tyranny. We are here to shield that flame so that the light of democracy will not go out in our country again."
>
> "That is why we are here today—to tell the people who want to stay in power by martial law or Charter change—no way and never again! Do your worst, we will do our best to stop you. And we, the people, will prevail."

After the ringing tones of Edsa Revolt II, President Ramos and those who wanted his term as president extended abandoned Cha-cha, Pirma and No-El. It is worth asking why they even attempted these efforts when it was so clear that any attempt to stir up the ghost of martial law would be met with strong resistance by the Church, militant organizations, cause-oriented groups, and, of course, the many "presidentiables" whose ambitions would be thwarted by Ramos' continuity in power.

There were a number of explanations for the apparent effort of President Ramos and his supporters to change the Constitution and remain in power. It was suggested that President Ramos was just interested in ensuring that he would not be treated as a "lame duck" president and that he would be taken seriously until the end of his term. People who advanced this proposition pointed out that President Ramos was keenly conscious of his role in history. It was extremely difficult for him, therefore, to be placed in a marginalized position of little or no power after having been such a powerful president.

There were also suggestions that President Ramos honestly thought that he was the only one who could manage the economic affairs of the Philippines and that, therefore, he should have been given the full authority to be elected so that he could finish the tasks that he had started. Although candidates like Erap said that they would be happy to continue the policies of trade liberalization, privatization and poverty alleviation if elected, President Ramos preferred to be the person in charge. The President had also formed a capable team of Cabinet officers who willingly did his bidding, and he felt that keeping these officers in the vicinity of Malacanang would ensure accomplishment of desired goals.

There was the possibility, of course, that President Ramos himself might have been quite willing to exit gracefully after his six year term but that people around him who would lose their authority and power when he was gone manipulated things to achieve advantages in their internal bickerings with each other. In the months before the official opening of the campaign season, a number of political observers pointed to the open conflicts among Lakas-NUCD key officials. Spokesperson Annabelle Abaya was at loggerheads with Gualberto Lumauig, who in turn did not seem to get along with Gabriel Claudio. Even among the Pirma advocates, things were sometimes not well between Pirma president Alberto Pedrosa and Pirma executive director Mike Policarpio. The disagreements among the Lakas-NUCD staff detracted from the single-minded dedication to achieving results that President Ramos is capable of. In turn, internal management inefficiencies must have contributed to the Lakas-NUCD failure to make their election campaign work.

The answers to the question of why Oplan No-El, Pirma and Fa-El failed will forever remain conjectural. The historical fact turned out to be that all the efforts to bring about Cha-cha, No-El, No-Proc and all the other schemes hatched in fervid strategic minds by Ramos partisans were demolished by the 11 May elections and the ascendancy of Erap Estrada to the presidency of the Philippines.

## Why Cha-cha and No-El Failed

It is useful to analyze how the failure of Cha-cha, No-El, No-Proc and all the various schemes hatched to thwart the 1998 elections actually influenced the patterns of politics in the Philippines. In particular, what effects did the machinations have on the outcome of the 11 May elections? With the benefit of hindsight, we draw the following conclusions.

First, the failure of Cha-cha and No-El revealed the strong commitment of Filipinos to the democratic process. The most serious miscalculation of the supporters of President Ramos was the belief that the money, power, governmental resources, and political machinery that gave the administration party such great advantages were sufficient conditions for winning the elections. Assessments of the accomplishments of the Ramos presidency, both local and international, were invariably positive. Analysts admitted that the Ramos government had transformed what used to be the sick man of Asia into a frisky economic tiger cub. The mistake of the administration party was in assuming that this was a sufficient reason for people to support continuity of the Ramos programs.

Second, the success of the 21 September anti-Cha-cha rally showed that the "people power" revolution that ended the Marcos dictatorship was still a force to reckon with in Philippine politics. Political analysts saw the Edsa revolt as the high noon of the middle classes. Led by Cory Aquino, Cardinal Sin, members of the clergy, religious sisters, cause-oriented groups and professionals, the Edsa revolt was able to chase Marcos out of the country without bloodshed.

By successfully invoking the spirit of people power at the 21 September rally, Cory Aquino and Cardinal Sin managed to stop dead in its tracks the ambitions of the Cha-cha forces to revise the fundamental law of the land to benefit one individual. They showed that there was still widespread suspicion and cynicism about the military in the country, that the memories of the Marcos dictatorship were still fresh in people's minds.

Third, it was obvious that Erap Estrada's participation in the anti-Cha-cha rally was of some benefit to him. Although Erap and Cory/Sin were on opposite camps in Philippine politics, the two principal rally organizers needed all the support they could get. They wanted to show that there was widespread resistance to the efforts to allow President Ramos to remain in power. The presence of Erap among the rallyists made their point but it was of even greater advantage to Erap.

Erap had traditionally been branded "a Marcos loyalist." He was one of the few individuals who was with the Marcos family in Malacanang on that fateful day in 1986 before the American helicopters flew in and took the Marcoses to Clark Air Force Base and then by plane to Honolulu. By actively participating in the anti-Cha-cha rally, Erap found himself, at last, on the good side. Earlier, Cardinal Sin, in drawing up a pastoral letter to guide the Catholic faithful whom to vote for, used participation in Edsa as an important criterion for supporting a candidate. Although Erap was not at Edsa, his presence at the anti-Cha-cha rally was of some help.

Fourth, the person most adversely affected by the September anti-Cha-cha rally was Secretary Renato de Villa. As an ardent aspirant for the "anointment" of President Ramos, de Villa had to excuse himself from the rally because of fear that he would antagonize the President. Unfortunately for de Villa, this action only served to heighten his image as a "clone" of President Ramos. By choosing political expediency to a matter of principle, de Villa, who had to demonstrate his personal loyalty to the President, lost quite a lot of support from cause-oriented individuals.

Fifth, the invoking of Edsa and people power showed the ability of organized religious bodies such as El Shaddai and other charismatic groups to mobilize their followers. It is generally believed in the Philippines that there is no such thing as a Catholic vote because by the very fact that the great majority of Filipinos are Catholics, it is almost impossible for them to be mobilized in a disciplined way to support a certain political line. However, the charismatic groups were shown to be responsive to the biddings of their leaders. It was interesting to observe whether such organized behavior could be converted into actual votes.

Finally, the defeat of Cha-cha, No-El and Fa-El could be traced to an utter failure of their proponents to properly gauge the dissatisfaction of the Filipino masses with the economic and social development policies of the Ramos administration. It was a case of the administration party strategists believing the very propaganda that they themselves produced . The main thread of Cha-cha, No-El and Fa-El was continuity. However, the Philippine economic situation had changed and the Ramos administration was rendered almost helpless by the collapse of the peso, high interest rates, high unemployment rates, and high inflation. When the Ramos partisans argued for the extension of Ramos' term for continuity, people, especially the masses, were likely to ask—continuity of what? Observing the seeming disregard of their socio-economic plight by the President's men, the masses whose living conditions have not significantly improved, rejected the party in power.

Although Erap and Cory/Sin became temporary allies in the fight against Cha-cha, subsequent months would show that the objections of the Edsa loyalists to Erap were more deep-seated and real. After it became clear that Ramos' ambition to remain in power would not be a threat anymore, Cory swung her support to Mayor Fred Lim. Cardinal Sin did not go to the extent of openly endorsing Lim but it was obvious that his "Anybody but Erap" feelings were very much alive.

In the end, Erap did not really need the support of Cory/Sin or the mantle of "I was at Edsa" identification to win the elections. His pro-poor campaign started to snowball and the public opinion polls showed this. Despite the Cardinal's admonition to the faithful not to be taken in by surveys and to vote only according to their conscience, many Catholics continued their support for Erap. For example, Erap got a sizable portion of the votes cast by members of El Shaddai, a Catholic charismatic group, even though its leader, Brother Mike Velarde did not openly endorse Erap. After the election, when Erap's victory was secure, he asked Brother Eddie instead of Cardinal Sin to deliver the inaugural invocation at the Barasoain Church in Malolos. This was the signal that Brother Mike, indeed, had secretly endorsed Erap during the El Shaddai rally and that the code words, "*Tiyak yon*" were for real.

This success of Erap with the religious vote contrasts sharply with the uncertainty of the support given to Speaker de Venecia by the Jesus is Lord Movement. Despite the open anointment by Brother Eddie Villanueva, De Venecia still did not get enough votes to really challenge Erap. Either the votes of JIL were not as many as originally claimed or the discipline of its members in voting for the person chosen by their leader is weak. Either way, the results were not so good for De Venecia.

# Chapter 4

# Erap as We Know Him

The voice on the phone seemed hurt and agitated. "What is this I hear that you are supporting *that man?* What has he done for the poor?" It was our former English teacher, a devout Catholic and lay apostolate, her voice still resonant at 74. She was aghast that we were supporting Joseph "Erap" Estrada for president. She could not even bring herself to mention his name. She was for Fred Lim—Cory Aquino's candidate. She said Cardinal Jaime Sin was probably for Lim as well. The Cardinal certainly did not hide his contempt for Erap, whom he called "morally unfit" to be President and a "probable disaster" for the whole country.

It was not a good way to get re-connected with a former teacher after 40 years of not seeing each other. More than half of those years we had spent abroad although we had kept in close touch with developments in the Philippines. Now, we were back in Manila as volunteers for Erap's presidential campaign. We had taken a six-month leave from the University of British Columbia, in Vancouver, Canada, to help Erap in whatever ways two political neophytes could. Many of our friends, many belonging to Manila's snooty literati and self-important intelligentsia thought we had taken leave of our senses. This was not the first time someone had asked us why we were supporting Erap. Before leaving Vancouver, a Canadian academic interested in Philippine affairs, after hearing about our planned Manila mission had asked us rather pointedly—"Why him?"

Our response was vintage Erap—"Why not?"

On the surface, we do not conform to the stereotype of Erap supporters. We may be classified A-B in the uniquely Filipino way of classifying voters—highly educated, comfortable but not filthy rich, more than a dozen books to our credit, international careers. Early in life, of course, Prod had been a D-E, growing up as a squatter in a Pasay slum, his life changed only because he won a Fulbright grant to get an MIT doctorate in political science after graduating from the U.P. in public administration. Eleanor's family would have been B—lawyer father, mother a nurse, nice home in Intramuros. However, her father's long illness forced Eleanor's family down to a C—not quite *masa* but acquainted with poverty, when her mother became a widow with five young kids to raise.

That was years ago. Now, we were *balikbayan* (returning former resident) researchers writing a book about the 1998 Philippine elections. And strongly partisan Erap campaigners—we were officially designated National Campaign Officers for Public Policies and Issues by the Management Committee of LAMMP on 11 February 1998. We also served on the LAMMP Policy-Media Caucus in recognition of Eleanor's past work with the *New York Times* in China.

In our hearts and minds, it was not that difficult to explain why we were supporting Erap. As Filipinos living abroad since the early 1960s, we had been avid observers of the Philippine scene. We also had a keen sense of history. Since 1898, the Philippines had been led by Presidents who identified with the economic and social interests of the elite—Aguinaldo, Quezon, Roxas, Quirino, Marcos—right down to Cory Aquino and Fidel Ramos—these presidents all belonged to the A-B group. There were two presidents who were *maka-masa* (for the masses), Ramon Magsaysay and Diosdado Macapagal. However, Magsaysay did not live long enough to effect any lasting changes and Macapagal was not able to carry out the agrarian reform and other social changes he set out to do. Marcos was too smart and wily for "the poor boy from Lubao."

Classical political theory has hypothesized that Philippine politics, from the very beginning, has been founded on the relationships between a small landed and moneyed elite and the teeming masses. In Remigio Agpalo's colorful analogy, Filipino politics is like the folk dance, *Pandanggo sa Ilaw.* The elites are the dancers, carefully and gracefully balancing lighted lamps on their heads and hands. The audience, clapping and cheering the dancers on, are the masses. The dancers are like politicians wooing voters. The rewards they get are theirs because of their agility and grace—they do not owe anything to their audience. After the dance, the audience are entertained but get little else.

Another theory saw Philippine politics as primarily involving bargaining among elites representing special interest groups. Jean Grossholtz, an American political scientist, proposed that Filipino politicians are primarily concerned with who gets what, when, how and how much. The bargaining, to Grossholtz, is mainly the prerogative of elite politicians. The currency used in such bargaining may be money, status, influence, authority or political power. In this bargaining process, the Filipino masses are rarely involved—as subservient followers of the elite, they are mere pawns in the political games of those who have control over what are euphemistically called "command votes."

Bargaining, of course, is a variation on the so-called "transactional theory" of political behavior. Under this theory, leaders and followers enjoy reciprocal relationships. Leaders enjoy superior authority and prestige but, at the same time, they provide security and benefits to their followers.

Other students of Philippine politics have made much of "patron-client relationships" as the foundation of political power. Carl Lande, Frank Lynch and Mary Racelis have theorized that these "dyadic relationships" and patterns of "reciprocity" were the main determinants of voting behavior. Despite the claim that the Philippines is a democracy, individual Filipino voters are not "free agents" who vote for the person they consider to be the best candidate. They follow the dictates of their elite patrons, who, in turn, look after their welfare. Winning an election, therefore, is a matter of crafting together a coalition of families, clans, and interest groups. This traditional politics means owing a lot of political IOUs which are, of course, encashed after an election.

## Changes in Philippine Society

In studying the 1998 elections, it was our view that after so many years of economic and political development, Philippine society had qualitatively changed. The communication revolution, we believed, had penetrated even the most remote Philippine villages. The print media, radio, television, the movies, video, karaoke and e-mail had reached most of Philippine society.

Movie stars, television anchors, sports heroes and other prominent people easily recognized by the people now enjoy status and prestige arising from their popularity. Not surprisingly, such popularity has been used by some prominent people as a passport to politics. In much the same way such stars endorse consumer products, they can now be marketed as political leaders themselves. In the tradition of "the medium is the message," the conveyors of messages have become more believable than the messages they convey.

Mass public education has allowed many poor Filipinos to get a degree and, even with their less than perfect English, many have been able to leave the country to work as overseas contract workers. The remittances of these workers had helped their relatives and friends get further education. Invested in small enterprises, the money earned abroad has enabled poor families to improve their lot.

With the globalization of human movements, dissemination of technological ideas and the international allocation of capital, the English-speaking Filipinos have participated actively in regional and international affairs. More than any other Asian country, the Philippines has opened up to the outside world. Economic and social changes in the Philippines have empowered the Filipinos, even the masses, to think for themselves. They have become less willing to blindly follow what their economic and political masters used to tell them to do.

## Erap and the Filipino Masses

The Erap phenomenon has puzzled many observers of Philippine politics. In Erap, despite his being what an acerbic columnist has called a "populist *burgis*" (bourgeois) we have a person with whom many poor people easily identify. Erap has direct appeal to the *masa*, the D and E voters, many of whom have grown up with his movies, seen him on TV, read about him in the tabloids, and heard his voice on the radio. In the still predominantly oral culture of the Filipinos, the proliferation of Erap jokes, the juicy stories about his womanizing, drinking and gambling and the supposedly unsavory friends he has around him have served to make him the hottest topic in every coffee shop chitchat, *sari-sari* (variety) store debate, or beer hall argument. Stories about Erap have made him larger than life. As a communication cliché has it—"it doesn't matter what people are saying about you, the important thing is that they talk about you."

Erap had what political campaign strategists call instant name recognition. A January 1998 SWS poll found 97% of people surveyed knew about Erap. Even his nickname *Erap*—a reversed play on *Pare* (a slang term for "buddy" which in turn is loosely based on a contraction of the Spanish *Compadre*) was a great aid to name recall. The masses readily identified with Erap and his party, the *Partido ng Masang Pilipino* (Party of the Philippine Masses). Erap's slogan, *Erap para sa Mahirap* (Erap for the Poor) was a master stroke of political communication and propaganda. But what made it effective was Erap's genuine empathy for the poor and the people's perception that he understands them.

The way we saw it, Erap's popularity and charisma made it possible for him to win the presidency without too many political entanglements. His direct appeal to the masses added to his "winnability." This meant that Erap could win without striking too many bargains and special arrangements that other candidates had depended on in the past. These compromises, special favors and "deals sealed in smoke-filled rooms" were, to us, at the root of graft and corruption in the Philippines.

To us, working for Erap posed the possibility of launching pro-poor people programs—affordable housing, clean water, sanitary toilets, garbage collection and disposal, good schools, efficient health services, smooth traffic, peace and order—all the things we tend to take for granted while living in Canada and the United States. In the past four decades, we have studied all these problems through research projects and consultancies that had taken us to as many as 88 countries worldwide. We thought we had picked up good ideas that could be tried in the Philippines to solve its low-cost housing problems. If Erap wins without depending too much on corrupt traditional politicians or *trapos* (literally, old dirty rags), maybe, just maybe, Erap would be able to make a difference in the country's plight.

Our studies have shown that more than 3.7 million houses are needed in the Philippines to keep up with rapid household formation and make up for the housing backlog (See Appendix 2). The bottom 36% of Filipino households can not afford to pay for even the cheapest house offered by the government (a unit costing P185,000). Water is one of the most serious problems in cities like Metro Manila and Cebu—about 45% of households in Manila depend on deep wells with squatter families having to buy drinking water by the can, paying seven times more than their wealthy neighbors for poorer quality water. Less than a fourth of homes in Metro Manila are connected to the sewer system. The raw sewage from septics is collected by private companies but this is just dumped into canals and rivers or into heavily polluted Manila Bay. Traffic in the National Capital Region averages 12 kilometers per hour during rush hour.

These are some of the problems blocking Philippine development. Erap, with his pro-poor commitment, was the kind of President who would make it possible to deal with these problems. We knew that he could subdue crime and maintain peace and order, that he would not tolerate graft and corruption in his administration, which was behind the government's inability to do anything constructive.

With his mass support, Erap could make hard decisions that would benefit the greatest majority of the Filipino people. He would pursue poverty alleviation programs and lead a government that will narrow the gap between the rich and the poor. We realize that six years may not be long enough to solve all these problems but at least the poor will get a break and a new direction for development would be set. Erap had promised all this and more.

**The Erap Connection**

Our links to Erap were Raul P. de Guzman, and his wife Patrocinio "Pat" Ejercito de Guzman—Erap's elder sister. Since the start of Erap's political career, Raul had been the head of Erap's "brain trust." He was Dean of the College of Public Administration, University of the Philippines, Director of the Local Government Center, Vice President of the U.P. for administration and finance, and Chancellor of the U.P. in Los Baños, before retiring in 1995. Raul also had an Asia-wide reputation as the long-time Secretary General of the Eastern Regional Organization for Public Administration (EROPA).

Raul had been Prod's professor in public administration at the U.P. in 1956. He was our *compadre,* godfather to our son, George. He was also Prod's boss, having been Director of the Local Government Center when Prod was Deputy Director. When we left for abroad in the late 1960s, Raul looked after our affairs in the Philippines. He had been friend, counselor, arranger, and patron. We never failed to see him and Pat in Manila whenever we were on home leave or just visiting. In some of those visits, we would sometimes meet Erap at his home in Greenhills, which was just adjacent to the home of Raul and Pat. When we first met Erap about 30 years ago, he was a young man with rugged good looks just starting his movie career. He had a poor man's smile—warm and disarming.

Pat de Guzman, has now retired from her position as National Deputy Director of the Food and Nutrition Reseach Institute. She refers to herself as "the Praying Sister." A devout Catholic (three daughters are with *Opus Dei*) Pat bombards heaven with prayers and petitions for her brother's success. In many long trips to the provinces during the 90-day campaign, she always had rosary beads running through her fingers. She was known in the Greenhills Group of campaigners as "Head of Prayer Department."

In his capacity as head of Erap's brain trust, Raul had helped conduct public opinion polls in San Juan that helped Erap win the mayoralty election. Once in power, Erap adopted Raul's recommendation to computerize San Juan's tax rolls, vastly expanding the town's tax income. Raul and his faculty members and students at the U.P. conducted organization and management studies and launched administrative reforms such as the professionalization of the San Juan police force. With Raul's help, San Juan became a model municipality and Erap was named one of the Philippines' "Ten Outstanding Young Men" in 1972 in the field of public administration. Raul himself was a TOYM awardee in 1965 while he was director of the Local Government Center under the U.P. College of Public Administration.

Since 1992, Raul had been running a Policy Studies Group in the Office of Vice President Estrada, despite the fact that he had suffered a stroke and had to undergo a quadruple bypass operation that left him with a speech impediment. This group analyzed the changing political situation, gave the Vice President policy advice, drafted some of his speeches, and recruited experts to focus on key policy issues. Raul invited us to participate in these policy sessions whenever we were in town. In many of those workshops, Raul and Pat would ask us if we would be willing to help in Erap's campaign for the presidency. Since we shared the same concerns about development in the country, we readily agreed.

## Getting to Know Erap

If there is a specific date when we first began to get involved in the Erap campaign, it would be 28 May 1996.

We were in Manila to participate in the launching of the *World Population Report*, 1996, released by the United Nations Population Fund (UNFPA). The UNFPA Country Representative, Satish Mehra, had invited Erap to be the guest speaker at a conference to be held at the Manila Hotel on 29 May. Erap had turned down the invitation. The excuse was that he was too busy —he had to fly off to Cebu to give a speech that day.

Satish, an old friend from UNFPA, had contacted us to see if we could help convince Erap to attend the conference. He had invited other high ranking officials to attend the event: Senator Leticia Shahani, President Ramos' younger sister; Congresswoman Tessie Aquino-Oreta; Secretary Cielito Habito of the National Economic and Development Authority; Secretary Carmencita Reodica of the Department of Health; and the chairperson of the Population Commission, Cecille Yasay. However, Satish wanted a star like Vice President Estrada to be the main speaker. We promised him that we would contact our friends, Raul and Pat, who agreed to arrange a meeting with Erap at his Greenhills home.

It was late in the afternoon when Raul ushered us into Erap's living room. With Erap was Robert Aventajado, who was President of *JEEP ni Erap*—a civic movement organized to jump-start Erap's presidential campaign by pushing for his social development programs at a time when outright campaigning was still banned by the Commission on Elections (Comelec). JEEP, according to Robert, stood for Justice, Economy, Environment and Peace. Then, with a mischievous grin, he said—"later on, of course, it can also stand for Joseph Ejercito Estrada for President."

When we brought up the UNFPA invitation, Erap was adamant. "Cardinal Sin will not like it," he said, "family planning is a sensitive topic in the Philippines." We immediately sensed that he really did not want to attend the conference.

We explained that the year's theme in the World Population Report was not family planning but urbanization. As a former Mayor of San Juan who solved the problems of housing, jobs, crime, and poverty in the town, he was in an excellent position to talk about his accomplishments. Danny Reyes, who had been one of Erap's main speech writers through the years, who was also in the meeting, said he would have no problem drafting Erap's speech for the Manila Hotel conference.

Erap was still very reluctant. It was hard for the host to say no face to face and harder still for the favor -seekers to accept the answer. Everyone around the table was starting to feel uncomfortable. "The conference will be full of family planning people," he said with a frown. "And the media will be there. They are very good at ambush interviews. What will I say if they ask me about my stand on abortion?"

It became quite clear that we would have a hard time convincing Erap to attend the conference. He explained that although there is no such thing as "a Catholic vote," pastoral letters written by Cardinal Sin and read in all the Metro Manila churches usually have negative effects.

"Look at what they did to Johnny Flavier in 1995," Erap said. "He could have been number one in the senatorial election but they nearly defeated him because of his stand on family planning."

Our discussions were mercifully interrupted as two maids brought in coffee, ice cream, and cakes for us and fresh orange juice for Erap. We found out later that a visit with Erap always involved being offered something to eat or drink. This is a very Filipino tradition that Erap, who loves to eat, dutifully observes. Erap's well-stocked ultra-modern kitchen could feed 5 or 50 guests at a moment's notice, in true Philippine hospitality fashion.

Raul mentioned that we were most interested in helping the Erap campaign. Ever prepared, he handed Erap our one-page CVs.

"You are two years older than I am," Erap told Prod, looking at his grey hair which contrasted sharply with Erap's jet black, Elvis Presley style, full head of hair. He did not say anything about our academic credentials, the many years of international experience, the long list of academic publications.

Robert was curious as to what prompted us to support Erap's candidacy.

We explained that we believed 1998 to be a historical moment in Philippine history in that for the first time in so many years, Filipinos have a chance to elect a President who really represents the *masa*. We said that as a person with direct appeal to the masses, Erap could become President without incurring too many IOUs from elite power brokers. That means he would be able to make the hard decisions to pursue his vision and implement social reforms to improve the standard of living of the masses.

"What policies would you like to see implemented by Erap?" Robert asked.

"If he can promise to build 1.2 million houses for squatters and slum dwellers, we will support him fully," we replied. We added that we are willing to spend six months in the Philippines at our own expense to help in the campaign. We would help deal with domestic issues such as housing and urban development as well as with international affairs involving the UN and bilateral relationships of the Philippines with other countries. We were both professional writers who could draft speeches, party platforms and press releases, and we had a wide network of contacts in the international press. We said that at this stage in our lives, we can afford to work for things we strongly believe in.

Erap reacted positively to what we said. We thought the "historical moment" of the 1998 elections appealed to him. The idea of a President with few or no entanglements to compromise his position also struck him as a good point. He started talking about his vision and program of governance. He stressed his fight against graft and corruption. He told many stories about his days as San Juan Mayor, how he resettled 1,800 squatter families to Taytay, Rizal, and gave each of them 100 square meters of land, good houses, clean water, electricity and other services; how he started the first build-operate-transfer (BOT) project in the San Juan Agora market complex; and how he left the municipality with a surplus of P24 million after 16 years as Mayor.

Robert also seemed impressed. He revealed that Vice President Al Gore had invited Erap to visit him in Washington on a "getting to know you" trip. He asked if Prod could find time for the trip. He revealed that most of the advisers of Erap were "political operatives" who knew how to win an election but that they do not have anybody yet who could see the "big picture" and incorporate this in a coherent political platform. They also needed someone with extensive international experience as Erap was mainly seen as a candidate whose interests were primarily domestic.

Towards the end of the meeting, we raised the issue of Erap's attendance at the UNFPA conference again.

Erap smiled and said he was still very reluctant to attend because population was such a touchy topic but—"How can I refuse you now?"

Apparently, our volunteered services were accepted. We were now officially within the Erap campaign.

**Erap the Man**

The best way to know the real Erap Estrada is to attend one of the Sunday *pochero* lunches held by the Ejercito clan at his Greenhills home. The focal point in these weekly get-togethers is Doña Maria Marcelo Ejercito, Erap's 93 year-old mother. Hunched in her seat at the edge of a huge round table, "Mama Mary" presides over her large brood, her voice resonant and commanding, receiving the *mano* (ritual touching of an honored person's hand on one's forehead, the ultimate Filipino act of respect) receiving and giving *beso-beso* (kisses) to loving family members and friends.

Mama Mary is proud of her Spanish ancestry. Erap delights in inflicting his broken Spanish on her, often recalling his meeting with Fidel Castro when, as Erap tells it in his self-deprecating way, he really confused the Cuban President with his mongrelized Spanish.

Erap also loves to tease his mother about her strong objections to his dropping out of school and going into the movies.

"You were so angry with me when I became a movie actor," Eraps chides his mother, "you did not even allow me to use the family name. Now, you are the mother of the Vice President." Mama Mary smiles indulgently but from the spark in her eyes, one can see the motherly pride for a son who had given her so much grief when he was growing up.

Now Erap was going to run for President.

Mama Mary had graduated from the Conservatory of Music. She played the piano and sang—she was a soprano. She met and married Emilio Ejercito shortly after he arrived from the United States where he took a degree in civil engineering from the University of Chicago. Her daugthers fondly remember her singing "*Ako'y Anak ng Dalita*" (I'm a Child of Poverty)—their father's favorite song—at family gatherings.

Pat, who acquired her mother's love for cooking, said that Mama Mary did not know how to cook at all when she and Don Emilio got married. To please her husband, who loved good food, Mama Mary enrolled in culinary arts at Far Eastern University. She also took private cooking and baking lessons with well-known teachers such as Mascunana Lobregat. Before long, she became an expert in cooking Spanish, French, Filipino and various types of European cooking. She also became much sought after for beautifully decorated multi-tiered cakes for high society weddings. She prepared bridal bouquets as well.

Mama Mary was a take-charge person—with ten children, seven of whom, at one time, were enrolled in universities and secondary schools, she had to run a very tight ship. Don Emilio was the family disciplinarian and Mama Mary was the caring and nurturing guide. Outgoing and friendly, Mama Mary at 93, still has a wide circle of friends. Every time Erap runs for political office, she writes to them personally, asking them to vote for her son.

Erap, in turn, dotes on his mother—he has specific orders for the whole family that her food be delivered every day in accordance with his instructions. Jackie, Erap's only daughter, calls this her grandmother's daily *rasyon* (care package)—which is carefully packed in Tupperware dishes and delivered to her home in San Juan. When he can, Erap cooks and prepares the food himself.

Even while on the campaign trail, Erap is likely to call home on Sundays and inquire if his mother and family members are having the family get together. He wants to know what they are eating, whether the food he has ordered for Mama Mary has arrived, or who of the family friends had been invited. Quite often, he complains about the quality of the food being served to him where he was—wishing he was with the family at these weekly lunches.

Despite his busy schedule, Erap tries his best to come home and attend the Sunday lunches. He usually walks in, makes *mano* to Mama Mary and sits on her right side. He then attacks the food with gusto—the popular *pochero* is his favorite but he is also partial to *lechon de leche* (roasted suckling pig), *kare kare* (beef or tripe in a peanut sauce), steamed crabs from Mindanao's Liguasan marsh, broiled prawns from Cebu, *kilawin* (marinated fish similar to *ceviche*), *callos* and salty *bacalao* cooked in tomatoes, garlic and onions.

Before Erap got busy with the campaign, whenever *callos* or *bacalao* appeared on the buffet table, it was usually cooked by him. Since the campaign started, however, Erap's ultra-modern stainless steel kitchen equipped with the latest appliances and gadgets has not seen much action—the Sunday food now comes mainly from caterers or is brought in pot-luck style by family members and friends.

Jackie, Erap's only daughter misses her father's cooking now that he is often away from home campaigning. In a newspaper interview, she revealed that "My Dad loves to cook—he is a much better cook than my Mom."

At these Sunday meals, Erap occasionally eats with his hands, shunning spoon and fork, especially when served crabs, prawns and other native dishes regularly served in these Sunday meals. He is a gracious host—urging guests to try this dish, giving tips on what the best morsels are. Now and then, he would even stand up, fill up a plate with a favorite dish and serve it to a special guest himself. He does this spontaneously and graciously as the kind and attentive host.

Interestingly, there is not much talk or bantering at the table. The Ejercito men, including Erap, are not much for small talk. Erap's brothers are all strong silent types, answering in monosyllables when asked something. They are all married to very quiet women. The only person who often breaks the ice is Pilarica, the eldest, who has been dubbed the *Kumander* by younger members of the family. Pil is another take-charge Ejercito who gets everybody organized.

Erap often complains that "his saliva gets stale" during these lunches—everyone is so quiet. There seems to be a conscious effort not to talk shop or discuss political issues. We found, however, that these lunches were the best times to get family members to talk about personal things—such as, how Erap was as a boy.

Mama Mary and Don Emilio Ejercito had ten children: Pilarica, a medical doctor; Emilio, Jr., another medical doctor who now lives in the United States; Paul, a lawyer who lives in an adjacent compound with his wife Margie; Pat, a nutritionist who also lives in an adjacent compound; Antonio, a political science graduate; Connie, who finished business administration (deceased); Marita, a retired World Bank official; Erap, who dropped out in his third year of engineering; George, a movie star (deceased); and Jesse, a chemical engineer turned movie producer. The Ejercito children were a group of over-achievers, motivated by a stern religious father whose word was law and a loving supportive mother who nevertheless demanded courtesy and obedience. Don Emilio reminded the children often that the best inheritance he and Mama Mary could give them was an education and he encouraged them all to finish their studies. Even after finishing their BA degrees, Don Emilio encouraged them to take up post-graduate degrees both in the Philippines and abroad.

## Father and Son

Asked once in an interview about his role models, Erap said that his father, Don Emilio, was the strongest influence in his life. In a TV interview, Erap revealed that he had promised his father that he would never cause dishonor or besmirch the Ejercito family name.

"I remember, my father 'kidnapped' me when I won the post of Mayor of San Juan," Erap said. "He told me—Joseph, all that I have given you is an honorable family name. Your entry into politics will subject you to a lot of temptations. Promise me that you will not succumb to such temptations and that you will give honor to the family name."

Erap said that he promised his father that he would not only give honor to the family name—he would even make it well known all over the world *(Hindi ko lamang pararangalan ang pangalang Ejercito, pasisikatin ko pa sa buong mundo).*

If there is a key insight into what drives Erap—the family "black sheep," the street-smart brawler who got into the movies and politics instead of becoming a professional like his brothers and sisters—it is this promise to his late father. It is as if, having failed to live up to his father's expectation to become an engineer, Erap is driven to succeed to lend honor to the family name. Being elected President of the Philippines is the ultimate offering to that family honor.

Erap's sister, Marita, says that Don Emilio was a devoted husband and a very religious man. She recalls that her father habitually woke up at four in the morning and walked to the Pinaglabanan church in San Juan to attend Mass. She laughs that since he usually arrived earlier than the *sacristan* (acolyte), the parish priest gave him a key so he could open the church door himself. After Mass, he would have breakfast and go to work at the Manila City Hall where he was the City Engineer in charge of all sanitary services. After work, he would go to church again or pray the rosary at the family altar.

Marita stressed that Mama Mary was the only woman in their father's life and that they were a loving and devoted couple.

Mama Mary says with a mixture of exasperation and motherly pride that Erap was always *pilyo* (naughty) the most troublesome child in her large brood. At six in the evening, every day, all the children were expected to be home at angelus time. All except Erap, who would be playing with his friends in a nearby squatter area. He would invariably sneak in late, dirty and sweaty, to join the evening prayers—avoiding the disapproving glare of his devout parents. Mama Mary said she eventually grew tired of twisting Erap's ears or punishing him for his unruly behavior.

Marita quotes her late father, Don Emilio, as saying that when he said the rosary, the first ten Hail Mary's were for nine of the children and the remaining 40 were for Erap. Pilarica recalls long closed door sessions between father and son whenever Erap was in trouble, which was often. She remembers, though, that their father treated all the children like adults, talking to them in a quiet voice, reasoning calmly but sternly.

The favorite Erap story was the case of the missing *pan de sal* (salted buns). Mama Mary said that every morning, the neighborhood baker would bring them a bag of breakfast buns. Often, the bag would be missing and they would complain to the baker. The baker swore, however, that he left the buns on top of the steel gate. The mystery of the missing buns was solved when it was discovered that Erap had been giving them to his friends in the squatter area.

Confronted with this, Erap had a simple answer—"*Nagugutom sila,*" he said (They were hungry).

Asked why Erap turned out to be the black sheep in the family, family members had interesting explanations. To Pilarica, who as the eldest was often in charge of family discipline when their parents were away, Erap loved to be with the kids in the squatter area because he was the acknowledged leader of their gang. Coming from a relatively well-to-do family, he could share his goodies with them. More than that, however, he was a tough brawler who could hold his own in a street fight. The kids from the squatter area, who often engaged in turf wars with gangs from other shanty neighborhoods, were happy to have such a strong, resourceful, and courageous leader.

Marita, born just a couple of years before Erap, said that her younger brother was not too keen on adopting the good behavior of his elder brothers—he wanted to be his own person. He was keenly aware of the fact that he looked different from them—they were fair-skinned *mestizos*, with high noses and wavy hair—they were always neatly dressed and well groomed. Erap was the darkest among the children (he loved being out in the hot sun), had thick unruly straight hair, and was always dressed in T-shirt and short pants.

Erap's elder brothers were taller and bigger than he was but in spite of this he was always trying to compete with them. Marita recalls that when Erap was around ten years old, he got into an accident because of his obsession to be as tall as his elder brothers. It was Easter Sunday, and, according to Filipino tradition, small boys and girls would grow taller if they jumped up and down when the church bells rang (the bells are silent from Good Friday to Easter Sunday to commemorate the death of Jesus). Erap was so desperate to grow tall that when the church bells rang, he jumped from a window, breaking his arm.

Marita said that Erap also resented wearing the hand-me-down clothes of his elder brothers and preferred rough clothes. He was respectful to his elder brothers and sisters and to his parents but he was also moody, taciturn, and hot tempered. He was not usually talkative but he could be counted on to have a witty remark.

Erap's wife, Dr. Loi Ejercito, a psychiatrist, says that Erap rebelled at an early age against the upper middle class values of his family. Although quite bright, he did not like to study too hard. He preferred to be tough rather than well-behaved. His father tried very hard to make him a good boy—he even arranged for him to serve as an altar boy at Mass. However, Erap preferred to do things his way.

Loi laughingly recalls that Erap once told her about an incident that happened when he was about six or seven. Don Emilio and Mama Mary went on a trip and left the children in the care of a very strict aunt. Erap promptly got into trouble with the aunt and, as punishment, she and a houseboy placed Erap in a jute sack, tied it with a long rope, and hang it from the rafters, with Erap kicking and screaming inside. Loi laughs at the story and says—"Nowadays, that would be called child abuse."

Pat says that Erap found it difficult to compete against his elder brothers and sisters who were always obedient, well-behaved, and went to exclusive private schools. They got excellent grades, went to church regularly, and rarely gave their parents any trouble. Erap preferred his *barkada* (gang) of tough kids from the slums and spent as much time with them as possible. He would often sneak out of the house even late at night to be with his friends, climbing down from a second floor window. To stop these night time escapades, his bed was placed between the beds of his two elder brothers. That apparently did not stop Erap. Once, while trying to sneak out of the window, Erap's arm got caught in the iron grills and was fractured. Pilarica says that, to this day, Erap's left arm is *komang* (crooked).

Erap's rebelliousness continued even when he attended high school at the Ateneo. As in San Juan, Erap became the leader of a gang of boys, who often got involved in mischief. His father was often summoned by the Principal because Erap had been involved in a fight, was late for school, or sneaked out of the room during class. Pilarica remembers accompanying her father on one of those visits to the Principal. They arrived and saw Erap marching up and down the Ateneo school yard—he was being punished for being disobedient to a teacher. Apparently, Erap had sneaked out of the room while the teacher was busy writing something on the blackboard. His friends started sneaking out one by one to follow him as he had dared them to do.

The Principal was quite blunt with Don Emilio—"We admire your son's leadership," the Principal said, "but not that kind of leadership."

Once they reached home, father and son had another long session behind closed doors.

How Erap got expelled from Ateneo was told by Reli German, one of Erap's classmates and closest advisers until he resigned when news broke that his wife Bunny had been using the Vice President's name to lure investors to a pyramid investment scam. Reli said that they had an American classmate, a Patrick Hilton, who was bullying one of Erap's Filipino friends. Erap told Patrick to pick on one his own size and they hied off to the boy's toilet to slug it out. Patrick was strong and stocky and Erap was getting the worst of it when their teacher barged into the toilet and broke up the fight. Both kids were expelled and Erap had to enroll at Mapua Institute of Technology. Erap has been looking for Patrick, inviting him to his inauguration as the President's guest, promising not to finish their fight then.

Despite his expulsion from Ateneo, some of his high school classmates continued to be friends. These Ateneo boys included Domingo Siazon, Jr., Tony Lopa, Roman Cruz, Jr. and Ducky Paredes. Their English teacher then, Emil Jurado, helped edit *Eraptions,* the best-selling collection of Erap jokes.

It would seem to indicate that his Erap *para sa mahirap* sentiments were rooted in Erap's childhood experiences. Rebelling against his family's upper middle class lifestyle took the form of identifying with the kids from the slums and squatter areas. Among them, Erap found the adulation and support that he could not get from his family of over-achievers. Among the poor boys from the slums, Erap was the acknowledged leader. In turn, he defended and protected them. He took on their mannerisms and lifestyle—Mama Mary remembered that one of the things she did not like about Erap's closeness with the slum kids was that he learned many "bad words." All these experiences were of great help when Erap decided to pursue a movie career where he often portrayed "diamond-in-the-rough" tough guys (jeepney drivers, market vendors, stevedores) who eventually triumph and win their lady love.

**The Most Successful Drop-out**

Don Emilio wanted Erap to follow in his footsteps and be an engineer. As a World War II veteran, he had a scholarship award that could be used by one of his children and Erap entered the Mapua Institute of Technology with this grant. The problem, however, was the inefficiency of the government in sending in the money. Erap complained bitterly that he would often be prevented from taking the final examinations because his tuition was not paid—the check from the government was always late. He also had to take the public bus to go to school while his brothers and sisters were chauffered in the family car because their schools were close to each other.

Although the Ejercitos were quite well off, at an early age, Erap wanted to earn his own money. He asked his parents to help him find a job and he was soon hired as a member of an ambulance crew at the National Orthopedic Hospital. He found out quickly, however, that the older workers were often giving him the toughest and most menial jobs. He went job-hunting.

A relative hired Erap as a clerk at the National Mental Hospital in Mandaluyong. There, he did such jobs as mimeographing, filing, taking messages from one office to another, and other clerical tasks. He was, however, the star in the hospital basketball team. The doctors at the hospital regularly watched the basketball team play against visiting teams. Dr. Luisa "Loi" Pimentel, one of the young doctors who regularly watched the game from the second floor window of her dorm, noticed the handsome basketball player who played so well and had such nice legs. The future Mrs. Ejercito would only say that one of the things that attracted her to Erap was that "he had very nice legs."

Erap's romantic charms were soon focused on Loi in relentless ways. Loi said that when her patients' records came from the office, each folder would have her name neatly stenciled on the cover, surrounded by drawings of flowers and ribbons and the papers within neatly mimeographed and collated. The records of other doctors were unadorned. When she was on duty, Erap would buy her fried chicken and other good things to eat. She knew that Erap did not earn much as a clerk and she felt guilty about accepting all his gifts but he was a persistent suitor.

Erap was also very resourceful. Once, Loi remembered, Erap gave her a Titus watch on her birthday. She objected, saying it was too expensive. Erap told her that, actually, he did not use his salary to buy the gift—he had gathered all the old newspapers in the hospital and at home, sold them to a dealer, and used the proceeds to buy the watch.

Even in those early days, according to Loi, Erap hated any form of discrimination. She recalls that the hospital cafeteria had a partition that separated the room where doctors and other professional staff ate and the section for the clerical and support staff. The love-struck Erap resented this partition because as a mere clerk, he could not sit down at the same table with Loi, a medical doctor. Erap, therefore, organized the support staff and wrote a petition soundly criticizing discrimination against support staff. Love and labor triumphed when the hospital administrators knocked down the partition.

## Into the Movie World

Erap's entry into the movie world happened almost by accident. Working at the hospital and studying at Mapua, he had very little time for other things. One thing he loved to do, however, was to go to the old Champion Studios to watch movies being made. One of his college friends was the son of Carlos Padilla, Jr., a famous movie star in the '50s.

One day, according to Erap, a movie director needed some extras in a scene. Erap's friends dared him to audition for the part. The director liked his acting and from then on, he started to play bit parts. The money was good and all those beautiful starlets were very friendly. Erap started to spend more and more time in the studios and missed many of his classes.

Erap kept his movie work from the family because he knew that his parents, especially his mother, would object. Mama Mary considered movies, especially Tagalog movies, beneath the family's social standing—an actor in the family was not someone to be proud of. Erap's secret came out, however, because he had been giving the Ejercito maids free passes to his movies. Pilarica, Erap's eldest sister heard them excitedly talking about *Kandilang Bakal* (The Steel Candle), one of Erap's earliest movies and, when confronted, the maids told her the truth. At about the same time, Mapua also called up and asked why Erap was not attending school. Pilarica confronted Erap, who told her about his secret life as a movie actor.

Erap's parents were in the United States at the time attending Pat's graduation at Columbia University. Pilarica wrote them and said they had a real problem with Joseph. Don Emilio and Mama Mary returned to the Philippines to deal with Erap. Mama Mary was beside herself—she ruled that if Erap insisted on becoming a movie actor, he was not allowed to use the Ejercito family name. Don Emilio was more calm. He told Erap that he had dreamed that one of his sons would follow in his footsteps as an engineer and that he was very disappointed that Erap did not seem to be inclined to do this. Finally, however, he told Erap "Being a movie actor is also a profession—if you really want to do it, then, you should try to be the best in the field."

Relieved at his father's understanding, Erap promised that he would do his best in the movie field. Heeding his mother's admonition, however, he decided to use the film name—Joseph Estrada. Later, students of the Erap phenomenon would say that Estrada, meaning "the street," was Erap's way of indicating his connection with poor street kids—the *kanto boys* (street corner toughs) he grew up with. Erap is more matter of fact—"Estrada just sounded nice," he says, "it is very easy to remember." He revealed that all he wanted to do was get a name that also started with the letter E—consulting the phone book, he came across the name Estrada.

As an actor, Erap specialized in action films. His favorite roles were of poor, insulted and belittled young men who fight for their rights and triumph in the end—winning the girl of their dreams in the bargain. Memorable roles were of gangsters with a golden heart such as *Asiong Salonga*, a Robin Hood type who fought exploitation of the poor by rich families. He played the roles of jeepney driver, ice cream vendor, tricycle driver, short order cook, stevedore, peasant farmer, Huk rebel, Muslim warrior, and many other depictions of the poor and the downtrodden. He also starred in an Erap series, where Boots Anson Roa played his partner (Erap goes to college, Erap becomes engaged, Erap becomes a father). Most of the Erap movies were not just financial successes—he won five FAMAS awards (the Philippine equivalent of the Oscar) and was given a lifetime achievement award for his contribution to the Philippine movie industry.

In his campaign speeches, Erap never tired of saying that it was in playing the roles of a poor person who triumphed over life's challenges that he developed a deeper understanding of the living conditions of the poor. Somehow, he internalized the feelings and emotions of the poor and the downtrodden in the roles that he played. Erap, as a character actor, was deeply influenced by Marlon Brando (quite a number of friends believe that Erap's tendency to mumble even when delivering a formal speech may be related to the Brando influence). In any case, Erap's empathy for the poor and underprivileged was reinforced by his movie roles.

Erap also admits that internalizing the emotional content of his movie roles was quite easy because he could delve into his rebellious childhood when he went against his parents wishes and played mainly with children from the shantytowns. His first hand experience as a young boy who had to pinch the family's supply of *pan de sal* to feed his poor hungry friends served him well in his movie roles. As a successful movie actor and producer, he never forgot that there were many poor people involved in movie-making (grips, drivers, electricians, make-up artists, stuntmen, bit players) who needed help. He organized and became the first President of the Movie Workers Welfare Fund (Mowelfund) which provided financial assistance to these workers during difficult times. The Mowelfund continues to provide this support to movie workers up to now.

The many physical fights he had to wage in his youth to defend his weaker friends did not only help Erap in his acting—they came in handy in real-life combat. With his friend, Ronnie Poe, Jr., Erap fought the gangster-style extortionists who preyed on movie actors and actresses. These thugs threatened to splash acid on the faces of movie stars or otherwise disfigure them if they did not come up with regular payments. In confrontations that aped their celluloid roles—but which were for real and dangerous—Erap, Ronnie and their friends stopped the extortionists.

It is clear that during his childhood, in high school, and his early years as an actor, Erap somehow developed a strong social conscience and a genuine desire to improve the lives of people less fortunate than he was. His leadership abilities, albeit shown in unorthodox ways, developed early. His desire to fight for the weak, the poor and the underprivileged became very strong—exemplified in both his reel and his real life. The emotions that have become so much a part of Erap's psyche—encapsulated in the slogan *Erap para sa mahirap*—evolved from his true life experiences and were enhanced by his make-believe film roles. They remain the most important clues to Erap's charisma and his great popularity.

## Complex Contradictions

Having known Erap for such a long time and working with him up close during the 1998 electoral campaign, we had come up with a number of observations about who he really is. It is obvious that Erap is a very complex person and that it is extremely difficult to try and understand what makes him tick.

First, we observed that Erap has neatly compartmentalized his life. Second, he is more of an instinctive person rather than a conceptual or methodical decision-maker. Third, he has very simple tests on what makes for a good decision—is it honest, will it help the poor, will it not harm the Ejercito family name? Fourth, Erap has a strong sense of morality that differs from what conventional society deems appropriate but to which he strictly adheres. Fifth, Erap is nationalistic in a way readily understandable to the Filipino masses. Finally, Erap listens to advice but makes his own decisions. He is very action-oriented, has a keen sense of power, and he takes full responsibility for his actions.

## A Neatly Compartmentalized Life

As an accomplished movie actor, Erap is used to playing many roles and has neatly compartmentalized his life in this way as well. His movie career was separated from his family life, which in turn, was set apart from his political life. For example, his marriage to Loi in the '60s was kept secret so it would not adversely affect the adulation of his fans. The glamour of showbiz, to his family, was only a job and a source of good income.

While his popularity as a movie actor initially helped Erap when he ventured into politics, he tried very hard to be known for his public accomplishments rather than merely basking in his popularity. As Erap himself says frequently, "while popularity helped me get elected as Mayor of San Juan the first time, it was my accomplishments that got me re-elected in subsequent elections."

Erap's compartmentalization of his life is best exemplified by his rather complicated domestic arrangements. Erap does not hide the fact that there have been other women in his life. It is also well known that he has other children other than the three he had with Loi.

When pointedly asked by reporters who the First Lady of the Philippines would be once he got elected, Erap's ready response is: "My mother, Mary Marcelo Ejercito."

In campaign rallies, Erap loved to introduce Loi as his "one and only wife," and, to the tittering laughter that inevitably followed, he would add "It seems you do not believe me." This never failed to get understanding laughter and applause. Then, Erap would bring the house down with the comment, "Of the many women I have loved, I have married only one—Dr. Loi Ejercito."

Once, at a luncheon meeting, the talk show host, Larry Henares, was discussing an Erap appearance on his TV show, "*Make my Day*." Larry suggested a dialogue where he would greet Erap and say, "And how is the Missus, and the Missus, and the Missus?"

Without batting an eyelash, Erap answered "Fine. Fine. Fine."

Larry suggested that, perhaps, Erap could sing a song during the show. Erap laughed again and said—""How about if I sing,To all the Girls I've Loved Before." However, this dialogue did not take place in the actual show.

All of Erap's children—he is secretive about their exact number—are well cared for. Most visible of the children are his children with Loi: Jinggoy, current Mayor of San Juan, Jackie, the only daughter, who is very active in KAME (*Kabataang Maka-Erap)* Foundation, and Jude, the son who is training to be a helicopter pilot in the United States.

Even critics of Erap marvel at how he is able to manage more than one household. Rather than take this as a negative element, Erap supporters see this as a compliment on his "management ability." An Erap supporter explains that his hero is an expert practitioner of "time and traffic management." One columnist, when asked about how Erap will manage the country, simply says—"he will run the country the way he manages his wives. Everyone is cared for, there are no complaints, they all seem to be happy."

The same compartmentalization can be seen in Erap's circle of friends. One of the negative issues Erap's opponents tried to use in the campaign against him was the so-called "Tell me who your friends are and I will tell you who you are" approach. They alleged that Erap was surrounded by unsavory characters—Atong Ang, David Tan, Peter Choi, and Le Peng Wee were often mentioned as shadowy Erap friends. Despite the fact that linking these men to him obviously hurts Erap, he refuses to turn his back on them. In fact, on certain occasions, he even defends them by saying no criminal charges have been filed against his friends.

To Erap, loyalty and one's word of honor is important. Of course, if a friend betrays him, Erap can become an unforgiving foe.

"People just do not like some of my friends because they are not high class," Erap once said. "They go for such things as *sabong* (cockfights). If they went for *jai alai* or other high-class gambling, maybe the elite will accept them."

In another compartment of Erap's life are his "Eraption buddies." Asked once what he did to relax, Erap quickly answered "swapping Erap jokes with my friends." The so-called Erap joking buddies which include Melo Santiago, Fernando Poe, Jr., and Reli German (before the Bunny scam) occupied another compartment of Erap's life. He enjoyed being with them in occasional "boys' night out," often at the 419 exclusive night club he co-owns with Ronnie Poe, Jr. While some of these friends also helped in the presidential campaign, they were there primarily for post-rally relaxation and comfort. Often, they supplied the jokes that Erap used in his speeches, press conferences and campaign rallies.

Less emotionally close to Erap but an increasingly important part of his life are his so-called political and economic advisers. They supply him with policy ideas and advice and often meet with him before an important public event—such as a televised debate. Foremost among these advisers are Edgardo Espiritu, the president of Westmont Bank, U.P. economics Professor Benjamin Diokno, banker Ding Pascual and businessman Robert Aventajado. On the political side, Erap confers with brothers Manny and Ronnie Zamora as well as with Orly Mercado, Jun Rivera, Frisco San Juan and Ike Zaldivar.

Most important to Erap, of course, are his family members. Elder sister Pilarica is leader of this group which includes brothers Paul and Jesse, brother-in-law Raul and his wife Pat, Marita, and his wife Loi and son Jinggoy. After a speech or a TV debate, Erap eagerly seeks out these family members and asks "Okay ba ako?" (Was I all right?). He is his own worst critic. Once, after a particular TV debate, he was in a bad mood because he felt he could have done better. The family said that he did all right. Finally, he asked—"So, how would you have ranked the participants?"

The family consensus was that he had scored number two to Renato de Villa.

Erap was crestfallen—"So, I was not the winner," he said. To Erap, number two was never good enough. He always tries to be the best at whatever he does. Before he delivers a speech he would go over a prepared speech very carefully, changing words here and there to make sure every word was appropriate. He would still be practicing the speech in the car on his way to the event often asking the speech writer or an adviser to join him in the car if he had any questions.

## An Instinctive Decision Maker

Faced with a decision, we noticed that Erap draws more on his personal experiences and instincts rather than use a conceptual model based on means and ends. Erap is not a strategic analyst who sets a goal and then analyzes the cost and benefits of the various options to achieve that goal. His personal experiences—some of them captured in favorite anecdotes—become the basis for his decisions. This mode of thinking makes Erap very decisive—he instinctively gets to the root of the situation and then decides on what to do.

For example, asked what he would do if a close relative abuses his influence and power, Erap tells the story of a husband of a cousin who was one of his supporters when he ran for Mayor of San Juan.

Apparently, the relative once got drunk and started smashing chairs on tables in a restaurant. The police, knowing he was Erap's relative, were reluctant to do anything. Learning about the incident, Erap himself arrested the guy and threw him in jail. "With the grace of God," Erap says, "the guy has not talked to me since."

The same reliance on gut feeling and instincts seems to govern Erap's judgment of people—whether a person is trustworthy or not. As a person who has been in the celebrity spotlight for a long time, Erap is amazingly immune to flattery. Effusive praise seems to make him visibly uncomfortable. At the same time, he is ultra-sensitive to what he perceives as unfair criticism and reacts aggressively to real or imagined personal affronts.

In starting to know a person, Erap is not impressed by a person's CV. He is not awed by educational background, work experience, or accomplishments. He seems to be guided more by what can only be called "inter-personal chemistry." Certain individuals, he takes into his confidence right away. Others take more time or never become his friends at all—despite the fact that he would work with them quite closely on very important issues.

True to his macho image, Erap does not like weak sycophants as friends. R.C. Constantino, a drinking buddy from way back says he has had really tough confrontations with Erap. "He wants you to argue your position with him," says R.C., "sometimes he plays devil's advocate just to get you to react violently. He loves to test people. However, after a heated discussion, he usually becomes very conciliatory and will do everything to smooth ruffled feathers. He will hate me for saying this but he is really a tender soul."

Erap has a prodigious capacity to remember names, places and events. Often, he would surprise his associates by recalling obscure events that happened a long time ago. In Philippine society, when one mentions a person's name, people immediately establish who that person's relatives are, how they are linked to him or her (classmate, friend, friend of a friend), past activities (including juicy scandals) and other bits of information. Erap stores these bits and uses them as guides—a most useful supplement to his stock of anecdotes and gut reaction judgments. Most of the time, his personal judgments are right on target.

The capacity to remember things is most marked in relation to promises Erap makes. Ike Gutierrez, Erap's ever-present spokesman who accompanies him on most of his trips remembers a particular incident that happened in Bacolod. While speaking at a rally, Erap noticed a woman who had been patiently waiting for a chance to talk to him. When she finally had the chance, the woman told Erap about her family difficulties and asked him for a letter of recommendation. Erap asked Ike to get the woman's name, address and other particulars and told him to draft a letter of recommendation.

Ike said he thought this was just one of those routine promises that politicians make. He got the woman's name and address but promptly forgot all about it. Six months later, Erap asked Ike if the son of the woman in Bacolod already got a job. Ike admitted that he had not done anything and, in fact, had all but forgotten the incident. But not Erap—he remembered the woman's problems in detail and the specifics of her request. He gave Ike such a severe tongue lashing about the incident that Ike had to rush home to find the woman's name and address from his notes. He frantically turned his files inside out and finally found the woman's particulars. He personally delivered the recommendation letter to Erap first thing in the morning. Ike said he never took any of Erap's instructions for granted after that incident.

## The Three-way Test

When Erap announced the names of his 30 economic advisers, his critics snickered and asked—how would he be able to resolve the conflicting proposals of his advisers—who range from extreme left to far right—when he himself admits he does not fully understand economics? To Erap, decision-making is quite simple because he does not usually meet problems head on. He unravels complex problems and breaks them down into solvable components. After some time, the complex elements of the problem fall into place and the main issues are resolved.

What makes decision-making so simple for Erap is the use of a three-way test that he consistently applies to issues: (a) Is it clean, honest and free of graft and corruption? (b) Will it achieve the greater good of the greater number, especially the poor? (c) Will it adversely affect the Ejercito family name? Applying this test, Erap can quickly respond to even the most complicated problems.

One of the most important accomplishments that Erap never fails to mention in all his campaign rallies—is that his name has never been linked to any case of graft and corruption. Having gotten this far in his political career, Erap says he will continue to apply this test to any issue facing him. Transparency and accountability are constantly noted in his public and private pronouncements. He has nothing but absolute disdain for grafters and corrupt officials.

Erap's concern for the poor is imbedded in his moral makeup. He has an uncanny ability to detect whether a proposed policy action will be good for the poor or not. When faced with a policy decision, he invariably asks how it will affect the welfare of the poor and the underprivileged. If there is any hint at all that the action will adversely affect the poor, he immediately rejects the proposal.

Erap's concern for keeping the Ejercito name clean is almost a fixation. He demands this commitment to the family name from all his relatives and friends. This is one of the reasons why Erap is so intent on upholding his *palabra de honor.* To Erap, a person's integrity is tied to keeping his word of honor.

Having such clear-cut criteria for deciding complex issues makes it easy for Erap to make decisions that cut through personal and moral dilemma. His uncompromising stand on graft and corruption, his unwavering commitment to improve the lives of the poor, and his absolute demand that the Ejercito family name not be tainted make his actions readily predictable. In his own way, therefore, Erap has simplified the process of decision making in his public and private life. While decidedly nonconformist in his personal life, Erap's adherence to traditional public values makes it easy for him to arrive at key political decisions.

**A Private Sense of Morality**

One of the most amazing things about Erap as a person is his adherence to a strict sense of morality that guides his actions. It is easily discernible, of course, that this sense of morality does not conform to what some members of Filipino society regard as normal. For example, Erap has transgressed social norms on womanizing, drinking, and gambling—and is blithely unrepentant of his actions. At the same time, Erap is strongly judgmental of the actions of other people and is quick to condemn others who violate his own sense of morals. In an oft-quoted aside, Erap has said "It is better to be a womanizer than a thief."

We remember once mentioning to Erap a candidate for governor in an island province who was seeking his support for re-election. Erap's face darkened at the mention of the person's name and said, no, it is impossible for him to support him.

Curious about this quick reaction, we asked why.

"The guy is a gigolo," he said, "he makes rich women fall in love with him and sucks all their money. Then, when they have no more money, he discards them. The guy is evil."

In a peculiar way, Erap's sense of morality dictates that women should be honored (he does not see as a contradiction the fact that by taking up with other women, he is not giving due honor to his legal wife—he justifies this by saying that he strayed when he and Loi were estranged). In his own way, Erap is totally against the exploitation of women. He is also fully committed to facing up to his obligations. If a person takes up with another, he has the obligation to make that person happy and comfortable. If he begets children, then he is bound to support the children and make life comfortable for them. A close friend of Erap told us that even if Erap is attracted to a woman, he never makes any advances if that woman is married, engaged or otherwise entangled. It is a matter of honor with him not to "put shit on another man's head."

Even as Erap clings to his own commitments to morality, he can be quite pragmatic about other things. For example, he thinks that graft and corruption in the government can be reduced drastically but perhaps, not entirely eradicated in his six-year term. We asked Erap once what he would do as president to a very rich businessman who owed the government billions of pesos in back taxes.

"I will call him to Malacanang for a private chat," Erap said. "I will tell him, look, you owe the government this much money. You have spent a lot of money for lawyers and the government has also spent a lot of money in litigation. All we are doing is enriching the lawyers. So, why don't we agree on a deal. We split your taxes you owe in half—you keep half, the government gets half. However, from then on, you pay taxes regularly. You clear your name, you save money on lawyers, the government gets its money. Everyone wins all around."

Erap is fond of saying that with him, it does not matter if a person is a friend or relative—if that person does something wrong, he or she will be punished. One story Erap likes to tell concerns a friend of his mother, who was in the business of butchering piglets and roasting them as *lechon.* Erap learned that this person was cooking piglets that had not been inspected by the Municipal Veterinarian, which was against the law. So one day Erap, with a contingent of policemen, raided the person's home and confiscated more than 50 roasted piglets.

The vendor went to Erap's mother and pleaded for Mama Mary to help him. Erap says that his mother called him in and berated him from head to toe. "This man supported your candidacy," she said, "he is my friend and look at what you did to his business."

Erap argued that the man was disobeying the law. It was dangerous to sell roasted piglets that were not inspected properly.

Usually, Erap's anecdote stops at that point of the story. However, one day, we pushed further and asked what happened to the 50 roasted piglets. Erap sheepishly admitted that he had to return them to his mother's friend because of Mama Mary's scolding. However, he said that he made the man promise that, from then on, only piglets that were inspected by the Municipal Veterinarian would be accepted as *lechon.* He was willing to heed his mother's words once but the right thing must be done afterwards. Erap said the man never sold "hot" meat again.

## Patriotic Champion of the Masses

In an election year that was also a celebration of the Philippine centennial, Erap's patriotism might have been a key factor in the massive support given him by the people. All the candidates vying for the Philippine presidency, of course, painted themselves patriotically for the campaign. Two of the candidates did not have to work too hard at it. Rene de Villa, a retired military general, and Alfredo Lim, a former police general, had good claims to patriotism, having spent their whole professional lives in uniform (the efforts of Lim's opponents accusing him of being Chinese and not a natural-born Filipino may have hurt him at the polls, however). Lito Osmeña, who is descended from one of the Philippines' most august statesmen, attempted to instill a nativist stance with his "back to the province" messages. Even Miriam Defensor Santiago, with her weird mix of Oxford and Ilonggo accents, claimed to be a true patriot by upholding the rule of law and the need to protect the poor from abuses.

It was Erap, however, who claimed nationalism as one of his most potent themes. This he did by linking nationalism to his use of Pilipino, largely based on Tagalog, as his main medium; the fact that his ancestors came from Cavite, where the 1898 proclamation of independence was held; his having been born in Tondo, the birthplace of the *Katipunan* and of the proletarian hero Andres Bonifacio; and his role in leading the Senate fight for closing of American military bases at Subic Bay and Clark.

Erap gained many electoral points by linking his love of country to his championing of the plight of the Filipino masses. At times, he came dangerously close to jingoism in criticizing the "unholy alliance" between the Filipino elite and exploitative foreigners. Erap had the Filipino masses' "sensitivity" to real or imagined insults to his country. Erap supporters never tire of telling the story of how security agents of President Bill Clinton tried to stop him from meeting the American President at the Manila International Airport during the APEC conference. Pushed aside by Clinton's security aides, Erap exploded.

"I am the Vice President of the Philippines and you don't push me around in my own country!"

His outburst did not only elicit an apology from Clinton's staff, it greatly endeared Erap to the Filipino masses who identified with his fight against domineering elites—local or foreign.

During the centennial celebrations, the "popular history" style of writing by historian Ambeth Ocampo created controversies about the role of the Hispanized elites or *ilustrados* in the Philippine Revolution. Many academic debates were fought on the role of President Emilio Aguinaldo in the death of Andres Bonifacio. Erap's pro-*masa* stand fitted in nicely into this elite vs. mass popularizing of Philippine history. Although many commentators did not quite subscribe to the theory that Erap's electoral victory was "the revenge of the masses," it was difficult to negate the fact that in this 1998 elections, it was mainly the D and E voters who carried the day for Erap.

Erap gave a hint of his nationalistic stance by speaking mainly in Tagalog in almost all of his campaign rallies. This is a necessity, of course, because Erap knows only Tagalog among the 76 or so languages and dialects spoken in the country. Erap's Tagalog is the common language of the streets—he is not at ease speaking in the classical or "literary Tagalog" that to him sounds stilted and unnatural. Most of the time, Erap uses "Taglish," the spontaneous mixture of Tagalog and English spoken by most educated Filipinos. To people who know him well, the alleged "murdering" of the English language by Erap (he loves to say that he speaks only *carabao* or "water buffalo" English) is a carefully contrived myth furthered by the publication of *Eraption—How to Speak English Without Really Trial.* Actually, Erap speaks excellent, if somewhat colloquial English. In delivering his speeches, Erap prefers English as his medium because he sometimes stumbles on polysyllabic and alliterative Tagalog words.

In his Tagalog speeches, however, Erap loved to occasionally throw in a few chosen English phrases ("You must remember, my friends, that a public office is a public trust." This always got a tremendous applause. Or sometimes, "The rule of law is the bulwark of democracy in the Philippines and no person, no matter how rich or powerful, is above the law."). Then, Erap would pause and say "*O, English yan, hah.*" (That is English, eh). After the appreciative laughter and cheering, Erap would add: "*Pag medyo seryoso tayo, paminsan minsan, nakakadale din tayo ng English.*" (When we get serious, we can sometimes speak English). The people lap this up.

Erap's story about his visit to Japan and his meeting with the Japanese Prime Minister even made it in the Tokyo papers. As Erap tells the story in his campaign rallies, he recalls that he went to Japan and after a 30-minute meeting with the Japanese Prime Minister, he noticed that his host spoke only two lines of English during their whole meeting—"Welcome" and "Thank You." Erap then pauses, smiles mischievously, and then says "*Mas mahusay ang English ni Erap dito*" (Erap speaks better English than this guy). The story never fails to elicit laughter and thunderous applause.

Erap loves to add that he also had a meeting with the President of South Korea and throughout the whole discussion, the Korean President did not utter a single word of English. And yet, Erap points out, while Japan and Korea are the two most prosperous countries in Asia, their heads of state prefer to speak in their own language in official meetings with foreigners and not English. In other words, says Erap, *Hindi nakukuha sa Inglisan yan* (You do not solve serious problems by speaking English). What is more important than the ability to speak English, is the leader's pride in his country and his cultural heritage. What is important is the leader's commitment to the greatest good of the greatest number—his true feelings for the people, especially the masses.

Erap never fails to mention in rallies that he was one of the few Senators who fought for the removal of American military bases in the Philippines. He recounts how the American Ambassador invited him to dinner once and then asked him—"Mr. Senator, how come you hate Americans so much?"

Erap's says his response was: "Mr. Ambassador, I do not hate Americans. I just believe that for as long as we have these American military bases here we will forever be mendicants in our own country. It is not that I love America less but I love the Philippines more."

Again, this story always elicits thunderous applause.

## A Ready Listener, a Quick Decision Maker

Erap, for all his larger than life reputation, is really quite humble. Unlike many public officials, he has the capacity to listen to advice. He seeks advice openly and eagerly—often calling up close friends and people he trusts to give their views on certain issues. He does not pretend he knows all the answers.

This trait is given as an explanation why so many academics, ideologues and professionals are attracted to Erap's candidacy. As columnist Adrian Cristobal said, it is one of the conceits of these people that they feel they have influence. With Erap, they have the chance to sell their ideological wares and be listened to. Erap does not always take their advice—in fact, he makes his own decisions and stands by them. The difference is that Erap knows how to listen.

Erap listens but he usually gets easily turned off by people who talk too much or over-explain things. One close adviser says Erap is a man of few words himself. It is quite easy to detect if Erap is not listening anymore—while he is often too polite to stop somebody from boring him, he usually has a quick joke or two that serves as the perfect squelch. Once, at a party, one guest was monopolizing the microphone. Erap, innocent as a lamb, asked the person if he had gone to school at AIM.

"No, I went to U.P." was the proud reply of the man, still clutching the microphone.

Somebody asked Erap what he meant by AIM. He explained that he was not referring to the Asian Institute of Management, a famous regional center for business administration—he said AIM was short for "*Ayaw Iwanan ang Mike*" (does not want to give up the microphone).

Erap is also unimpressed by people who backbite. You rarely hear him say negative things about a person—not even against his enemies. Ike Gutierrez, who knows him well, says that Erap believes a person who says negative things about somebody cannot be trusted because that person would be capable of saying nasty things about him too. He says that, at times, Erap tests other people by saying negative things about another person. If the person he is testing takes the bait and starts badmouthing that person, he has failed Erap's test.

It is the most natural thing for Erap to back the underdog. He is ever-ready to take up the cudgels for the poor in any discussion or confrontation. Since his childhood, he has been in quite a few scrapes to protect weaker friends. His sisters say that when he was a sophomore in college, he was almost killed in a fight while protecting a classmate. He was stabbed in the chest with a *balisong* (fan knife) which, luckly hit his sternum instead of penetrating his lungs.

Erap is not always a very patient listener. His attention span is quite short—especially since there are usually a thousand and one things clamoring for his attention. Amazingly, Erap is quick to grasp the essence of any subject being discussed. People who know him well attribute this ability to the way Tagalog movies are made. Often, detailed scripts are not used—a simple story line is given to actors and they are expected to ad lib and make up the dialogue. With this training, Erap has developed the ability to absorb ideas quickly. He does not memorize what he wants to say but relies on his quick wit and instinctive understanding of the situation.

Erap is also not too fond of reading long memos—his usual reaction to a speech draft is *"Masiyadong mahaba naman ito" (*This is too long). The daily briefing memos we prepared for him during the campaign never exceeded two pages—and they were printed in 16 points bold. Ike Gutierrez, who briefs Erap on most things, says that Erap prefers "bullets style" memos. "If you can't fit it on one page," says Ike, "you have not solved the issue yet."

It is one of Erap's notable assets that when he is talking with you, he gives you his undivided attention. It may be only a moment but for that brief time, you feel you are the most important person to him. And he always has a number of persons around to take messages and give him reminders—Ike Gutierrez when he is in the field, Malou Florendo or Cheryl Jimenea at his home in Greenhills. He quickly tells them to take note of what was discussed and expects them do something about it.

Erap sometimes uses a sly technique to get the best advice from his staff. We found this out in our speech writing chores. When faced with an important speech,

Erap does not rely on only one person to draft it. He goes to one person and says, this speech is very important, I want you to prepare for me the best speech you can write. Then, he goes to another aide and says the same thing. At the end of the week, there may be three drafts of the same speech from different persons who have put in their best efforts into the task.

Erap then looks at all the drafts and selects what he considers to be the best. Sometimes, he will call in one of the speech writers and asks him to choose the best one among the drafts. If the person chooses the draft of another person and says it is better than the one he prepared, Erap laughs and says—"I was only testing you, I thought that draft was the best too." He does not apologize for "using" people this way—it is part of "creative tension"—his way of making sure that he will get the best advice or the best output. The staff on the other hand enjoys the challenge of the competition.

What usually saves the situation when Erap has a problem with others is his great sense of humor. He has a great capacity to laugh—and he does not mind if the joke is on him. The great success of his *Eraptions* book is due to the fact that instead of being defensive about his English malapropisms and alleged simple mindedness, he actually turned these to his advantage. When faced with an awkward moment, Erap is quick to defuse tensions with a witticism or a joke. Filipinos say that the most serious things are often said in jest—Erap has this unique talent to use humor effectively in his dealings with others.

As an accomplished movie actor, Erap has perfect timing. He can demolish a long-winded speaker by a sharp one-liner. People who are close to him say that he does not want to be pressed or otherwise prevailed upon to do something he is not completely in agreement with. If one has to raise a delicate issue or a request for a favor, timing is most important. If you catch him at a bad time, you can end up with a quick rejection or worse.

Erap can be moody, which some people sometimes mistakenly interpret as having a temper. When he is tired, harassed or under pressure, he can be abrupt. However, if he loses his temper with anyone, he usually feels bad about it afterwards and tries his best to make amends. But he rarely apologizes directly—he shows he is sorry by sending a gift, suddenly becoming very solicitous, or—the ultimate Erap signal for amity—an invitation to a sumptuous meal. One Erap subordinate who has been on the receiving end of such treatment insists that Erap is actually *Pusong Mamon* (a softie). He likes to look gruff and tough but, deep down, he is all heart.

Erap listens but once he has made up his mind, he acts and sticks to his decision. He is decisive and eager to do something about a problem rather than talk about it. He is keenly aware of the powers of the Presidency. He knows that, once at the top, "the buck stops with him." Contrary to what some people believe, Erap understands the powers of the Presidency and he feels quite comfortable with the fact that he knows how to wield those powers.

What will make running the country quite easy for Erap is the fact that he is able to choose the best people for even the toughest jobs. He is an excellent judge of character. More important, he commands the respect, love and undying loyalty of the people around him. He truly knows how to inspire and motivate people. Among the ablest people around Erap at present are quite a few he had inherited from previous offices, such as the Office of the Vice President under Laurel. There are members of his staff who have been with him since he was Mayor of San Juan.

Once it became known that Erap had won the presidency, he set up a Selection Committee composed of Manny Zamora, Edong Angara, Raul de Guzman, Ed Espiritu, Orly Mercado and Ronnie Zamora to help him choose the key officials that will make up his Cabinet and run the most important offices. His main instruction to the committee was: "You don't have to change everybody; retain as many people as possible."

Erap explained that if incumbent officials had honestly and efficiently carried out their jobs, it was more useful to keep them. Continuity of work in the office was important. There is less disruption when people are allowed to keep their jobs.

"That is what I did in San Juan when I was Mayor," he said. "I told the key officials, I know you are a good person and I trust you. I am asking you to continue working with me. The officials were so grateful that they did an excellent job. I do not believe in changing people, I change their attitudes."

# PART II

## THE CAMPAIGN

## CHAPTER 5

# HOW TO WIN AN ELECTION

Erap was in a good mood after the traditional *pochero* lunch held every Sunday by the Ejercito clan. It was the last Sunday in March, exactly 43 days before the election. He had gone to bed at four in the morning after a massive rally in Taytay, Rizal but he looked amazingly refreshed.

"I can get by on four hours of sleep," he says *"dinadaan ko na lang sa kain"* (I just make up for it by eating).

We moved to the music room of Erap's sprawling Greenhills home for coffee. He was in his usual checkered short-sleeved shirt, denim pants and loafers. Erap walked with a limp favoring his left leg. This was due to an old basketball game injury that still bothered him despite repeated surgical operations, the last one done in the United States in December 1997.

We asked Erap how he hoped to win the 1998 elections with a weak political party. The LAMMP coalition was still struggling to set up a nation-wide political machine, De Venecia had so much more money—the government's resources had been pledged by President Ramos to a De Venecia victory and key segments of the Army and Police seemed ready and able to commit fraud in apparent collusion with the Commission on Elections.

"Popularity," Erap said—"the public opinion polls show I lead all candidates in popularity ratings."

Erap noted that name recognition was a salient factor in his candidacy. He pointed out that the latest SWS survey found that 97% of voters interviewed recognized Erap's name without any prompting and most people who knew about Erap were inclined to vote for him. No other presidential candidate has come close to 97% in name recognition.

How about regional blocs?" we asked, "people say you do not have a power base—the polls show you may even lose Metro Manila, which may be considered your bailiwick, to Mayor Lim?"

"What others call my weakness is actually my strength" Erap said with a laugh, "the whole country is my political base. My appeal to the people, especially the *masa* is direct. I do not need local bosses, political strongmen or elite families to endorse or support me. The Erap support cuts across all political blocs."

Erap explained that Senator Roco was strong in the Bicol region, Governor Osmeña in Cebu, Senator Santiago in Iloilo, Imelda Marcos in Leyte, Speaker De Venecia in Pangasinan and Secretary de Villa in Batangas. Each one of these power bases, however, could not deliver enough votes to ensure victory. It takes nation-wide appeal to get elected.

We asked Erap what will happen if the so-called "LORD Covenant" came about (this was a call by former President Cory Aquino and some church leaders for a coalition among several candidates to form a "Third Force" for a "Stop Erap" drive. LORD stood for Lim, Osmeña, Roco, and De Villa. It was rumored that Cory was asking all four candidates to unite, using the "equity of the survey" principle as a basis for choice (whoever tops the next two public opinion surveys will become the unity candidate, those not chosen will withdraw and support the official one).

"I don't think they will succeed in forming a Third Force," Erap said—"who will slide down or give up his ambition this late in the game? *Napasubo na sila.*" (They have put in too much in the campaign already).

"Besides," said Erap, "the poll data on voters' 'second choices' are in my favor. Votes are not necessarily transferable. The coalition's choice of one candi-date does not mean that supporters of other candidates will automatically vote for him. My pollsters tell me that among supporters who do not choose Erap as their first bet, I am the favored second choice. If a voter's first choice quits, he goes for Erap."

That Sunday in March, Erap was quite confident that he had found the right formula for winning the Philippine presidency. With his almost 30-year experience in politics, Erap has become one of the most astute public servants around. He does not like to be called a politician. He believes he owes his position to the people who voted him into office and he had an instinctive feel for what the voters and his constituents want.

## Key Factors for Election Victory

Many studies have been conducted on how one wins a Philippine election. A number of elements have been identified as key factors to electoral victory. Some of these are:

- Popularity and charisma;
- Party machines;
- Alliances with elite families;
- Regionalistic or linguistic ties;
- Access to governmental resources; pork barrel and patronage.

## Popularity and Charisma

In April 1996 Erap was invited by U.S. Vice President Al Gore to visit Washington, D.C. This was an early Washington effort to get acquainted with Gore's Philippine counterpart.

According to Erap, Vice President Gore asked him how he had managed to be so popular after so many years in politics.

"I was a movie actor before entering politics," Erap replied.

Gore, who was facing a re-election contest, deadpanned—"It is rather too late for me to try that. What else can I do?"

"You can smile more," said Erap, "or you can sing and dance."

"Gore must have thought his candidacy was dead," laughed Erap, recalling the incident. "He could not even do a decent *macarena*."

In the past there have been a number of movie actors who have ventured into Philippine politics. The first was the handsome matinee idol Rogelio de la Rosa who ran for the Senate and won, inspiring him to think that he could also be president. De Ia Rosa filed his candidacy for president but later withdrew and was appointed ambassador soon after that. There had been other attempts from the movie industry to penetrate politics but without much success. Until Erap.

Erap, elected Mayor of San Juan in 1967, but allowed to hold office only in 1969 because of cheating, has been the most successful actor-turned-politician. In fact, many attribute the current proliferation of actors, sports, and media personalities in politics to Erap's success. In 1998, Tito Sotto, Freddie Webb, Loren Legarda, Rene Cayetano, Robert Jaworski, Ramon Revilla and Ray Langit were running for Senator; Dennis Roldan, Jose Mari Gonzales, and Franz Pumaren wanted to be congressmen; Vilma Santos, Jinggoy Estrada, Ray Malonzo, Joey Marquez, and Herb Bautista were candidates for Mayor; candidates for governor included Bong Revilla, Bong Carrion, and Lito Lapid, all up for re-election; Imelda Papin and Romeo Vasquez were running for Vice Governor; and Edu Manzano, Paquito Diaz, Connie Angeles, Bong Daza and Rio Diaz were running for Vice Mayor.

The "starization" of Philippine politics has not been welcomed by some people. The columnist, Amando Doronila, laments the entry of showbiz personalities into politics, arguing that "while these new entrants certainly made politics more democratic...they have also brought down the level of political discourse to entertainment and burlesque."

> The widening of the political arena to all ambitious entrants...permitted people like Estrada to take themselves seriously...How Estrada or the cabal of actors and entertainers got the idea that they could govern the country and run it well on the basis of skills unrelated to politics is hard to explain. ("Explaining Estrada," *Philippine Daily Inquirer*, 17/4/1998, p. 9).

People readily agree that Erap has charisma defined by German sociologist Max Weber as "personal magnetism or charm that inspires others to follow one's lead." Erap exudes an aura of stardom, he has poise, sex appeal, self-confidence and dominance. One feels this when Erap walks into a room, in the way people react when he comes up to the microphone to talk, when he waves to people from a passing car. He leaves so many smiling and glowing people behind in his motorcades. It is an outpouring of emotion, elation, joy—a reaching out to touch his hand, an eagerness to be near him.

Erap's charisma has certainly been an asset in his political career. In Philippine politics, popularity is a most important factor. Popularity arises from real or attributed personal traits or characteristics—eloquence, good looks, intellectual prowess, athletic ability, personal courage, family background or an enhanced reputation—as a nationalist, a war hero, a poor person who made good, or as an honest incorruptible person. To succeed in Philippine politics, one has to be larger than life, lifted to a different level of character or reputation.

Most Filipino presidents stood out on their own. Manuel L. Quezon was a temperamental *mestizo* who mesmerized others with his eloquence—he used nationalism as an issue, encapsulating this in his most famous quote: "I prefer a government run like hell by Filipinos to one run like heaven by Americans." The flamboyant Quezon easily won over the quieter, more formal, Sergio Osmeña. In one of the worst political miscalculations in Philippine history, Osmeña decided not to openly campaign during the 1935 elections, hoping that people will recognize the many things he had accomplished. He lost miserably to Quezon.

Ferdinand E. Marcos had good looks, eloquence, intellectual brilliance, sex appeal, and personal courage—he also carefully cultivated his image as a war hero (critics later charged that his many war medals were fake or were bought). With his beauty-queen wife, Imelda, Marcos kept Filipino audiences enthralled, using television, print and personal appearances to full effect (their love song duets were key features in their campaign rallies). Early in his career, Marcos encouraged the proliferation of myths about him—arrested and accused of murdering his father's political opponent, he reviewed for his bar examinations in jail and topped the exams. Marcos' sexual dalliances kept Manila society intrigued and titillated. Even during the height of his martial law regime, Marcos took pains to justify his authoritarianism in sophisticated legal treatises. Books were written by Onofre Corpuz, Adrian Cristobal and other prominent intellectuals extolling the vision and governance ideas of Marcos.

Diosdado Macapagal could have been a movie actor—his childhood friends Rogelio and Jaime de la Rosa went from acting in provincial *zarsuelas* to Filipino movie stardom. Macapagal could have joined them had he not decided to get on a political platform instead of the theatrical stage. Macapagal had matinee idol looks, bombastic eloquence, and, most important of all, he nurtured a reputation as "the poor boy from Lubao," whose singular dedication, honesty and academic brilliance enabled him to achieve the Philippine presidency.

Jose P. Laurel exemplified courage and a sense of honor—his biography, *Days of Courage: the Legacy of Dr. Jose P. Laurel*, stated that he fought for Philippine freedom even when he was forced to act as puppet president by the Japanese during the Second World War. Laurel also understood the meaning of symbols—it was said he always wore a white suit and a black armband as a sign of penance for killing a man when he was young.

Manuel Roxas typified the American-educated *pensionado,* returning to the Philippines to assume the mantle of leadership after several years of studies abroad. Roxas was handsome, eloquent, an excellent writer and orator. Running for president immediately after World War II, he carefully nurtured a reputation as a nationalist despite criticisms that he had collaborated with the enemy.

Ramon Magsaysay was probably the first president who became popular because of careful image building. Portrayed as coming from a simple background (Magsaysay's biography *Bare Feet in the Palace* made much of the fact that he started out as a lowly mechanic) the former Defense Secretary became popular ("Magsaysay is my guy") because of his identification with the common *tao* (people), his vaunted honesty, his fight against graft and corruption, his courage in fighting the Communist insurgents, and his championing of democracy ("Our democracy will die, if there is no Magsaysay").

The alleged "selling" of Magsaysay as a hero was attributed to the CIA, especially to Colonel Ed Lansdale, the supposed model for the hero of Graham Greene's *The Ugly American.* Magsaysay was portrayed as a tough Defense Secretary who could slug it out against the Huks and a caring and sympathetic friend to surrendered Communist rebels. His civic action program pioneered an approach later used by the Americans in Vietnam. It was regretted by many that Magsaysay died so early in his term, in an airplane crash. Still, there are some Filipinos who believe that Magsaysay's reputation was saved by his untimely death—there were doubts that he could have sustained the carefully crafted popularity and image that was mounted to lift him beyond simple human proportions.

A docile housewife like Corazon Aquino, thrust into the limelight by the assassination of her husband, Ninoy, owed her popularity to reflected glory from a charismatic martyr. Cory's handlers, of course, enhanced her popularity even more by a carefully managed publicity campaign—the trademark yellow ribbons and yellow dress, her magnificently grafted speeches by Teddy Boy Locsin, her religious rituals and personal piety, the careful evocation of her image as a brave widow fighting the evil forces of militarism and violence—these all seemed so natural and effortless, although, according to those who worked with Cory these were all carefully scripted and orchestrated. Cory also had the benefit of recalling the ideas of her late husband Ninoy which helped her in running the country. It was said that she often "consulted" with him.

The "Cory Magic" was part simple sincerity and part hype, rooted in the Filipino's sympathy for the innocent visited by misfortune. The image was carefully burnished and stage-managed. In Cory, frailty was seen as strength, ignorance perceived as innocence, and incompetence became genuine well meaning attempts to do good. To her credit, Cory remained sincere and honest throughout her presidential years—many critics attribute the loss of the Cory magic to the abuses perpetrated by some corrupt relatives, what one journalist has called *Kamag-anak, Incorporated* (the Family Syndicate).

Elected as a rather colorless retired military man, Fidel V. Ramos also became popular due to a well orchestrated image building program. This involved personal image-making—the unlit cigar (the identification with his *tukayo* Fidel Castro is obvious) the athleticism of a physically fit oldster who could jump like a crazed rapper, the reputation for hard work rather than intellectual brilliance ("Steady Eddie"), the plastic smile, the use of slogans and hyperbole (the Philippines as a "tiger cub economy," Philippines 2000, "pole vaulting" strategy, *Kaya natin iyan!*).

Ramos had a reputation as a plodder but he blossomed with his presidential power. In the waning years of his presidency, he was practically incandescent. It must have been a heroic effort to fade away.

Economists have clearly shown that Ramos' development policies were flawed. However, due to effective public relations, sloganeering and gimmickry and a big dose of psychological-war tactics, Ramos enjoyed six years of popularity that were nearly translated into a longer reign (until anti-Cha-cha managed to stop him).

Among the crop of presidential candidates for the 1998 elections, Erap was the one who easily attracted the wild cheers and ovations that drove people to agitated frenzy. Aside from his own aura as a former movie actor, Erap also sought the help of Fernando Poe. Jr., ("The King of Philippine Movies") and the "super-star" Nora Aunor to join him in campaign rallies and motorcades. In many provinces, the LAMMP campaign relied on motorcades and big rallies featuring such movie stars as Rudy Fernandez, Philip Salvador, Mikee Villanueva and Jinggoy Estrada. The Erap entourage also included international beauty contest winners such as Gemma Cruz and Myrna Borromeo. For brief shining moments, these mega-stars and beautiful people kept the voting public bedazzled enough to forget their everyday concerns.

In 1992, Miriam Defensor Santiago had evoked the same kind of mass adulation that Erap and his showbiz friends got in 1998. Maid Miriam was particularly popular among young students and the intelligentsia, who saw her pistol-packing persona as the antidote to widespread criminality and corruption. In 1998, however, the Miriam magic seemed gone. Her razor-sharp wit and wicked attacks were still there but, somehow, they had become bizarre and unreal. An early attempt to cast her as a returning Princess Leah in the Star Wars movie fantasies failed. Her sequined, colorful gowns and bold make up, while attracting attention, seemed merely gauche and inappropriate.

After 1992, when Miriam launched an acrimonious protest against President Ramos whom she accused of stealing the election from her, Miriam's detractors started spreading malicious rumors that she was emotionally and mentally unstable. They started calling her *Brenda* which was short for "Brain Damaged." This wicked appellation stuck. There were also rumors that she had abandoned and left frustrated, her young supporters.

In televised debates and talk shows, Miriam was a popular participant. Audiences could depend on her for the wicked turn of phrase and the quick riposte. She could mount an attack, complete with encyclopedic legal citations, that could wilt even the strongest opponent. However, there were many indications that to most people, this had become entertainment, a quick escape from the drudgeries of everyday life. Miriam's staccato speeches delivered in a weird foreign accent (one wit called it *Bringo* or a combination of British and Ilonggo) had merely become theatrical and glib. They had lost their political bite.

In many college campuses, Raul Roco had taken over Miriam's role as the darling of young people. Lacking a political machinery and funds, Roco concentrated on addressing his campaign to students and women (Roco became a self-styled "Honorary Woman"). Choosing as his running mate Inday Santiago, who had earned a reputation as a fiery delegate to the U.N. Beijing Women's Conference, Roco started building up his popularity based on intellectual capability, eloquence and conceptual brilliance. He attracted small but emotionally charged crowds, especially in university campuses. There was a strong feeling among political observers, however, that Roco was really running for president in 2004—1998 was merely a launching pad and pilot test for that grand ambition. If true, Roco's rapidly increasing popularity would certainly be an important factor in the next presidential elections.

Try as they might, the other presidential candidates just did not have the charisma to drive people into frenzied adulation. Fred Lim started drawing raves, especially after Cory Aquino's endorsement and the obviously manipulated rumor of a possible romance between the two. Lim, however, did not have the oratorical skills and eloquence to mesmerize people. He was a ramrod-straight policeman with grey hair and a hard mien, a wooden speaker who often stumbled over English and Tagalog phrases. Lim got some public sympathy when he cried on television after the verbously mellifluous Teddy Benigno goaded him into talking about his poverty stricken childhood. People said that "Dirty Harry" had a soft heart and was a human being after all. This incident, however, did not turn into the "one defining moment" that could turn the election around, as a bombastic Benigno bent on raising his TV ratings had hoped would happen.

The most pathetic of all the 1998 presidential candidates was Imelda Marcos. During the height of the martial law years, Imelda had, like Evita Peron of Argentina, attracted the adulation of the masses. Pop psychologists attribute this to folk Catholicism where an Imelda or an Evita could evoke images of the Virgin Mary and of Caucasian-looking angels. Dressed in beautifully embroidered gowns and wearing golden tiaras, Imelda became the personification of the unattainable beauty, power and prestige that the masses could only dream about. This kind of self-indulgent adulation may be seen, to this day, in a fresco at the Agoo, La Union, basilica where Imelda is painted as an idealized winged angel.

In 1998, however, Imelda had lost her popularity and had become merely a caricature of her old self. Walking on her knees and prostrating before the altar at the Manila Cathedral was seen by some as grotesquely theatrical. Her frequent crying episodes in public, charges of malicious persecution, and her pleadings of personal penury (shattered later by her revelation that she was ready to share $800 million of her hidden wealth with the Filipino people if elected) became the running jokes of the campaign. There were rumors that she became a candidate only to avoid going to jail. She had been convicted of fraud early in 1998 over some real estate deal she had arranged when she was governor of Metro Manila. The case has been appealed.

The least charismatic of the candidates was the administration candidate, Joe de Venecia. JdV's main problem was his face—a sad looking mien flanked by two big ears, etched by downcast sloping eyebrows. The irrepressibly malicious TV commentator Larry Henares had told De Venecia on national television that people would find it hard to vote for him because he looked like Yoda in Star Wars. To his credit, De Venecia said he does not mind being likened to Yoda because Yoda is wise, "and the force is with me." Undeterred, Henares said that De Venecia looked like Mickey Mouse. Again, De Venecia retorted by saying his wife thinks he is very handsome.

De Venecia's witty retorts to Henares were the exception to his usual boring speaking style. Even strong backers of De Venecia admitted that he talks too much. He was also an incurable self-promoter who tended to promise anything and claim credit for everything. In many televised debates, De Venecia was often cut off for exceeding his time limit. He also spoke in a lifeless monotone. To many De Venecia supporters, his main strength was not in being a popular charismatic figure but as a deal maker and bargainer. They called him a good *trapo* or traditional politician, a master at working out compromise to achieve the best deal. His best work was done in smoke-filled rooms, not out there in the bright lights of an open political stage.

## Popularity *vs.* Party Machine

To observers of Philippine politics, the 1998 elections witnessed the classic contest between personal popularity and party machinery.

Students of Philippine politics have theorized that Filipinos tend to vote for individuals rather than parties or political aggrupations. Ticket splitting, or the tendency of Filipinos to vote for a candidate from one party for president and for another person from a different party for vice president is given as proof of this proposition. The tendency to vote for individuals is seen both as arising from a personal trait and an institutional construct—"block voting" which was used in the immediate post-war years had been abolished. Despite the cumbersome process of writing in the names of individuals in the longest ballot known in modern-day elections, Filipino voters are encouraged to exercise their right to carefully choose individuals rather than blindly vote for blocks or parties when they go to the polls.

On the other hand, some political analysts insist that factors other than personal popularity, such as money and influence derived from a party machinery, are key elements in winning an election. They argue that individual voters may express a choice but when they actually cast their ballots in the election booth, they are influenced by what their political leaders tell them to do, their loyalty to a highly respected individual, or the fact that they had already sold their vote to a political operator. To analyst Antonio Gatmaitan, for example, it is political machinery and not personal choice that wins elections. Political science professor and newspaper columnist Alex Magno also believes that it is "command votes," derived from party machines, which ultimately decide electoral outcomes. (Both predicted a De Venecia victory because of "command votes." Both are now feasting on crow.) The Lakas-NUCD strategy for 1998 was predicated on party machinery—and it failed.

In the 16-18 April 1998 SWS survey, a random sample of individuals were asked to respond to the following question: *In the coming election, candidates with money and influence will probably win over candidates who are competent but without money and influence.*

The response to this question was interesting. About 44% of those asked agreed with the statement and 40% of them disagreed. In other words, taking the 3% margin of error inherent in a survey of 1,500 respondents into consideration, people were evenly split between those who believed that money and influence (and therefore political machinery) were crucial and those who thought personal popularity as the key to winning an election.

## Popularity is the Key

Erap Estrada, a former movie actor, the butt of Erap jokes, a master of the sound bite and witty one-liners, the object of whispers and gossip related to womanizing, drinking and gambling, a telegenic TV guest and ad-libbing radio commentator, enjoyed great popularity with the Philippine masses. This fact was a given in the campaign strategy worked out by the Erap camp. Although a nation-wide party machinery based on the LAMMP coalition was cobbled together during the 90-day campaign period, it was seen primarily as a supplement to Erap's popularity. Personal popularity was also an important factor in the LAMMP choice of senatorial candidates resulting in the selection of candidates like Robert Jaworski, Tito Sotto, Freddie Webb, and Tessie Aquino—individuals who enjoyed mass appeal and instant name recognition.

The SWS polls of 7-16 March 1998 revealed that 97% of 3,300 respondents nation-wide were aware or have heard of Erap. Of interviewees from urban areas, 100% said they knew about Erap. It was not just the fact that Erap had been a popular movie actor—the SWS survey showed that 29% of voters aged 18-24 who were probably too young to have seen an Erap movie were still supporting Erap. The Erap phenomenon was based on complex emotional-psychological elements at play in the rapidly changing Philippine society.

A careful analysis of the foundations of Erap's personality reveals the following:

- Erap is seen as *maka-mahirap* (for the poor) or *maka-masa* (for the masses). To analyst Dennis Arroyo, Erap had "the *masa* edge." He drew his main support from people with only an elementary level education,

37% of whom expressed the intention to vote for him. He was perceived as being sincerely concerned with basic issues like food, jobs, prices and peace and order. According to Arroyo, knowing this, the Erap strategists coined the slogans "*Trabaho para sa Pilipino*" (Jobs for the Filipino); *Hustong suweldo* (A sufficient and just wage); and *Kontra sa pagtaas ng presyo* (Fight increasing food prices).

- There is a clearly defined personal image of Erap in people's minds—his face, his Elvis Presley hairdo, his moustache and even his trademark wristband—are instantly recognized. The nickname, Erap, is one of the greatest aids to name recall. Translated roughly into English as "buddy" or "close friend," Erap in Tagalog has that emotional nuance and connotation of intimate relationship that is impossible to capture outside Philippine cultural dynamics. No other Filipino candidate enjoyed that much emotional attachment to his name.

- Erap is seen as pro-poor and approachable. Among the most important personality traits voters were looking for in a candidate, according to a December 1996 SWS poll, being pro-poor (63%); approachable (40%); never been involved in graft and corruption (34%); and enemy of criminals (24%) were considered the most important. These were also the exact traits that Erap projected in his campaign.

- Personal attacks on Erap for his alleged marital infidelity did not seem to deter people from voting for him. Asked in a SWS survey to respond to the statement "A person suspected of marital infidelity should not be elected to a high position in government" about 53% of respondents agreed with the statement and 32% disagreed. However, among those who agreed with the statement, Erap was still the strongest choice for president (27%).

During the campaign, a story, which every person telling it swore was absolutely true, spread very rapidly. We heard it from LAMMP senatorial candidate Tessie Aquino. It seemed that Speaker Jose de Venecia, Jr., was haranguing the crowd in a big rally. After attacking Erap Estrada, JdV asked the crowd:

"Will you vote for a person who has many wives?" The response was a thundering "No!"

"Will you vote for a drunkard?" Another resounding "No!"

"Will you vote for a habitual gambler?" An even louder "No!"

"Will you vote for a person who does not know anything?" "No!"

"Will you vote for Erap?"

"YES! Erap! Erap! Erap!"

**Master of the Well-oiled Machine**

Lined up against Erap Estrada in the May 1998 elections was Speaker Jose de Venecia, Jr., the masterly negotiator and coalition builder, the best practitioner of the art of the deal in the halls of Congress, the arbiter and distributor of massive pork barrel funds, the ultimate "good trapo" whose bargaining and negotiating skills have created probably the best organized and most well-endowed political machines since Marcos. JdV had built up the Lakas party which had only a handful of legislators when President Ramos and he won in 1992. His Rainbow Coalition in the House of Representatives had efficiently supported the Ramos legislative program. The Lakas-NUCD supporters boasted that their campaign chests were full. Furthermore, the party in power had access to massive government funds, including congressional pork barrels and the President's own intelligence fund. How could such machinery lose?

De Venecia partisans argued throughout the campaign that popularity does not necessarily translate into votes. They calculated that the anointment of De Venecia by President Ramos was roughly equivalent to 10% of the votes. Taking out their calculators, De Venecia strategists added up the numbers: (a) the six million signatures gathered by the Pirma initiative could amount to the same number of votes for JDV; (b) the Joshua anointment of JdV by the Jesus is Lord and the Jesus Miracle Crusade movements was good for at least another 4 million votes; (c ) the fact that 44 governatorial and city mayoralty contests had Lakas-NUCD candidates running unopposed meant another 2 million JdV votes; and (d) the endorsement of the El Shaddai charismatic group elicited by Manay Gina de Venecia could translate into another 1 million votes.

All these machine-related command votes could mean more than 13 million votes for De Venecia—surely, an unbeatable margin considering that only 27 million voters are expected to actually cast their ballots come election day. In the 1998 elections, however, party machine proved no match to popularity.

## Alliances with Elite Families

In *An Anarchy of Families*, McCoy (1994) noted that, in the Philippines, "elite families can be seen as both object and subject of history." He argued that "instead of treating the Philippine past solely as the interaction among state, private institutions and popular movements, historians might well analyze its political history through the paradigm of elite families."

The role of elites has been a traditional feature of Philippine social analysis. Political scientist Remigio Agpalo captured the principal character of Philippine politics as a spectator sport through the imagery of his book on Occidental Mindoro politics titled *Pandanggo sa Ilaw* (The reference is to a Filipino folk dance where dancers balance lighted oil lamps on their heads and hands. Agpalo likened the dancers to elite politicians and the audience to common voters. The most agile, graceful and flamboyant dancers got the applause—and the votes).

It was Agpalo's contention that although electoral politics had been introduced in the Philippines since the 1900s, it has not actually improved the lives of people too much. This was because of the dominance of elite families which used elections to decide who among them would reign supreme after achieving electoral victory. The Philippine masses were entertained and made to believe they were electing a new leadership every election time. In reality, what happened was a mere "changing of the guard," if such a change occurred at all, the interests of the elites always prevailed. Under these circumstances, winning a Philippine election was merely a matter of crafting together a network of elite families, each one in control of so-called "command votes."

The importance of elite families in Philippine politics was carefully documented by *The Ties that Bind: A Guide to Family, Business and other Interests in the Ninth House of Representatives* (Gutierrez, 1994). What emerged from the study was "a web of interlocking family, business, and professional connections that link the members of the House to one another and to other sections of the countries economic and political elite."

The political role of the House members was explained as follows:

> To their constituents, representatives are patrons or benefactors as well as political bosses. Transactions between the representative and the represented involve mostly particularistic demands ranging from jobs, medical help, and intervention in disputes, to

> business favors and solicitations. Members of the House refer to these requests as 'district matters' and attend to them because they translate into votes and political support.

The book called the Philippine legislature "a House of families"—two of every three representatives come from families whose members have held political office for years." Sheila Coronel, the book's editor, indicated that "The findings of the study attest to the continuity of the Philippine political elite." However, she also noted that "changes in the composition of the elite have taken place" and that analyzing these changes is one of the main challenges to Philippine political science.

The elite-mass nature of Philippine politics was noted by Lande in 1964, when he characterized Philippine political behavior as arising from traditional "patron-client relationships." According to Lande, political patrons commanded the votes of their clients through traditional social ties—the patron provided economic sustenance, dependence, and identification with an elite group. In exchange, clients offered blind obedience arising from *utang na loob* (a debt of gratitude arising from favors given that is impossible to repay).

The patron-client relationship was not an adversarial but a symbiotic one—in a traditional *hacienda*, for example, the landlord allowed the tenant to plant crops on his land (for a share of the harvest), lent him money for seeds, fertilizers and other inputs, arranged for medical help when the tenant or his family were sick, gave the tenant status and prestige by acting as sponsor at baptisms or weddings, attended the tenant's feast during the town *fiesta*, helped in the education of the tenant's children, etc. In turn, the tenant dutifully delivered the landlord's share of the harvest, his wife and young children worked as unpaid servants in the landlord's big house, brought chickens, pigs, vegetables, rice and other offerings when the landlord held a party, and, of course, voted blindly for the candidate chosen by the landlord come election time.

Anthropologists Frank Lynch and Mary R. Hollnsteiner explained the patron-client phenomenon in terms of "dyadic relationships" involving "reciprocity" and exchanges of favors, traditional village society, the reciprocal relationships offered a sense of stability and safety to poor tenant farmers who were often subjected to extreme uncertainties arising from natural and human-made calamities. It also provided patrons the power and influence required for maintaining their elite position in society. While the relationship was of mutual benefit to the parties involved, the patron definitely had the upper hand.

Even as Gutierrez documented the role of elite families in Philippine politics he also noted many societal changes that have influenced political relationships. For one, many traditional Filipino elite families have not been able to maintain their economic dominance—a new class of rich families had made it to the upper levels of Philippine society. Some of these families progressed because of commerce, others enriched themselves through graft and corruption. The power of the traditional landlords also declined with the migration of their tenants' children to cities where they got good education and landed better jobs. Soon the children were inviting their parents to join them in the cities.

Many factors are responsible for the weakening of political families. The 1987 Constitution, for example, introduced the need for sectoral organizations to be represented in Congress. For the first time in Philippine history, the party list system would be tried out in the 1998 elections. Through this system, cause-oriented groups and small parties belonging to marginalized organizations will be allowed to nominate their candidates. Any accredited group able to garner 2% of the party list votes will be entitled to one representative, another nominee can get elected for another 2% and a third one can get elected by another 2%.

The party list system, first advocated in the 1930s by philosopher Ricardo Pascual of the University of the Philippines in his book *Partyless Democracy*, will probably finish off the two-party system in the Philippines—not that this had any more influence, anyway—the Philippine polity had been multi-party in the past 30 years or so.

In the absence of ideologically distinct and well organized political parties, it becomes most important for any aspiring politician to organize a network of elite families in order to win an election. Even if "command votes" by elite families have waned, other "command votes" have taken their place.Trade unions, for example, have been important mobilization structures for votes. It is also one of the traditions in Philippine politics that the Iglesia ni Cristo, a local sect, can deliver the votes of all its members. The latest groups that can reputedly deliver blocks of votes are the religious groups such as the *El Shaddai*, led by Mike Velarde and the *Jesus is Lord* (JIL) movement, led by Eddie Villanueva.

Ironically, the popularity and mass appeal of Erap and the many movie, sports and media stars who have entered politics has contributed to the weakening of elite networks. By becoming widely known by the people and appealing directly for their support, these popular politicians have been able to by-pass the mediating influences of landlords, political *liders* and warlords.

It is true that in some provinces (in Ilocos Norte, Ilocos Sur, Cavite, and Nueva Ecija, for example), political overlords still hold sway. It is also believed that huge chunks of "command votes" can still be controlled and delivered in Muslim Mindanao. There are suggestions that traditional political machines persist in low income communities in Metro Manila—the Cuneta machine in Pasay City, for example, the Jojo Binay machine in Makati or the Mel Mathay machine in Quezon City. In general, however, Philippine politics has become more free, even anarchistic. The atomization of political action, name recognition, charisma, popularity and mass appeal have become the major factor in electoral victory.

## Regionalism and Linguistic Politics

The 1998 elections were seen by many as proof that regionalism and linguistic or "tribal politics" were the main influence in Philippine elections. A *Manila Standard* editorial (25/3/98) lamented that just when the Philippine centennial as a free country was being celebrated "the surveys indicate a revival of tribalism in voter behavior brought about by the breakdown of the political party system."

Political tribalism was blamed when candidates espoused policies of benefit to their regions and appealed to linguistic groups to vote for candidates from their own areas.

This tribal politics pattern, however, is belied by the candidacy of Joseph "Erap" Estrada. Erap's bailiwick is the Tagalog-speaking region of Laguna, Cavite, Rizal, Quezon and Bulacan. However, the results of the Social Weather Stations public opinion poll of 16-21 March 1998 revealed that Estrada was pulling votes from all regions as follows:

- Regions 1 and 2 (Ilocos & Cagayan Valley) 33%
- Region III (Central Luzon) 41%
- Region IV (Southern Tagalog) 38%
- Region VIII (Eastern Visayas) 31%
- Regions IX and XII (Western & Central Mindanao) 34%
- Region X (Northern Mindanao) 31%
- Region XI (Southern Mindanao) 36%

The only regions where Erap had less votes than other candidates (7-16 March SWS survey) were in the following:

- Region V (Bicol): Roco 66% vs. Erap 14%
- Region VI (Western Visayas): Santiago 25% vs. Erap 19%
- Region VII (Central Visayas): Osmeña 49% vs. Erap 15%
- National Capital Region: Lim 28% vs. Erap 26%

One measure of tribalism was the preference of people speaking a specific language or dialect. The 7-16 March SWS survey results were as follows:

- First language Tagalog: For Erap 34% followed by Lim 20%
- Cebuano: Erap 27% tied with Osmeña 27%
- Ilocano: Erap 37% followed by De Venecia 16%
- Capampangan: Erap 34% followed by Lim 30%
- Other Visayan: Erap 35% followed by Lim 17%

The only other language groups where another candidate received more votes than Estrada were as follows:

- Ilonggo: Santiago 25% vs. Erap 21%
- Bicol: Roco 65% vs. Erap 14%
- Pangasinense: De Venecia 57% vs. Erap 19%

Among the three linguistic groups, Erap was the second choice of all the voters polled.

Interestingly, the candidate with the widest national (as against tribal) appeal was Gloria Macapagal Arroyo who was the first choice of people interviewed in all the country's regions except people speaking Pangasinense. Among this group, Governor Orbos was preferred by 39% of voters vs. Macapagal-Arroyo's 38%.

The pattern of voters' choices indicate that it was possible for candidates to be widely chosen. Some of the reasons for this ability to cut across tribal politics were:

- Personal popularity—Estrada was a successful movie actor before turning to politics. Macapagal-Arroyo was the daughter of a former Philippine president and has campaigned widely throughout the whole country.

- Name recognition—because of the candidate's popularity, people could recall his or her name easily.

One of the most enduring traditions in Philippine elections is the "north-south balance"—if a candidate for President hails from the northern island of Luzon, the vice presidential candidate must come from Visayas or Mindanao. The belief was that Filipinos vote along regional linguistic, religious or "tribal" lines. One has to have a "favorite son or daughter" in an electoral line up in order to mobilize enough votes to win nation-wide.

In 1998, nearly all the major political parties violated this rule. Erap, with roots in Laguna, Bulacan and Metro Manila, chose as his running mate, Edong Angara, from Quezon, who has lived mostly in Metro Manila. Joe de Venecia, from the Central Luzon (Pangasinan), was running with Gloria Macapagal, who also has family roots in Central Luzon, in the province of Pampanga. De Villa from Batangas got Oscar Orbos from Pangasinan as his running mate, also both from Luzon. The only two presidential candidates who went with regional balance were Fred Lim (Metro Manila) who chose Serge Osmeña III (Visayas) from Cebu as his running mate, and Raul Roco, from Bicol in Luzon, who chose Inday Santiago from Mindanao as his tandem.

Public opinion polls, however, point to the persistence of geographical preference or tribal politics in the behavior of voters. The across-the-board popularity of Erap Estrada was more of an exception than the rule. The SWS survey results for a nation-wide poll taken 16-21 March 1998 yielded the following results:

**Presidential Preference by First Language (in %)**

| Language | Estrada | Lim | JdV | Osmeña | Roco | De Villa | Santiago |
|---|---|---|---|---|---|---|---|
| Tagalog | 34 | 20 | 7 | 1 | 11 | 11 | 3 |
| Cebuano | 27 | 10 | 8 | 27 | 2 | 3 | 2 |
| Ilocano | 37 | 15 | 16 | 1 | 3 | 2 | 0.3 |
| Ilonggo | 21 | 16 | 7 | 9 | 2 | 2 | 25 |
| Bicol | 14 | 4 | 5 | 1 | 65 | 2 | 1 |
| Pampango | 34 | 30 | 15 | 2 | 4 | 3 | 1 |
| Pangasinan | 19 | 9 | 57 | 1 | 4 | 2 | 0 |
| Philippines | 30 | 16 | 10 | 9 | 8 | 6 | 4 |

From the survey results, it is clear that Bicolanos are the most regionalistic among Philippine language groups, with 65% of those polled preferring Roco. Pangasinenses were the second most regionalistic, with 57% choosing De Venecia. Although Ilonggos preferred their "favorite daughter" Miriam Santiago over any other candidate, the percentage of people preferring her (25%) is a lot lower than the share Santiago had in the 1992 elections.

An interesting pattern shown by the survey results is the across-the-board popularity of Erap Estrada who was the first choice of Tagalogs, Ilocanos, and Pampangos. Erap even tied with Cebuano candidate Osmeña, whose one-issue campaign *(Probinsiya Muna or Promdi)* is focused on winning the Cebuano vote.

Although Lim did not get any top ratings among all language groups, his popularity is shown to also cut across such groups gaining high preference ratings among Pampangos (the Cory endorsement might be at play here), Tagalogs (Lim hails from Bulacan and Metro Manila), Ilonggos and Ilocanos.

A noteworthy finding in the survey is the candidate preference of people who adhere to the Islamic religion (who are concentrated in ethnic enclaves in Mindanao). According to the SWS finding, 41% of those polled preferred Erap for president, followed by Lim (16%) De Venecia (14%) and De Villa (7%). Although Erap was preferred by (Catholics (30%), other Christian denominations (30%) and the Iglesia ni Cristo (37%), people belonging to these religious groups do not tend to belong to specific ethno-linguistic groups. The voter preference patterns, however, consistently point to the across-the-board popularity of Erap. Muslims say they like Erap because he is macho. His detractors say Erap is popular with the Muslims only because like them, he has many wives.

**Access to Government Resources**

In the Philippines, the candidate of the party in power has undue advantage over all others because of his or her access to the vast resources of the government. This is why, the "anointment" of a candidate by the outgoing President of the Philippines is important. Some political analysts have even proposed that the anointment of President Ramos of Speaker De Venecia was worth 10% of the votes.

The most important asset available to the ruling party candidate are the "pork barrel" funds available to Congressmen, Senators, the Vice President and the President. In 1995, the pork barrel budget (known as the Countrywide Development Fund or CDF and the Congressional Initiative Allotments or CIA) amounted to P54.5 billion. Although these funds were supposed to be allocated among legislators and executives, those who do not tow the party line may find their allocations delayed or stopped. Since the CDFs and CIAs are the main sources for specific projects that are designed to benefit specific bailiwicks, they are important elements in an election victory.

In the 1998 elections, the importance of access to government resources was shown in the mad scramble of local politicians to be officially chosen as the candidates of the Lakas-NUCD. One of the boasts of De Venecia, in fact, was that only the administration party had a complete slate of candidates in all the local governments and congressional districts in the Philippines. To De Venecia and leaders of the party in power, this meant that these local candidates would "carry" the national presidential, vice presidential and senatorial candidates through their party machines.

One problem with this strategy, however, was that for every local person chosen by the Lakas-NUCD as official candidate, there were several who were frustrated because they felt rejected and left out of the opportunity to avail of public resources in their campaigns. Once the local nominating processes were finished, there was a stampede of rejected candidates who wanted to join the opposition LAMMP and other parties.

Access to government and ruling party resources were important to the "anointed" candidates but many of these people were keenly aware of the popularity of Erap, too. Thus, many of the official Lakas-NUCD candidates worked out private side deals with Erap and the LAMMP. The most common deals were as follows: (a) do not field a candidate against me in this election and I will secretly support you for the presidential, vice presidential and senatorial contest; (b) just ask Erap not to campaign against me in my province or city and I will support him; (c ) give me a little time to receive the money from the Lakas-NUCD; as soon as I receive my share of the national campaign funds, I will shift my support to Erap and the LAMMP candidates; and (d) declare our province or city as a "free zone," and you get my support.

The LAMMP strategists were probably exaggerating but, after election day when the extent of the rout of the party in power became obvious, Ronnie Zamora, in charge of political operations and Orly Mercado, campaign manager, claimed that 90% of the Lakas-NUCD candidates who ran unopposed and who received funding from the party in power had actually entered into private side deals with Erap. All they wanted was to get the resources from the government and the party in power. After they got that, they told their followers to vote for Erap.

The final results of the 1998 elections partly confirm the importance of governmental resources and access to Lakas-NUCD party funds as key reasons for electoral victory. While Erap won as president and the senatorial results had the opposition LAMMP victorious at 7–5, the majority of conrgressmen, governors, mayors, provincial board members and municipal council members were from the Lakas-NUCD camp. Locally, it was still the public funds and the resources of the party in power that made all the difference. Most of the victorious candidates were re-electionists or they were the spouses or relatives of officials who had "graduated" and who could not run for political office any more. They had relied heavily on government and national party resources to keep themselves in power.

Analysts of the Philippine political situation point to other significant changes that could be discerned from the results of the 1998 elections.

First, the importance of personal popularity and charisma in winning an election was proven by the victory of Erap, Gloria Macapagal Arroyo, Loren Legarda, Rene Cayetano, Tito Sotto , Robert Jaworski and other showbiz and sports personalities. Name recognition was the game. With the "anaconda" ballot as long as it was, having a difficult name that voters could not readily recognize was lethal inside the polling booth.

Second, alliances with elite families was important but, in the case of Erap, it was not absolutely necessary for victory. Most Filipino voters chose Erap because they liked him and identified with him—they refused to be told about whom to vote for by leaders and traditional controllers of command votes.

Third, regionalistic ties and tribal politics were important but they were not sufficient conditions to defeat Erap nor many of the popular candidates.

Fourth, access to government resources and the funds of the party in power was very important in the election victory of local candidates. In the national contest for president, vice president and senators where it counted most, government and party resources were less important.

Fifth, the importance of so-called "command votes," whether controlled by local machine bosses, religious leaders, or local influentials was negated by the 1998 election results. With the exception of the Iglesia ni Cristo, whose votes went to Erap and Gloria Macapagal Arroyo, the other command votes were not delivered. There was no evidence that the charismatic religious groups were able to sway their followers to blindly follow the choices of their leaders. The final results of the El Shaddai votes were very interesting—perhaps, Brother Mike Velarde will confirm soon whether there was, indeed, a "code word" given to Erap that signaled he was the chosen one. The more important question, however, was whether Brother Mike's endorsement would have been necessary—the SWS and other polls already revealed a sizable Erap following among the El Shaddai members.

Finally, the results of the 1998 elections revealed how fickle the electorate were. The Cory magic, the Miriam magic and the Cardinal Sin magic were all gone. While Cory and the Cardinal could mobilize thousands to go against Cha-cha, their influence could not stop the Erap votes. The Makati Business Club and other economic elites could not influence their workers and staff members to junk Erap either. In the exclusive compounds and tightly guarded villages, the votes of the maids, drivers, gardeners, caretakers, nursemaids and laborers that far out-numbered the votes of their masters heavily went to Erap. In the whole country, demographics won—the fact that 90% of the Philippine electorate was made up of D and E social classes and that these groups voted overwhelmingly for Erap was the most deciding factor of all.

The strategies on how a Philippine election can be won has definitely changed. The role of the mass media—the primary channel for popularity, name recognition and fame—has been confirmed. But the media in the 1998 elections was tainted by corruption which resulted in its blatant partisanship. Public opinion polling as a science and an art has definitely become a necessary part of election campaigns. The political parties and local party machinery are important but they are not what they used to be. Money alone, or political power and governmental advantage are not sufficient to win elections.

Political pundits will debate for a very long time whether the Philippine 1998 elections heralded the emergence of class-based politics in the country. Our own reading of the situation is that there were definite class identifications and elite *versus* mass patterns in the electoral campaign. There may even be tendencies in the future for political alignments to follow socio-economic lines similar to the tendency in the United States for the working classes and new immigrants to vote Democratic and rich business people and the country club set to vote Republican.

To win an election in the Philippines, however, does not require class-based revolution in the Marxist-Leninist sense. Ideology is very dead in the Philippines—the so-called "revolt of the *masa*" is more like a fiesta or a raucous *miting de avance.* When all the shouting and the singing and the dancing is over, all that the Filipino electorate can do is wait to see if the political promises will be fulfilled. With Erap Estrada as the newly elected president, there seems to be greater expectations on the part of the electorate that these promises will be remembered and realized.

An important factor in this nascent formation of two socio-economic blocks (the elite and the mass) is the institutional change introduced only in 1998, the party list system. Left to develop on its own, the party list system will probably encourage fragmentation and atomization of social groupings because the patttern of vote allocation after the election is based on the formation of many groups. Its emphasis on community-level action also poses some difficulties in mobilizing resources at a higher political/administrative level.

The implementation of the party list system in 1998 was marked by confusion, lack of information about the process from the Comelec and other groups, very low interest on the part of the electorate and great difficulties in tabulating results. The party list process was so cumbersome that in many precincts, tabulation of party list results had to be postponed in order to finish the count for national and local government contests.

The party list system, with its fragmenting tendency, need not get in the way of the elite-mass social formation. In fact, with very few exceptions, many candidates running for party list positions were coming from the NGO, civic and cause-oriented groups sector. As such, they will have a strong tendency to identify and work with the leaders of the Erap Estrada system of governance.

In implementing Erap's program of government, it is most important to keep and strengthen the political party machinery as a structure both for people's mobilization and for enforcing party discipline. In this regard, it may be more useful for Erap to strengthen the *Partido ng Masang Pilipino* (PMP) rather than LAMMP during the six years of his term. The coalition that created LAMMP was a key factor to win the election. After the victory parade, however, it is more crucial to actually carry out the dream plans and development scenarios now. Pursuing Erap's legislative program will require quite a number of congressional members and senators who will help the new president in getting his pet bills approved. Erap's proposed abolition of the pork barrel will not endear him to many legislators. This is why, within the next 100 days it is most critical that PMP be strengthened and the party leaders be supported in their valuable roles.

# Chapter 6

# Campaign Strategies

On 18 February 1998, the Policy and Media Group met at LAMMP headquarters on Shaw Boulevard for the first time. We became officially affiliated with the campaign as Campaign Officers for Public Policies and Issues upon receiving a formal letter of appointment signed by Senator Orly Mercado, LAMMP National Campaign Manager.

The group was chaired by Orly and had as members Rod Reyes, in charge of Media, Susy Pineda Mercado, (Orly's wife) who was assisting him with Operations, Ding Gageloña, who worked with Rod, Paul Bograd, an American political strategy consultant, R.J. Esteban, and us.

It was obvious from the outset that there was some uneasiness between the Rod and the Orly groups. Orly had called for the meeting at 9:00 A.M. and Rod arrived at 10:30. He said that he had set his alarm clock at 6:00, left his home at 7:00 and still made it to LAMMP headquarters only by 10:30 because of traffic. Was it necessary to hold these meetings every day at 9:00 A.M.?

Orly was very conciliatory—he said his call for the meeting was meant to acquaint all individuals involved in the campaign with each other. This was not an attempt on his part to impose a bureaucratic structure to the campaign. However, it was indicative of something amiss that all of us were meeting each other for the first time—three months before election day. He recognized that all of us had been doing something for the campaign for some time—indeed, the Policy Studies Group under Raul de Guzman had been in operation for the past six years in the Office of the Vice President. Rod's Media group had been active for months, working from the offices of Manny Zamora, the main PMP financier.

However, a formal campaign structure had now been established and some kind of coordination was needed. That organization had Orly as National

Campaign Manager in charge of Operations, Ronnie Zamora in charge of Political Affairs, Jesse Ejercito in charge of Finance and Administration, and Rod Reyes in charge of Press and Media Relations. The Policy Studies Group headed by Raul had been invited to participate in the campaign. We were the representatives of Raul's group.

**The Political Situation**

The meeting started with a "situationer" (one of those neologisms peculiar to Filipinos, meaning, the situation, another is"presidentiable" for presidential candidate). Paul talked about the results of a November 1997 survey conducted by Philippine Survey Research Center (PSRC) headed by R.J. Esteban. The survey had a sample of 5,000 nation-wide and had a margin of error of plus or minus 3%.

The Philippine political situation, according to the survey, was as follows:

- People were dissatisfied with their living conditions under the Ramos administration—a full 38% were very dissatisfied and only 15% said they were very satisfied.
- Crime, especially kidnapping for ransom, was of deep concern to people, especially the rich who felt unsafe when venturing outside their "gated communities." Graft and corruption were also important issues to those who had to deal with the government. Asked who among the candidates would be able to solve these problems, 40% said Erap was their choice.
- The economy was considered by the masses as the most important issue—jobs, prices of prime commodities, salaries and wages, and food security were uppermost in people's minds. Here, Gloria Macapagal Arroyo, got a 45% rating; Erap came in a poor 4$^{th}$, behind Osmeña and Roco.
- The people were looking for a leader who could understand their plight—someone caring and compassionate who shared their misery. They wanted a leader who would listen. Erap scored highest in this category (75%).

With this situation, the group agreed that the main elements of the Erap campaign strategy would be as follows: (a) concentrate on the economy as the main campaign issue; (b) focus on population centers where the votes were; (c) stress poverty alleviation and the concerns of the poor and underprivileged; (d) wage both a community-based civic effort and a traditional political mobilization campaign; and (e) manage the campaign scheduling well.

## The Economy as Campaign Issue

The economy was to be the main area of concentration since people were most concerned with it. More effort was needed in economics, also, because the surveys showed that Erap was perceived to be weakest in that area. The economy issue, however, should not be framed in terms of complicated macro-economic models involving complex variables such as monetary policy, fiscal management, balance of payments, current accounts deficits, etc. Rather, the issues would be boiled down to four basic elements of utmost concern to the masses:

- *Trabaho para sa Pilipino* (Work for the Filipino).
- *Hustong suweldo para sa lahat (*Adequate salary for all).
- *Presyong abot-kaya (*Affordable prices).
- *Agrikultura at kabuhayan sa nayon (*Agriculture and countryside development).

It was agreed that Erap and the whole campaign media blitz would hammer away at these four messages. A ten-minute "staple speech" for Erap would be crafted, focused on the themes. Briefing memos on specific cities and provinces to be prepared before each campaign sortie would seek out problems on the four issues. The candidates would bring these issues to the people during the provincial sorties.

Special local circumstances highlighting any of the themes were to be inserted in the staple speech and the briefing memos. For example, Nueva Ecija farmers were concerned with irrigation as the El Niño drought had forced the government to divert water from agriculture to respond to Metro Manila's water needs. People in Mindanao were demonstrating against high interest rates as these have adversely affected investments, resulting in firms closing and laying off thousands of workers. Cebu's rapidly growing population demands more affordable housing, with more than 60% of families living in depressed areas that were chronically short of drinking water, sanitation and waste disposal services. Bicolanos were complaining that they pay the highest rates for electricity even though the country's hydro power sources are in the Bicol region.

## Regional Concentration

The group decided that campaign efforts would be focused on the most densely populated provinces and cities where votes were concentrated. The Philippine archipelago covers a vast territory and transportation linkages are grossly underdeveloped. Even with three helicopters and three planes devoted to Erap's personal use in the campaign, bringing the candidate to all the places would be an extremely difficult exercise.

The Comelec had registered 34,146,194 voters (December 1997) all over the country. The bulk of these votes were concentrated in 15 provinces and regions where aggregated votes made up 53.4% of the total. These key provinces/regions were as follows:

| Region/Province | No. of Reg. Voters | Percent |
|---|---|---|
| National Capital Region (NCR) | 5,150,194 | 15.1 |
| Cebu (Region VII) | 1,526,448 | 4.5 |
| Negros Occidental (Region VI) | 1,139,100 | 3.3 |
| Pangasinan (Region 1) | 1,078,161 | 3.1 |
| Bulacan (Region III) | 1,013,718 | 3.0 |
| Cavite (Region IV) | 902,828 | 2.7 |
| Laguna (Region IV) | 898,390 | 2.6 |
| Batangas (Region IV) | 895,658 | 2.6 |
| Davao del Sur (Region XI) | 874,378 | 2.6 |
| Iloilo (Region VI) | 870,316 | 2.5 |
| Pampanga (Region III) | 848,539 | 2.5 |
| Zamboanga del Sur (Region IX) | 811,021 | 2.4 |
| Nueva Ecija (Region III) | 773,874 | 2.3 |
| Leyte (Region VIII) | 701,982 | 2.1 |
| Quezon (Region IV) | 700,320 | 2.1 |

In deciding where to concentrate their campaign efforts, the LAMMP strategists did not only focus on total number of registered voters. Attention given to a province/region was weighted in accordance with the possibility of getting votes in the place. One factor used was the share of Erap votes during the 1992 vice presidential contest. Another important factor was the Erap voting preference rating in the latest SWS survey.

In 1992, Erap had done very well in Pangasinan (42.6% of the votes), Bulacan (49.8%), Cavite (37.9%), Laguna (52.6%), Batangas (34.9%), and Davao del Sur (33.8%). He did not do so well in the NCR (25%), Cebu (10%), and Negros Occidental (24.8%).

The February 1998 SWS surveys revealed that Erap was still not doing that well in Metro Manila (26.3%), the Bicol region (13.8%), Iloilo and Western Visayas (19.2%) and Cebu and Central Visayas (16.3%). His popular vote in Pangasinan might get eroded because of Jose de Venecia's candidacy. The same situation might happen in Batangas, where favorite son, Renato de Villa, might get many votes. The candidacy of Lito Osmeña would most likely cost Erap a lot of votes in Cebu and Central Visayas as well as in the Western Visayas (Iloilo and Negros Occidental). The Bicol region, of course, was expected to go heavily for Roco, who was projected to win 66.7% of the regional vote. The LAMMP strategy group assumed that the traditional Filipino patterns of "tribal politics" would continue in 1998, with favorite son candidates garnering most of the votes in their bailiwicks.

## Man of the Masses- Focus on Poverty Alleviation

For campaign purposes, the LAMMP political strategists divided Filipino society into five categories. The A-B-C group, which made up 10% of the voting population, was composed of mainly urban, high income, educated and politically aware individuals. Survey findings showed that this group was most fearful of an Erap presidency. Some A-B-C voters even said that, if Erap won the presidency, they would leave the country. Erap's televised response to that threat was a nonchalant "they can start packing."

It was estimated that 30% of Metro Manila voters belonged to the A-B-C categories. This correlated quite well with the survey finding that only about 25% of voters interviewed by SWS would vote for Erap in the NCR (National Capital Region). About 10% of voters in the Southern Tagalog region, 8% of those in Cebu and Central Visayas, and 7% of those in Central Luzon were A-B-C. In these places, it was probably ethnic identification or "tribal politics" rather than socio-economic grouping that was responsible for some of the low voter preference for Erap (Batangas voters preferred de Villa, Cebuanos went for Osmeña and Bicolanos were for Roco).

Most Filipinos (about 72%) belonged to the D group, roughly divided into middle income (D-1), making up 43% and lower income (D-2), making up 29%. These groups made up the *masang Pilipino,* who are really quite poor. Most people belonging to this category were mid-level farmers tilling less than three hectares of land, low level employees in the public and private sectors, small scale entrepreneurs, fishermen, and petty traders. They would have barely achieved a high school education. They were concentrated in small towns, larger villages and in low income settlements in urban areas.

The SWS survey respondents belonging to the D group were mainly concentrated in Ilocos and Cagayan Valley regions (88%), in Central Luzon (83%) and in the Southern Tagalog region (83%). The Bicol region (78%), Western Visayas (75%) and Central Visayas (70%) also had heavy concentrations of D voters. The lowest concentration of D voters were in the Metro Manila area (45%).

With the exception of provinces with favorite sons, the places with high concentrations of D voters tended to support Erap. In these places, therefore, the political strategy called for protection and maintenance of Erap's votes. To the strategists, this could be done by working out alliances with local leaders, repeatedly relaying pro-poor messages relevant to local conditions, and actually showing up in motorcades and rallies in these target areas.

The poorest groups belonging to the Philippine masses, (E) made up 18% of the total sampled voting population. They were landless agricultural workers, artisan fisherfolk, migratory farm laborers, slash and burn agriculturists, urban squatters and slum dwellers, and the grossly under-employed and unemployed. The poor were highly concentrated in Eastern Visayas and Northern Mindanao where they made up 34% of voter respondents, as well as in Central and Western Mindanao (28%). They could also be found in Southern Mindanao (25%), Central Visayas (22%), and Western Visayas (22%).

SWS surveys have repeatedly found that Erap's main political support was drawn from the D and E groups. Nation-wide, among A-B-C voters, Erap was preferred by 18%. About 30% of D voters preferred Erap but among E voters, this preference went up to 39%. In contrast, Alfredo Lim, the second ranking candidate, was supported by 31% of ABC voters, 16% by D voters and 7% by E voters.

The LAMMP political strategists noted a tendency of the LAMMP campaign officials to focus more heavily on the A-B-C groups. This was particularly notable among the Media group, who tended to concentrate on the mainstream Manila press, television and radio. The Manila-based media people's reason for this was that provincial media pick up their stories from Manila media anyway. The pollsters argued that provincial concerns were different from Manila's.

Group discussions often revolved around what this or that columnist said, how Erap did in a televised debate, how the Makati business crowd will react to a particular Erap pronouncement, or which clan or prominent family criticized Erap.

It must be mentioned, that despite their commitment to Erap's candidacy, almost all the key members in the LAMMP campaign staff actually belonged to the A-B-C categories. Their intellectual predisposition, world-view and lifestyle found kinship with those of the economic and intellectual elites. Only those among them with strong ideological leanings, social science analytical capabilities, and emotional capacity to empathize could grasp the importance of understanding the D and E groups. Erap himself, and his immediate family members, lived a comfortable upper middle class life. It was one of the supreme ironies of the 1998 campaign that the champion of the masses and the strategists who supported him were actually hopelessly *burgis,* albeit populist ones.

The SWS survey results called for greater attention to the D and E voters. This meant more reliance on face-to-face approaches such as campaign rallies and motorcades, working with local leaders, campaigning in places where people were concentrated (markets, bus depots, factories), and in urban poor depressed areas (slum and squatter settlements). Instead of glossy brochures, the strategy called for Pilipino *komiks*. The orange Erap wristband served as a colorful identity symbol but, when distributing campaign materials, it was found that people preferred T-shirts, hats, sunshades, small calendars, and other useful items. Particularly sought after items were made-in-Singapore wristwatches with Erap's smiling face.

Based on the survey findings that people preferred Erap because of his compassionate, caring, and sympathetic nature, the LAMMP campaign strategists decided that radio and TV programs that targeted the concerns of the poor would work best. Thus, the radio program, "Jeep ni Erap," which featured Erap and Orly Mercado, was launched. The format allowed people to call up Erap and Orly by telephone so that they could air their problems. Erap and Orly would then indicate how they could help solve these problems. This format enhanced Erap's image that he was one who knew how to listen (*Marunong makinig).*

Another campaign approach was to bring Erap more closely to the people through "press the flesh" sorties. He was pictured having a modest lunch with a squatter family. He had long discussions with former San Juan families in Taytay, Rizal, who had been relocated there during Erap's term as Mayor (each family was given a 100 square meter lot, a house, and access to water, sanitation and electricity). The community had its own school, church and health center.

An Erap video showed him directly untangling a traffic jam. To increase Erap's identification with the lowly jeepney, Erap and all the LAMMP candidates drove to the Commission on Elections on board the colorful vehicles when they filed their candidacy papers.

In his campaign sorties, Erap wore a checkered shirt, denim or khaki pants, and an orange and blue campaign vest. However, in all these efforts to dress up like the common man, Erap drew the line on head gear. In a photograph in Marawi City where Erap was signing a memorandum of understanding with Muslim leaders, he was the only one, among the LAMMP officials, not wearing a Muslim cap. Although he distributed thousands of hats and caps, Erap refused to wear one except when he drove a jeep to Comelec to file his candidacy. It would mess up his hair.

**Campaign Organization**

When Erap openly declared his bid for the presidency in 1994, he had a very weak political party, the *Partido ng Masang Pilipino (PMP)*. He then entered into a coalition with the *Laban ng Demokratikong Pilipino (LDP)* and the *National People's Coalition (NPC)* to form the *Laban ng Makabayang Masang Pilipino (LAMMP)*. LAMMP selected Erap for its presidential candidate and the LDP's Edgardo Angara for vice president. Senator Ernesto Maceda, the NPC president, decided to pull out of the coalition when his ambition to be the vice presidential candidate was thwarted. He decided to run for Mayor of Manila, instead.

As early as 1994, Erap and his friend, Robert Aventajado, had thought of organizing a civic movement to support Erap's candidacy for president. This was JEEP, styled as a Citizens Movement for Justice, Economy, Environment and Peace. JEEP envisioned a "corps of dedicated, trained, highly motivated cadres deployed at all precincts of the country." It would employ a "social mobilization model" focused on advocacy, capability building, coalition building, communication, and organization.

JEEP was headed by Robert as President, with Horacio "Boy" Morales as Secretary General. The JEEP Secretariat headed by Boy had Area Coordinators, Training Officers, Liaison Officers with Sectoral Groups, a Head for Monitoring operations and a person in charge of a computerized Data Base unit. At the provincial level, JEEP Provincial Councils headed by a Chairperson were organized, supported by Area Trainer Organizations. Similar councils and Organizers were set up at the municipal and *barangay* (village) levels.

From the very beginning, JEEP was unabashedly partisan. Its mission, according to the official JEEP brochure was "To campaign and secure votes for Erap." The JEEP immediate goal was—The Presidency!

Despite JEEP's emphasis on process and organization, individual personalities marred its operations somewhat. For example, the JEEP organization for the National Capital Region (JEEP/NCR) was run by Roberto "Bobby" Oca, an experienced labor leader who was very close to Erap. Bobby was the son of Roberto Oca, Sr., who ran for Mayor of Manila in the early 1960s but lost. He inherited his father's political machine revolving around labor unions, especially those at the Manila north and south harbors and the working-class district of Tondo. Bobby refused to be coordinated by Robert so it was decided that JEEP/NCR would do its own thing, fully independent of Robert's operations.

Aside from Robert and Boy Morales, the key JEEP officials were Ed de la Torre, a former priest who had become an activist and Felicidad Villareal, a former nun, who also turned to activism to alleviate poverty among the masses. Ed and Fely were professional organizers and trainers—Fely had spent more than a decade with the Food and Agriculture Organization (FAO) of the United Nations and had been awarded the Sen Medal of Achievement for her work in China organizing women's self-help groups. Ed was president of a grassroots foundation that conducted regular seminars for the rural and urban poor. Both Fely and Ed worked with Salvador "Buddy" Garbanzos, a training consultant who was hired by JEEP to actually conduct the seminars, workshops and training programs for card-carrying JEEP members.

When the LAMMP coalition was formed, further personality problems ensued. The key PMP (and later LAMMP) officials were the brothers Manny and Ronnie Zamora. Manny was a banker with extensive interests in the mining industry—he provided the major financial support for PMP and LAMMP. Ronnie was the elected NPC Congressman for San Juan, Rizal, and House Minority Leader. Erap's primary political base was San Juan where his son, Jinggoy, was Mayor.

While Manny controlled the purse strings, Ronnie, chief back room negotiator and political strategist, parlayed his talents into political alliances that would deliver votes. Unfortunately, the Zamora brothers and Robert Aventajado could not see eye to eye. When Robert aspired to play a key role in LAMMP, the Zamora brothers vehemently objected and blocked his ambition with the support of other power brokers who did not trust Aventajado. Erap was forced to withdraw his support for Robert. That left the JEEP operations as the main responsibility of Robert.

In its efforts to work out formal working relationships with LAMMP, JEEP formulated a division of responsibilities as follows:

a. LAMMP would be in charge of party organizing, recruiting people for partisan politics, and establishing linkages with political candidates and personalities.

b. JEEP, in turn, would be a social movement. It would help mobilize sectoral groups that share its social goals. It would affiliate with appropriate organizations and those with shared local-specific concerns. It would be a mass-based movement with card carrying members dedicated to a cause—social justice, economic well being, environment protection and conservation, and peace and order.

**Campaign Scheduling**

Scheduling campaign activities was the most difficult activity in Erap's campaign strategy. The campaign got off to a rousing start with the LAMMP party convention on Sunday, 18 January 1998, held at the Folk Arts Theater on Roxas Boulevard. However, this was not really a convention because everything had been agreed upon in caucus before the event. It was decided that Erap would be the candidate for President, Angara would be for vice president, and 12 senatorial candidates were also proclaimed.

Initial difficulties were encountered in finding a person who would be in full charge of scheduling. Orly Mercado, assisted by Susy supported Lito Banayo, who belonged to the group of the Zamoras. Eventually, however, the choice fell on Jimmie Policarpio, who had been Chief of Staff in Senator Maceda's office (and whose loyalties, therefore, were suspect). Jimmie mentioned to us that he had talked with Maceda before accepting the job and they both agreed that this was a good thing for him to do.

Proper scheduling was crucial to an efficient campaign because the campaign period is limited to 90 days, starting on 10 February and ending on 10 May. Within that compressed period, all provincial and local sorties, motorcades, speeches, debates, proclamation rallies, teas, lunches, dinners and other occasions had to be orchestrated. Aside from organizing the events, campaign materials had to be prepared and distributed, speeches written, logistics arranged and all 14 major candidates notified and their supporters mobilized.

The physical mechanics for scheduling rallies were worked out in the Operational Manual encapsulated in the LAMMP Guidelines for Organizing Local Activities and Rallies. In reality, however, scheduling turned out to be a messy affair characterized by communication mix ups, misplaced supplies and equipment, missed appointments and frayed nerves.

One particularly ingenious reason for the frequent changes in campaign schedules was "to confuse our opponents." Another often used excuse was "for security purposes." The real reasons, of course, arose more from the many demands on the candidate's time. These demands came not only from the political strategists but from friends, big money donors, important local leaders and supporters, and even close family members.

By the middle of March 1998, family members were urging Jimmie Policarpio to ease up on Erap's campaign sorties. He had been running 16-hour days since mid-January, barely having three or four hour sleep in between rallies, motorcades, breakfast meetings, luncheon speeches, dinner parties, wedding receptions, and private meetings. From 10 February when the campaign officially started to mid-March, the LAMMP candidates had campaigned in 18 provinces, 13 cities and 14 municipalities in the National Capital Region. Jimmie altered the schedules so that Erap could rest on Mondays. As much as possible, mornings were also kept free, with campaign activities being arranged after lunch.

It was found, however, that these changes in the schedule did not really work. The Erap residence at Polk Street in Greenhills, San Juan, saw a constant stream of people wanting to see him. There were local candidates for mayor, governor, city council or provincial boards who wanted their pictures taken, with Erap raising their hands. There were newspaper people demanding interviews, businessmen wanting to get Erap's supports for deals, diplomats wanting to get advanced ideas on what an Erap administration would mean for their countries, job seekers, volunteers, book writers, favor seekers. Erap had prided himself on being a man of the masses, an accessible person who knew how to listen. It became obvious, however, that if no one managed this flow of people wanting a bit of the candidate's time, he would never find the time to rest and be ready for the next sortie.

### The Mobile Cinema: The Erap Roadshow

Jesse Ejercito, Erap's youngest brother and a movie producer, was the production czar of the campaign. He produced the spectacular rallies with a cast of thousands including the big-name movie stars who attended them and provided entertainment. He monitored provincial rallies by remote control: the cell phone. He produced CDs and video casettes of campaign jingles, video tapes of excerpts from Erap's old movies, video films of campaign events, and a box office hit of a documentary on Erap's life. Jesse was also in charge of producing every campaign material bearing Erap's face or name: posters big and small, calendars for wallets or walls, magnetic car stickers, colorful stickers for tricycles and jeepneys, big ones for cars and vans, orange vests, T-shirts, fans, caps,visors, wristbands, headbands, hand towels, anything that can be worn, stuck on a wall or used in any way to advertise our candidate.

As Chief of Administration and Finance at LAMMP headquarters, he oversees the LAMMP membership drive, the legions of campaign volunteers and thousands of field operatives. He leads the Monday morning staff Mass at HQ and makes sure all volunteers are given their daily lunch within the P86/meal allowance budget. But most of all, Jesse is best known for his mobile cinema.

Long before the official campaign began, the mobile cinema has been traveling all over the country showing Erap's documentary in every town and village of every province of the land accessible by land or sea. It has also penetrated the interiors of depressed squatter areas in Metro Manila and other municipalities in the National Capital Region. The mobile cinema was composed of 12 tall white vans with a loudspeaker on top. Each van was equipped with a VHS machine, a sound system and a built-in collapsible movie screen. The main feature of the roadshow was the 45-minute documentary on Erap's life. This was followed by an old Erap movie. There were no explicit campaign messages in the films asking people to vote for Erap. The films were primarily meant to just introduce Erap to the crowds as a pro-people, caring, honest and patriotic public servant.

When we first previewed the documentary, we found some sections "corny" and told Jesse so. When our comments reached Erap, Erap did not agree with us. He thought those scene were good and he refused to have them cut out. It turned out that those were the most applauded parts of the film when it was shown to the masses, proving once again that Erap understands the masses and what they want. After all he made his fortune in the movies with box-office hits.

The Erap campaign strategies, then, were a complex amalgam of scientific public opinion polls, press the flesh rallies, organized meetings and other local activities, meticulous scheduling, media events and showbiz razzle-dazzle. There were, of course, a variety of "dirty tricks" that were really meant more to anticipate what the opponents were cooking up rather than focusing on cheating or doing illegal things. Funding such a massive campaign was a real issue—the Zamora brothers initially supported the operations but it soon became apparent that greater resources were needed. The top secret financing strategy focused more on depending on a few large donors rather than incurring too many small IOUs all over the country. The feeling was, it was more efficient to owe big bucks to a few rich donors (who would probably be less "hungry" after the campaign) than to depend on thousands of *trapos* who would probably take the winning candidate to the cleaners after inauguration day.

Somehow, it all worked. The crush of volunteers who jammed the LAMMP headquarters on Shaw Boulevard day in and day out was overwhelming. Despite the lack of formal coordination mechanisms among all the various groups (LAMMP, JEEP, the Angara Group, the Greenhills Group) personal linkages through meetings, fax, e-mail and cell phones got it all together. The main reason for the strategies' success was the dedication of the campaign staff, almost all of whom were volunteers. The Erap campaign became a cause that pre-empted everything—regular jobs, family life, social obligations, love interests—they were all neglected during those 90 days of the campaign. The Erap victory on 11 May 1998 made it all well worth it.

All in all, the campaign strategies used by LAMMP in getting Erap and the senatorial slate elected were guided ably by the use of scientifically conducted surveys. Most of the activities proposed—the concentration on only a few themes in the Erap platform, the appeal to the *masa,* the focus on poverty alleviation, the decision to go more for motorcades and rallies rather than television or other media ads, the use of the party and the party satellites like JEEP and the reliance on old Erap films as a way of attracting people to the Erap campaign were all suggested by the social surveys.

Surveys, of course, were terribly expensive. However, despite the expense, LAMMP occasionally hired at least two agencies to conduct side by side polls—the SWS and the PSRC. Happily, throughout the campaign, the two surveys came up with very similar findings. This did not only confirm the validity and reliability of the survey findings—it also allowed the LAMMP strategists to release the results favorable to Erap in such a way that there was a reinforcing of findings on both sides.

A potential source of difficulty in the campaign was the lack of coordination between the party machinery on the one hand and the NGO efforts on the other.

Until the last periods in the campaign, when coordination became absolutely vital, LAMMP and JEEP had been allowed to operate quite independently. Furthermore, even within JEEP, the NCR unit under Bobby Oca worked independently of the national JEEP structure. The many NGO efforts personally committed to Erap (the Samahang LAMMP Federation) more or less acted on their own. Again, it was not until the last minute that these different groups were able to get their act together and even this was accomplished through interpersonal relations rather than structural or institutional action.

In the final analysis, then, it was the tens of thousands of volunteers and committed individuals who gave flesh and blood to the campaign strategy that made it work. Herein, perhaps, lies the lesson of the 1998 Erap elections as far as a winning strategy is concerned. Popularity will always beat machinery. However, it is not abstract popularity between the popular figure and the masses of adoring public alone that wins elections—it is the voluntary effort and mass mobilization appeal of many NGOs, CBOs and other civic organizations supporting the popular figure that translated the adulation into votes that is responsible for Erap's victory.

# Chapter 7

# Motorcades and Rallies

Candon, Ilocos Sur. High Noon, 17 March. Some 15,000 people had been waiting for Erap, Edong and the senatorial candidates since 8:30 A.M. under a gigantic bamboo canopy covered with coconut fronds to shield the throngs from the searing sun. Local *barangay tanods* (village patrols) had almost given up trying to direct traffic as the national highway was jammed with buses, jeepneys, trucks, tricycles, cars and bullock carts. Hundreds of vehicles were parked, helter skelter in nearby rice fields and along the highway. Most of them bore hand-made signs indicating the towns the people came from.

Outside the canopy, lunch boxes and soft drinks were being distributed. Nearby enterprising vendors were selling ice-cold bottled water, ice cream, soft drinks and rice cakes. Inside, however, the people patiently waited. Don Pepot and Inday Pusit, veteran comics from Manila were heroically trying to keep the crowd entertained with off color jokes. However, they were speaking in Tagalog and this crowd was one hundred percent Ilocano and they were not connecting too well.

Lieutenant Colonel Rodolfo Diaz, Erap's chief of security on this mission, was anxious. Only two senatorial candidates had come—Ruben Torres and Pong Biazon. He prevailed upon Torres to speak first. Torres was happy to do so—"This way, I get to talk for more than seven minutes," he said, "it pays to arrive early."

Torres, who comes from Botolan, Zambales, is warmly received by the crowd when he addresses them in Ilocano. His accent is not quite right—he admitted later that he can barely speak his native tongue as he has lived in Manila since child-hood—but he had memorized some lines.

He wows the crowd when he jokes that, actually, he is an Italiano—"I am part Aeta," he says, referring to aboriginal negroid tribes from Zambales, " and I am part Ilocano—thus, an Aetaliano." Loud laughter. He goes into his favorite spiel of having been an activist during the Marcos martial law years. He claims proud ownership of the title "Kadre," the title of a movie made of his life (which unfortunately flopped at the box office).

Torres ends his speech by explaining why he quit the Ramos administration (as Executive Secretary, he was Ramos' "Little President") to join the opposition LAMMP party. "I could not stomach their corrupt ways anymore," he shouts—"I realized that all my life, I really belong to the party that has the interest of the masses at heart. Now, I am with my true friends."

The crowd gives him a tremendous ovation.

"They are two hours late," Colonel Diaz says. "This crowd is getting impatient. Their choppers just left Vigan."

A TV crew from Nine Network Australia led by Hamish Thomson, producer of "60 Minutes" arrives but their way is blocked by Security. Colonel Diaz intervenes and, after finding out who they are, allows them to get inside the cordoned area near the stage. The 60 Minutes reporter plants himself along the entry path, cordoned off by security, in the hope of getting an ambush interview.

Colonel Diaz taps his shoulders—"You will be wasting your time," he said. "When he arrives, there will be pandemonium. You will be swept away by the crowd."

The reporter, heads and shoulders above the crowd, smiles. "I will take my chances," he said. He signals his cameraman to focus on him and the narrow path Erap and the other candidates will take on their way up the stage.

Four young local beauties stand at the foot of the stage with sampaguita garlands. They are good naturedly discussing who would put her garland around Erap's neck. The tallest and prettiest of them all boldly says—"Basta, I will do it. I want to kiss him!"

One of the ladies complains—"But you already kissed Tito Sotto, you must give others a chance."

"And you kissed Freddie Webb," retorts the tall one.

Another girl laughs—"Just give me Dondon Bagatsing," she says, "he is as dark as I am." All the girls giggle and patiently wait.

The sound of helicopters stirs the crowd. Inday Pusit breaks off her jokes and says "*Narito na po ang ating pinakahihintay! Mabuhay si Erap Estrada!*" (The person we have been waiting for has arrived. Long live Erap Estrada!).

The crowd rises to its feet and screams *Mabuhay!* Chants of Erap! Erap! Erap! break out spontaneously.

The lead helicopter stirs up a horrendous cloud of dust that blankets the whole crowd. Black bits of straw from the burned rice fields cling to everyone. The crowd rushes towards the helicopter, barely controlled by security men in their orange Erap vests.

The helicopter passengers alight—Tessie Aquino, Dr. Loi Ejercito (Erap's wife), Dondon Bagatsing and Tito Sotto are cheered by the crowd. Security clears a path for them and they rush to the stage area.

Another two helicopters arrive and the crowds disperse because of the dust. Erap and Edong come out of the third one. They walk toward the stage in their campaign poster pose—arm in arm. The crowd braves the cloud of dust and surges forward. Security men link arms and line the path to the stage.

Everyone along the path is swept away by security men. The 60 Minutes reporter was helplessly pushed away by the crowd. Everyone was cheering, extending their arms to touch Erap or shake his hand. Edong valiantly tries to keep up. They reach the stage, clambering up as fast as they can. The crowd kept cheering all the while.

The four young ladies did not get a chance to present Erap and the other candidates their garlands. Not to be deterred, the tall one went up the stage when the path was cleared, garlanded Erap, and kissed her idol on the cheek.

The others pinched her when she scampered down happily. "Sobra ka naman," (You're too much) one of them chided her.

"Basta, I said I will kiss him," she said, her eyes all lit up. She was jumping up and down and clapping her hands like a little girl.

Inday Pusit screams into the mike—"*Mga kababayan. Ang susunod na Presidente ng Filipinas—si Erap Estrada!*" (My countrymen. The next President of the Philippines—Erap Estrada!).

Claps, cheers and whistles. The crowd had been on its feet since the helicopters arrived. Now, Inday Pusit asks everyone to please sit down so that the program could continue.

Tessie Aquino was introduced as *Ang bunsong kapatid ni Ninoy!* (The youngest sister of Ninoy Aquino). She takes the microphone amidst thunderous applause.

"I hope she does not go into her *Buto, Bituka, Bulsa* routine again," a veteran watcher of rallies mutters. But Tessie was already well into it.

"I have only three things to offer you if you elect me, she says. "The first one is *Buto (*Bones). This means you will stretch your bones so you can work—our political party will give you jobs!" (*Applause*). "We will set up employment creation projects by giving easy credit, strengthening manufacturing and providing inputs to agriculture."

"The second thing we will provide is *Bituka."* (Intestines). "This stands for food security. If you elect Erap, Edong and the 12 senatorial candidates, every Filipino will have three square meals a day." (More applause). Tessie promises that LAMMP will support agriculture, unlike the Ramos administration that had paid little attention to it. She says irrigation fees will be abolishedt fertilizer will be sold tax free and agricultural extension will be more efficient.

"The third thing we will give you is *Bulsa."* (Pockets). "If you elect the candidates of LAMMP, you will have money in your pockets." The crowd loves this appeal and gives Tessie another rousing ovation.

Melancholic, Tessie recalls to the crowd the last time she talked with her martyred brother. "When Ninoy decided to return to the Philippines," Tessie said, "we tried to dissuade him. Something bad might happen to you, we said."

However, Tessie said Ninoy was adamant. Tessie recalled Ninoy telling her—"If something happens to me, Tessie, promise me just one thing—you will love the Filipino." A hushed silence sweeps over the crowd.

"*Mahalin mo ang Filipino"* (Love the Filipino), Tessie says, her voice almost breaking. "This is why, despite all the troubles, despite all the problems, I am campaigning for the Senate—because of my promise to my dear departed brother that I will love and serve the Filipino!"

Tessie stops amidst thundering applause and bows her head. She hands the mike over to Inday Pusit and takes her seat. Other candidates stand up and shake her hand. She sits down beside Erap, happy that she had connected emotionally with the crowd.

Senator Pong Biazon was introduced next as a military general who was one of the leaders who rebelled against former President Marcos. Don Pepot said that there are many candidates who are brave and known as fighters. There are those who eat bullets before breakfast. "Our next speaker," Don Pepot says, "does not only eat bullets—he lunches on cannons and tanks."

Biazon wows the crowd by addressing them in Ilocano. "I was born in Batac, Ilocos Norte," he says proudly. (The home town of former President Marcos). The crowd takes him as one of their own. Amazingly, like Ruben Torres, Biazon's Ilocano did not quite have the right accent because he had also grown up in Manila.

Biazon had a different gimmick. He asked a small boy, around seven years old, to join him on the stage.

"What is your name?" Biazon asks the boy. The boy murmurs something.

"What do you want to be when you grow up?" Biazon asks.

"A soldier like you," the boy answers smartly. Loud applause.

Biazon takes that cue to ask a rhetorical question—"who will assure that this young boy will be able to fulfill his ambition when he grows up?"

The boy still by his side, Biazon recalls his poverty-stricken childhood, how his mother used to do laundry for rich neighbors and he had to deliver the laundry himself. He recalled being a working student who was lucky enough to get accepted into the Philippine Military Academy.

"Education," thundered Biazon, "education is the ladder to fulfilling one's dreams." If the LAMMP candidates are elected, they will offer free public education to everyone. That way, people will have jobs and their lives will improve.

Biazon then tells how the present Ramos administration cheated him in the last senatorial elections. "I was a victim of *Dagdag-Bawas,*" (Vote Adding and Shaving) he shouts. "Please make sure that this will not happen again. By May 11, you should not only vote—you should make sure that your votes are counted and safeguarded."

Biazon ended his speech before his seven minutes were up. He strode, proud and erect, toward his seat, every inch the soldier.

Pandemonium broke loose with the introduction of the next speaker—the basketball star, Robert Jaworski. Cheers of "Jawo, Jawo, Jawo" filled the air.

Jaworski, slightly balding and athletically stooped, took the microphone. People, especially young ladies, were jumping up and down and cheering. Jaworski smiled and everyone grew crazy. He went to the edge of the stage and started making high fives with people he could reach. When the cheering died down, Jaworski went into his set speech. He said that his success in life was due to his having learned to play basketball when he was young. Like Biazon, he emphasized education—the fact that he got a basketball scholarship was his ticket to a college education and a bright future.

*"Ako po ay mahusay maglaro ng bola pero hindi ako nambobola,"* he says, making atrocious Tagalog puns (I play ball but I do not fool and flatter other people). He then starts throwing small balls into the crowd, which goes crazy again.

Like Biazon, Jaworski keeps within his time limit. His speech was simple and prosaic, entirely lacking in style or message. But he did not have to talk eloquently—being Jaworski was good enough!

The speeches were interrupted by a musical number. Mikee Villanueva, in a tight-feeding sheath dress sang and undulated in front of the crowd. Whistles and cheers. She throws her orange Erap wristband into the crowd, creating a major tustle among some young men. She wiggles her way down the stage into a waiting air conditioned bus.

The next speaker introduced was Dondon Bagatsing. Don Pepot introduces him as the son of a former Mayor of Manila. He is also referred to as "Mr. Computer Education" because he promises that, if elected, he will install a computer in every village high school in the country.

"Oh no," sighed a familiar rally kibitzer, "here comes the *Ibon* (Bird) story again." Everyone laughs—most veteran rally followers have heard Bagatsing's bird story and have asked him not to use it too often but he loves the story.

Bagatsing tells the story of a young man who claims to be the smartest person in the whole village. People tell him that an old man was smarter than he was so the young man goes to him.

"Grandfather," the young man says, "they tell me you are very smart. I have a puzzle for you." The young man shows the old man a bird in his hand and says—"Tell me, Grandfather, is this bird dead or alive?"

The old man says—"you are, indeed, a smart young man. If I tell you the bird is dead, you will set it free and it will fly away, very much alive. If I tell you the bird is alive, you will crush it in your hands and it will be dead. My answer to you is—the truth is entirely in your hands."

Bagatsing then takes a theatrical pause and exclaims—"My countrymen, like the old man says, the truth is entirely in your hands—my fate is entirely in your hands."

The story is good and dramatic but Bagatsing tells it so slowly and lugubriously that he spends three of his precious seven minutes telling it. As a finale, his short farewell is much more effective. "I cannot force you to love me," he says, "but please don't stop me from loving you." This usually draws appreciative applause.

Easily the most effective speaker among the senatorial candidates came next—Senator Tito Sotto. In Candon, Ilocos Sur, Sotto was accompanied on stage by his wife, the movie star, Helen Gamboa. The crowd went wild when husband and wife greeted them with a short song.

Sotto, who used to star in a TV comedy show, is a master of timing and ad lib. He immediately went into his self-deprecating story.

"I want to thank the people of Candon, Ilocos Sur, for their most warm welcome," he said. "During the motorcade, a young woman grabbed me and held my face," he says *(Laughter)*. "Then she kissed me hard!" *(Louder laughter)*. Then she exclaimed—"Wow, ang pogi ni Vic!" (Wow, Vic is so handsome!—referring to Sotto's younger brother, Vic Sotto, who is still the star of a long running TV show). (*Loud laughter, followed by enthusiastic applause*).

Sotto turns serious and says how the present administration has tried to demolish his reputation (they had accused him of being linked to drug smugglers and protecting drug lords).

"They hit me with sledge hammers," he exaggerated. "They hit me with two by fours." Pause. "Then, they nailed me to the cross."

Drawing a somewhat inappropriate analogy, Sotto then says, "but they forget—like our Lord whom they nailed on the cross, I will rise again come May 11 with the support of your votes." (*Thunderous applause*). The crowds are forgiving of the sacrilegious analogy between a TV comic turned politician and Jesus Christ, even this close to the Lenten season.

The next speaker introduced by Inday Pusit is the acknowledged tail-ender among the 12 LAMMP senatorial candidates. Mike Romero is an earnest, hard working congressman but this is his first nation-wide campaign. He has been losing his voice but talks at the top of his voice anyway. His campaign staff, dressed in their blue and orange vests, loyally cheer him on.

Romero's speech dwells on his humble beginnings as a young boy in Negros. He says his family was so poor that his grandfather did not buy a pair of shoes until his father managed to graduate from law school in Manila. Romero credits education for his success. This is the reason, he said, why he devoted much of his pork barrel allocations to provide scholarships to poor young men and women.

Romero then goes into his rather long-winded story of Binoy, or his old "shine-shoe boy." As Romero tells it, Binoy earned his living shining shoes—a humble but honest occupation. With his meagre earnings, he was able to send his children to school. When his eldest son graduated with a commerce degree, he applied for a job and one of the questions asked in the application form was: What is the occupation of your father?

The young man asked Romero how to answer this question, whereupon, the candidate goes into a long sermon: "Do not be ashamed of your father's occupation as a shine-shoe boy. Your father earns his money honestly. He has sacrificed so that you will be able to have a good education. Be proud of the fact that your father is a shine-shoe boy."

Romero dramatically pauses. He then says that Binoy's son writes down on the form as his father's occupation: Shine-shoe boy. He gets the job. Now, he is Assistant Manager in a big bank.

The moral of the story, Romero thunders, is that education is the key to human progress. That is why, if elected senator, he will give all his pork barrel allocations to scholarships for the poor. There is polite clapping but it was not very enthusiastic. Romero takes his seat and another senatorial candidate is introduced.

Tall, handsome and a well known basketball player and movie actor before getting into politics, Freddie Webb gets instant recognition and a warm applause. He extols the virtues of education, too, by saying that his success has been due to athletic scholarships. He calls on the young people in the audience to study hard to have a better life.

Unfortunately for Webb, his political career has been marred by one of his son's involvement in a sordid case of drug-related rape and murder. Like a good father, he defended his son and said that he had been wrongly accused. While his pleading voice was touching, the audience, made up mostly of poor people who usually complain that the children of the rich get away with murder, does not seem too impressed. There is not much enthusiasm when Webb ends his speech and sits down, wiping sweat from his tanned face.

The "Dean of the Senate"—Senator Blas Ople, is then introduced. Ople is a chain-smoking elderly veteran who had been a hard-hitting journalist, labor leader, and former Secretary of Labor. Now, old age is creeping up on him although he has not lost his fire. He lurches into a vicious attack on the "mad dogs" let loose by the administration on Erap Estrada and his fellow LAMMP candidates. He says that the Lakas-NUCD had been spying on the LAMMP rallies and taking video shots of the huge crowds. In contrast, he says, the Lakas rallies have to rely on *hakot* (fetching and paying people to attend the rallies).

There is a great deal of respect for the old man and people listen intently. However, it was now almost two in the afternoon and the people have not eaten yet. Polite applause after his talk but not much enthusiasm.

The last of the senatorial speakers was Aquilino "Nene" Pimentel. He is introduced as the victim of *dagdag-bawas*, who should have been in the Senate since 1995 if he was not cheated by the administration. Like Romero, Pimentel had been losing his voice but he is game. He reminds the crowd that he is known as "Mr. Local Governments" because he had authored the Local Government Code of 1991. Pimentel enumerates the many pieces of legislation he had authored in the Senate but it was obvious that the crowd was not much impressed with how many laws and statutes one had sponsored or supported in the legislature. The crowd was getting restless and hungry. It is not good to be the last speaker. People are already tired and hot and fanning themselves non-stop.

At this point, the rally arrives at the second most important event of the day. It is almost 2:30 P.M. and the crowd had not eaten lunch yet—styrofoam lunch kits provided by local organizers are wrapped in huge plastic bags strategically placed among the people but no one dares to open them.

The candidate for Governor of Ilocos Sur introduces Senator Edgardo "Edong" Angara, who is running as Erap's vice presidential candidate. Edong is hailed as a former President of the University of the Philippines, the Integrated Bar Association of the Philippines, and the Philippine Senate.

Unfortunately, Edong Angara is a rather wooden speaker. He enumerates his accomplishments in the Senate—the passage of the agricultural modernization law, a statute raising the salaries of teachers, another law giving benefits to the elderly. He traces his origins as a poor boy from Baler, Quezon, who managed to get a law degree from the prestigious University of the Philippines. He heaps praises on Erap, saying that the welfare of the poor will be assured if he and Erap are elected as a tandem.

In spite of his valiant efforts, it was obvious that, somehow, despite his academic brilliance and great accomplishments, Angara just did not have any charisma. There was no emotional spark between him and the people. He gave his speech in a loud haranguing style. When he ended, there was polite applause but no real frenzy among the listeners.

There were loud squeals of delight and frenzied applause when the superstar of Philippine movies, Nora Aunor, was invited to sing a song. Dressed in tight fitting jeans, high cowboy boots, an orange vest and an orange Erap headband, Nora greeted the audience who responded with hand waves and screams. Huge banners of "Noranians for Erap" were waved wildly amidst the crowd. Many men and women took out handkerchiefs and waved them to and fro.

Nora started with an English love song. People swayed, both arms high in the air, singing along with her. She quickly moved from one end of the stage to the other while singing, making the sound technicians scramble on stage to keep her from tripping over the long microphone cord.

The crowd insisted on an encore and Nora started singing her hit song, "*Munting Bayani,*" ( The Small Hero) which extolled the sacrifices of Overseas Contract Workers. She walked to the edge of the stage to shake hands with her adoring fans and she is almost dragged down by enthusiastic greeters.

More requests for another encore. Nora agrees but asks people to listen to her own request first. She appeals to the crowd to vote for Erap, Edong and the entire LAMMP senatorial slate. People scream yes. She then warns them to be watchful on election day—"If the administration candidates give you money, accept it," was her pragmatic reply—"then, go into the booth and vote for Erap, Edong and the straight LAMMP ticket."

Nora sings a Tagalog love song. Thunderous applause and squeals and screams when Fernando Poe, Jr., was asked by Nora to join her in the song. FPJ sings a few bars and, almost shyly, returns to his seat. The crowd goes wild. Nora steps closer to Erap on stage. The crowd explodes into wild applause when she approaches Erap and asks him to sing along with her. Nora and Erap go into a duet, their practiced voices blending beautifully. Cheers, whistles, applause when Erap returns to his seat and Nora finishes the song.

By almost 3:00 P.M., Governor Luis "Chavit" Singson started introducing Erap Estrada. He delivered his speech almost entirely in Ilocano, complete with flowery flourishes and high phrases. The introduction lasted almost ten minutes.

The crowd shoots up on its feet when Erap takes the microphone to address the rally. He greets the crowd good afternoon and they enthusiastically answer back.

"I would like to thank Governor Chavit Singson for his enthusiastic introduction," Erap says, "unfortunately, I did not understand a word he said because he spoke in Ilocano." (*Loud laughter*).

Erap then greets all the prominent people on stage. His PR man, Ike Gutierrez, had painstakingly prepared the list of people for him so he would be able to greet them one by one. This was an important ritual in all rallies which was also the opportunity for endorsing local candidates. Ike always carried a big black pentel pen and white sheets of paper for preparing this list.

Erap's voice was soft, conversational. He took great pains to pronounce the names of people correctly, indicating in detail, also, their positions, titles and links to him and the party.

When it came to the part where he was to introduce his wife, Loi Estrada, a naughty glint flashes in his eyes. "I want you to meet, my one and only wife," he says. Embarrassed smiles and tittering laughter—most people did not miss the sly reference to the fact that he had several women in his life.

Erap pauses, looks at the crowd, and then says—"You don't seem to believe me." Loud laughter, this time.

"I would like to tell you formally," he says, "that among so many women I have loved, there is only one woman I married—Dr. Loi Estrada." Applause and laughter.

"She does not seem to believe me," Erap says, looking at Loi. Loi stands up and walks toward Erap—More clapping and cheering.

Loi takes the microphone and is greeted with wild applause when she speaks in Ilocano. "My mother was born in Piddig, Ilocos Norte," she says, "so I am a genuine Ilocano." Actually, Loi had grown up in Zambales and Manila but she had kept her mother tongue.

Loi's short speech was rewarded with enthusiastic applause. There were more gales of laughter when Erap observes—"she spent many days memorizing that speech and I still did not understand a word of it."

Turning serious now, Erap goes into his standard campaign speech. Despite the fact that many LAMMP campaigners had heard the rally speech many times before, they still enthusiastically laughed at the familiar jokes.

The Erap campaign rally speech had four distinct parts.

First, Erap went into his movie career—pointing out, specifically, that it was the support of the masses that was responsible for his success.

"When I became a movie actor," he said, "it was the poor people, the so-called *bakya* (wooden shoe wearing) crowd, that supported my movies. Without the poor people, I would not have succeeded in getting five FAMAS best actor awards" (the Filipino equivalent of the Oscars).

At this point in his speech, Erap starts referring to his friend, Fernando Poe, Jr. "Ronnie Poe and I have been friends for a long time," he would say. "He is good but, I am more handsome than he is." (*Pause. Gales of laughter*). "He is now the King of Philippine movies—but that is only because I am no longer in the movie business." (*More laughter*). Ronnie, seated at the back of the stage, stands up when he hears his name mentioned. He shakes his head at the friendly criticism hurled at him by his candidate.

"I have won five FAMAS best actor awards," Erap continues the attack, "Ronnie Poe only has three." (*Laughter*). "I got so bored waiting for him to catch up that I decided to quit the movies and go into politics." (*More laughter*).

The crowd breaks into wild applause when Fernando Poe, Jr., starts walking from the back of the stage and joins Erap out front. He takes another microphone.

"Excuse me for interrupting," Ronnie Poe says, amidst thunderous applause. "I just wanted to greet the people and set the record straight."

"Actually, early in our careers, Erap and I agreed on our respective roles," Ronnie Poe says—"one will enter politics and another will just be a supporter. I am the supporter. I have not regretted this because Erap has turned out to be a good public servant."

"It is not true that Erap is a better actor though—actually, I am just giving him some leeway—people may say that I do not know how to respect the elderly." (*Laughter and cheering*). Ronnie Poe smiles and the people laugh along with him. "But I am happy that Erap has decided to get into politics—he has become a good Mayor, a Senator, and the Vice President of our country. I will be happier, still, if you vote Erap for President."

Erap thanks Ronnie Poe for his support. He recounts how they campaigned together when he ran for Senator—they had so little money they had to take commercial planes. He chides Ronnie Poe for being a tightwad and for refusing to spend money for his campaign. This elicits even more laughter and cheering.

Ronnie Poe thanks the audience for supporting Erap. He then takes his exit line, saying "I better stop talking now. Otherwise, Erap might think that I am the one running for President." This brings the house down.

The second part of Erap's speech dwells on his early career as Mayor of San Juan. He tells the audience how many people, mainly members of San Juan elite families, looked down on him, a mere movie actor, who had the ambition to run for Mayor. He peppers his speech with funny stories.

"When I first ran for Mayor, people laughed at me," he would say, "what did I know? I was just a movie actor—what did I know about running a municipality? People said that if I won for Mayor, I would appoint as my Chief of Police, the villain Max Alvarado." (*Gales of laughter*).

"I won the election but there was an electoral protest. It was two years before I could get into office. I had won by 192 votes."

"While it could be said that I won my first election because of my popularity, I would like to think that the second time around, I had won the election because of my performance. Against the same candidate, a medical doctor, I got more than 42,000 votes. My opponent received less than 2,000 votes. I wanted to protest because, I thought, he does not have that many relatives in San Juan to vote for him" (*Laughter*).

Erap lists his accomplishments as Mayor. He is proud of having set up the Agora market—the first build-operate-transfer (BOT) project in the Philippines, he says, and he did it more than 25 years ago. He also mentions the computerization of tax rolls in San Juan, an action that enabled him to more than quadruple real-estate tax collections in the town. He is also proud of the relocation project, where he took squatter families to a resettlement site in Taytay, Rixal, where they were provided with about 100 square meter of land, a house, water, electricity and other amenities.

Erap jokes about his accomplishments as Mayor. He decided that the town should provide free medical services, especially assistance at child birth. "The trouble with this," he says, "is that when people found out that all maternity services were free, everyone started having babies."

He also decided to provide free burial to poor people. "The problem with this," he said, "is that when people found out that burial was free, more and more of them died. Even residents from other towns decided to die in San Juan so they could have a free coffin, free church blessings, and even a police escort to the cemetery."

Erap also proudly says that he had all the major and minor streets in San Juan paved. "I had every road and pathway cemented, he said. In fact, I ran out of roads to pave. My political opponents started getting scared because they feared that I was so efficient that I would start cementing their faces."

Erap makes fun of the rich and educated people who belittled his efforts and looked down on him because he was a movie actor. They said he did not speak good English—how would he fare if the heads of state of the United States and other countries visited the Philippines? How will he communicate with foreigners when he goes on official state visits? Will he embarrass the Philippines by telling Erap jokes in public?

Erap says one does not need to speak good English in order to be a good president. He recalls that when he was in the Senate and he was leading the fight against the continued operation of American military bases in the Philippines, he was invited by the American Ambassador to dinner.

"Tell me Mr. Senator," the American Ambassador was supposed to have said, "why do you hate Americans?"

Erap said that his response to the Ambassador was: "Mr. Ambassador, I do not hate Americans. I am against the continued operation of bases in the Philippines because for as long as the bases are here, we will forever be mendicants in our own country. It is not that I hate Americans but that I love Filipinos."

Thunderous applause. Erap pauses, looks at the crowd with a teasing glint in his eyes—"You just heard me speak English," he says. Loud applause and laughter. "When I get serious, I break out into English, " he says, amidst loud cheering.

Continuing on his nationalistic theme of using Pilipino instead of English, Erap reports on a recent trip to South Korea. "I spent 30 minutes with the President of Korea," Erap says—"we had interpreters, he did not speak a single word of English."

Erap said he also visited the Prime Minister of Japan in Tokyo. "He only spoke two lines of English," he laughs—"Welcome. Thank you." Erap said he spoke much better English than that.

Erap turns serious. "In other words," he says, "accomplishments and service to the people do not depend on whether you speak good English or not. Korea and Japan are two of the most progressive countries in the world. Their heads of state do not speak any English but the Korean and Japanese people have the highest incomes and their countries are the most progressive in Asia."

The fourth and final part of Erap's campaign speech focuses on his vision and program of governance. He repeatedly goes through his mantra—*Trabaho para sa Filipino* (jobs for all Filipinos); *Hustong suweldo* (a decent living wage); *Presyong abot-kaya* (affordable prices for basic commodities). He adds to this three priority items, control of crime and minimization if not eradication of graft and corruption.

Erap closes by repeating his thanks to the poor for supporting him in his movie and political careers. He says that this run for the presidency is his last performance.

He is running for President so he will be able to change the elite control over Philippine politics. He winds up with the slogan—*Kung hindi sa mga mahihirap, wala si Erap.* (If the poor are not there, there would be no Erap). This message is drowned in an explosion of applause, screams and whistles.

The sound technician plays the the Sha la la Erap and Edong theme song. The local candidates line up on stage for their pictures taken while saying their oaths before Erap as official candidates of the LAMMP. Erap shows them the open palm "LAMMP salute" saying that the open palm means nothing is being hidden from the people. Finally, at 4:15 PM the lunch boxes are opened and people start eating.

The candidates and their supporters get into their vans. Erap's car is the first to move out with his police escort clearing the way. The rest follow. Next stop: Vigan. People are already starting to gather at the grandstand for the rally there that evening.

# CHAPTER 8

# BATTLE OF THE SURVEYS

The 1998 presidential elections saw the use of surveys and public opinion polls as the basis for strategy formulation as well as propaganda instruments. For LAMMP, in-house polls were conducted by Philippine Survey and Research Center (PSRC) headed by Raul J. Esteban, or R.J.

In addition, JEEP commissioned special polls from Social Weather Stations (SWS), headed by Mahar Mangahas. For the party in power, polls were taken by Asia Research Organization (ARO) and HB & A—the Philippine partner firm of Louis Harris and Associates (LHA) and Gordon S. Black Corp (GSBC). The campaign office of Speaker Jose de Venecia, Jr., also used a small outfit called Facts Base, Incorporated (FBI).

The extensive use of public opinion surveys in the 1998 elections generated a great deal of controversy. Predictably, candidates who were shown by the survey to be on top trumpeted the survey results. LAMMP, in fact, often timed the release of PSRC survey results with that of SWS because the consistency of the findings of both surveys tended to "validate" their findings. The simultaneous release of poll results also maximized the public relations impact of the surveys.

It is common knowledge among people who manage election campaigns that surveys favoring a specific candidate have a strong "band wagon effect." Filipinos, like other nationalities, hate to support a loser. A candidate's consistently high ratings in a survey has a demoralizing effect on opponents—*Baka masayang lang ang boto ninyo kung talunan ang susuportahan ninyo* (You might just be wasting your vote if you support someone doing poorly in surveys). This is the usual sales pitch of supporters promoting a candidate who is leading in the polls. At the same time, supporters of a candidate doing well in surveys get a positive jolt to their morale. Although they know that survey data have certain limitations, the tantalizing promise of victory is an excellent emotional booster.

An important effect of public opinion polls was that surveys brought in the money. Contributors and supporters flocked to candidates doing well in surveys. In the case of Erap, his consistently good survey ratings meant that funding was never a problem despite the fact that he was in the opposition and the administration had the power to make life difficult for donors. Conversely, candidates doing poorly in public opinion polls often found that the flow of funds quickly dried up. Although some contributors may play it safe by donating funds to all candidates, the general practice is for candidates doing well in surveys to get a bigger share of campaign funds.

From the very first time that Erap openly declared his candidacy for President, the public opinion polls indicated he was the man to beat. The SWS had conducted surveys on 16-23 January 1998, 21-27 February, 7-16 March, 16-21 March and 12-16 April. These polls showed Erap's popularity to have consistently been between 28% to 30%. A parallel survey conducted by PSRC on 15-19 April showed Erap's ratings to have reached 34%.

Essentially, then, the surveys indicated a see-sawing battle for number two among candidates competing with Erap. In the 16-23 January SWS survey, the number two spot (17% voter's preference) went to Lito Osmeña, followed by Lim (14%), De Venecia (11%) and Roco (10%). Osmeña's high poll rating, which surprised many people, could have been caused by the expensive ads put out by the candidate prior to the official launching of his candidacy—a neat trick that circumvented the political ad ban.

The 21-27 February survey shifted the number 2 spot to Fred Lim (14%), as Osmeña's voter preference score went down from 17 to 13% and De Venecia went up slightly from 11 to 12%. Roco slid down slightly from 10 to 9%. At this time, Lim's candidacy received a significant boost from the endorsement of former President Cory Aquino and the general impression that Lim was the preferred candidate of the Catholic Church.

Lim's hold on the number 2 spot solidified some more during the 7-16 March surveys. De Venecia slid down a bit from 12 to 10% while Osmeña (9%) and Roco (9%) also dipped slightly. Lim's continued improvement was also due to his popularity in Metro Manila, where he outpolled Estrada 28% to 26% respectively.

The 16-21 March poll was De Venecia's round despite the fact that he and Lim were tied for number 2 (both at 14%). What was significant in this poll was the increase of De Venecia from 10% to 14 while Lim slid down from16% to 14. The main reason for De Venecia's improved rating could be attributed to the Lakas-NUCD's vaunted political machinery. At this time, the selection of all congressional and local government candidates by the ruling party had been done and these candidates threw their followers behind De Venecia. The fact that LAMMP had not been able to field candidates in all contested areas was seen as a disadvantage to the main opposition party.

The 8-16 April survey tied Lim and Osmeña for second place (13%) with De Venecia slightly behind (12%) and Roco not too far behind (10%). De Venecia's slide from 14 to 12% was significant, especially since his marked improvement in the 7-16 survey. Lim's slight decrease may have been due to his citizenship problem which happened just before the survey. His original birth certificate showed he was not a natural-born Filipino. Roco's improvement was due to his increasing popularity among A and B voters in Metro Manila, especially students and women's group.

The high media attention given to survey results generated varied reactions from all political partisans. Since most other candidates fared poorly compared to Erap, there was much admonition from their camps that "surveys don't win elections," "surveys are unreliable," "surveys are being manipulated," "popularity needs to be translated into votes," "machinery and organization are the ones that count, not surveys," and even that "surveys should be banned because they are obscene." Even Cardinal Jaime Sin warned his flock not to be swayed by surveys—on 24 April, he issued a pastoral letter urging the faithful to make their decision with their conscience rather than allowing themselves to be influenced by survey results. The Cardinal said that "the most probable winner could probably be the most disastrous for the country and referred to surveys as "forces of darkness."

The Lakas-NUCD camp did their best to belittle the surveys, saying they were "massaged" by the parties that commissioned them. The Lakas spokesman, Cesar Sarino, made much of the fact that in an earlier memo from R.J. Esteban to Erap, De Venecia was rated at 12% while the final PSRC result released gave him 11%. The response of Erap to that was—"how about the SWS survey?" One columnist, in fact, took Sarino to task for questioning a "measly one percent" which was well within the survey's margin of error.

The 1998 elections showed, therefore, that surveys were mainly useful for two things: for propaganda purposes if a candidate is rating highly and for formulating an internal strategy based on the survey results. In the case of LAMMP, the PSRC surveys were fully utilized for both purposes.

### The March 1998 Survey

As mentioned previously, survey results may be used for political propaganda or they may be used as guides to the formulation of specific strategies. For the LAMMP campaign strategists, the results of the 23-27 March sample survey for Metro Manila served as guides in working out specific campaign strategies.

On 2 April 1998, Paul Bograd, an American consultant, and R.J. gave a briefing on the results of a survey conducted 23-27 March. Since Paul's role as a foreigner in the Erap campaign had been questioned by the Government, we held the meeting at the Club Filipino at 7:00 P.M. In attendance were Senator Orly Mercado (Operations), Rod Reyes (Media), Jimmie Policarpio (Scheduling), and Raul de Guzman (Policy Studies). We were asked by Raul to attend the briefing as part of the Policy Studies Group.

Upon entering the room, Jimmie kiddingly told Paul, "Commissioner Adaza is looking for you."

Paul smiled sheepishly and asked—"who is he?"

Jimmie said "He is the new Immigration Commissioner. He is asking about your work permit, whether you are paying local taxes or not. I think he wants to add you to the Indians he just deported."

Paul thought it was all a big joke but he went along anyway. He said, "all my papers are in order."

Just then, Senator Orly Mercado came. "Why are we hiding here?" he asked. "This looks like a very secure place."

Still, when the waiters came in to take our orders for dinner, all discussions stopped as everyone was extra careful not to say anything that was confidential. Either the group was feeling extra paranoid about the snooping powers of the opposition or years of political backroom activities had made secrecy second nature to them. In any case, the door was locked when the briefing on the survey results began. Waiters had to knock before they could bring in food, water or other things.

This March 1998 survey was confined to Metro Manila and involved only 250 respondents.Survey findings had a margin of error of plus or minus 3%. The main purpose of this survey was to determine the extent of damage, if any, caused by the administration's black propaganda against our candidate. The concerted attacks on Erap by JdV's ruling Lakas-NUCD óperations included:

1. The Morato release of videotapes showing Erap gambling at the Heritage Casino which was released on national television on 4 January.

2. The so-called Bunny German pyramid investment scam which happened the first week in March. Bunny is the wife of Erap's media advisor, Reli German.

3. The Berroya assassination expose (3rd week in March), where a former military man and *kumpadre* of Erap charged that Erap ordered him to kill President Ramos on at least three occasions.

The polls looked into "awareness" by people of the three attacks noted above. They revealed that 74% of the sample interviewees had heard of the Morato tapes; 58% were aware of the Bunny scam; and 58% had heard of the Berroya assassination charges. All in all, 27% of the sample had not heard of any of the three negative charges against Erap.

What were the effects and impact of the attacks?

## Effects and Impact of Negative Attacks

The survey revealed that the attacks on Erap have had some negative effects. The "favorable" attitude score of Erap went down from 59 to 55%. Considering the margin of error in the survey (arising from the small size of the sample), this decline was not statistically significant.

An interesting aspect of the findings, however, was the fact that the "voter preference" scores for Erap did not seem to be affected by the decline in "favorable" attitude—this remained at 28%. This indicated that the decline in the favorable-unfavorable attitude scores were not translating into votes lost.

A very significant finding in the survey is that the concerted attacks of JDV's camp on Erap tended to have adverse effects on the attackers themselves. The study revealed that JdV's "favorable" scores went down significantly from 52 to 38%. In other words, the lesson learned is that when a political group starts slinging mud, some of that mud sticks to the slinger.

A very important element in the finding was the steep decline in JdV's vote preference score which went down from 11 to 5%. This showed that in the case of JdV, the decline in favorable-unfavorable scores actually translated into loss of votes as measured by preference scores. It may be concluded, then, that *negative campaign attacks may hurt the candidate being attacked but it also hurts the attacker.*

In the case of JdV, the boomerang effects were probably strong because of his image as a *trapo* and the general view that his camp will use dirty tricks and black propaganda in order to win. This is consistent with a growing perception among political observers that the only way JdV can win in the elections is by the use of massive cheating through *dagdag-bawas* (adding-shaving of votes)and other tricks.

The survey questionnaire also had a question on the "favorable" rating of President Ramos because of the fact that, as the chief endorser and campaign manager of JdV, the people's attitude toward him would significantly affect the LAMMP strategy. The survey revealed that the "favorable" score of the President went down from 53 to 46%. This may have been due to the general perception that since President Ramos had taken on a very partisan stand on behalf of JdV, he must have been also involved in the attacks on Erap. In other words, the fallout from the negative attacks was also hitting the President.

The main beneficiary of the strong JdV attacks on Erap seems to have been Senator Raul Roco, whose "favorable" rating went up from 71 to 73%. Most significantly, Roco's voter preference score shot up from 9 to 19%. In analyzing this survey finding, the LAMMP strategists reasoned that *since the negative attacks were harming both Erap and JdV, voters had to find an alternative candidate to whom they could transfer their feelings* . Senator Roco, with his image of being an honest, clean, articulate, intelligent and principled politician seem to have become the chosen alternative candidate and was getting the disaffected votes.

The other candidate who seemed to have benefited from the "dirt bombs" was Secretary Renato de Villa. His voter preference went up slightly from 3 to 4%. However, considering the small size of the sample, this increase was not statistically significant. It is worth noting only because the scores of other candidates mostly went down.

The LAMMP analysts tried to determine the demographic foundations of the survey results. Cross tabulation of the data showed that the A and B groups as well as the "higher C's" were the one's most influenced by the attacks on Erap. Among these groups, Erap's voting preference scores went down from 27 to 20%. In analyzing this finding, the LAMMP analysts noted that the A-B-C groups, because of their greater exposure to the media, had a much higher "knowledge" and "awareness" of the negative incidents. The negative reactions were also not surprising because the A-B-C groups were the ones most critical of Erap's candidacy in the first place.

In sharp contrast with the attitudes of the A-B-C groups were the reactions of the D and E groups to the attacks. The voter preference for Erap among D and E groups went up from 29 to 36%. The analysts came up with at least three explanations for this. First, the so-called "sympathy" for the "underdog" candidate seems to have been aroused by the concerted attack on Erap. The D-E groups' attitude may be characterized as: "The rich people are ganging up on our candidate—let us defend and support him."

One other reason advanced for the increase in the D and E groups' support was related to the so-called "sleeper effect." It was reasoned by the LAMMP analysts that the D-E groups' support for Erap was already there when the attacks came. The delay in the revelation of the support, and its sudden acceleration may have been triggered by the attacks themselves. In other words, the support for Erap was already increasing before the attacks, it just snowballed because of the attacks.

A third possible explanation for the increased support by the D-E groups was their low awareness of the Morato, Bunny and Berroya incidents. The survey revealed that among all socio-economic groups the D and E had the lowest access to print, radio, TV and other media outlets. It was possible that a higher percentage of the D-E voters had not heard of the attacks so their voter preference scores were not affected.

An interesting element considered in the analysis of survey results focused on respondents' "second choices". The question for this item determined a respondent's second choice in case his or her first choice was not in the running anymore. The results from this question are good measures of a candidate's "favorable" scores—adding first and second choices together provides a gross measure of a candidate's general "preferability."

The survey revealed that if other candidates withdrew from the race, Erap's "second choice" preference went up slightly from 11 to 13%. Lim's score also went up slightly from 20 to 21%. Most interestingly, Senator Roco's voter preference scores jumped from 10 to 18%, confirming the initial finding that Roco was the one most benefited by the exchanges of negative attacks among the leading candidates.

**Limitations of Negative Attacks**

The use of negative attacks during political campaigns has been widespread only in recent years. The experience with negative attacks showed that their effects and impacts tend to be of short duration. Based on this awareness, the LAMMP analysts discussed why the negative attacks on Erap did not seem to hurt him seriously.

First, the analysts concluded that there were too many attacks launched by the Lakas-NUCD camp. Almost like "time-released pills," the attacks came rapidly one after another, so that they gave the semblance of an "overkill." Since media coverage of the attacks was so intense, each succeeding attack tended to displace the previous one, relegating it to the inside pages where it tended to be ignored. After a while, people just glossed over the attacks as their attention was saturated with all the concerted efforts.

Second, some of the attacks were exaggerated and unbelievable. Berroya's expose that Erap told him to assassinate President Ramos reflected more on him and his state of mind than Erap's known persona. People also concluded that the sources used for the attacks were "polluted." They had very obvious motives for joining the attack on Erap and that lowered their credibility.

Third, the attacks seemed too organized, giving the impression that they were being orchestrated and manipulated. Newspapers widely reported Morato's negative attitudes towards Erap. The release of Berroya from jail was also widely covered. The appearance of a pre-meditated and well organized negative attacks campaign did not sit in too well with the general public. People did not like the feeling that they were being manipulated and started not believing the attacks.

The LAMMP analysts also complimented the party's Media Bureau for dealing effectively with the negative attacks. To begin with, the Media Bureau had adopted the "inoculation technique" as a way of dealing with negative attacks. According to this technique, one could steal the thunder from an attacking group if the public is informed beforehand that such an attack is coming. In the case of Lakas-NUCD attacks, for example, constant reminders by LAMMP that the administration would use dirty tricks, such as announcing that Erap was backing out of the race for health reasons, would not only make people aware and wary of these possibilities, they would also condition their minds that these are just dirty tricks. When the negative attacks came, they did not have the shock value and high profile that they would otherwise have, had the LAMMP strategists been taken by surprise.

In the case of the Morato casino tapes, the LAMMP strategists knew in advance that Morato was planning to expose them. The inoculation took the form of revealing in advance that Morato's candidacy for President was primarily motivated by his efforts to "Stop Erap."

The Bunny pyramid investment scam came as a big surprise to the LAMMP group. When it broke, one exasperated member of the group exclaimed—"we should stop shooting ourselves in the foot." Efforts at "damage control" were critically hampered by the fact that the mainstream media hates being manipulated by "spin doctors" who withhold information or selectively leak information to friendly channels. In this particular case, Malou Mangahas, editor-in-chief of the *Manila Times* raised hell about the fact that the Bunny scam news was scooped by the *Philippine Daily Inquirer.* A *Times* editorial raged against efforts at a "spin" and accused the LAMMP Media Bureau of manipulating the media.

By the time the Berroya accusations came out, the inoculation process was well on its way. The LAMMP Media Bureau came up with advanced information that more attacks on Erap would be forthcoming . The newspapers picked this up. Sample headline: "Erap says opposition will next throw the toilet bowl against him—after the kitchen sink." The approach was vintage Erap—it served to blunt the negative attacks by informing and warning the people that damaging news would come.

Another approach used by the Media Bureau stressed the fact that any attacks that would come from the Lakas-NUCD camp was part of a concerted effort at "black propaganda." A vague blanket category like black propaganda, *mga paninira* (demolition jobs), *gawa gawa lamang ang mga ito ng mga kalaban* (the work of enemies), diffused negative attacks. In this, the negative reputation of Lakas-NUCD, with their history of dirty tricks, *dagdag- bawas*, and other negative practices worked in favor of LAMMP.

In a political campaign, as in war, the best defense is a strong offense. The LAMMP strategists decided to release its own negative attacks on the administration focused on the PEA-Amari deal, the Alabang land deal, the leaked plan of the party in power of an assassination plan against Erap himself. The idea was to come up with counter punches that would keep the opponents busy trying to respond to the attacks. Happily for LAMMP, quite a number of individuals, sensing, perhaps, that LAMMP and Erap will probably win the May elections, started volunteering sensitive information about corrupt deals involving key government officials and Lakas-NUCD partisans. Many of these individuals had special axes to grind but some of them seemed genuinely interested in having justice done and the truth told.

A few were even willing to come out in the open, at some risk to themselves, to expose anomalies and corrupt deals.

Part of the survey questions zeroed in on specific negative attacks. For example, respondents were asked if they believed that Erap had ordered Berroya to kill President Ramos. The survey showed that 13% of respondents found the accusation "Strongly believable" while 42% found it "Strongly unbelievable."

The survey then probed how respondents perceived the general response from LAMMP that the Berroya attacks were part of a black propaganda campaign. Here, 34% of respondents found the LAMMP response "Strongly believable."

Focusing on the Bunny German scam, respondents were asked how they found the Lakas-NUCD accusation that since Bunny and Reli German were "very close to Erap," the Vice President knew about the scam and that some of the money taken from victims were contributed to the LAMMP campaign funds. About 11% of the respondents found this accusation "Strongly believable." On the other hand, 36% of the respondents found the accusations "Strongly unbelievable."

The LAMMP Media Bureau had countered the accusation with the assertion that Erap could not have been a party to the scam because his own wife and daughter were victimized by Bunny German. About 12% of respondents found this assertion "Strongly believable." However, 22% of the respondents found the response "Strongly unbelievable."

## Recommended Actions Based on Survey Results

After a thorough analysis of the survey results, the LAMMP strategy group discussed what could be done. The "lessons learned" from the survey findings were synthesized and, on the basis of the derived patterns, specific recommendations for action were made. Some of these key recommendations included the following:

1. It was not useful for LAMMP to respond to each attack in detail or to dissect each accusation point by point. It was more effective to lump all the accusations as part of an "orchestrated scheme of black propaganda". In this way, it was the credibility of the attacker that was questioned, not the guilt or innocence of the group being attacked.

2. The responsibility for responding to the attack should not be placed on Erap's shoulders. If possible, other people not directly linked to Erap would be the ones to respond. This made the issue less partisan and, if the Erap defender was credible, the response would be more effective because it seemed less self-serving.

3. Use other damaging goods on the rival candidates for counter-punching. The thing was to keep the enemies so busy defending themselves that they would have less time to mount a concerted attack.

4. If advanced information was available, the public would be inoculated by revealing the nature of the attack earlier. In that way, the element of surprise would be lost and the accusation would fall flat.

5. The survey results pointed to the need to keep hammering away at the basic platform messages of jobs, food security, prices, interest rates, the collapse of the peso, the climbing foreign debt, and other things wrong with the economy. These were the issues that would be responsible for Erap's strong voter preference. Returning to these issues whenever possible would maintain Erap's ratings.

6. Specific authority figures who attacked Erap should not be answered too aggressively. For example, the best reaction to Cardinal Sin's pastoral letter attacking Erap is to say "The good Cardinal is entitled to his own opinion but he should not take advantage of his eminent position to impose his will on other people." Don't repeat the statement that "Nobody listens to him anyway." There is more to lose in attacking the Cardinal, who has a large following among Catholics.

7. President Ramos must not be pressed too much as he is likely to take extreme response. Since he is so concerned about his place in history, it was not wise to threaten him with jail in case Erap wins. The prospect of him being charged with plunder and then jailed (like South Korea's president) would be enough to drive him to extreme action.

8. It was not useful to attack Dick Gordon, Chairman of Subic Bay Metropolitan Authority, by threatening to sack him when Erap wins. It only served to antagonize his followers, many of whom might vote for Erap anyway. Until election day, it was best not to use too many negative attacks.

9. Select battles that can be won. Some attacks are best ignored.

10. Erap should rise above the fray and start being presidential.

## The April 1998 Survey

On 23 April, with only 18 days left before the 11 May elections, PSRC invited us at the Club Filipino again for a presentation on the results of a survey they conducted 15-19 April. Erap's numbers were excellent. He was getting 34% of the votes, with Raul Roco a distant second with 12%. The other candidates (Lim, De Venecia) were tied for third place at 11% while Osmeña was fourth at 10%. The rest of the candidates were lagging way behind—De Villa, 6%; Santiago, 4%; Marcos, 3%; Enrile, 1%; and Morato and Dumlao, 0.5% each.

The PSRC figures "validated" the results of another SWS survey conducted a week earlier (8 to 16 April). In the SWS survey also released on 23 April, Erap got 30% of the votes, followed by Lim and Osmeña (both at 13%); De Venecia, 12%; Roco, 10%; De Villa, 5%; Santiago, 4%; Marcos and Enrile (both 2%); Dumlao, 0.3%; and Morato, 0.2%. The results of both surveys were very consistent with each other as they fell within the margin of error accepted by both (plus or minus 3% for SWS and plus or minus 2.19% with a 95% confidence level for PSRC).

The results of the PSRC and SWS surveys both contradicted the findings of an FBI survey released on 12 April claiming that De Venecia had narrowed the lead of Erap to just 5 points. FBI claimed that Erap's votes had gone down from 28 to 26% while De Venecia had gone up from 14 to 21%. Based on the survey results, FBI claimed that De Venecia will overtake Erap by the last week in April and then win the elections with a narrow margin. De Venecia supporters likened the contest to one between the tortoise and the hare—they predicted that De Venecia's slow but sure rise in the ratings will eventually win him the elections.

"The May 1998 elections represent a contest between popularity on the one hand and machinery and organization on the other," said Cesar Sarino, Lakas-NUCD campaign manager, over national television. He said that on the final day, De Venecia's machinery would win, and that the Lakas-NUCD had more than 40 local officials running unopposed and they would give De Venecia their uncontested votes.

The PSRC survey gave some indication that, indeed, De Venecia's political machine and organizational efforts were having a slight effect. For example, the survey revealed that Erap's voting preference among rural voters went down slightly from 39 to 37%. In contrast, De Venecia's preference ratings went up from 7 to 12% among rural voters. Since poor rural voters are the ones most likely to be influenced by the appeals of traditional political leaders, the favorable results for De Venecia may be his reward for focusing machine efforts on the rural poor.

Another indication that De Venecia's machinery efforts were gaining votes was seen by looking at voter preference in geographical areas where "command votes" by local leaders were strong. In Muslim Mindanao (basically the ARMM, Lanao and Maguindanao), De Venecia's preference rating went up from 6 to 13%. De Venecia also had positive voting patterns in the Western Visayas (up from 4 to 8%). Of course, De Venecia had good results in Northern and Central Luzon, especially in Pangasinan, the home province of both President Ramos and De Venecia.

The positive results for De Venecia among rural voters have been upset by Erap's gains in urban areas. The SWS survey showed that Erap went up from 25 to 30% among NCR voters while Alfredo Lim went down from 27 in March to 19% in April. After Lim was Roco, who garnered 19% of the votes.

## The Exit Poll

The survey that nailed whatever chances the Lakas-NUCD camp had of claiming victory in the 1998 elections was the SWS exit poll released by Mahar Mangahas barely a day after the polls closed. That survey showed that Erap was the presidential choice of 38.7% of the 4,800 voters interviewed in their homes after casting their ballots. Speaker De Venecia got only 16.4% of the votes while Raul Roco garnered 13.6%. Lito Osmeña of Promdi got 11.6% of the votes and Fred Lim 9.3%. De Villa was a distant 4.7%, Defensor-Santiago, 2.9%, Enrile and Imelda Marcos, 1% each, Dumlao had 0.2% and Morato, 0.03%. For vice president, Macapagal-Arroyo got 51% of the votes, Angara, 21%, Orbos, 12% and Osmeña, 10%. The exit polls, commissioned by ABS-CBN were very consistent with the results of another poll conducted by radio station dzRH which had Erap leading with 34.6% of the votes.

Speaker De Venecia strongly objected to the release of the exit poll results. The Comelec also said that exit poll results were "not conclusive" and asked people to wait for their official tabulations. Cardinal Sin, in a last gasp pastoral statement asked the faithful not to be misled by exit poll results and unofficial sources warning that "misinformation" had been shown by history to have been used "by the forces of darkness to subvert the will of the people."

The exit poll results, however, were loudly hailed by the Estrada camp. They showed that Erap had won in all the regions in the Philippines except in Bicol, where Roco got more votes, in the Ilocos, which favored De Venecia and in he Central Visayas, which went to Osmeña. However, in the Western Visayas, Erap defeated Defensor-Santiago, garnering 41% as against Miriam's 23%. Enrile also lost to Erap in his own bailiwick, the Cagayan Valley, receiving 31% of the votes against Erap's 46%. Even De Villa, who claimed Batangas as his territory, lost to Erap in the Southern Tagalog region, getting 19% of the votes, which was way behind Erap's 46%.

The year 1998, then, could very well come down in history as the time public opinion polling came of age in the Philippines. To be sure, the SWS results were more than 1% off the final tabulation of 40.0% for Erap that served as the basis for his official proclamation of President on 29 May. The SWS was also off by one senator, indicating a 6 to 6 tie while in the final tally, LAMMP had 7 while Lakas-NUCD got 5. Still, the poll results were close enough to the final results, vindicating the science of statistical forecasting.

In earlier efforts to discredit surveys, the Lakas-NUCD had said De Venecia would do a Truman and defeat Erap, in the same way that Dewey was defeated in that infamous American election that showed that polls could be disastrously wrong. Responding to the charge, Mangahas had said that the Truman-Dewey polls were done more than four decades ago—the science of public opinion polling had improved tremendously since then. Mangahas rightfully observed that polling is an act where the final election tabulation always revealed whether the poll results were accurate or not. In the case of the 1998 elections, the SWS results were all within the acceptable margin of error in such surveys.

It can be safely predicted, then, that future electoral campaigns in the Philippines would rely heavily on public opinion polls and pollsters like Mangahas and R.J. Esteban need not look for other jobs yet. This has serious implications for campaign financing for public opinion polls can be awfully expensive (the rumored price of a nation-wide poll was about P2 million).

The 1998 elections were not too kind to political analysts, though. The stock of self-proclaimed pundits like Antonio Gatmaitan, Alex Magno, Amando Doronila and Frankie Llaguno was not helped too much by the Erap victory as the prognostication of these analysts did not give him too much of a chance to win. Of course, more partisan interpreters of the political scene such as Cesar Sarino, Gabriel Claudio, Chit Pedrosa, Belinda Olivares-Cunanan and Neal Cruz might have to sharpen their statistical skills. Some of them, unlike the pollsters, might have to find other jobs.

# Chapter 9

# The Byron Hotel Operation

The Byron Hotel is a grey unimposing pseudo-Romanesque structure perched on a steep embankment off Epifanio de los Santos Avenue (EDSA), Metro Manila's main thoroughfare. It is tucked away on a side street where Boni Avenue turns into a tunnel passing under EDSA in Mandaluyong City. Located almost mid-way between the plush hotels of the Ortigas mega-mall complex and the five-star luxury hotels in Makati, the Byron advertises itself as "a European style boutique hotel." The Byron's lively Pelican bar is a favorite watering-hole for Metro Manila's yuppy entrepreneurs and political operatives.

In mid-February 1998, the fifth floor of the Byron started filling up with people wearing the orange uniforms of the opposition party—the *Laban ng Makabayang Masang Pilipino* (LAMMP). Computers, TV sets, desks, maps, thick files and other office paraphernalia were brought in by the truckload. The hotel's two small elevators started getting jammed with scores of people coming in from the provinces—important-looking officials in *barongs* with their bodyguards, sun-burnt persons in plaid shirts and denim pants clutching briefcases, ladies in the trade mark LAMMP orange outfits, men in heavy jackets who wore dark glasses even at nighttime.

The harried woman at the hotel desk would only say that the fifth floor had become the headquarters of *Bantay Halalan '98 (*Elections Watch, '98), also referred to as Task Force '98. Access to the fifth floor was strictly controlled by burly security men—visitors were escorted from the lobby, into the elevators, and to the fifth floor reception area. Visits were by appointment only—guests had to be fetched by the person they had an appointment with before being allowed past the security desk.

Jaded political observers learning of the Byron Hotel goings on said they were reminded of the Sulo Hotel which housed *Oplan Dagdag-Bawas* (Operation Adding/Shaving of votes) in 1992. Like the Byron, the Sulo Hotel was a nondescript meeting place favored by political operatives in suburban Quezon City. The Sulo was conveniently located not too far from the Office of the National Security Adviser, General Jose "JoAl" Almonte, reputedly the chief political strategist and psychological-war expert of President Ramos. Appropriately, the Sulo was famous for an underwater ballet show, which could symbolize the murky undercover activities of many of its patrons. The Byron, in turn, had *Café Botanica,* the perfect setting for the many shadowy denizens that frequented it.

In 1995, the Sulo Hotel operatives were alleged to have carried out *dagdag-bawas* activities that helped elect to the Senate Juan Ponce Enrile, who eased out Ferdinand "Bongbong" Marcos, Jr., and Gregorio "Gringo" Honasan who eased out General Rodolfo "Pong" Biazon. Senator Aquilino "Nene" Pimentel also became a victim of *dagdag-bawas.* Official protests were made by the defeated Senatorial candidates but there were many delays. In the 1998 elections, Biazon and Pimentel ran for the Senate once more, arguing that the voters' will should not be vexed this time.

In one of those strange twists of fate, some of the people who had denied victory to Biazon and Pimentel were now working for their candidacy. In 1998, it was alleged by many persons that some of the same Sulo Hotel political operatives who carried out *dagdag-bawas* were now seen buzzing around the corridors of the Byron Hotel.

The rationale for *LAMMP Bantay Halalan '98* (LAMMP Elections Watch '98) was a call for "nationwide vigilant action to stop the recurrence of any form of fraudulent electoral practice and to ensure honest, credible, orderly, and peaceful elections."

In this master stroke along the lines of "to catch a thief" political operatives who were allegedly associated with past electoral fraud had been recruited to counter dirty tricks efforts of the ruling Lakas-NUCD Party. As one Bantay Halalan operative admitted quite proudly in an interview, "If you want to stop cheating in the coming elections, you go to the expert cheaters. You leave the real job to us professionals—we know who the cheaters are—it takes one to know one."

The objectives of BH '98 were as follows:

- Preserving the integrity of the upcoming May 11 polls;
- Providing a presence that will deter any electoral fraud;

- Keeping vigilant watch over the tabulation process, so as to ensure honest, orderly, and peaceful elections;
- Working together with the National Movement for Free Elections (Namfrel) by providing assistance and information;
- Establishing linkages with other poll-watch groups;
- Maintaining vigilance until the proclamation of winning candidates.

To achieve the objectives mentioned above, BH '98 carried out seven types of activities:

1. It established a reliable nation-wide communication system that would link BH '98 headquarters with operatives in all municipalities, cities and provinces as well as all local units with each other.
2. It submitted reports particularly on identified election trouble spots.
3. It established linkages with the National Movement for Free Elections (NAMFREL), Parish Pastoral Council for Responsible Voting (PPCRV), VoteCare, Integrated Bar of the Philippines (IBP) and other Comelec-accredited poll watch groups.
4. It disseminated information on Comelec rules and procedures and guidelines for the 1998 May elections.
5. It ensured media coverage of uncovered election irregularities and fraudulent acts.
6. It assisted LAMMP poll watchers and local counsels of the Lawyers for Estrada, Angara and Democracy (LEAD) in their poll watching duties, particularly in identifying and reporting electoral fraud and anomalies.
7. It secured data needed to conduct a LAMMP "Operation Quick Count."

As structured, BH '98 operated principally at the precinct level. The organization served as the support arm of precinct poll watchers officially designated by LAMMP upon the recommendation of local candidates and/or party officials. It was the duty of BH '98 operatives to make sure that the tabulated results at each precinct (election returns) were efficiently carried by poll watchers to the Municipal or City Board of Canvassers (BOC).

The tallied municipal election returns were transferred to Provincial canvasses and conveyed to the Provincial Board of Canvassers in the provincial capitol. At that stage, watching the election returns and preventing fraud fell on the shoulders of LEAD (Lawyers for Estrada, Angara and Democracy), who watched the operations of Comelec and Congress, all the way up to the proclamation of elected senators, the vice president and president of the country by the Electoral Tribunal.

In carrying out its tasks, BH '98 was particularly worried about the possibility of a No-Proc (No Proclamation) scenario. Under this troublesome possibility, LAMMP expected that President Ramos and the party in power would try their best to prevent the proclamation of Vice President Estrada (or any other candidate for that matter) before 12 June 1998. President Ramos is widely known to be almost obsessed with being the only "Centennial President" to preside over the country's 100th Independence Day celebrations that would cap his career. Having Erap proclaimed before 12 June, will mean sharing the limelight with the president-elect, a most humiliating occasion for President Ramos.

A variation of No-Proc would see the party in power delaying the counting of ballots for the presidential contest. This could be done by lodging innumerable protests that would require the opening of ballot boxes and re-counting of ballots. If the protests are unresolved by 30 June, the date specified by the Constitution as the deadline for proclaiming a new President, there would be a Constitutional crisis. If the contest for the Vice President went smoothly and Gloria Macapagal Arroyo was proclaimed the winner, she could assume the presidency.

Another problem scenario, tagged Fa-El (Failure of Elections) anticipated massive cheating by the party in power. This would spark rebellious demonstrations and even riots by disgruntled LAMMP partisans. This, in turn, could trigger off harsh military reprisals. In the midst of such violent disturbances, a state of emergency or even martial law would be declared. President Ramos could then do a Marcos—keeping the reins of power because the State was in peril.

As election day approached, the strategists at the Byron Hotel went about their tasks gathering intelligence from the field, talking to local officials to persuade them to shift to the Erap camp, preparing training plans for poll watchers, establishing contacts with like-minded election watch organizations, and removing kinks and bugs in their communication systems. Ever alert for sabotage, the group set up stand-by generators in case their opponents cut off their electricity supply. The most modern wireless telephones with anti-bugging devices were purchased and put into operation. All calls to the BH '98 were screened by the switchboard operator. Callers wanting to speak with Ronnie Puno were told to leave a message. Ronnie had no phone. Code names for operatives were routinely changed. Computers were programmed to set up "firewalls" around secure channels that led to top decision makers. Precautions reached near paranoid proportions as the BH '98 crews approached election day.

Aside from the Byron Hotel operations, two other parallel organizations were set up in top secret safe houses. Layers of "redundancies" were built into systems as "fail safe" precautions. Thorough checks were made of people recruited for specific jobs. Knowing very well that the BH '98 group was up against highly trained military operatives, it took all the precautionary measures necessary to carry out its mission effectively and efficiently.

## Leave it to the Professionals

Masterminding the Byron Hotel activities was a professional campaign organizer named Ronaldo "Ronnie" Puno, who had been brought back specially from the United States to head BH '98. Puno had been Undersecretary of the Department of the Interior and Local Governments (DILG) under the Marcos administration, working with then Secretary and former Governor Jose Roño.

Before entering government, Puno owned a computer company where he specialized in installing tax assessment and collection systems for local governments. Jun Veron Cruz, who was Puno's computer whiz even in those early days, remembered that one of their company's earliest clients was the town of San Juan, whose Mayor then was Joseph Erap Estrada.

"We had many clients in those days and we paid kickback regularly," recalled Jun, "but the only Mayor who did not ask for a kickback—even if it was SOP then—was Erap." Jun said that they had a normal business agreement with San Juan. They provided the service, they got paid on time.

"I was very impressed with Erap even then," said Jun. "When he won the TOYM (Ten Outstanding Young Men) award in public administration I remembered thinking that this underestimated actor would go far."

In the early 1970s, Puno and Jun came to the attention of Secretary Roño because of their computerization work with local governments. Their access to data enabled them to quickly respond to questions asked by the Secretary. Soon, many of the Secretary's questions focused on political matters—which political group is that Mayor supporting? Which political clan does he belong to? Who are his allies and his enemies? How many votes did he get in previous elections? How many votes can he deliver?

Even when martial law was declared in September 1972 and no real elections were held in the Philippines, knowing about voting patterns was still important. The late President Ferdinand Marcos, in a twisted desire to cloak his naked power with legalistic niceties, felt compelled to conduct plebiscites, referenda and other "formal consultations" with the people to legitimize his rule. Since these exercises in formalistic consultations needed a nation-wide system of controlling votes, Puno's network of political operatives which provided an efficient way of conducting "surveys" became very useful and it rapidly expanded.

When we visited Ronnie Puno at the Byron Hotel on 30 April 1998, he did not hide the fact that he had worked with Marcos, Ramos and Speaker De Venecia in the past. On the contrary, he was proud of his "track record" as a professional political organizer. That day, Puno gave a briefing to the Policy Studies Group of Vice President Estrada on the operations involved in *Bantay Halalan* '98.

"What you have here," Puno explained, "is a real professional political operation. Most campaigns involve enthusiastic volunteers and amateurs—relatives, friends, fraternity brothers, former classmates. They are okay but if you want to win an election, you need the professionals."

Puno gave the visiting Erap policy group members a tour of the facilities. In one room, banks of computers linked to regional area networks continuously received data from more than 3,500 operatives from across the country. They were organized by regions, with big cities like Cebu and Davao, having their own terminals.

The "operations room" walls were full of maps, with blue, red, orange and pink pins stuck on them. The color-coded pins indicated if Erap's voter preference was virtually uncontested (blue), if he was being contested by another strong candidate (red), if the contests were almost tied (orange), and if he was way behind in votes (pink). Other maps classified the municipalities and cities according to their political situation—a blue pin meant that a dominant leader controlled the electorate and could deliver so-called "command votes"; a red pin meant the place was "leader-oriented" but no one leader was dominant; and an orange pin meant that the place was "voter-oriented" and there were no strong political leaders who could deliver big blocks of votes.

A media monitoring group occupied another room where a dozen TV sets were turned on. These were playing taped broadcasts from provincial TV stations that were flown into Manila every day. Campaign workers who knew the languages and dialects monitored all these broadcasts, doing content analysis of the messages, indicating if pro-Erap or anti-Erap materials were being broadcast.

The heart of the Byron Hotel operations was the "political intelligence" group that received and processed information from the field. Here, skilled political operatives received data by phone, fax, e-mail and other means on the political situation in every municipality, city and province. They sorted out what was gossip and rumor, soft or hard data, believable or unbelievable information. On that day in April, each local area operative was required to contact the Byron Hotel at least once a day. A week before election day, Puno explained, they will be required to come in at last twice a day or any time something "hot" came along.

Puno was obviously very proud of the thoroughness of their operations. He said that very often, the LAMMP Management Committee were caught by surprise at how quickly they received information on local conditions. Puno also said that the political campaign managers of De Venecia were wary of their capabilities.

"We know all the dirty tricks that the current administration can use," Puno boasted, "we know all the people doing them. I used to work with Jo Almonte, Gabby Claudio, Rey Maclang and Cesar Sarino. They are all old friends. They enjoy the game as much as we do."

Puno explained that in 1992, he was one of the organizers that ran the Ramos campaign. He said they got Ramos elected a minority president with 24% of the national vote. In the 1992 elections, Puno predicted that President Ramos would win by around 800,000 votes. SWS and other polling organizations called it a much closer race. When Ramos won with the exact plurality predicted by Puno, the political operative got a reputation as a master strategist. There were those, of course, who believed that Puno resorted to cheating and dirty tricks—how could he have predicted the margin of victory so accurately otherwise?

Puno revealed that the Ramos 1992 campaign effort was thrown together in a great hurry—Ramos contacted him on 3 March, as soon as he was "anointed" by

President Corazon Aquino as her candidate, and he started working on 15 March. In contrast, Puno said that in joining the LAMMP campaign he had a little bit more time—contacted by Manny and Ronnie Zamora, the real "king makers" in the LAMMP operations in December 1997, he actually did not have to join the fray until January 1998. It took a bit of time for the negotiations to get under way because he was then already working for De Venecia's campaign.

In helping run the Ramos campaign, Puno's main assets were his personal contacts with governors, mayors, provincial board members, city council members, barangay captains, and other local officials located in various parts of the country. He had known most of these officials since his days as DILG Undersecretary and had taken pains to maintain contact with them through the years. As he launched BH '98, he renewed contacts with this network of old friends and acquaintances who were affiliated with almost all the competing parties and groups involved in the coming elections. Renewing friendships, calling in old political IOUs, and cashing in on the strong popularity of his chosen presidential candidate, Puno had no trouble convincing many political operatives to join him.

Drawing from the lessons of the 1992 elections, Puno's main concern was to make sure that the LAMMP would not be able to "do a Mitra" on his chosen candidate. Puno recalled that after the ruling *Lakas ng Demokratikong Pilipino* party had nominated Speaker Ramon Mitra as official candidate, they expected Fidel V. Ramos to conform with the decision and withdraw his candidacy. Instead, Ramos decided to run as an independent, with the active support of President Corazon Aquino.

Puno went with Ramos and found the campaign rather tough going. Mitra had the political machinery. Puno and others in the Ramos camp had to rely on enthusiastic but completely inexperienced Cory volunteers, armed forces personnel, both retired and still in the service, and some civil servants, for the campaign. The anointment of Cory Aquino helped a great deal, as did the volunteer forces of middle class and Church-oriented people mobilized with the help of the President. As he pursued the campaign, Puno had to rely on this motley crew, which he called "naïve but enthusiastic amateurs."

The only solid support to the Ramos campaign, according to Puno, was a very large contribution from a certain lady who was engaged in politics recently. The alleged support of the moneyed elite to Ramos, said Puno, was a myth; a well-known Makati landowner actually gave only P5 million to the campaign. There were rumored contributions from wealthy Taiwanese taipans (the candidate's father, Narciso Ramos, had been Philippine Ambassador to Taiwan) but Puno denied any knowledge of these. A small group of New York based Filipinos were also said to have helped finance the campaign.

Interestingly, Puno claimed that there was no widespread cheating in the 1992 presidential elections—that Ramos won fair and square. Pressed on this issue, however, Puno quickly added that a lot of cheating occurred at the local level—"Local candidates habitually engage in dirty tricks because the margin of electoral victory in local elections can be very small and every vote counts."

Some of the "dirty tricks" that Puno's group carried out during the Ramos campaign were laughably amateurish, Puno said. For example, they hired men to carry out the "Sticker topping operation." This meant that new posters for President Ramos were stuck on top of posters of Santiago, Mitra and other candidates. More successful were direct personal appeals, accompanied by lucrative offers, to local officials. Puno said that upon launching the campaign, he found out that there were about 800 mayors who belonged to the party in power—not a single one was for Ramos. He sent personal emissaries to these officials and talked to many of them directly, promising specific things if Ramos won. Puno proudly said that by election day, 550 of the mayors had left Speaker Ramon Mitra to join Ramos' camp.

After the Ramos victory, Puno was rewarded with heading the two television companies sequestered by the Government, Channels 9 and 13. He said that the running of these TV companies became the plum of the Media Bureau that had originally ran Cory Aquino's public relations office and who were determined to claim their just rewards. Upon assuming this post, however, Puno learned that the TV companies were being bled white by the group. He decided to terminate the contracts of the press gang, who promptly complained to President Ramos. Fed up with the problems, Puno quit and went to the United States to work as a consultant to a public opinion polling company that also handled political campaigns.

When the 1998 election season opened, Puno said he was first approached by Speaker De Venecia to join his team. He was offered a huge sum in legislative spending authority (good as cash) for his services. He said De Venecia promised to give him whatever he needed to set up his operations.

Puno revived the "survey network" he had set up using DILG personnel, including those who had retired and who now had more time to devote to political intelligence gathering. Reviving the network required a lot of money. To Puno's surprise, the promised support from Speaker De Venecia did not come. Puno had made a lot of commitments to members of his network and he said he lost face because he could not pay them. This unhappy relationship forced Puno to end his services to De Venecia's campaign. He said that in frank conversations with De Venecia, he told him that he could not work for the speaker's candidacy anymore because the Speaker had not kept his word.

"Joe de V is basically a deal maker and a great compromiser," Puno said. "He is very good at convincing people to join him. He will promise you everything to get you to agree with him—that is why people jokingly call him "the most promising politician. "The problem is, once you join him, he fails to deliver what he promised."

According to Puno, because De Venecia was the master of the art of the deal, he did not stand firmly for anything. "The compromise agreement is all—the Speaker is not guided by any ideological or moral values." Puno explained that is the reason why the Speaker was such a great deal maker. That was also the reason why Puno quit the De Venecia campaign—"The country needs a leader, not a broker," Puno said.

Another reason why Puno left De Venecia was the fact that he found the Speaker "a tough product to sell"—*mabigat dalhin* (a very heavy load to carry). The image of De Venecia as a *trapo* stuck. Both in person and on stage, De Venecia talked too much and rarely listened to what others had to say. All sorts of rumors linking him to graft and corruption circulated widely. Puno said that when he first did a survey for De Venecia, he found that more than half of the Mayors were supportive of Erap. Many of them were openly saying they were for De Venecia because they were waiting for the government funds that were promised to them but in their hearts, they were for Erap.

When approached by the Zamora brothers in late 1997, Puno said he needed very little convincing to work for Erap's candidacy. He had known Erap before and he knew that, unlike De Venecia, the Vice President valued his *palabra de honor* (word of honor). Puno's talk with Erap was effortless. As Puno said later, "For me, it was an easy decision to make. I looked forward to a fun campaign. We did not even discuss how I would be paid."

"This is the irony of the whole thing," Puno said, "the Lakas camp says I was paid P500 million for this job. After all, they had offered me a large sum. What they don't know is that I am doing this mostly as a labor of love." Another ironic thing Puno mentioned was that he had just learned that he was on the assassination list of the Alex Boncayao Brigade (ABB), also known as the Revolutionary Proletarian

Army (RPA). In mid-April 1998, the ABB-RPA kidnapped Dante Marcelo, a Lakas-NUCD lawyer, whom they accused of having participated in the *Oplan Dagdag Bawas,* electoral fraud committed in 1992 and further electoral cheating during the senatorial elections in 1995. Puno said that the ABB-RPA got documented evidence from Marcelo indicating plans for cheating in the 1998 elections. Marcelo was manacled to a lamp post and warned that if he got involved in any more electoral fraud, he would be killed.

Later in the month, ABB-PRA issued a "hit list" of officials they accused of being involved in plans for electoral fraud. The list included Chairman Bernardo Pardo and Commissioner Manolo Gorospe, both of Comelec, congressional candidate Elaine Cuneta of Pasay, Representative Dante Tinga of Tagig, and Ronnie Puno. Puno laughed off the threat even as Pardo and Gorospe asked for more bodyguards. "The ABB is going after the wrong persons," Puno said, "I am a very small potato. The ABB should check the documents they got from Marcelo and go after the masterminds."

## A Unique Polling Method

One of the most interesting activities in the Byron Hotel operations was the "survey methodology" developed by Puno which was applied to the Erap campaign. Based on his past work in the DILG, Puno had developed this unique approach. Essentially, it was based on the premise that individual Filipino voters in many rural and urban poor areas *do not decide whom to vote for themselves*—they are convinced, told, coerced or otherwise influenced by *liders* (local political ward heelers), warlords, clan patriarchs, powerful relatives, and other influentials. Winning an election, therefore, was a matter of aggregating enough of these "command votes" through techniques of attraction, enticements, incentives, bribery, intimidation, and other means.

"Public opinion surveys based on random samples are okay," Puno said. "However, they are very expensive and give you information only for a specific slice in time. The problem with random surveys is that they are based on the assumption that respondents interviewed make their own decisions as individuals. That is okay in the United States, England or Canada where people vote as individuals even when they belong to a political party. Sociologically, the Filipino votes as part of a group—a family, clan, a fraternity or sorority, alumni of a certain school, an ethnic group speaking a specific dialect. Thus, it is most important to know about these loyalties and entanglements that influence voting decisions."

To Puno, if the voting decision was made by leaders or influentials, then, it would be more efficient to poll all of these leaders and influentials rather than the individual voters themselves. "You have a universe, a complete census, rather than a random sample," Puno explains. "This means that, statistically, you get more valid information."

For the 1998 elections, the 17,263 positions being contested were:

- 1 President
- 1 Vice President
- 12 Senators
- 207 Members of Congress
- 79 Governors
- 79 Vice Governors
- 722 Provincial Board Members
- 72 City Mayors
- 72 City Vice Mayors
- 1,536 Municipal Mayors
- 1,536 Municipal Vice Mayors
- 13,124 Municipal Councilors

For his unique survey, Puno's operatives set up a list of all officials, leaders and influentials in 79 provinces and autonomous regions, 72 cities and highly urbanized municipalities in the National Capital Region, and 1,536 municipalities. Included in the list were all candidates for congressmen, governors, vice governors, provincial board members, city mayors, vice mayors, city council members, municipal mayors, vice mayors and municipal council members. In most areas, local *barangay* captains were also included in the list.

Also included were civic leaders, religious leaders and other influentials who could affect voting patterns in each area.

Puno recruited about 3,500 political operatives to closely monitor the political activities of each of the leaders and influentials who could influence the votes in all the contests mentioned above. Based on in-depth information (each operative was a political professional who came from the place) an estimate was made of the number of votes that each leader or influential was likely to deliver. Then, an educated guess was made of the likely number of votes that each leader or influential could deliver to Erap, De Venecia, Lim, Roco, and other presidential candidates.

Puno admitted that his methodology involved primarily qualitative judgment. However, since the estimate was being made by astute professional political observers, it was likely to have very high validity. In giving instructions to observers, Puno said he tried not to put in too many instructions on how the ratings would be made. The person doing the rating was assumed to be more knowledgeable about the local political situation than the researcher in Manila.

The questions asked of the field people doing the ratings were mainly designed to elicit valid data. For example, has the leader run for political office in the past? If so, how many votes did he or she get? Are these votes likely to be cast again for the same leader or his or her candidate? Is the leader related to a big political clan? If so, how many votes from family members and followers can they most likely mobilize? Puno admitted that the estimate of the likely number of votes that may go to a candidate in this methodology was an "educated guess." However, the personal assessment of the political operative was a professional one—based on long experience and knowledge as a politician. It was hoped, then, that the assessment would be valid and reliable.

Puno laughed when asked if his surveys are "objective"? "This is not a scientific poll," he said, "we are not after statistical validity." What Puno wanted is politically useful information. The survey was at the same time a political campaign. The field data gatherers did not only watch the political activities of leaders and influentials—they actually approached them to vote for Erap and the LAMMP ticket.

"Others may call this "dirty " but our field men merely reminded the people they were surveying that Vice President Estrada said he would be the Secretary of DILG when he wins," Puno said. "Then, we left it up to them to worry how they would fare as local officials if it was known that they campaigned actively against Erap".

For the period 9-16 April 1998, the LAMMP unique survey summarized the voting preferences in all the local government units in the Philippines into three categories: (a) LGUs where Erap is the first choice among ten candidates; (b) areas where Erap is tied for first place with another candidate; and (c) areas where Erap is the second choice.

Looking at first choices only, the survey revealed that Erap was first choice in 69.2% of voters in 78 provinces; first choice of 59.2% of voters in 76 cities and highly urbanized local units within the National Capital Region; and first choice of 53.3% of voters in 1,532 municipalities all over the country.

De Venecia was a distant second as follows: 20.5% of voters in provinces; 18.4% of voters in cities and NCR units; and 25.6% among voters in 1,532 municipalities. Lim was an even more remote first choice among candidates: 0 in 78 provinces, 7.8% in cities and NCR; and 3.1% among municipalities.

Interestingly, Roco was doing better than Lim from the LAMMP survey. He was first choice of 3.8% of provinces, 3.9% of voters in cities and NCR and 5.2% of voters in municipalities. Even Osmeña did better than Lim, who had 2.5% of the votes in provinces, 5.2% in cities and NCR, and 6.5% in 1,532 municipalities.

The methodology devised by Puno was also most interesting in that it allowed for tracking trends in candidates' support. On 4 May 1998, the Byron Hotel survey indicated that as of 29 April 1998, Erap garnered 29.2% of the votes while De Venecia was second at 22.6%.

The 29 April figures from the LAMMP survey contrasted quite sharply with the SWS survey conducted the week of 8-16 April. According to SWS, Erap had 30% of the votes while De Venecia had only 12%. Asked about this significant discrepancy, Puno theorized that the SWS survey probably did not capture the significance of the so-called "command votes" that De Venecia, with his access to massive government resources and the Lakas-NUCD machinery could muster. The LAMMP survey, in contrast, was almost completely based on the importance of command votes.

In his campaign speeches, De Venecia constantly reminded his listeners that LAMMP does not have official candidates in 29 congressional districts, 40 provinces and 150 municipalities. This meant, according to him, that the political leaders and influentials in these places are carrying the Lakas-NUCD national candidates unchallenged. While Puno does not completely swallow this argument (he contends that many Lakas-NUCD official candidates are secretly supporting Erap because the mass of voters are for Erap), he does not underestimate the capacity of local leaders, supported with massive resources from the party in power, to get the votes.

Another command votes block that the SWS surveys may not adequately cover are the religious denominations like the Iglesia ni Cristo, El Shaddai, Jesus is Lord Movement, etc. The small size of the SWS sample might not adequately cover the significance of these blocks of votes. The LAMMP survey, however, takes these religious groups into consideration, accounting for the higher ratings of De Venecia, who has been endorsed by three of these groups.

# Chapter 10

# *Bayanihan* Style Politics

Erap's overwhelming victory in the 1998 elections was partly due to the massive efforts of non-governmental organizations (NGOs) that made the Erap campaign a truly cooperative effort. The most conspicuous NGO efforts were carried out by six separate and uncoordinated organizations and movements which, somehow, in the end, managed to win without getting their acts together. These were: (a) the *Samahang LAMMP* Confederation made up of at least nine Erap-focused associations; (b) the JEEP Movement, a unique alliance of leftists, big business types and World Bank economists; (c) the Mare women's group made up of orange-vested society ladies including former beauty queens; (d) the Policy Studies Group composed of academics and policy administrators; (e) movie fans such as the Noranians for Erap led by Nora Aunor; and (f) the Greenhills Group of relatives and close family friends.

While the official political parties like LAMMP and PMP did most of the activities that translated Erap's popularity into actual votes, the voluntary civic and family associations provided the energy, creativity, enthusiasm and verve that made the 1998 elections so exciting and remarkably successful.

Each of the organized civic and family efforts on behalf of Erap's candidacy was pursued in true *bayanihan* style. Most of the key leaders and members of these organizations were unpaid volunteers. In the Mare organization, for example, each official member even donated P100,000 to the campaign in addition to their personal and family efforts. Some of the key organizers and trainers in JEEP had their operating costs reimbursed but what they received was a pittance compared to the true value of their efforts. In our case, as volunteer advisers for Erap, we had gone on six months leave from the University of British Columbia and paid our way throughout the whole campaign. Even when an exasperated Erap insisted on paying some of our hotel bills during provincial campaign sorties, we had stubbornly refused to allow him to do this to maintain our true volunteer status. In truth, the non-party efforts that helped Erap win the presidency were carried out by tens of thousands of idealistic people who lived for politics rather than off politics.

The most amazing thing about these family, community and civic organization efforts was that, somehow, they worked. It's true the personal and civic activities were confused, fragmented, overlapping, conflicting, contradictory and vastly complicated by incompatible personalities and poor chemistry. For example, when JEEP ni Erap was organized, the group in charge of the national capital region (NCR) led by Roberto "Bobby" Oca absolutely refused to be placed under the control of the JEEP ni Erap national office led by Robert Aventajado. The Samahang LAMMP confederation started out as nine different organizations, each one with special contacts and direct lines of communication to Erap. The Mare group efforts, led by Erap's wife, Loi, had to be kept completely separate from the activities of another ladies organization. Even the platform committee efforts of the JEEP ni Erap and the Policy Studies Group led by Erap's brother-in-law, Raul de Guzman, found it difficult to avoid territorial conflict. In the end, another policy group in the LAMMP headquarters produced the official platform distributed at the convention.

Despite the confusion, fragmentation, redundancies, wasted funds, petty quarrels, jealousies, intrigues, personality conflicts, and the maddening lack of coordination, the sheer energy of the whole Erap campaign coalesced into a tidal wave of actions that eventually won the presidency for Erap. In the end, everything just miraculously fitted together. If, as they say, defeat is an orphan and victory has many parents, the personal and civic efforts that combined to give victory to Erap may indicate that somehow, there is reason in madness and there is something to recommend *bayanihan* as a way of heroically doing momentous things. As the painfully slow counting of votes heralded an Erap victory, two contrasting images stand out—the raucous partying of Erap supporters at the Estrada home on Polk Street, Greenhills and the dark silence at the house on Magnolia Street, Dasmarinas Village, where the De Venecias live. Finally, the Filipino people, especially the masses who overwhelmingly backed Erap, had their voices heard.

## The Samahang LAMMP Confederation

The Powerhouse building at 123 A. Lake Street in Barangay Salapan, San Juan, is a sprawling three-story structure that gives one the feeling of a cavernous barn. As one enters the compound past the creaking iron gate, rows upon rows of plastic chairs arranged around a makeshift stage grab one's attentions. On one side is a long glass-enclosed case of ready-to-eat food, laid out *turo-turo* (literally, "point to your choice") style. Past the cafeteria line are square formica-topped tables and more plastic chairs. Farther down, are offices and cubicles where serious looking personnel officers are interviewing a long line of eager-looking campaign volunteers. At any time, day or night, the place is jammed with people.

In normal times, Powerhouse is a recruitment agency that sends overseas Filipino workers (OFWs) to Hong Kong, Singapore, Japan, Korea, the Middle East and North America. Since January 1998, however, it has been headquarters to the *Samahang LAMMP Confederation* (SLC), one of the voluntary civic organizations set up to support Erap's campaign. The company is owned by William Go, a *Chinoy* (Chinese-Filipino) businessman. William's major partner is Guia Gomez, a former movie actress who lived with Erap when he and his first wife, Loi were estranged and Loi and the three Estrada children lived in the United States. Erap has one son with Guia, Jayvee Estrada, a young up and coming entrepreneur who is President of the Philippine Junior Chamber of Commerce (Jaycees) and a key leader in both Kampil and YUPPEE in the SLC. The back of the makeshift stage in the Powerhouse compound bears a sign in big, bold orange letters saying *Samahang LAMMP Coordinating Council* (SLCC) and lists its members as follows:

- Inaanak ni Erap Foundation, Incorporated
  (The Godchildren of Erap Foundation, Inc.)
- Kabataan ng Masang Pilipino (KAMPIL)
  (Youth of the Philippine Masses Association)
- Kaibigan ni Erap Movement
  (Friends of Erap Movement)
- Magnificent Group
  (A woman's association in the Filipino-Chinese community)
- Masang Pilipino Volunteers for Erap Movement
  (Philippine Masses Volunteers for Erap Movement)
- Media for Erap Movement
  (An association of journalists and broadcasters)
- People's Golden Circle, Incorporated (PGC)
  (A senior citizens association)

- Young Professionals for Erap Movement (YUPPEE)
  (An association of young professionals)

- Samahang Erap Movement, Inc. (SEM)
  (Associations for Erap Movement, Inc.)

A multi-colored brochure issued by SLCC describes the Council as "an aggrupation of multi-sectoral and people's organizations that serves as a core group to coordinate the activities of the various organizations that support the campaign of the *Laban ng Makabayang Masang Pilipino (LAMMP)."* The nine organizations that made up SLCC were independently organized at different times. In early 1998, they decided to band together into a council in order to allocate specific responsibilities to each group, share personnel and resources and effect cooperation and coordination in their single-minded effort to get Erap elected President.

The main goal that encouraged the NGOs to pool their efforts arose from the realization that the campaign was heating up and the other parties, especially the Lakas-NUCD, were mobilizing rich resources that could spell trouble for Erap. At one level, Erap's campaign was going extremely well (indeed, the Social Weather Stations or SWS public opinion poll was showing that Erap had reached an approval rating of 30% in March 1998). There was a danger, however, that "Erap might win the balloting but lose in the counting." There was widespread belief among the SLC officers and members that the only way the Lakas-NUCD party could win was through massive cheating. The SLCC was specifically organized to counter that threat and ensure clean elections.

The rationale for setting up SLCC was stated in the organization's brochure in the following way:

> In the past few months, several organizations supporting the presidential bid of Vice President Joseph E. Estrada have been organized by "die-hard" supporters of Erap. Some of these organizations have been formally organized and they have started programs in line with the political campaign. Yet, there have been no continuous programs and strategies that would coordinate efforts to achieve our goals. There is fear of "wholesale" election fraud that may be initiated by the administration in the form of so-called *dagdag-bawas*. Hence, what is needed for the organizations or movements supporting the Estrada-Angara and the whole LAMMP senatorial ticket is unified action to combat election fraud.

In an organizational meeting held on 18 April, the confederation of NGOs elected the following officers to the SLCC: Pabling Casimina, Over-all Chairman, William Go, Co-Chairman, Charo Yu, Finance Officer, and Mely Puzon, Chief of the Secretariat. Members of the council representing their own organizations were: Boy Arceo, William Tiu, Julius Topacio, Allan Lee, Gilbert Cubias, Lito Caballero and Jun S. Bustamante.

Overall Chairman Casimina was originally from the *Partido ng Masang Pilipino* (PMP), and was an old hand at ward-level politics. He had worked with the Asistio political machine that had dominated Caloocan City politics for many years. Go was new to politics—his main role was to help raise the funds for the SLCC efforts, particularly from donations from the Filipino-Chinese community. Yu was another *Chinoy* who was an expert at fundraising. Her husband worked with the richest *taipan* in the Philippines, Lucio Tan, who owned Asia Brewery, Fortune Tobacco and Philippine Airlines among others. Puzon, a hardworking NGO organizer was perfect for her role as secretary to the council.

To effectively carry out its tasks, the Coordinating Council created eight working groups, each one headed by a Coordinator, as follows:

- Finance and Logistical Support Group—Charo Yu
- Information and Communications Support Group—William Go
- Voters List and Project of Precincts Group—Felix Serina
- Elections Procedures and Monitoring Support Group—Lito Caballero
- Coordination with Namfrel Support Group—Ralph Mangubat
- Training and Seminars Support Group—Gilbert Cubias
- Task Force Poll Watchers Support Group—Totit Dulay
- Mass Action Support Group—Rolly Lauchang

The coordinators of the working groups were mostly active NGO workers with very little political experience. Serina was a lawyer who specialized in labor law—he had a penchant for delivering long-winded speeches that sometimes frustrated the whole group. Caballero was a young activist who also knew election laws and procedures, having worked as a poll watcher for a local candidate in the past. Mangubat has had a lot of experience in national and local elections—he had been an active member of Namfrel in the past. He was also a high official in the PMP. Cubias was a young trainer—prior to this political involvement, he had mainly trained workers before they left for abroad. Dulay also knew election procedures from past work as a poll watcher for a local candidate in the 1992 and 1995 elections. The leader of the Mass Action Group, Lauchang, has had plenty of experience in the labor movement and he had lots of contacts with urban poor communities who could be counted on in case a mass demonstration was needed. "You want a thousand warm bodies for a demo," said Luchang, "just give me one day and I will deliver them to you."

Before the organization of SLCC, each of the nine organizations did their own thing to support Erap's candidacy. They also had their own special linkages and communication lines to Erap. For example, the *Inaanak ni Erap Foundation, Inc.*, which was headed by Julius Topacio and Mario Ponce was made up of more than 3,000 individuals who were the "godchildren" of Erap when he had served as a sponsor to their weddings, baptisms, confirmations and other rituals, thus establishing a kinship tie of sorts. The People's Golden Circle, Inc., headed by Noli Dacalos and Jun S. Bustamante, counted among its members retired individuals who were grateful for the old age benefits that Erap and his running mate, Edong had worked for in the Senate. Kampil or the *Kabataan ng Masang Pilipino* was headed by Erap's son Jayvee and had more than 3,000 active members. The *Kaibigan ni Erap Movement*, led by Mely Puzon, was mainly composed of friends and neighbors of Erap's family, particularly in the town of San Juan.

The challenge facing the SLCC in early 1998 was how to effectively coordinate their individual activities so that they could become an efficient structure for helping achieve Erap's goal of capturing the presidency of the country.

## From *Bayanihan* to Coordinated Action

The source of strength (and the cause of serious problems) of cooperative actions such as the ones attempted by the Samahang LAMMP Coordinating Council (SLCC) is a traditional form of organized action called *bayanihan.* The original reason for using *bayanihan* is rooted in cooperative traditions of mutual aid common to wet rice cultivation in monsoon Southeast Asia. In fact, the practice is also found in Indonesia where it is known as *gotong royong.*

In the often harsh climatic conditions in the Philippines, farmers usually have to pool their labor and other resources together in order to effectively carry out their myriad tasks. In many villages where people depend on the rains for growing crops, the ground preparation, planting, and harvesting seasons are very short. An individual farmer attempting to plow his fields as soon as the rains come, therefore, has to depend on the assistance of friends and neighbors. Groups of farmers have learned to pool their plows and water buffaloes together and agree on a set day when each person's field will be plowed. All the farmers, using the *bayanihan* approach, get their fields plowed according to a mutually agreed upon schedule.

The traditional symbol for *bayanihan* is a group of peasants moving a small house. Long bamboo poles are placed beneath the joists of the house. All the people, shouldering the poles, lift in one coordinated motion. The understanding is that every person must exert his effort at the same time in a coordinated manner. *Bayanihan* requires this voluntary coordinated action arising from agreement on a common objective and an acceptable process or procedure. In this joint effort, no one plays the role of coordinator or leader. Co-equal participants pool their resources to accomplish a task and goodwill and internalized rules of doing things make the achievement of the task possible.

The ideal of *bayanihan* still guides most community-based activities in the Philippines. It was not surprising, therefore, that the nine NGOs supporting the Erap and LAMMP political goals set up SLCC as a coordinating council. In *bayanihan*, there is no boss who can give orders—everyone pitches in according to specific skills and capabilities. The group spirit that energizes a *bayanihan* effort is its main source of strength. The *bayanihan* system works best when people know exactly what is expected of them and each person carries out his or her tasks in accordance with customary knowledge of roles.

The problem with a political campaign, however, is that culturally determined roles are not always very clear. Some kind of coordinating body is needed to assign specific tasks and to monitor whether these tasks are being carried out in time and with the proper effort and emphasis. To do this, SLCC was very lucky to have had the services of Professor Luzviminda Tancangco of the College of Public Administration, University of the Philippines, an expert on electoral processes and procedures, and electoral fraud.

Tancangco had been team leader of the UP-CPA research team that had studied the elections since 1984. Her book, *The Anatomy of Electoral Fraud*, is widely regarded as the authoritative documentation on *dagdag-bawas* (vote adding and shaving), the infamous cheating method that adds votes to chosen candidates and shaves them from opposing candidates. The findings of the UP-CPA research project were presented to the Senate in 1991. The Senate Technical Committee upheld the findings of the study. Despite a number of methodological quibbles that questioned a number of findings in Tancangco's study, it was widely recognized that the book led to better understanding of what fraudulent means were used by officials in power to get themselves elected through crooked means.

In a number of workshops, Tancangco walked the SLC officers and members through the whole electoral process—from the registration of voters, to voting, to counting, tabulation, and canvassing of ballots as well as the official reporting of election returns. Tancangco pointed out that cheating in an election occurs at all stages of the process. The designers of electoral procedures, in fact, may be the chief perpetrators of fraud. The electoral procedures have been designed precisely to make them complex and cumbersome. In this way, the powers of election officials are maximized—each point in the process requiring discretionary powers becomes an opportunity for exacting bribes.

Tancangco, by clarifying the various steps in the electoral process, provided the organizational basis for the various groups organized by the SLCC. She explained that cheating usually starts with the preparation of the list of voters, which may be padded with names of people who have already moved from a place or even those who have already died. Tancangco estimated that the 1998 computerized voters' list prepared by Comelec might have had as many as 4 million "reserve" voters whose names could be used for fraud.

To guard against the problem of the padded list, SLCC created the Voters' List and Project of Precincts Support Group headed by Felix Serina. The task of the group was to obtain copies of the Computerized Voters List (CVL) for each precinct and the Project of Precincts (POP) document, which listed all the precincts in every local government unit as well as the total number of voters per precinct. These lists could then be scrutinized by the group to find out if there were "flying voters" or other fraudulent names on the lists.

Another step in the process was to understand the detailed election procedures and to figure out where the points for fraud were likely to occur. SLCC organized the Election Procedures and Monitoring Support Group under the leadership of Lito Caballero for this purpose. The group was to collect documents detailing election procedures, paying special attention to recent changes that could facilitate cheating. These documents were then studied and simplified for use in the training program for poll watchers.

In the Tancangco analysis, because the local officials, LAMMP, JEEP and the SLCC were deploying thousands of people to act as poll watchers on election day, there was a need for a comprehensive "training of trainors" program that would help these volunteers identify key decision points in the process and to figure out if they were being duped. A training group, headed by Gilbert Cubia, was organized to do this cumbersome chore.

A key step in preventing fraud was watching the voting process itself on election day. Thus, the SLCC organized the Task Force Poll Watchers Support Group led by Gilbert Cubia of the *Inaanak ni Erap* group. Some 1.1 million poll watchers were needed nation-wide and the SLCC decided to focus its efforts mainly in the Metro Manila area which needed about 153,000 watchers. The watchers were to work in pairs, and would rotate every three or four hours. The total number of watchers was required by the fact that there were about 25,500 clustered precincts in Metro Manila and each one would need at least six watchers. The poll watchers would be recruited by the local LAMMP candidates in Metro Manila.

On its part, the SLCC estimated that it would need 4,018 individuals to carry out its poll watching and "operation quick count" activities. Needed were one computer tabulator, two data receivers at headquarters, 738 polling place tabulators (one each for every polling center) and 3,277 data retrievers (one retriever for every 10 precincts).

In terms of equipment and supplies, SLCC estimated that it would need two vehicles, two drivers, 30 hand-held radios, as many cell phones as could be borrowed for each of the data retrievers, and gasoline money for the cars.

Finally, Tancangco said that the SLCC needed to be ready for a "show of force" in case electoral fraud incidents required mass protests. The SLCC organized the Mass Action Support Group for this purpose, headed by Rolly Lauchang of the "thousand warm bodies." The group would rapidly mobilize people for protest rallies at Comelec, at City Halls or at the Electoral Tribunal, if needed. It therefore needed sufficient resources to send enough protesters to any point in Metro Manila at very short notice.

With the volunteer groups now organized into specific teams, the need for coordination was solved, at least conceptually. A far more difficult job was developing a spirit of cooperation and camaraderie among the various individuals that made up the Council and its members. Here, Guia Gomez played a very important role. She organized a formal induction ceremony, complete with a huge banquet in her San Juan home, where she extolled the capabilities of the individuals chosen as group leaders. She also conducted small meetings involving group leaders so that all the officers and members would get to know each other.

The efficiency of the SLCC was greatly aided by conscious efforts to effect institutional coordination. While interpersonal relations helped a lot, it was made clear to the volunteers that certain processes and procedures were needed to achieve coordinated action. To begin with, each officer or member of SLCC was issued an official identification card that had the name, address, and position in SLCC. The ID card had a picture of the holder taken with a special polaroid camera that automatically indicated a serial number. Each member had to attend a workshop for poll watchers and a special certificate was given to those who completed the workshop. SLCC had its own newsletter edited by Jun Bustamante of Goodheart International Publishing Company, Inc. The newsletter had special sections on the tasks of each group and reported on the activities of various committees.

Molding the SLCC volunteers into a coherent force was helped by pinpointing a common enemy—the party in power that was expected to cheat in the coming elections. Workshops were held, therefore, where the various cheating techniques were discussed in order to allow the participants to figure out how to counter them. In these workshops, the following "dirty tricks" were analyzed:

- The "ballot chain" or *kadena* technique. In this trick, official ballots bought or stolen from the printers or Comelec officials are filled in with the names of the cheating candidates. A voter will be bribed to use this ballot. If a voter is paid P500, the first installment of P200 is paid before voting and the remaining P300 is handed over when the candidate gives the unused ballot to the crooked vote buyer. The process is repeated, using the blank ballots of each succeeding voter in the "chain."

- The "carbon paper" method. Bribed voters are told to place a carbon paper and a white sheet beneath the official ballot. The copy is submitted to vote buyers as proof that they voted for the "buying" candidate.

- Ballot stuffing and ballot box switching. Ballot boxes are stuffed with prepared ballots. During times of confusion (say during an electrical brownout), they are switched with the official ballot boxes. In some cases, armed men may actually snatch the official ballot boxes and then replace them with stuffed ones.

- Reading out the wrong names. Some election officials (or poorly paid school teachers susceptible to bribery) may actually read the name of a favored candidate instead of the one actually voted for during the tabulation process.

- Vote adding or *dagdag*. A candidate with only 23 votes in the tabulation is recorded as having received 123 by simpling adding a 1 before 23.

- Vote subtraction or shaving *(bawas)*. The board of election inspectors whose members have been bribed may report that a candidate got only 23 votes when the actual tally was 123—the digit 1 is just erased from the tally sheet.

By carefully describing the various techniques used for cheating, the poll watchers being trained were able to come up with creative solutions on how to detect and counter these. In this way, the workshop participants developed a common sense of mission. The tasks they were going to perform were also made a lot more exciting and even dangerous. This strong sense of mission was a source of strong motivation for the workshop participants as they felt they were part of a crusade not only to get Erap elected but to stop the forces of evil from winning.

On election day and the suspense-filled days that followed, the well coordinated voluntary actions of the SLCC and component groups proved their worth. Two days before election day itself, the JEEP branch for Metro Manila revealed that it did not have enough people and resources to help coordinate poll watching. Roberto "Bobby" Oca, head of JEEP NCR had asked LAMMP for a huge amount of money to pay for his people. When that amount was not forthcoming, he said he would not be able to do his job.

In many Metro Manila communities, the SLCC people stepped into the gaps. They moved from precinct to precinct, picking up the election returns and conveying these to *Bantay Halalan '98* located at the Byron Hotel and the JEEP-AMA quick count being run from the Pacific Star building. The SLCC volunteers mobilized food brigades to feed poll watchers—there were ugly rumors that unscrupulous opponents were planning to give tainted food to LAMMP watchers that would cause diarrhea (pre-prepared ballots would then be stuffed in ballot boxes or ballot boxes would be switched while the LAMMP poll watchers were rushing to the toilets). The SLCC people reported cases of electoral fraud immediately. They filed detailed protests when necessary. Many of the SLCC people accompanied the ballot boxes from the precincts to the municipal hall and then on to the provincial capitol. In other words, they helped immensely in safeguarding the ballots for Erap and the whole LAMMP ticket.

### JEEP ni Erap Citizens Movement

One of the most effective NGOs supporting Erap's candidacy was the citizen movement for Justice, Economy, Environment and Peace or JEEP. It was organized by Robert Aventajado, an old friend of Erap from his San Juan days. When Erap decided to leave San Juan to run for the Senate, he had asked Robert to run for the same position. At first, Robert agreed but then decided to move to the United States with his family. However, after martial law, Robert returned to the Philippines and set up the Asia-Pacific Planning and Evaluation Company, Inc. (APP&E) which represented a number of American and Japanese business interests. In 1994, Robert and Erap agreed to set up JEEP. Since there was a ban on campaigning activities until 90 days before the election, JEEP was organized as a civic movement. Come the election season, of course, the real meaning of JEEP could be revealed as Joseph Ejercito Estrada for President.

According to its official brochures, JEEP's mission was:

- a society where justice and freedom reign.

- a community where all Filipinos can fully expand their potential for goodness.

- a society that cradles, as a national patrimony, the environment in its bosom.

- a society where all God's creatures live in harmony and where peace dwells.

The people sharing these high-sounding ideals belonged to four different groups that under normal circumstances would not have cooperated with each other. One group was composed of "leftists" who saw in Erap's candidacy a chance to achieve their social development and poverty alleviation goals. It was headed by Horacio "Boy" Morales, president of the Philippine Rural Reconstruction Movement (PRRM). Morales had been one of the original technocratic "Salas boys" carefully nurtured by then Marcos Executive Secretary Rafael M. Salas, who was obsessed with becoming President of the Philippines some day.

During the Marcos martial law years, Morales joined the New People's Army and went underground. He was captured and tortured but was released in 1986 when Cory Aquino was elected President. Salas, in turn, died in 1987, having left the Philippines years earlier to set up the United Nations Fund for Population Activities (UNFPA). At first, Morales played a key role in the Aquino government (he and Louie Villafuerte headed the Selection Committee that screened applicants for top positions in the Cory administration) but the marginalization of the "cause-oriented groups" became worse as the power of Cory's relatives, the so-called *Kamag-anak Incorporated* (The Corporate Body of Relatives) became more dominant. He was forced out and later agreed to head the PRRM.

Another key member of the leftist group in JEEP was Edicio "Father Ed" de la Torre, a former priest who followed the example of the Colombian priest Camilo Torres and took up arms against the Marcos government. Father Ed was also captured, tortured and then released after martial law. He set up an NGO that focused on training rural and urban poor activists for community work. He was also a popular column writer for the prestigious *Manila Times* newspaper. When Father Ed became really active in JEEP, he gave up his column and concentrated on helping run training programs for JEEP members.

Boy and Fr. Ed were later joined by another progressive reformer who had spent almost two decades as a nun, then quit to become a social activist, a United Nations official and then a consultant on training processes. Fely "Inday" Villareal came from a political family in Capiz—her father, Speaker Cornelio "Kune" Villareal, dominated the Capiz political scene for more than three decades. Fely's brother, Dodoy was elected Governor of Capiz for several terms. Another brother, Gabriel, serves as the legal adviser for Erap supporter and former candidate for President in 1992, Eduardo "Danding" Cojuangco. Her youngest brother, Willy, is also an Erap supporter. When Fely retired from the Food and Agriculture Organization (FAO), we recruited her to join the campaign. She joined JEEP in 1996 and took charge of the political organization and training programs for community workers in the provinces, particularly the Western Visayas.

The other group in JEEP was made up of about a dozen Filipinos living in Washingon, D.C., most of them working with the World Bank. Prominent members of this group were Vic Paqueo, Ed Quisumbing, Orly Sacay and Ed Campos. In 1992, this group had assisted President Ramos in formulating an economic program that stressed trade liberalization, privatization, and opening up Philippine trade to the outside world. In 1996, during a visit by Erap to Washington, D.C. at the invitation of Vice President Al Gore, he met with the group (the meeting was arranged by Robert Aventajado who knew most of them from their U.P. days in the School of Economics). The group members agreed to formulate a draft economic program for Erap. Subsequently, members of the group visited the Philippines at different times and fleshed out their proposed economic program. Orly Sacay retired from the World Bank, returned to the Philippines, and proceeded to formulate more detailed plans for the organization of credit cooperatives throughout the whole country.

An important member of the Washington, D.C. group actually lived in Baltimore. Jose "Oying" Rimon, Jr., runs the population communication and information program at Johns Hopkins University. In his work for the Erap campaign, Rimon was strongly supported by Benjamin "Benjie" Lozare, who works in the same Johns Hopkins program. Before leaving for abroad, Rimon was Executive Director of the Philippine Population Commission (Popcom). His area of expertise is communication and propaganda, especially the use of public opinion polls and market surveys to determine "social marketing" of contraceptives and other consumer items. We recruited Oying to join the Erap camp while we were working together on a UN project in Egypt in 1992. Because of many large population projects in the Philippines and other Asian countries, Rimon was in the Philippines frequently to help in interpreting survey results and translating them into communication strategies. It was Rimon who suggested the slogan *Bawat Isa, Mahalaga* to balance the original Erap slogan of *Erap para sa Mahirap,* which, to him, had overtones of class conflict. Rimon also suggested the focus on key communication themes and the repetition of these themes in all media—Jobs, Fair Wages, and Affordable Prices. Instead of putting money into the Manila mainstream press, Rimon advocated investing in radio programs and face-to-face communications by field workers in villages and towns, where almost 90% of the electorate favorable to Erap actually reside.

The third group in JEEP was made up of business entrepreneurs in Makati City. Leader of this group was Jose "Titoy" Pardo, one of the Makati businessmen to throw his lot in with Erap at a time when it was not even polite to mention his name in mixed company. Another early JEEP recruit was Art Alvendia, a management consultant with a penchant for transforming any policy proposal into a cold structural-functional matrix. The banker Abraham Co, former president of Bank of America actively participated in the early JEEP policy sessions, especially during the formulation of the Erap economic program. There were other business people who sympathized with Erap's candidacy but they hesitated to be openly associated with him for fear that the party in power would punish them for this.

A fourth group in JEEP was composed of economists, mainly from the School of Economics, University of the Philippines. Playing a key role, especially in finalizing the proposed JEEP economics program was Gonzalo "Gonz" Jurado, who also worked with the United Nations office in Bangkok. Another very active participant was Benjamin Diokno, who, aside from teaching economics in U.P. was also Undersecretary of the Department of the Budget. Felipe "Philip" Medalla was a frequent participant in JEEP bull sessions. The problem was, these U.P. economists often disagreed vehemently about the right prescriptions for the Philippine economy. There were a number of heated arguments when Jurado, for example, would heatedly take the "professor's prerogative" in arguing certain points with Diokno and Medalla (both of whom had been his students). The sessions were liveliest when the World Bank economists, almost all of whom were alumni of the U.P. School of Economics, were present and each of the workshop participants would insist on pressing for his own theories.

There are at least four areas where JEEP significantly contributed to the Erap victory. First, as the earliest NGO effort extolling the virtues of Erap, JEEP helped to legitimize the Vice President's aspirations, especially to groups who did not believe in him initially (e.g., the Makati business community, academicians, and the leftist true believers). Second, JEEP played a major role in formulating the Erap program of governance, especially the economic development planks in the platform. Third, JEEP set up a formidable machinery of trained NGO workers covering a third of the country, complete with a monitoring and quick count operation that relied heavily on the resources of the AMA computer school system. Finally, JEEP engaged in a number of covert activities, whose effects may not be known for a long time considering the "dirty tricks" proclivities of the party in power.

A serious problem with JEEP, a source both of its strength and its weakness, is its commitment to an uncompromising social equity agenda. To some JEEP leaders such as Boy Morales, Father Ed de la Torre and Fely Villareal, Erap's winning the presidency is "just a means to an end." They were more committed to their ideological ends—Erap was a convenient and winnable instrument but, their efforts did not start or end with him. If Erap had lost the elections, JEEP would have continued in its quest for social equity. Now that Erap has won, JEEP feels it has brighter prospects of achieving its ends.

Part of the problems from JEEP arose from personality differences between its national president, Robert Aventajado and some of the more "traditional politicians" around Erap such as Ronnie and Manny Zamora. From day one, tensions already existed between these two camps. In October 1997, when PMP, LDP and NPC coalesced to form LAMMP, Aventajado had hoped that he would be made Secretary General of the party. Instead, the Management Committee (ManCom) made Ronnie Zamora in charge of political operations, Orly Mercado the national campaign manager, Rod Reyes the media coordinator and Jesse Ejercito the finance and administration chief. Robert was eased out from LAMMP although he was allowed to raise funds and run JEEP as an autonomous operation.

A crisis of sorts came about in early 1998 when JEEP decided to register as a party list organization and nominated Boy Morales, Ed de la Torre and Fely Villareal as its official candidates. This move was condemned immediately by progressive leftist groups such as Akbayan, Sanlakas, Abanse Pinay, and Bisig. Their arguments were quite strong and critical of Erap—how could Erap object to the fielding by Lakas-NUCD of so-called "satellite parties" for the party list (such as Gloria's GLOW) when JEEP, openly identified as an Erap supporter, was also running in the party list contest?

In a meeting we helped to organize between Robert, Boy, Father Ed and Fely on the one hand and Francisco "Dodong" Nemenzo, Jr., of Akbayan, the wide gulf between the leftists and JEEP became easily discernible. Nemenzo said that it was unfair of JEEP to be competing with marginalized cause-oriented groups because it is well funded by Erap contributors. Nemenzo also said that it was "immoral" for JEEP to enter the party list contest because it is obviously not a marginalized group. Nemenzo argued that the votes that JEEP would get for its nominees would be taken away from the more legitimate marginalized groups such as the peasants, the urban poor, the handicapped, and the underprivileged.

Robert, on the other hand argued that the nominees of JEEP—Boy Morales, Ed de la Torre and Fely Villareal—were real progressives who had the true interests of the masses at heart. He said that with JEEP's political strength, it was at least assured that three progressive minded individuals would join the House of Representatives. Nemenzo did not buy this argument—he said that the JEEP movement had turned into another *trapo* organization that was willing to take advantage of its power position to achieve its own selfish goals.

It took the intervention of Renato "RC" Constantino, Jr., to resolve this JEEP as party list organization dilemma. RC wrote a letter to Erap strongly stating his objection to JEEP's entry into the party list, stating more or less, the same arguments brought out by Nemenzo. He cornered Robert in the Music Room of Erap's Greenhills home and showed him a copy of his letter. Later, when Erap realized the extent of the left's objections to JEEP, he personally talked to Robert to withdraw JEEP from the party list. Thus, although JEEP could have easily won three seats in the party list contest, it backed down and did not participate at all.

## Mare and the Beautiful People

One of the most visible fixtures in many Erap campaign rallies in cities and towns all over Luzon was a long air conditioned bus with airplane-type reclining seats, tinted windows, curtained compartments, and even its own toilet facilities.

This was the vehicle that carried officers and members of Mare, the women's civic organization headed by Justa K. Tantoco and friends to support Loi Ejercito's efforts to help her husband campaign. Decked out in their orange vests (comic Ai Ai de las Alas referred to them as the "Beta Carotene Ladies" during the LAMMP convention), the Mare ladies were guaranteed show stoppers. Trooping up the campaign rally stage in their well-coiffed elegance, the Mare beautiful people lent a touch of class to the sometimes tawdry business of political campaigning. Erap never failed to acknowledge their presence in his introductory speeches often singling out Justa Tantoco and former beauty queens Gemma Cruz and Myrna Borromeo who waved to the crowds like seasoned politicians and flashed their winsome smiles.

*Mare* is a Tagalog contraction of *Comadre* which is the feminine form of *Pare* (Compadre) which when reversed becomes "Erap." The organization was headed by Justa Tantoco, a prominent member of the well-to-do Tantoco clan of Bulacan and Batangas. Cynical observers of the Philippine social scene see the Mare as the natural successor to the "Blue Ladies" of Imelda Marcos—high society matrons who adorned social functions at the presidential palace in Malacanang. Die-hard members of Mare, however, angrily reject the odious comparison. They say they are serious believers in the social equity vision of Erap and have no interest at all in the glitzy court life in a future Malacanang. To prove their point, each Mare member had contributed P100,000 to the campaign chest of Erap. They also offered their homes in both Metro Manila and in the provinces as rest stops for weary campaigners, often serving endless meals for all the campaign supporters.

At one of the organizational sessions of Mare held in Justa Tantoco's home in Makati's exclusive Dasmarinas Village, veteran politician, Jimmie Policarpio, briefed the eager political neophytes on the do's and don't's of campaigning. Jimmie had been chief of staff of Senator Ernesto Maceda, who originally helped set up the LAMMP coalition, bringing in his Nationalist People's Coalition (NPC) to merge with Angara's *Laban ng Demokratikong Pilipino* and Erap's *Partido ng Masang Pilipino*. When Maceda, failing to get picked as Erap's vice presential candidate, bolted the coalition and decided to run for Mayor of Manila, Jimmie elected to stay with Erap and was appointed Campaign Officer in charge of scheduling ralllies and other political events. The successful "Erap Express" whistle-stop campaign on the railroad from Manila to Alabang was his idea.

The most important thing to remember, said Jimmie, is that *Erap para sa Mahirap* (Erap for the Poor) is not just a campaign slogan. Erap sincerely believes in his mission to help the poor and the underprivileged. Thus, nothing should be "plastic" (false, insincere, hypocritical) in the way Mare members deal with the people. The Filipino *masa* are ultra sensitive to real or imagined slights and they easily get insulted by intended or unintended actions. Some of the important no-no's indicated by Jimmie included the following:

- Don't shake hands with a limp hand—grasp the other person's hand firmly and fully. Convey warmth and sincerity, look into the other person's eyes and smile while saying how do you do?

- Never never be seen in public cleansing your hands with rubbing alcohol, not even after campaigning in a smelly public market and shaking the hands of fish vendors and butchers.

- Don't wrinkle your nose when you smell something awful (garbage in an open dump, stink from a clogged estero or small canal, over-ripe body odor). Don't take out your dainty handkerchief and put it to your nose. If you can't stand stink, you have no business joining the campaign.

- Don't offer money to even the most pitiable cases. Pocketbook generosity will not solve the problems of poverty. Besides, you may be accused of vote buying and endanger the chances of your candidate.

- Leave your gold jewelry and diamonds at home and don't wear fancy accessories—they are insulting to the poverty-stricken people you will meet on the campaign trail. Besides, it is not safe—you run the risk of getting robbed if you flaunt your wealth.

Aside from their colorful presence at rallies and motorcades, the Mare campaigners were most active in visits to markets, shopping centers, and depressed area communities. Led by Loi and Justa, they went from stall to stall in public markets and house to house in slum and squatter communities handing out Erap wristbands, the comics version of Erap's biography, stickers, posters, calendars, hats, T-shirts, and other campaign paraphernalia. They targeted jeepneys and tricycles, especially those where drivers were willing to attach Erap stickers to their vehicles.

Most of all, the Mare maidens prayed. They organized Masses, vigils and novenas to pray for Erap's safety and victory in the elections. They sponsored special Masses. Since the campaign season coincided with Holy Week, campaign trips often turned into impromptu *visitas iglesias* (church pilgrimage visits) where groups of Mare campaigners dropped by provincial churches and cathedrals and recited interminable litanies of Our Father's, Hail Mary's and Glory Be's. Catholics believe that reciting set prayers when visiting a church for the first time entitles one to special indulgences and guarantees fulfillment of a fervent wish. The Mare maidens bombarded heaven with their wishes for an Erap victory. On one campaign trip to Quezon province, the Mare group in our van recited the Rosary every hour or so. We also took side trips to churches with famous miraculous images of the Blessed Virgin, such as the one in the town of Lucban. Combining piety with political practicality, the Mare campaigners also went house to house and store to store distributing campaign materials. In the process, they practically bought out the town's supply of spicy Lucban home-made *langonisas* (sausages).

Another thing the Mare did very well was feed the multitudes. During campaign rallies, they could be relied on to bring sandwiches or order fast-food packages from Jollibee or Macdonalds to feed campaign workers. Pot luck lunches or dinners at Loi's Greenhills home would see Mare members and their maids bringing in trays of lasagna, fried chicken, noodles, salads, cakes and cookies for the streams of guests and campaign volunteers. In the true *fiesta* spirit of a political campaign, calorie counting and cholesterol cautions were thrown to the winds, to be dealt with later with aerobics sessions and herbal wraps, shiatsu massage and diet pills.

It is extremely difficult to assess the contribution of the Mare campaign to Erap's electoral victory. On the positive side, the Mare presence added class and glamour to the rallies and motorcades. The beautiful people, especially the former beauty queens, had the same effect as movie stars, entertainers and other showbiz types that attracted people to LAMMP rallies. Imelda Marcos, who in her own way probably understood the psychological yearnings of the masses best, loved to say that she always dressed up in her glittering finery when meeting the poor because it was her way of showing respect for them. As a young girl in Leyte, Imelda said she resented the insulting behavior of the "old rich" who dressed shabbily and did not even comb their hair before meeting the poor because they were only the *masa* anyway. To Imelda, the poor needed to identify with beauty and culture and the fantasy world of the elite they can only dream about. By personally bringing all this to the masses, she believed that she was honoring them. Perhaps, in their own way, the well dressed ladies of Mare were performing the same functions.

It may also be said that the presence of Mare campaigners in Erap's entourage symbolized his concern for the *masa.* A number of political analysts have pointed out that despite Erap's well-known identification with the poor, he actually comes from an upper middle class family background and his past and current life style is anything but poverty stricken. What is important is the fact that the poor perceive Erap as being for them and they believe in his pledge that he gives highest priority to their welfare. The Mare campaign, therefore, was another proof of Erap's commitment to the poor. By bringing the *malalaking tao* (the big people) and the *magagandang tao* (beautiful people) with him in his campaign, Erap was conveying to the people his main message of equity and social justice.

# Part III

## THE ELECTIONS

FOR VICE
PARA

## Chapter 11

# Dynasties, Regionalism and Tribal Politics

The 72 million Filipinos today speak more than 76 distinct languages and dialects. Unlike China, India, Indonesia or even Thailand and Vietnam, there was no unified Philippine state when European colonizers stumbled upon the islands during the first half of the 16th century. What the Spanish *conquistadores* found were isolated villages (*barangays*) or small federations of villages owing loyalty to petty chiefs. The Filipino nation, therefore, was cobbled together by force of superior arms and fear of sin—the sword and the cross, the hallmarks of the Spanish colonial empire.

At the turn of the century, the United States took over the Philippines and attempted to "Christianize" what was then the only predominantly Catholic country in Asia. The American experiment with bumbling colonialism was marked by naive idealism on the one hand and economic opportunism on the other. The introduction of compulsory mass public education revolutionized Philippine society by enabling poor but bright boys and girls to become upwardly mobile. At the same time, opening up Philippine natural resources to extraction by American business interests and forced revision of the Philippine Constitution, to give American entrepreneurs the same rights as Filipinos, were high prices to pay for the meager war damage payments that the Americans grudgingly gave to the Filipinos after World War II.

Democratic institutions introduced by the Americans such as elections based on one-person, one-vote, a merit-based civil service, separation of Church and State, an open and sometimes even licentious free press, and encouragement of community-based and civil society efforts in public life have had massive leveling effects on Filipino society. However, an inability to appreciate the cultural and psychological nuances on why such institutions imported from America did not quite work in the same way in the Philippines added to the frustration of American scholars who found it difficult to understand Philippine style politics.

While the elite-mass structure of Philippine society remained pyramidal even after years of American tutelage, quite a number of individuals and families who used to belong to the masses started to gain entry into the ranks of the indigenous elite. A few upwardly mobile individuals managed to achieve middle class status but this segment remained quite thin—the Philippine bourgeoisie unlike its classical European counterpart, was not composed of wealthy grasping insecure merchants lusting to buy themselves elite status. The Filipino *burgis* was made up mostly of medium-scale landowners, professionals like doctors and lawyers, salaried officials, local entrepreneurs, and successful local politicians.

Any member of the masses who achieved fame and fortune was readily co-opted and smoothly absorbed by the ruling elite. Even greedy individuals who became wealthy through shady means became acceptable members of high society in one generation or two, their dark pasts conveniently forgotten and their social status achieved painlessly by money, family connections, social influence and political power. As shown by the resurrection of the Marcos family during the 1998 elections, Filipinos, generally, have very short memories.

Four hundred years after Spanish colonization and a full century after proclaiming itself free from colonial domination, the Philippines prides itself in having evolved into a democratic state with one republican government, a Constitution, one flag, and one national anthem. However, the divisive calls of regionalism and adherence to (the politically incorrect notion of) "tribalism" are never far below the surface in Philippine society. To many Filipinos, the family and the home village or town of origin remain the most important units of society and not the nation-state. The Filipino's loyalty flows from some deep pool of blood ties and ancestor worship, his strongest emotional affects are rooted deep in the rich dark soil of his native village. Scratch a Filipino and you will most likely find a *promdi*—a person "from the" province. Many Filipinos still see themselves as Ilocano, Cebuano, Bicolano or Pangasinense first and Filipino second. As Edu Manzano, a candidate for vice mayor of Makati who was disqualified by the Comelec for being an American citizen said while tearing up his U.S. passport, "I am not an American, I am an Ilonggo."

Having lived abroad for most of our lives, this harking back to primordial roots and identities has always fascinated us. For example, we have found that when two Filipinos meet, one of the first questions that gets asked is: *Taga saan ka ba sa atin?* (Which part of the Philippines are you from?) Once the province, city, town or village of origin is established, the next question is "Do you know so and so?" In most instances, normal discourse starts only after the provincial origin, linguistic roots, ethnic identity, family connection, school background, or other elements of a person's identity are firmly established. A Filipino is never just a person—he or she is part of an invisible network of aggrupations with real or imagined characteristics of physical attributes, habits, beliefs and idiosyncratic features.

Many years ago, when we decided impetuously to get married in Bangkok and informed our parents about it (having so many relatives we wanted to avoid the expense of a large wedding), the first telegraphed question from Eleanor's relatives, from Laguna and Iloilo, was not "who is he" but "where is he from?" When informed Prod was from Pampanga province, the immediate reaction was "Oh, no! Call the wedding off—Capampangan men are wife beaters. And they eat dogs."

Similar stereotypes persist among some Filipinos even today, despite long years of education and the enlightening evidence of experience. Ilocanos are stingy, Visayans are fun loving, Bicolanos either become priests or taxi dancers, Capampangans love good food and like to show off. What matters most to many Filipinos, it seems, is not the individual but the family, clan or ethnic group to which they belong.

In this line of thinking, the voting decision is not a rational choice based on calculations of merits and demerits of a candidate or an analytical assessment of a candidate's political platform and ideological stand. Rather, that is how a self-proclaimed Manila intellectual would like to vote. A true-blooded Filipino's vote is the emotional distillation of a gut-felt choice rooted in highly charged biases and prejudices. It is based on personal loyalties, how other members of the family are reacting, on real or imagined hurts and slights, on irrational likes and dislikes. Most important of all, the vote is based on how other members of the family or clan are voting. This is probably the reason why political dynasties thrive in the Philippines despite constitutional efforts to ban them.

Although the Philippines has been an organized nation-state for at least a century, there are quite a number of social scientists who believe that Philippine society remains fragmented along ethnic, family and regional lines. This particularistic regionalism has been the main consideration in traditional politics in the past. The Philippine House of Representatives is the ultimate instrument for legitimizing regionalism as the main objective of the members seems to be to maximize the benefits they can extract from the central government to be allocated to their own bailiwicks. The institution of the pork barrel, in turn, is the main channel for the extraction of those funds.

At an even more basic level is the strong attachment to the family or clan as the basis of political power. After the long dark years of martial law, a Constitutional Commission was struck to wipe the political slate clean. In that commission where, in the words of one newspaper columnist "political correctness and wishful-thinking were given free rein," the framers of the 1987 "Cory Constitution" adopted a provision banning political dynasties. The Philippine Congress, however, has never passed supporting legislation to implement that constitutional provision. During the 1998 elections, therefore, political dynasties played a most important role.

## Political Dynasties and Local Politics

In his column of 16 March 1998, the lugubriously prolix Max Soliven who must pay himself by the column inch in his otherwise well-edited *Philippine Star,* raised the question: "where politics has become a 'family monopoly,' can we call ourselves a democracy?" Soliven had trained his tart pen on Makati Mayor Jojo Binay, who, banned from running a third time, was fielding his wife, Elenita for Mayor. He also noted that with Ramon Revilla running for re-election in the Senate, his son Bong Revilla running for Governor of Cavite and his son-in-law Robert Jaworski also running for the Senate, what we will have is a "family reunion" instead of a political gathering.

Indeed, one of the most remarkable aspects of the 1998 elections was the great number of wives, husbands, sons, daughters, in-laws, cousins and other relatives running for political office to replace many "graduating" incumbents banned from running beyond three consecutive terms. The influential Catholic Bishops Conference of the Philippines, in its pastoral letters, cited the continued existence of political dynasties as a serious defect in the Philippine political system.

"Instead of skill or track record and commitment to the common good, the people are forced to choose by bloodlines," wrote the CBCP. Putting the blame directly on the administration of President Ramos, the Bishops asked: "If the government is sincere in removing political dynasties, why did they not pass an enabling law?"

The issue of political dynasties is one where not one person in the Philippines is able and willing to cast the first stone. President Ramos himself is the founder of a political dynasty—he supported his sister Leticia Shahani in her bid for Governor of Pangasinan as well as the candidacy of her son, Ranjit, for congressman. A grand-uncle, Simeon Valdez, was running for congressman in Ilocos Norte, up against another relative, Imee Marcos, daughter of his cousin, former President Ferdinand Marcos. The family of the late dictator himself was staging a strong come back bid—aside from Imelda's quixotic run for the presidency, son Bongbong was also running for governor.

Even President-elect, Erap Estrada, despite his efforts not to be branded a practitioner of traditional politics, can be accused of having a political dynasty of sorts. His son, Jinggoy, has been re-elected as Mayor of San Juan, where Erap started his political career more than 30 years ago.

*Landlord-Tenant System*

Because of the stubborn persistence of political dynasties, winning an election in the Philippines has traditionally involved working out a coalition among prominent families and clans that dominated political life in provinces, cities and regions. The roots of this dynastic system can be traced to the system of land ownership early in the nation's history when land formed the most basic source of wealth. During the Spanish colonial era, the Crown rewarded local *ilustrados* with land grants or *encomiendas* for their good services. Many of the prominent families in the Philippines today (the Ayalas, Zobels, Madrigals, Aranetas, Escalers and Gonzaleses) have derived their economic dominance and high social status from this colonial practice.

Under the traditional landlord-tenant system, *hacienda* owners exercised dominant influence over the political attitudes and actions of their sharecroppers and laborers. In many instances, this was not the result of exploitative patron-client relationships where the masses were coerced to vote for the candidate chosen by the landowner. It was more of a paternalistic relationship where the landlord provided a means of livelihood, welfare services and emotional guidance to sharecroppers and laborers, who, in turn, willingly followed the wishes of the landlord from a strong sense of loyalty, debt of gratitude and a grateful desire to repay the landlord's benevolence and concern. It was a nice cozy system—the oligarchic families looked after the basic needs of their dependent charges, the poor and disadvantaged, in turn, looked up to their masters for economic sustenance and spiritual/ emotional guidance.

The stark reality nowadays, however, is that in the Philippines, the business of politics has become the most lucrative business of all. In a society where the economic benefits are often "rationed" from the capital city of Manila through pork barrel fund allocations, business contracts, franchises and permits, special concessions and favors, and various preferential arrangements, holding a political office has become a most desirable plum. Politicians have become the main channels for economic and social benefits. Charging the usual 10% to 20% of the value of any public transaction, skimming off up to 40% of pork barrel public works contracts, exacting a "facilitation fee," or commission or bribe whenever a signature is needed, a politician can become rich very quickly. As political office has become more lucrative, the price of running an electoral campaign has escalated, which, in turn has increased the pressures on the politician to avail of corrupt money to recoup the huge expense of the campaign. And so, the vicious cycle goes on, with families and clans protecting their power and wealth by ensuring that a member of the family gets elected always.

Not surprisingly, local political power in the Philippines has become the preserve of what the American political scientist Harold Lasswell has called "agglutinated elites." In this system, the politically powerful are also the economically dominant; the ones who own the most lands are also the business entrepreneurs; families with the most money also possess the highest social status and prestige; the parents with the best education also make sure that their children go to the best schools; and the families that have money, land, social status, education, prestige and political power are also the ones who have a monopoly over the means of violence through their bodyguards, private armies and goon squads. In politics as in Philippine native desserts, the rice grains that stick together are sweetened together.

*Command Vote Politics*

In areas such as the Ilocos region, in Nueva Ecija, in Cavite and parts of Mindanao, the politically powerful also have the strongest private armies with the deadliest firepower. We remember during one of Erap's campaign sorties being the guest of an Ilocos Sur town Mayor who was giving us the basic lessons on "command vote" politics. We had arrived at his home at seven in the morning and his yard was already full of people. Despite the electoral gun ban, a couple of men with armalite rifles were lolling around while another group was having breakfast. Our LAMMP Orange Book indicated that the town had a voting population of 85,000. Our host asked us how many votes we wanted from his town. We told him what was written in our Orange Book and he laughed. Just tell me how many votes you want me to deliver, he said. Don't worry about what your guide book says. We were awfully glad he was on our side.

There have been quite a number of efforts to limit or even ban the proliferation of dynasties in Philippine political life but they have all failed. The limitation on the number of terms an official can hold, as already pointed out, has only seen spouses and other relatives assuming the vacated posts. Local political machines are inherited from elders like so much land or chattel. Elective political office has become just one more account in the commercial and business portfolios owned by families and clans.

But are political dynasties really that bad for Philippine society? After all, aren't the Filipino voters the ultimate determinant on whether a person gets elected or not? And if the voters in a certain political area support the son, spouse or daughter of a prominent political leader, what is wrong with that? (Nothing is wrong, of course, if there is no coercion, intimidation or terrorism used to force someone to vote in a certain way).

If we trust that Filipino voters are free in selecting the candidates they vote for, does it really matter if they support members of a family dynasty? Some of our best leaders have been supplied by political dynasties. For example, in Cebu, no less than seven members of the Osmeña clan were running for political office in 1998: Lito for President, cousin Serge III for vice president, brother John for senator, John's son John-John for provincial board member, Serge's brother Tomas for congressman, Lito's cousins Renato and Rogelio were running for Cebu City vice mayor and councilor respectively. Considering that the late President Sergio Osmeña had 17 children, those candidates were only a small segment of the clan. To many of these descendants, the honorable name of Osmeña was not enough to get them elected as they lost miserably in the polls.

The decision of the voters also hit the Ramos family in Pangasinan. Leticia Shahani, the sister of President Ramos, lost the governorship to a son of former Governor Agbayani. Ranjit Shahani, Leticia's son, won as congressman but that may be a pretty thin victory to base a dynasty on. Taking the verdict of the people in stride, Letty Shahani made her peace with Erap Estrada less than two weeks after election day. Visiting Erap at his home, the President's sister congratulated the "president-elect" and said that, on her personal capacity, she was acknowledging his victory. Ever the gracious and magnanimous victor, Erap thanked Ms. Shahani and said she could have a position in his government. This early capitulation of the President's sister was very significant because Ms. Shahani revealed that her own tally of the Pangasinan votes revealed that, contrary to the claim of Speaker de Venecia, Erap had won in the majority of Pangasinan towns.

In Tarlac, the Aquino clan suffered a most humiliating rout—Margarita "Tingting" Cojuangco, wife of Congressman Peping Cojuangco lost her bid for governor (Noynoy Aquino, the former President's son, won as congressman). In Bulacan, Felix Ople, son of LAMMP Senator Blas Ople won while another son, Raul Ople, lost.

The results of the 1998 elections as far as candidates belonging to political dynasties were concerned revealed that Filipino voters are quite independent in making their electoral choices. While belonging to a political family may help some people get elected, it is not a foolproof guarantee that it will always ensure victory. In some instances, as in Makati, being the wife of the former Mayor who could not run for office anymore, helped Ms. Elenita Binay in getting her elected. In nearby Pasay City, the wife of Mayor Pablo Cuneta, who had ruled the city for more than four decades, lost.

As far as political dynasties are concerned, maybe the pragmatic attitude of President Ramos on this issue is worth repeating here. Reminded that the Constitution prohibits political dynasties but that they seem to thrive anyway, the President said: "I do not encourage it (running as part of a political dynasty), but I guess it is necessitated by the desire to win and to survive the coming May elections... If you don't accept it as a reality that it's there, there's nothing else to counter it with." In other words, there is really very little we can do about political dynasties except trust in the wisdom and maturity of Filipino voters. Passing legislation curbing it will probably only mean that politicians will find loopholes to thwart the intent of the laws.

Political dynasties, in any case, are hardly confined to the Philippines. In the United States, the Kennedy clan in Massachusetts has always had a member of the family in power or running for a political position at one time or another. In Indonesia, the Suharto family's influence and power extends not only to political but to business as well. In due time, the people themselves will decide—as they have just done so in the case of the Suhartos. In the days when political power in the Philippines was being transferred from one political party to another, in a relatively peaceful manner, the scenes of bloody riots and angry demonstrators in Indonesia, forcing Suharto to resign, provided a sharp contrast. If there is any lesson to be learned here, it is that in the final analysis, the wisdom of the people will triumph in the end.

## Regionalism

In 1998, the Philippines celebrates its centennial and its proclamation as an independent state. Despite a hundred years of national history lessons, patriotic pledges and affirmations of love to the nation, weekly Monday morning flag raising ceremonies, recitations of the lives of national heroes, and various brainwashing attempts at nation-building, the average Filipino remains a bundle of petty identities and loyalties. Each one of the primordial linguistic "tribes" that makes up the Philippine nation-state is a microcosm of emotional ties that often exercise a stronger hold on a person's consciousness than the artificial notion of nationhood.

It is not surprising, therefore, that one of the fundamental rules of traditional electoral politics in the Philippines is the need for "regional balance." Thus, if the candidate for president is from Luzon, the vice presidential candidate must be from the Visayas or Mindanao. The members of a good senatorial ticket should represent different regions in the country. To win nationally, a political party needs to piece together a coalition of political leaders, clans, local machines and warlord fiefdoms that could be relied upon to deliver the votes.

*Tribal Politics*

The 1998 elections provided an empirical test of whether ethnic identity, regional loyalty or "tribalism" is still a strong factor in Philippine politics. As an editorial of the *Manila Standard* (25/3/98) noted, it was rather ironic that in a year when the Philippine centennial as a free country was being celebrated "the (political) surveys indicate a revival of tribalism in voter behavior brought about by the breakdown of the political party system."

Proof of political regionalism and tribalism were advanced as follows:

- Most presidential candidates based their electoral strategies on their ethnolinguistic bailiwicks. Raul Roco was counting on his strong political following in Bicol, Santiago in the Ilonggo-speaking Visayas, Osmeña in the Cebuano-speaking southern islands and Mindanao, De Venecia in the Ilocos region, De Villa in the Southern Tagalog region, and Imelda Marcos in Leyte and in the Ilocos region of her late husband.

- Most candidates strongly supported policies and programs that would benefit their regions. The most unabashedly jingoistic was Osmeña whose political party *Promdi* or *Probinsiya Muna* (The Province First) was almost wholly founded on what was good for Cebu. Osmeña's campaign was based on what he had done for Cebu. His program of government promised that he would develop the whole country as he had developed his home province of Cebu.

- Most candidates appealed to the linguistic groups to which they belonged and proudly addressed their *kababayans* (provincemates) in their native tongue: Pangasinenses and Ilocanos for De Venecia, Tagalogs for De Villa, Ilonggos for Santiago, Cebuanos for Osmeña, Bicolanos for Roco, and Warays for Imelda. Even when the candidates were not fluent in the language or dialect anymore because they had lived outside the region for years, they still memorized native lines and delivered them with ethnic pride.

- Most candidates cultivated affiliation or tried their best to be identified with prominent provincial or regional families and clans. They courted the support of political "dynasties" such as the Osmeñas of Cebu, Laurels of Batangas, Singsons of Ilocos Sur, Cojuangcos of Tarlac, Josons of Nueva Ecija, and Duranos of Danao City. One of the indispensable tools in any political operative's kit bag is the Center for Investigative Journalism's *The Ties that Bind* as this details the complex kinship and other linkages among the Filipino elite families that control the Philippine House of Representatives.

In other words, during the good old days of traditional politics, one needed alliances to win nation-wide in a Philippine election. Old line politicians lived by the maxim attributed to the late Eulogio "Amang" Rodriguez that "Politics is addition." Winning nationally was a matter of putting together a coalition of families and clans. Even enemies who suddenly turned around, if only temporarily, are now friends and allies. This called for deals, bargains, compromises, special arrangements, accommodations, and washing of each other's hands, or scratching of each other's backs. To win in an election, one needed to belong to the "system," follow its rules and adhere to its unwritten codes. Most of the time, to enter Philippine politics was to take the first steps towards the slippery slope of personal and institutionalized corruption.

## Breaking the Mold

The situation changed during the 1998 elections.

One of the most fascinating things about the 1998 elections was the fact that the presidential campaign of Erap Estrada did not conform with the need to depend on regionalism and local machines. Despite the fact that Erap himself had been in politics for more than 30 years his campaign strategy differed significantly from the one that his opponents used, at least as far as regional alliances were concerned.

It is interesting to analyze how and why this situation came about.

In choosing Edong Angara as Erap's vice presidential running mate, LAMMP did not follow the rule of regional balance. Both Erap and Edong were from the southern Tagalog region, with Erap identified with Metro Manila, Cavite and Laguna and Edong with Quezon and Nueva Ecija. Although Erap sometimes referred to his Tagalog ethnic roots in his provincial rallies, this reliance on regional support did not play a major role in his campaign. The major thrust of the Erap electoral strategy, in fact, was his acceptability to *all* Filipinos, not just to a specific ethnic group or region.

The national rather than regional basis of Erap's popularity among Filipino voters was revealed in the results of the SWS public opinion polls of 7-16 March, 17-21 March, and 16-18 April 1998. The following poll results revealed Erap's nation-wide popularity:

- In Region 1 (Ilocos) and Region 2 (Cagayan Valley) about 33% of registered voters interviewed said they were voting for Erap. In this vaunted "solid north" region, supposedly guaranteed as De Venecia territory, only 26% of the voters actually supported De Venecia. The ties of regionalism were true only of the pure Pangasinenses who went overwhelmingly for De Venecia (about 89% of respondents that had Pangasinan as their mother tongue said they were going to vote for De Venecia). The April 1998 survey showed however, that there were Ilocanos and other ethnic groups in Pangasinan province and they did not solidly support De Venecia. Among residents of Pangasinan province who spoke Ilocano, 28% said they supported Erap which was not too far behind the proportion of those who supported De Venecia (30%). In other provinces within Northern Luzon where Ilocano speakers predominated, most voters supported Erap.

- More than 41% of voters interviewed in Central Luzon were for Erap. In the April survey, Erap was first among Tagalog speakers living in Luzon south of Manila (36%). Despite Roco's 76% share of the Bicol-speaking vote, this lead was reduced from a 7 percentage point advantage for Roco in March to a 15 point deficit in April.

- In Region VIII (Eastern Visayas) Lito Osmeña got 42% of the votes, as against Erap's 19%. A breakdown of vote preferences by language spoken showed that Cebuano speakers went predominantly for Osmeña

(39%) compared to Erap's 19%. Eastern Visayas, therefore, confirmed the importance of regionalism in people's voting preferences.

- Among Ilonggo speakers, Erap got 36% of the votes, and "native daughter" Miriam Santiago got only 16%. This was a significant triumph for Erap and confirmed the fact that the so-called Miriam magic, which nearly got her elected president in 1992, had faded away in 1998. Osmeña got even more votes than Santiago (16%) in the latter's traditional bailiwick.

- In Regions IX and XII (Western & Central Mindanao) Erap's portion of the votes improved from 33% in March to 35% in April. Osmeña, counting on the migrant Cebuano votes in Mindanao got only 13% and Lim and De Venecia garnered 12% each. All in all, the Muslim vote was 48% for Erap and only 27% for De Venecia.

What, then, was responsible for Erap's nation-wide victory in the polls and his breaking of the mold of region-based and tribal politics?

The most likely explanation for Erap's near universal appeal and transcendence over regional cleavages is the support of the Filipino masses. In other words, we could hypothesize that regionalistic politics got replaced by class-based politics in the case of Erap. Instead of people seeing him as a favored son of any one particular region, Erap was perceived by most people as the champion of the *masa.* Since there are more members of the *masa* than members of the elite nation-wide, Erap won overwhelmingly over other candidates whose main appeal was regional.

Some political analysts have interpreted Erap's electoral victory as a manifestation of the "revolt of the masses." This is pure hyperbole and shows lack of appreciation of the lessons of history and inadequate understanding of political theory. If Marxist analysis is used here, one can hardly say that the objective conditions prevailing in the Philippines in 1998 signaled the formation of a new class. In fact, the opposite situation probably existed—in 1998, more and more low income Filipinos were becoming "empowerd" by expanding economic opportunities and the increasing strength of civil society. The improvements in the lives of the common *tao,* (especially those among them with relatives living abroad as overseas contract workers who remitted billions of dollars to the Philippine economy) increased their aspirations to become more *burgis* than proletarian.

The Erap phenomenon, in other words, was not an earth-shaking political event with revolutionary significance. It was more a situation where a candidate liked by the people was able to convince them to vote for him—no more, no less. And they did.

The Erap phenomenon meant that Filipino voters saw in Erap a candidate who understood their plight, was sympathetic to their situation and was willing to listen to their wishes and aspirations. The masses liked Erap, they identified with him, they saw him as potentially helping them get out of their misery, they were fascinated with his colorful life, mesmerized and entertained by him and his touring company of showbiz stars. However, they did not see him as their savior. Despite his macho fighter image, they probably never regarded him as their leader in a historical process of "class struggle." One doubts if they would have laid down their lives for him.

Happily, the theory that the masses would have stormed the barricades if their hero had been cheated in the polls was never tested—the electoral process resulting in an Erap victory was relatively peaceful. As of the latest Namfrel count (18 May 1998), with 70.3 of the votes counted, Erap had obtained 7,165,638 (37.3%) of the votes as against De Venecia's 2,935,983 (15.3%).

What the *masa* vote for Erap suggests is their strong preference for a candidate who championed their cause. Erap was someone they could strongly identify with. As shown in the results of the SWS 16-18 April 1998 poll, the people decided to place their trust in Erap as they perceived him to be:

| | |
|---|---|
| Pro-poor | (63%) |
| Approachable | (40%) |
| Decisive | (27%) |
| Honest (never been involved in corruption) | (34%) |

The SWS pollsters broke down the Philippine voting population into five categories corresponding to the first five letters of the alphabet. "A" voters had high income, were highly educated, were predominantly urban and well traveled. "B" voters were upper middle class, also highly educated and well tuned to the mass media. "C" voters were middle class, with medium level incomes, resident in towns and small cities, probably professionals and entrepreneurs with more than a high school education. The "D" voters were the typical *masa,* with low income, literate but with probably an elementary school education, engaged in farming or low-level trading. "E" voters had very low income, probably semi-literate, eked out a livelihood as a small farmer or farm laborer, probably lived in a slum or squatter area if an urbanite.

The sample of the 7-16 March 1998 SWS survey was made up of socio-economic classes broken down by region as follows:

| | **A-B-C** | **D** | **E** |
|---|---|---|---|
| **All Philippines** | 10% | 72% | 18% |
| Metro Manila (NCR) | 30 | 45 | 15 |
| CAR, Ilocos (R-I & II) | 4 | 88 | 8 |
| Central Luzon (Reg. III) | 7 | 82 | 18 |
| Southern Tagalog (R-IV) | 10 | 83 | 7 |
| Bicol Region (Region V) | 2 | 78 | 19 |
| Panay (Region VI) | 3 | 75 | 22 |
| Cebu/Bohol (Region VII) | 8 | 70 | 22 |
| Samar/Leyte (Region VIII) | 1 | 65 | 34 |
| Basilan/Zamboanga (R-IX) | 5 | 68 | 28 |
| Agusan/Misamis (R-X) | 2 | 64 | 28 |
| Davao/Cotabato (R-XI) | 0 | 75 | 25 |

From the socio-economic categories noted above, it is obvious that the great bulk of Philippine society (and of the voting public) belonged to the common *masa* (about 72%) and the very poor often marginalized, underprivileged and poverty-stricken *masa* (18%). Only 10% of the population could be classed as elite and most of those were concentrated in the very large urban centers such as Metro Manila (30%) and Cebu (8%).

Even in the relatively rich agricultural regions of Northern Luzon and the Southern Tagalog regions, the common *masa* predominated. The poorest of the poor, the E classes, were concentrated in the Eastern and Central Visayas as well as Northern and Central Mindanao.

With the regional class patterns noted above, the Erap strategy for winning the votes of the masses became quite clear. First, concentrate on the large centers of *masa* which, happily for Erap were also heavily in the Tagalog speaking provinces and cities. Second, rely less on the mass media and more on face-to-face dealings with the masses, which meant rallies and motorcades. Third, stress the basic needs of the masses for food, jobs, prices, housing and education. Finally, take on the role of the underdog, cast the personal attacks on Erap as direct attacks on the masses, and gain the sympathy of the people thereby.

From the very beginning, the Erap campaign focused on his populist image. In the Tagalog provinces, his mangling of the English language and insistence on the use of Tagalog in his speeches got him a lot of sympathy and support. In rally after rally, Erap stressed the point that it was the patronage of the Tagalog movie fans that made him successful. Touching on the very Filipino virtue of *utang na loob* (debt of gratitude), Erap said that his desire to become President of the country was based on his desire to repay the masses who flocked to his movies by serving them in Malacanang.

Erap's populist image played really well in massive provincial rallies and motorcades where he pressed the flesh. Early in the campaign, Erap avoided television and campus debates that, he said, were mainly designed to entertain the snobbish intelligentsia. Aware that about 90% of the Philippine electorate belonged to the D and E groups, Erap decided to bring the campaign to them. He ignored the petulant complaints of columnists and so-called intellectuals and their calls and challenges for televised debates. In the long run, this seemed to have paid off because the rural and small town voters overwhelmingly went for Erap.

Erap's campaign platform and his set speeches tirelessly focused on the themes of *Trabaho para sa Pilipino* (Jobs for the Filipino), *Hustong Suweldo* (Adequate pay), and *Presyong abot-kaya ng lahat* (Affordable prices). The commissioned public polls said these were the main issues people were interested in so Erap's messages repeated them endlessly. Erap committed himself to putting the highest priority on agriculture (abolition of irrigation fees, tax-free sale of fertilizers, seeds and other inputs, farm to market roads). He promised low-cost housing, health services, and education and feeding programs for the children. He told people he was listening to their plight and that, when elected, he would launch the programs that would help them get out of poverty.

It was in playing the underdog that Erap got the most cheers and applause from his *masa* audience. The relentless attack on his lack of education, womanizing, gambling, drinking and association with undesirable characters helped make Erap even more popular with the masses because they felt he was being ganged up on by the elites and their hearts went out to him. Erap delighted his *masa* audience whenever he went on the attack against graft and corruption, "hoodlums in robes" and "rogues in uniform." He aroused the people's sympathy when he pointed out that the personal attacks on him were also attacks on the masses. By linking his campaign to the interests and aspirations of the masses, Erap was able to get their support, rise above regional interests and achieve an overwhelming nation-wide popularity that led to victory.

The 1998 presidential election requires political scientists interested in Philippine electoral behavior to rethink their conceptual frameworks and methods of analysis. In general, the old notions of patron-client relationships, dyadic relationships, the reliance on political elites and dynasties, regionalism and the use of tribal politics have to be either abandoned or re-conceptualized. In some regions (the Ilocos region, Cavite, Muslim Mindanao) local political machines still existed. However, the command votes they used to rely on have been weakened considerably. Even when political ward heelers thought they could "deliver" the votes, the old-line *trapos* found that this did not really happen. In many places, the people decided to vote their hearts and they voted for Erap.

# CHAPTER 12

# PRAISE THE LORD AND CAST YOUR BALLOTS

"BISHOPS TELL VOTERS: ANYBODY BUT ERAP."

The headline of the *Philippine Daily Inquirer* on election day, 11 May, was typical of the sudden importance of religion in the 1998 elections. The news item that followed revealed that the pastoral letter issued by the Catholic Bishops Conference of the Philippines (CBCP) to guide the faithful as they went out to vote that day, did not actually mention Erap Estrada's name. The pastoral letter, simply urged members of the flock to "Vote for persons who morally, intellectually and physically show themselves capable of inspiring the whole nation toward a hopeful future."

The *Inquirer* based its headline on the fact that the CBCP pastoral letter said "The things that will yield the death blow to our democracy and freedom will be false principles, *a disregard for the sacredness of the marriage vow and the obligations of family life* and a blindness to prevalent social injustices." The *Inquirer* simply linked the highlighted portion of this statement to the gratuitous observation that Erap "admits to a history of womanizing and boozing." To the sensation-seeking headline writer, this was enough to report that Erap had been completely rejected by the Bishops.

## The Church in Philippine Politics

The 1998 elections may be remembered as the first-time religious groups in the Philippines got involved in politics in such a blatant way. The Philippine Constitution adheres to the principle of separation of Church and State. Although the country's population is about 85% Roman Catholic, it is openly acknowledged that "there is no such thing as a Catholic vote." But this has not stopped the Catholic Church leadership from trying to create such a bloc.

A number of candidates in the past and at present have tried to get votes by being on the right side of the Church. The late Francisco "Soc" Rodrigo was known to have won a Senate seat because of Church support. Francisco "Kit" Tatad may owe his election to the Senate to his *Opus Dei* affiliation and the support of the Church. Corazon Aquino's personal piety, of course, and the support of Cardinal Jaime Sin, the vocal Archbishop of Manila, won her the presidency after the 1986 EDSA revolution. By and large, however, Filipino candidates avoid being too strongly associated with the Church, even as they avoid being identified as being against certain policy positions of the Church such as abortion, family planning, gambling, drinking or immorality.

To most political analysts, the Catholic Church in the Philippines has rarely been able to muster enough votes to get its chosen candidates elected. If the Church voted as a block, argued a political analyst, Ferdinand Marcos, an Aglipayan and Fidel V. Ramos, a Protestant, would not have been elected President. Dr.Juan Flavier, who opposed the Church's stand on family planning, and on the distribution of condoms, won a seat in the Senate despite a strong Church-backed campaign against him. In 1998, Cory Aquino's personal choice, Mayor Fred Lim, who was also strongly supported by many Church leaders, fared poorly at the polls. Senator Kit Tatad, the moral crusader, was never a serious contender in the vice presidential race. Nor was the pious Santiago Dumlao a serious presidential candidate.

How does one explain, then, the complex role of the Church in Philippine politics?

Most Filipinos are said to be "Sunday Catholics" if indeed, they bother to go to Church at all. In remote villages, people practice a form of folk Catholicism, a strange amalgam of animism, ancestor worship and superstition revealing traces of a pre-Spanish system of beliefs. Such bizarre rituals as nailing penitents on crosses on Good Friday, the belief in *anting-anting* (amulets) as a protection against bullets, or the adoration of Jose Rizal as a religious deity have more or less the same importance as the novenas to Our Lady of Perpetual Help or belief in Saint Jude as the patron of lost causes in the Filipino's pantheon of beliefs. It is not uncommon for corrupt officials, who will not do anything unless they are bribed, to have pictures of Jesus and the Holy Family beneath their glass table tops or for Filipino men to attend Mass on Sundays before visiting their mistresses.

The dominance of Catholics in the country's population works against the formation of a strong committed band of people and the need to act together as a disciplined group. On the other hand, members of local sects such as the Iglesia ni

Cristo, Aglipayans, and other groups such as Seventh Day Adventists, Mormons, Baptists and Presbyterians have little problem sharing a common identity and acting as a group. Not so the numerous Catholics, whose identity is muddled by other affiliations such as family, clan, province of origin, language spoken or school attended.

The Filipino's ambivalent attitude toward religion may be rooted in the country's perception of history. The main thrust of Filipino nationalism has a decidedly anti-clerical streak. The novels of the foremost national hero, Jose Rizal (*Noli me Tangere, El Filibusterismo),* that helped spark the revolution against Spain, drew up a portrait of the church as oppressive, manipulative and tyrannical and of friars as abusive, treacherous and lecherous. The revolution against Spain, in fact, was waged both to achieve political freedom and to free the people from the conservative hold of the Catholic Church. It was no accident that many of the key leaders of the Philippine revolution against Spain were Free Masons, who had strong anti-Church inclinations.

American colonization of the Philippines introduced compulsory mass public education that broke the hold of exclusive Church-run schools that had formerly educated and trained the children of the Filipino elite. The Americans also brought in thousands of Protestant missionaries who preached a more participatory style of worship and expounded democratic ideas (people actually spoke in their congregations freely and they sang hymns, unlike in Catholic rituals where liturgical prayers were recited by rote). Many Filipinos who wanted to be "modern" like the Americans embraced Protestantism in the 1920s and 1930s.

After World War II, many Filipino intellectuals flirted with Communism, which regarded religion as the opiate of the people. The University of the Philippines, where the nation's best and brightest students competitively went, strictly adhered to the principle of separation of church and state. The Americanization of Filipino culture through Hollywood movies and the mass media also helped to encourage questioning of traditional values, including those related to religion. Emphasis on achieving material progress and increased secularism also eroded the influence of the Church.

During the martial law years under Marcos, the palpable difference between the Filipino elite and the downtrodden rural and urban poor did not only fire up activists from the Left—many firm believers in the Catholic Church also advocated "Liberation theology" as a way of fighting social injustice. Quite a number of rebel priests in the Latin American tradition went to the hills to fight for justice and freedom. Nuns and priests, in fact, were at the forefront of the anti-Marcos struggle and they were most visible during the EDSA revolution. Such activism was fueled by many Papal Encyclicals such as *Veritate Splendor* in 1986 by Pope John Paul II, which stated that the Church has the right and obligation to participate in public life when a nation's leaders are losing touch with the people, arrogating powers unto themselves, and are adversely affecting justice and freedom.

The sudden growth of charismatic and "born again" Christian groups in the Philippines is of relatively recent vintage. Many people trace the advent of these groups to the successful crusades of evangelists in the United States which enterprising Filipino religious leaders have successfully copied. Television, of course, has given evangelical groups great popularity. The Protestant Jesus is Lord and Jesus Miracle Crusade are home-grown versions of popular movements in the United States.

To many poor and underprivileged Filipinos, the chance to participate in weekly televised activities, where people in their finest clothes sing and recite stories of miraculous religious conversions provide a strong psychological attraction. In El Shaddai, JIL, JMC and other born again groups, one can have his or her one minute of fame—shining in the glare of TV kleig lights. It is no surprise, then, that the intense rivalry between JIL and JMC does not revolve around differences in religious doctrine but over ownership of a television franchise. From the competition over a TV channel, it is only a few steps to an open contest for political power and influence.

## Church Groups in the 1998 Elections

While the Catholic Church has not been able to marshall votes to convincingly win elections, there have been cases in Philippine history when local religious sects have actively participated in politics. In the 1934 elections, the main opponent of the fiery Manuel L. Quezon for the presidency of the Philippine Commonwealth was Bishop Gregorio Aglipay of the Philippine Independent Church. Aglipay lost miserably but the nationalist church, which refuses to follow the dictates of Rome, has continued to thrive.

Since its founding, the Iglesia ni Cristo (INC) has delivered its "command votes" to candidates chosen by the sect's leaders, who base their decision on a scriptural call derived from the teachings of Saint Paul that the church must be "of one mind and one judgment." Under the leadership of its founder, Felix Manalo, the INC had no problem in exacting unwavering obedience from its members in voting for a chosen candidate. In recent years, questions have been raised about the ability of current leader, Eraño Manalo, to impose his will over more educated and enlightened followers. In 1998, the INC discreetly endorsed the presidential candidacy of LAMMP's Erap Estrada but split its ticket by also supporting Senator Gloria Macapagal Arroyo of Lakas-NUCD for vice president.

On 26 April 1998, the Jesus is Lord (JIL) charismatic movement, a Protestant "born again" group openly endorsed Speaker De Venecia as its candidate for president in a five-hour televised prayer rally at Manila's Luneta Park. Dubbed the Jesus Declaration of Victory (few missed the fact that the first letters of the rally's banner were Jose de Venecia's initials) the rally saw President Fidel Ramos liken De Venecia to Joshua, who received the "rod of authority" from Moses, the role Ramos appropriated for himself. De Venecia was formally anointed with holy oil by Brother Eddie Villanueva, declaring that "the President's choice is actually God's choice as our country's next leader." JIL and De Venecia claimed that more than three million people attended the rally. Police estimated the crowd at half that number.

On 3 May 1995, it was the turn of the Jesus Miracle Crusade (JMC) group to endorse Speaker Jose de Venecia's candidacy. Again, President Ramos was there to root for his chosen successor. In this rally, JMC head, Brother Wilde Almeda got so carried away with his endorsement that he announced that if De Venecia was not elected president, he would be willing to be shot at the Luneta. Cooler heads reminded him that they have stopped killing people by firing squad at the Luneta for more than a hundred years.

The largest charismatic Catholic group in the Philippines (claiming total membership of eight million people) is El Shaddai, headed by Brother Mike Velarde. In the week before the 11 May elections, there was widespread speculation on which candidates the group would support. On 3 May, banner headlines declared "El Shaddai Goes for Estrada, Tatad." The story went around that Brother Mike, attempting to avoid the intense pressures from both the government and the opposition, decided to reveal his choice through a secret code. Months before the election, Erap met with Brother Mike in Hong Kong where Brother Mike pledged his support to Erap and gave him the secret code words to shout at the end of his speech in a rally to be arranged. In a rally where all the presidential candidates were to give speeches to the group, the El Shaddai faithful was advised that any candidate saying the code words *Tiyak 'yon* (That's for sure) would be the one. At the rally, both Erap Estrada and Kit Tatad uttered the code words in their speeches and, each time, their pronouncements were greeted with thunderous applause.

The alleged endorsement by El Shaddai of Erap Estrada met with strong pressures from the party in power. It was reported that Brother Mike was facing serious charges of malversation of funds and that he was vulnerable to such pressures. On 10 May, a majority of the elders of El Shaddai announced that they were voting for De Venecia. However, Brother Mike himself adamantly refused to endorse anyone for president.

On 10 May, the day before the elections, the LAMMP Media Bureau and Mrs. Gina de Venecia tried to get Brother Mike to issue a statement endorsing their own candidate. Mrs. de Venecia had been booed in an earlier El Shaddai rally for promoting her husband too aggressively. In a wild Keystone Cops chase through three restaurants in Ayala, Alabang, the opposing camps tried to get the El Shaddai head to reveal his choice. When Velarde's statement finally came, read by Velarde's eldest son Franklin, it announced that he was not endorsing any one for President. Instead, he was allowing his flock to "vote freely and according to their conscience as it is their right to do so."

If the El Shaddai members are given complete freedom in voting for the candidate of their choice, the LAMMP claimed that they would vote for Estrada. In a public opinion poll conducted 15 to 28 April, the Asia Research Organization (ARO) revealed that among 1,350 respondents belonging to El Shaddai, 25% said they would vote for Estrada, 18% for Roco, 16% for Lim, 14% for De Venecia, 12% for De Villa, 3% for Imelda Marcos, 2% for Santiago, and 1% for Osmeña. Enrile, Morato and Dumlao got less than 1% each. In the Vice Presidential race, Gloria Macapagal got 53%, Orbos, 12%, Angara, 10%, Serge Osmeña, 8%, Tatad, 3% and Irene Santiago, 1%.

## The INC's "Egg" Farm

The Iglesia ni Cristo (INC) is the only religious group in the Philippines that can truly claim to deliver "command votes." At the New Era High School which had 31 precincts with 5,565 registered voters, 99% of whom are INC members, the election results showed the INC leadership's strong influence on its followers.

Estrada, the INC-supported presidential candidate garnered 3,278 votes while JdV and Roco received only eight votes each. Macapagal-Arroyo, the INC's candidate for VP got 3,279 votes while Erap's running mate Angara received only six. All 12 INC-supported senatorial candidates received more than 4,000 votes each. The rest of the candidates all got zero. Members of the Board of Election Inspectors who conducted the polls at the school have nicknamed the place the "egg" farm.

## The Sin-Aquino Anti-Cha-cha Rally

Easily the most important role the Catholic Church has played in recent Philippine politics is its active resistance to efforts to amend the Constitution to allow President Ramos and other incumbent officials to remain in office after 30 June 1998. This could have been done by lifting the Constitutional provision limiting a President's tenure to one term. It was also proposed that the terms of office of other elective officials be synchronized so that incumbent officials can remain in office until the year 2000.

The so-called Charter change or Cha-cha proposal was hatched by people close to President Ramos (the President himself insisted that he did not support the initiative, repeatedly announcing that he would "graduate" by 30 June 1998). Most ardent advocates for Cha-cha were former Ambassador Alberto Pedrosa and his wife Carmen who set up the People's Initiative for Reform, Modernization and Action (PIRMA). They were supported by government officials fearful of having to account for their misdeeds under a new administration or of losing their political clout to protect their selfish interest. Their goal was to gather more than six million signatures for a constitutional change (which requires 12% of the total number of registered voters) requesting that the presidential term limit be lifted so that President Ramos could run for re-election.

The Cha-cha proposal is allowed under Section 2, Article XVII of the Constitution that grants the people the right to directly propose constitutional amendments through initiative. This provision was implemented by Republic Act No. 6735, which was, however, ruled as "fatally flawed" and considered an insufficient basis to amend the Constitution by the Supreme Court on 19 March 1997. It set back the Charter changers somewhat but they remained undaunted.

It was the Cardinal Sin-Cory Aquino prayer rally at the Luneta, backed by all opposition parties, and attended by 1.5 million loudly protesting Filipinos, that showed President Ramos beyond any doubt, that the people would not allow anyone to tamper with the Constitution again.

How important is religion, then, in Philippine politics?

To casual observers, the 1998 elections seem to suggest that the leadership of the Catholic Church received a drubbing in the overwhelming votes that went to Erap. After Cardinal Sin called Erap morally unfit to be president and a probable disaster to the country, the people still voted for him. They also ignored the pastoral letter of the Catholic Bishops Conference not to vote for a person who has not lived up to his moral marital vows.

Even as the formal leadership of the Catholic Church was not listened to by the people, a charismatic sect within the Church, El Shaddai very heavily supported Erap. Despite strong pressures from the government and the administration party, members of the sect still went for Erap. The ruling factor in this vote, however, might not be religion at all. As the SWS poll revealed, most of the members of El Shaddai are drawn from the D and E voting groups. Thus, the support for Erap may be rooted more in the socio-economic origins of the El Shaddai members than on their religious membership.

It is interesting to speculate on the effects and impact of the strong endorsement by the JIL and JMC Protestant born-again groups for Speaker de Venecia on the future of these two political organizations in politics. As a tolerant individual, Erap is not one to vindictively go against people who did not support him. The more likely effect of the JIL and JMC action is the formation of some kind of a backlash among rabid Catholic and activist sections in the church. Until these two Protestant groups came out so openly for a candidate, they were generally tolerated and ignored. Now that the extent of their near-fanatical support for a candidate supported by their leaders has become apparent, some form of backlash might come about from more militant members of the Catholic Church.

# CHAPTER 13

# ELITES, MEDIA AND THE INTELLECTUALS

Our friend, Sandy Burton of *Time* magazine looked perplexed. "What do Filipinos mean when they say someone belongs to the A group?" she asked. "And how do you define D and E voters?"

Sandy was interviewing us for a piece she was writing for *Time* on the 1998 elections. We explained that some social scientists have divided Philippine society into five categories. The A group are the super-rich. They include tycoons living in exclusive "villages" in Makati or Mandaluyong, blue-blood *hacienda* owners in Negros or Tarlac province, rich loggers or mine owners in Mindanao, and top business leaders usually of Spanish or Chinese ancestry. Some of these tycoons are not even Filipinos, we said. They are likely to have several passports and have other homes in Spain or the United States. They are inclined more to give donations to political parties or back certain candidates rather than run for political office themselves. They probably hate politics.

The B group are the normal rich, high officials holding political office, successful entrepreneurs, people who are well educated, who tend to travel a lot and send their children abroad to study. They tend to have Chinese ancestry and prefer to live close together in compounds as extended families. You are likely to find them in less tony villages in Makati, Mandaluyong or Quezon City. Some of the older families have big compounds in San Juan, which used to be the preferred "suburb" of the rich.

The C group are middle class, with a high school or a college degree, both husband and wife working, receiving a comfortable salary or running a fairly profitable business but now and then concerned about the mortgage or not trading in the old car for a new one until the repair bills become too excessive. This would be the Filipino *burgis* which should not be confused with the European bourgeoisie. They are mostly professionals with high aspirations, concerned with raising their children properly and dreaming of sending them off to college abroad, if only they can get a scholarship. This is the middle class which liberal-minded social analysts hope will grow to make the Philippines a true democracy.

The D people are the *masa*, probably with elementary or high school education, employees in a small business or clerks in a government agency, small landowners working farms of less than three hectares, jeepney or taxi drivers working to meet their "boundaries," salesmen on commissions. They may be fishermen who own small boats, small time traders who buy and sell agricultural produce, stall owners in public markets. If employed in large companies, they are likely to be union members. The pollster Mahar Mangahas of SWS fame divides the D group into D-1 and D-2, the former roughly corresponding to the middle middle class and the latter the lower middle class.

The poorest group would be the E—which include migrant agricultural workers, laborers hauling cargo at the pier, ambulant vendors on the periphery of public markets, tenant farmers, persons who rent a small room in a crowded slum, or a squatter in a shanty town. The E group include the poorest of the poor—the unemployed, the sick, the handicapped, those who are dependent on the charity of others.

Proportionately, the A-B-C groups make up about 10% of Philippine society, the D group roughly 72% and the E 18%. The government says that 35.5% of Filipino families live below the poverty line. The World Bank says that is too optimistic—about 60% of Filipinos make do with an income of less than $100/ month.

Sandy wanted to know the significance of the candidacy of Erap Estrada, the importance of his popular slogan *Erap para sa mahirap,* and the reaction of the elite to the fact that Erap might end up the country's president. We explained that Erap probably had the middle and upper classes of society worried about the future. They are not too happy entrusting their future in the hands of a college drop-out, a self-confessed womanizer, gambler and hard drinker, although Erap has assured everyone that he has mellowed and changed.

With Erap's strong identification with the masses, it was not surprising that his candidacy was immediately rejected by the elite members of society. The more the common citizens and the poor people flocked to Erap's cause, the more strident the attacks on him became. The Catholic Church, especially Cardinal Sin and the Catholic Bishops Conference of the Philippines issued pastoral letters questioning Erap's moral fitness—they didn't think he would be such a great role model for the Filipino youth. Landowners worried about his intentions to really implement a land reform program. Business people, especially those linked to foreign markets were concerned about his leftist friends who might pursue an anti-foreign and protectionist economic policy. The Filipino *burgis* class, with its bloated sense of morality and intellectual pretensions shivered at the thought of a former movie actor, with a shady past who did not even finish college and who associates with questionable characters, as the leader of their country.

In the Philippines it is not easy to differentiate between the economic elite, the intellectual elite, the social elite and the political elite. As in other hierarchical societies, the Philippine elite monopolizes the factors that make for eliteness. If one is rich, one is also likely to be politically powerful, socially prominent, highly educated, well traveled and probably, physically beautiful or handsome as well. As Erap loves to say, once you are tops, you own all the marbles.

The elite's rejection of Erap may not be that difficult to understand in the context of Philippine social dynamics. On the surface, Erap is very much like the elite classes that look down on him. His family origins are upper middle class, he lives in the exclusive subdivision of North Greenhills, he has money, and he leads a life style that is not too different from the one led by the economic elites. That he was a movie actor who made his money from *bakya* crowd movies makes him less acceptable than opera singers or ballet dancers to rich elites with aesthetic and cultural pretensions. Having been kicked out of prestigious Ateneo and not finishing college would have been reason enough for elites with intellectual aspirations to reject him as well.

It is probably Erap's unembarrassed and complete identification with the plight of the *masa*, however, that has turned local elites against him and his candidacy. From the safety of their militarily guarded gated communities, the elites probably saw the threat of a candidate, who should be on their side, leading the charge of the barbarians at the gates. Erap's platform of social justice, his cry for land reform, his demand for social housing for squatters and slum dwellers are threatening to those who have already made it and want to protect what they own from those who would like to change things. That the person who is leading this clamor for radical changes is supposed to be one of their own probably heightens the sense of middle class and elite betrayal.

Whatever the reasons for the elite's rejection of Erap, the idea hit close to home when he lost in his own community of Greenhills on election day. This did not prevent the Greenhills Homeowners Association, however, from hoisting a huge banner saying "CONGRATULATIONS PRESIDENT-ELECT ERAP" the day after elections.

As one of Erap's die-hard supporters said upon seeing the sign, it's so like the elite to stab you in the back and embrace you at the same time.

## Erap and the Business Elite

No other group in the Philippines has probably been more anti-Erap than the super-rich business elites in the Makati Business Club, the Philippine Chamber of Commerce and Industry, and the American Chamber of Commerce and Industry. Some club members, worried about the dangers to business of an Erap presidency, raised funds to mount lobbies against the Erap campaign. Others members of the business elites supported their own candidates: the Zobel de Ayalas, for example, openly campaigned for Reforma's Renato de Villa. A newspaper item published an interview with a young child of a business elite family who shocked her peers by saying that if she could vote, she would vote for Erap. Her reason was simple—"My Mom and Dad said that if Erap wins, we will move to the United States."

Members of the Philippine business elite cautioned against capital flight in case of an Erap victory. They said that foreigners will not invest in the Philippines with Erap as president as they will be worried that Erap would not be able to manage the country. They expressed fear of a resurgence of crony capitalism as a number of business people associated with the late President Marcos are rumored to be strongly linked with Erap and are just raring to stage a comeback.

One of the LAMMP responses to the business elites' concerns about Erap was the announcement of the names of his "30 economic advisers." On the one hand, the open support of such business people as Cesar Virata, Edgardo Espiritu, Federico "Ding" Pascual, Jose Luis Yulo, Jose "Titoy" Pardo, Rafael Buenaventura, and Miguel Varela served to reassure the business elites that Erap would follow free market based economic policies. On the other hand, there were fears that the wide ideological differences among the Erap advisers—whose backgrounds ranged from protectionist nationalism to absolute *laissez-faire*—would send out confusing signals not just to local business but the regional and global communities.

There were some concerns, also, that some powerful business people would be "more equal than others" in an Erap administration, despite Erap's promise of a level playing field. Some names viewed with concern by the business elites were: Danding Cojuangco, Lucio Tan, William Gatchalian and John Gokongwei. It was feared that these business leaders, because of their known political links to Erap, might lord it over others during his presidency.

Calming the anxiety of the business elite succeeded somewhat at a P1,000 a plate lunch held at the New World Hotel on 19 May 1998. In a closed door dialogue with the Employers Confederation of the Philippines, the Makati Business Club, the Philippine Chamber of Commerce and Industry and the Management Association of the Philippines, Erap enunciated his philosophy that "Good economics is also governance and good social policy." Erap promised the business elites that his government would have "the least amount of regulations and the greatest number of opportunities." He also assured them that they would "always be consulted in all economic policies which we will put together."

With his background as a movie producer, an investor in real estate, and as owner of a number of business enterprises, it was not difficult for Erap to gain some of the confidence and the grudging support of the business elite. The support of some key members of this group helped. Some formerly anti-Erap business elites seemed pragmatically resigned to the fact that Erap had been elected by the people. They were anxious to make the best of what the political situation had dealt them.

The initial concerns and misunderstandings about Erap's alleged anti-business elite attitudes probably came from his close association with people ideologically identified with the left such as Boy Morales, Father Ed de la Torre, Karina Constantino David, Renato Constantino, Jr., Dodong Nemenzo, Liling Briones and other U.P. activist-academicians. It is worth noting, however, that almost all these progressively minded supporters of Erap have mellowed through the years.

Now married and probably more worried about child rearing than making revolution, the former firebrands of the left have turned progressive-liberal. Briones, for example, has not been active in the Freedom From Debt Coalition for the past two years—FDC is now headed by Ma. Teresa Diokno-Pascual. Briones is currently more concerned with balancing the U.P.'s budget as vice president for finance than waging an anti-IMF demonstration. Boy Morales has devoted his attention full time to the Philippine Rural Reconstruction Movement, although in the past five months or so, he had been active also in JEEP. Aside from accepting Erap's invitation to head the Agrarian Reform Commission, Boy has also agreed to devote his energies to doing everything to achieve food security in the country.

R.C. Constantino was initially active in the party list campaign of Sanlakas and Akbayan but he has recently spent more time on his private business concerns. His sister, Karina has accepted to be the head of the Anti-Poverty Commission. Father Ed gave up writing his newspaper column to work more actively in JEEP. Nemenzo now advocates parliamentary struggle and was active in the party list campaign for Akbayan despite his personal qualms about Ricardo Pascual's "partyless democracy" and its roots in the late U.P. professor's fascination with Italian fascism. He is mentioned as a likely candidate for U.P. president when Emil Javier finishes his term in 1999.

With Erap's leftist friends agreeing to join the establishment and respected members of the business elite supporting him fully, there is great anticipation in the business community that the initial suspicions about the economic directions of an Erap presidency would ease a bit. Erap is fully aware of the importance of business in the economic resurgence and continued development of the Philippines. He looks to business as the creator of wealth and the generator of jobs that would solve the high unemployment rates in the country. He is eager to establish confidence in the economy so that foreign investors would enter into partnerships with local business elites to set up more joint ventures.

## Erap and the Media

The Philippine media, made up of print, television, radio, the movies and the recording industry constitutes one of the most complex and ungovernable aggregation of egos, wealth and power in the country. It is not surprising, therefore, that different sectors in the media had different reactions to the Erap candidacy. Actually, there are as many sectors of media as there are channels and it is inaccurate to deal with media as if it is a coherent entity. For starters, it may be worthwhile dividing media into the money-making side of the business and the information collection and dissemination side.

Easily the item that grabbed the interest of the media in the 1998 elections was the political ad ban. The government, in an attempt to make entry into politics more accessible to people who may not have the money to support a full blown campaign prohibited the buying of advertising and other propaganda materials by candidates and their parties. This ban, of course, hit the media moguls where it hurts them most—in their pockets. During the 1998 elections, therefore, there were concerted efforts on the part of media owners to reconsider the political ad ban.

## The Ad Ban

Early in 1998 the Philippine media tried its best to have the ad ban lifted. All the Manila-based newspapers (*BusinessWorld*, *Isyu*, *Malaya*, *Manila Standard*, *The*

*Manila Chronicle*, *The Manila Times*, *The Philippine Daily Inquirer*, *The Philippine Journal*, *The Philippine Star* and *Today*), various media associations (The Philippine Press Institute, The National Association of Newspapers, and the National Association of Broadcasters in the Philippines) took out full-page ads in the papers explaining why Republic Act 6646, the law banning political advertisements, should be repealed. The petitioners were later joined by the Telecommunications and Broadcast Attorneys of the Philippines and GMA Network. The announcement was followed by forums, debates and workshops televised and/or broadcast over radios. Newspaper columnists, TV talk show hosts and radio commentators extolled the virtues of freedom of the press and the enlightening effect on the public of unfettered political advertising at least during the 90-day campaign period.

Republic Act 6646 was passed in 1987, under the Cory Aquino government, to level the playing field for all candidates. In the words of the Supreme Court, the goal of the political ad ban was "to equalize the situations of the rich and poor candidates by preventing the former from enjoying the undue advantage offered by huge campaign war chests."

The proponents of lifting the ad ban argued that RA 6646 had not succeeded in its noble goal. They said that the incumbent officials, showbiz and sports personalities and prominent media people turned politicians enjoyed an undue advantage over relatively unknown candidates because they were already well known—as celebrities, they did not have to advertise. It was the relatively unknown candidates who had to advertise to make the voters know more about them, especially the fact that they tend to be more qualified than the celebrities. The ad ban prevents them from doing that.

The lift-the-ad-ban advocates pointed out that while rich candidates may not advertise in newspapers, TV or radio, they can spend their money on other campaign activities and materials that are unaffordable to their poor rivals. Thus, the ban does not really level the playing field. It just denies candidates the chance to be better known. It also prevents the media owners from earning more money, of course.

Arguing that the 1998 elections were crucial, because the country would be electing a president that would preside over a country hit by the Asian economic crisis, going into the next millennium, and that an estimated 100,000 candidates were vying for 17,000 elective posts, the media proponents of lifting the ad ban urged the Senate to repeal the ban in time for the start of the 1998 campaign period. The Senate responded by shelving the bill to lift the ad ban thus committing it to its doom, at least for the May 1998 elections.

Presidential aspirant Lito Osmeña petitioned the Supreme Court to lift the ban on political advertising. The Supreme Court played Osmeña an April Fools joke by dismissing the petition on 1 April. By a vote of 10-4 the high court upheld the mandate of the Comelec "to procure and itself allocate to the candidates space and time in the media."

The petitioners contended that the Comelec is ineffective in supervising publicity campaigns in radio, television and newspapers of almost 100,000 candidates and 17,000 national and local positions which works to the disadvantage and deprivation of unknown but better qualified candidates.

The Comelec asked the Supreme Court to dismiss the petition claiming the SC has already upheld the constitutionality of the law in the 1991 case "National Press Club vs Comelec."

"The Supreme Court having already examined the law in question and upheld its validity, its pronouncements, therefore is stamped with finality," the poll body said. And the ad ban controversy was laid to rest at least until the next election.

Actually the media people did not seem to really care about leveling the playing field for rich and poor candidates. Their combined efforts to lift the ad ban were more driven by the need for ad revenue than concern for competent candidates with limited campaign funds. So it did not take long for the media and the politicians to find ways and means to get around the ad ban.

Because the ad ban was not lifted, hurting media owners have tried many schemes to circumvent it. In this, a number of candidates have become willing accomplices. For example, some candidates launched their political communication efforts before they actually filed their certificates of candidacy. In this way, they were able to take advantage of the technicality that the messages they were airing were not political advertising. Technically, because they were not candidates yet, they were not in violation of the ad ban.

There were also widespread rumors that because the media could not make money legitimately, they had "sold" their editorial pages (or space and time in the case of radio and TV) to the highest bidders. As media analysts in LAMMP, we spent many hours doing content analysis of the columns and editorials of all the mainstream newspapers to detect any political biases which resulted from these "purchases." We also spent hours listening to radio broadcasts and watching TV programs to detect any slants in treatment, especially against our candidate.

We did note that many columnists did not even try to hide their partisanship. At least four columnists used their writings to blatantly campaign for their chosen candidates. One constantly printed the results of university mock polls showing his candidate winning in even the most obscure provincial diploma mill institution. Another took advantage of every opportunity to attack and needle Erap—when we inquired from Erap supporters and family members why this person had such a vitriolic attitude toward our candidate, we were informed that he once approached Erap for money to support a project and he was turned down. There was the columnist who used the column unashamedly to push for a candidate who could in turn do something for a spouse's career. Two columnists were so convinced of their own genius and analytical prowess that they could not see anything right in Erap's candidacy—they regarded Erap as simple-minded, attacked him for refusing to engage in intellectual debates, made fun of his 30 advisers, and aired dire warnings of confusion when the advisers start making *bulong* (whispers) in Erap's ears and he would not know how to decide because he had nothing between his ears.

In Philippine journalism, the tradition of reporters and columnists on the take is part of the carefully nurtured image of the tough hard-bitten newspaper person as observer-chronicler-participant cynically existing in the "real world." The term "envelopmental journalism" has become a cliche—it means that when reporters are invited to attend a press conference, it is customary for the public official inviting them to hand out little envelops with cash inside. It does not matter how one calls the bribe. *Pamasahe lang 'yan* (Just for transportation expenses) is the usual excuse. The amounts are often quite modest—P2,000 to P4,000—unless a "special favor" is requested (a press release to be printed, a sensitive story to be killed). Then, the amounts become quite significant.

Journalist salaries are very low in the Philippines and that is the usual excuse for receiving money from politicians and other people needing publicity and other services. The most common service provided is ghost writing—politicians are quite willing to pay journalists for drafting speeches, writing special reports, preparing "vanity publications" such as biographies or books for election purposes, etc. From such rather innocent and above-board services, journalists may turn to darker activities. For example, "dirty secrets" dug up by journalists about public officials may be withdrawn from publication for the right price. Such arrangements may reach the point where it already involves blackmail and criminal extortion. During the 1998 campaign, a number of "white papers" circulated widely, giving graphic details of the sexcapades of candidates and supposedly secret information about corrupt deals. These aberrations we saw as not only parts of dirty tricks but often as preludes to blackmail.

A week into the official opening of the campaign season in January 1998, we were approached by a well known journalist offering a "package of services" for Erap. The journalist said that he and his friends noticed that Erap was not getting a very good press. Many of the good things he was doing were not getting into print. However, negative things were coming out all the time. To our practiced friend's eye, it was obvious that no one was actively managing the information about our candidate. Our visitor said that he knew that Rod Reyes, who is the LAMMP Campaign Officer in charge of media, is an honest and straight guy. Maybe that was the problem—good guys don't get good press in this business.

Our journalist visitor had an interesting proposition. He and four of his friends will handle Erap's media relations full time. They will guarantee that only good things about Erap will be printed, broadcast or disseminated. They will not confine their work to Metro Manila—in fact, for Erap to win, it is more important to get him greater exposure in the provinces and non-metropolitan cities. The services will cover all media—print, radio, TV. It will also include communication in English, Tagalog and all the major languages and dialects.

The group would be be happy to base the payment for their services on a "performance standard" basis. Thus, if Erap's approval rating as measured by SWS polls is 28% at a certain date, they will guarantee that this approval rating will reach 35% or more within two months. If the SWS poll does not reach the desired target, they will not bill us for their service fees—only for actual operational expenses. However, if the polls exceed the set target, they will be expecting a bonus. The package deal offered to us was priced at P10 million. It was a very professional offer but we did not even take it to the party's management committee. It was just too much money for the campaign to handle. Besides, LAMMP already had a full-time Media Bureau and hiring another outfit, whose operations will most likely be quite sensitive was just too much.

## Media Elitism and Arrogance

A far more difficult task to deal with in media relations has to do with the inflated egos and intellectual arrogance of media personalities such as columnists, TV anchors, radio broadcasters, editors, etc. As Campaign Officers involved in Policy Issues and Media Relations, it was one of our duties to ensure that ideas atrributed to Erap were accurate, verifiable, and truthful. This usually involved monitoring news items, editorials, column materials and opinion pieces. It also included writing letters to the editor, at times, usually about some trivial affair that could have been prevented if someone just took the trouble to check data or to talk to the right source.

One particular letter to the editor we enjoyed writing concerned a *Philippine Daily Inquirer* headline on 21 February 1998 that read: CARDINAL'S MESSAGE: NO TO ERAP. We noted that the pastoral letter of Cardinal Sin never really mentioned Erap's name when giving instructions to the faithful on how to choose a candidate. We argued that the paper was "putting word's in Sin's mouth" since all the Cardinal said in his pastoral letter was that people should vote according to their conscience and guard against being manipulated by popularity surveys. The headline writer concluded that the Cardinal was referring to Erap because he was leading in the surveys. To our surprise, the *Inquirer* printed our letter.

It was an even bigger surprise when we received a letter from Cardinal Sin himself, thanking us for our clarification. "You are very kind," the good Cardinal wrote, "Please accept my pastoral affection."

Much of the media elite's concern about an Erap presidency arises from the traditional idea of what an ideal presidential candidate should be. Unfortunately, in the eyes of the elite, Erap (or any of the 11 candidates for the presidency for that matter) just do not measure up. The columnist, Teddy Benigno, typifies this harking back to the past:

> There was a time in the '50s and '60s, and earlier during the Commonwealth Period, when we Filipinos set the tone and the model for an emerging Third World democracy. We had some of the best technocrats in Asia, our education and literacy were one of the highest. Our presidential system of governance was envied. And that was not surprising at all for we had giants like Manuel Quezon, Claro Recto, Sergio Osmeña, Jose Laurel, Lorenzo Sumulong, Benigno Aquino, Jr., Jose Diokno and Ramos Magsaysay, each of whom did or would have done our country proud as chief of state.

Alas, according to Benigno, in the 1998 elections, "...what passes for a presidential campaign today, with eleven 'serious' candidates, has become aimless, boisterously empty, so downright disgusting. We are not given the choice of the best and the brightest but the choice of the celebrity and the machine."

In this ideal presidential contest, according to the media elites, the candidates would all have high IQ, college degrees, scholarly capabilities, courage, humility and honesty. The candidates would be untainted by any accusation of graft and corruption. They would all lead clean moral lives, love their spouses (only one per candidate allowed at any one time), devote quality time to their children, and live in a simple but comfortable home. The candidates would have risen from poverty and succeeded only by dint of intellectual brilliance, hard work, perseverance and clean living. The candidates will have only honest loyal friends (no shadowy underworld characters), play their roles happily as community leaders, and attend church regularly. They should dress neatly, simply and not gaudily, be handsome or beautiful or at least, charming, be cheerful and not be seen having a tantrum or a bad hair day, and never never be seen having a foul mood.

Electoral campaigns in this ideal world will feature the airing of the candidates' views in the market place of ideas. There would be high-minded debates where the key issues in the campaign would be discussed. The candidates would represent political parties whose principled stands on the key development issues would be eloquently articulated. The electorate would choose the best candidate from this list of the ablest and the best. The elections would be honest, orderly, and peaceful.

After the elections, all the bitter rivals will respect the people's will. The winners will be magnanimous in victory and the losers will be good sports and show this by cooperating with the victorious ones. Everyone will participate in the inauguration rituals and the winning party will formulate and implement its program of governance based on the best ideas of both the winning and losing political parties. Programs and projects will be implemented until the next election campaign comes. Then, the whole rational cycle starts all over again.

This ideal situation, of course, exists only in the imagination of the media elite. Even they, in their coldly rational moments, probably know that it is impossible to achieve the ideal campaign in reality. However, the elites maintain the dream because it is theirs—if the teeming masses come up with a new idea or a candidate challenges the dream, it is there to be used to belittle such efforts. In the Philippines, the members of the intelligentsia are quick to trot out the dream when a credible threat comes around. The most vociferous of these elites are the newspaper columnists, about 120 of them just for the three top English language newspapers in Manila and they never fail to foist the dream on the public when needed. In 1998, Erap's candidacy was measured against the dream and, of course, was found wanting.

Not just Erap but all the candidates contesting the 1998 elections were described as mediocre by the media elites—arrogant media pundits advised people to vote "None of the Above" when faced with the list. The worst insults were aimed at Erap—he was judged to be morally unfit to be president, a poor role model for the young, a person incapable of representing the Philippines in front of other prominent leaders, probably a potential disaster for the country. The media elite all hailed the importance of democracy in the country but it was to be democracy on their own terms. The *masang tanga* (stupid masses) were adjudged incapable of choosing their own candidates. Thus, the individual vote of a person belonging to the masses was not equal to the vote of a member of the media elite. Since the masses were voting for Erap, the election of Erap was unacceptable.

## The Media for Sale

With the political ad ban, candidates could no longer buy newspaper space or airtime on TV or radio to advertise their many virtues and accomplishments. This affected not only the candiates' campaign but the media people's pockets as well. After all, advertising revenues, not subscriptions, are what keep the newspapers, TV networks and radio stations afloat. Something had to be done about revenue.

Fortunately for the candidates, the Philippine media was for sale in many more ways than just buying advertising space and time. The low salaries paid to journalists and other media people easily justified earning money on the sides. It has been reported that some editors of newspapers were quite willing to be on "retainers" earning as much as P50,000 per week for regularly putting out favorable stories about favored clients. Some editors and reporters get paid by the piece or by the column inch. A media handler for a candidate revealed to us that at a national daily, the going rate for a page 1 photo was P5,000, P1,000 of which went to the reporter as broker and P4,000 to the editor who agreed to put it out. The candidate's media bureau was happy over this arrangement because it was cheaper than the price of a similar sized paid advertisement in the inside pages.

A presidential candidate's photo on the front page may cost P15,000; a senatorial candidate pays only P10,000 for the same space. A banner story costs P25,000, a front page above the fold, P20,000, and a short press release without photo is P,5000. At these rates, a P50,000 weekly retainer to an editor seemed like a bargain.

Some magazines allegedly charged Media Bureaus P50,000 for a cover story, favorable to their candidate, especially if the item is disguised as news. The candidate gets 10,000 copies of the magazine for free. Some publications will even distribute these free copies in remote areas where the candidate is not known.

Even the venerable Radio Veritas-Global Broadcasting System, Inc. which played a vital role during the Edsa Revolution of 1986 that toppled the Marcos dictatorship, was alleged to have succumbed to selling airtime for political promotional materials in exchange for payoffs, according to a *Manila Times* report on election day. For "pre-arranged" coverage of political events and interviews, the following rates applied: studio-phone guesting with ZNN stations from 8:00 to 9:00 A.M., P20,000 for presidential and VP candidates, P10,000 for senatorial candidates and P5,000 for local candidates. For phone interviews lasting for five to 10 minutes, P5,000 for presidential and VP candidates, P2,500 for senatorial candidates, P2,000 for local candidates. For straight news with voice clips, P750, and P500 for those without voice clips. For field reports with interview with candidate, P1,000, and P500 for those without any interview with the candidate.

Special contracts were allegedly offered by Radio Veritas to political parties at a bargain price of P5 million for radio "pre-arranged coverage" from February, the start of the campaign period until June when the successful candidates were to be proclaimed.

During the campaign, there was a proliferation of journalists moonlighting as media consultants offering full media coverage (print, TV and radio) for a fee. Some newspaper columnists, TV talk show hosts, and radio commentators were shamelessly partisan raising the question of whether they were on the payroll of certain candidates or not.

Several letters to the editor of the *Philippine Daily Inquirer* condemned Belinda Olivares Cunanan, an *Inquirer* columnist, for her blatant use of her column to promote her candidate, Jose de Venecia, President Ramos' anointed one. One reader claimed that Cunanan's bias was due to the appointment of her husband, General Thelmo Cunanan, as ambassador by President Ramos. There were calls for Cunanan to resign for ethical reasons, or at least to take a leave of absence if she wanted to continue her propaganda work for JdV. She did not resign. Nor was she fired by the *Inquirer* for unethical conduct. There was widespread belief among Manila's media circles that the top management of the paper was known to support a particular candidate.

Manila-based media did not have a monopoly on media corruption. In the provinces, the practices associated with *warik* and *tigbas* were quite widespread. *Warik* is Cebuano slang denoting an unscrupulous person; *tigbas* is the Cebuano word for "cut" equivalent to the Tagalog term *taga.* Both words mean exacting a fee or price from a person being victimized. Thus, in Cebu, Davao, Cagayan de Oro or

General Santos, politicians and local officials are sometimes subjected to extortionist demands by journalists. If they do not come up with the accustomed cut, unsavory information about them might be published.

*Wariks* usually buy blocks of time on AM radio stations for their programs. They then use these programs to either extol those who have given them money or attack those who have not. An hour of blocktime usually costs P3,500. *Warik* blocktimers pass themselves off as legitimate public affairs programs but their main occupation is extortion and blackmail.

Horror stories about the *wariks* and *tigbas* have been reported in Manila's mainstream papers. According to these reports, *wariks* and *tigbas* have victimized presidential candidate Lito Osmeña who was once stuck with a P10,000 restaurant bill for an alleged press conference. That's peanuts compared to the P100,000 another presidential candidate was supposed to have paid a mainstream legitimate journalist to facilitate a press conference in Davao City. A *warik* who came late and missed the bounty that senatorial candidate Lisandro Abadia had distributed to other earlier reporters, grabbed Abadia's wallet after Abadia supposedly said he had run out of money. Another presidential candidate, Fred Lim, was supposedly offered a favorable banner story for P10,000.

The media hustlers are known to knock on candidate's hotel rooms in the dead of night, either to solicit advertisements or simply extort money. They work in cahoots with hotel personnel and restaurant waiters who give them tips they can use for or against a candidate.

Publishers practicing *tigbas* usually have no qualms about using their papers to earn money from politicians. Some publications appear only during election time precisely for this purpose. Some *tigbas* editors would even publish a favorable article about a candidate the day before that candidate visits the city so the *tigbas* reporter could show the candidate a copy and say that the paper was favorably inclined toward him or her. Editors of these fly-by-night papers justify the corrupt practices by saying that community reporters are paid so little that they have to be corrupt in order to survive. Many provincial reporters of community papers receive only allowances ranging from P1,000 to P2,000 a month.

In Iloilo province, radio blocktimers are known to specialize in mudslinging. Blocktime radio programs are sponsored by politicians whose names are promoted by their anchors. They are not covered by the political ad ban because the promotion is presented as legitimate news or as a public affairs program. The radio hosts would also attack his sponsor's political foes. Womanizing, gambling and fabricated corruption stories dominate these programs.

Around ten known blocktime programs were aired by DYBQ, a radio station previously owned by former Ambassador Roberto Benedicto but sequestered by the government in 1986. DYBQ is the only radio station in Iloilo without a morning, noontime and evening newscast because these time slots had been leased to blocktimers. Other radio stations allowed blocktimers only on weekends.

It was common practice for radio stations to precede a blocktimer program with a disclaimer to protect the station against libel and damage suits. According to industry sources, a political blocktime in Iloilo usually costs between P5,000 and P8,000 an hour, depending on the time slot. Blocktimers do not have regular sponsors. The hosts have to court politicians to pay for the airtime, salaries and production costs. News anchors and talk-show hosts usually end up in the candidate's payroll as well because they also come under the influence of blocktime promoters.

The spread of corruption through all ranks of the media—from publishers and editors down to the most junior cub reporter—has spawned a number of terms for these types of corrupt media people. In addition to *wariks* and *tigbas,* they are also called *iswis, pitpit*, and *"taga"* press. The mercenery media people have also coined some new terms to describe their operations: AC-DC is not a term in electrical engineering nor the appellation for a bisexual person—in the murky world of corrupt Philippine media, it means Attack/Collect - Defend/Collect. "Envelopmental" journalists have been replaced by ATM journalists. The old fashioned job of ad soliciting has been replaced by "Orbiting," which is journalese for a media person who regularly goes the rounds of politicians, business leaders, and others needing publicity asking for trips abroad, money to pay school expenses for their children or for hospital bills, or a down payment for a house and lot. Such soliciting often becomes extortion especially when the patrons have something to hide.

The Philippine media is famous (or notorious) for its freedom and excesses. It is not surprising, therefore, that during an election campaign, media practitioners see themselves as important people who can either make or break a person. In some instances, the media people cease to become king makers and become the kings and queens themselves. With the "starization" of Philippine politics, Loren Legarda and Rene Cayetano have moved on from becoming media luminaries to senators.

Corruption in the media, however, has become the concern of many Filipinos who worry about the future of the country. Are media people to blame for accepting the bribes and special offers of politicians or are politicians to blame for corrupting the media? The moral dilemma is difficult to solve, especially since, in some instances, the media people themselves become the politicians.

In the case of the Erap candidacy, quite a number of the media elite took it upon themselves to question the candidate's qualifications, his moral background, and his program of government. To the extent that they were expressing their views as opinion leaders, that was entirely legitimate. There were some media elites who attacked Erap because they believed that another person they were supporting was a better candidate. Again, provided that the attacks on Erap were factual and not fabricated, there was nothing wrong about that.

It is in cases where the media elites attacked Erap because they were paid to do so, or they were on the payroll of some anti-Erap group, that the media corruption in the Philippines becomes a real cause for concern. Of course, in the case of media entrepreneurs and blocktimers who used their programs to extract money or who blackmailed candidates, there is no doubt that in these cases, we are dealing with criminality.

The role of media in a democracy like the Philippines deserves more research and attention. In some instances, the media as the Fourth Estate idealistically safeguards political freedom. At other times, media becomes an instrument of propaganda and serves to stifle that very freedom. In the 1998 elections, there were corrupt journalists and idealistic and clean journalists. In the words of a hard-boiled journalist friend of ours who has seen it all, "Why will you expect an honest media in a corrupt society?" Why, indeed?

## Erap and the Intellectuals

Another group that initially rejected Erap as a presidential candidate were the intellectuals. Resident intellectuals in college campuses, research centers and other academic institutions, university administrators, faculty members and student leaders were not attracted to the Erap camp, with the exception of some U.P. professors and leftist intellectuals who had seen Erap as a sincere advocate of social justice and as a person who was willing to listen to their social reform plans.

In the Philippines, being an intellectual is associated with four things. First, intellectuals are in the groves of academe—they teach, they write, they do research, they publish books and journal articles. Second, intellectuals are ideologues, they passionately believe in certain things—Communism, nationalism, social justice, agrarian reform—they are committed to a cause. Third, intellectuals are creative—they write novels, poems, short stories, plays—they are advocates of an indigenous Filipino art and believe in a national genius. Finally, intellectuals are supposed to be impractical, not concerned with wealth, status or fame, they look at politics with disdain, they expect recognition to come to them, they will never seek out something that will result in personal gain.

With these popular images of intellectuals, Erap, with his lack of an academic record, is seemingly at a disadvantage when dealing with them. In truth, however, Erap has more intellectual friends and advisers than most Filipino leaders. The reason for this has been mentioned by many—intellectuals see Erap as a person who seeks advice, who is willing to listen. Unemcumbered by a self-image as an intellectual, Erap is quite able to talk with intellectuals on his own terms. Thus, intellectual elites with specific policy goals see Erap as sympathetic and supportive of those goals. He gives them the opportunity to translate their abstract concepts into real action that will benefit the people.

Erap, however, seems most at ease with intellectuals of an artistic and cultural bent. His years in the movies enable him to empathize with these creative people. His strong sense of nationalism is inspiring to lovers of culture, songs, dance, literature, sculpture, painting, and the arts. Erap is regarded as a strong supporter and patron of artistic activities. His aesthetic sense is respected by many intellectuals, especially since he is able to translate it into something financially successful, like the movies.

Despite these positive aspects, there were intellectuals of course, who were not supporters of Erap's presidential aspirations.The general intellectual dissatisfaction with Erap expressed itself in disappointment over his refusal to defend his program of government before them in university forums and symposia. They sometimes expressed this dissatisfaction by making available to the media the results of small university mock polls showing Lim, Roco, De Villa or Santiago as the candidates of choice in campuses, with Erap invariably trailing way behind. The only cheerful note to the Erap strategists was the fact that De Venecia was even getting worse treatment on campuses than Erap.

The refusal to appear in university campuses, however, was not universal. Erap readily accepted invitations to speak before students in universities and colleges outside Manila. In such institutions as the Central Luzon Agricultural University in Munoz, Nueva Ecija, at the Polytechnic University of Pangasinan in

Dagupan, and in other rural-based institutions, Erap met with the students and faculty and discussed his vision and plans for the country's development. In these campuses, Erap was received very well. It was in the elitist unfriendly campuses of the large universities in Metro Manila where Erap encountered some opposition.

Presidential forums were organized by the political science department of U.P., the College of Law of Ateneo University, the business management department of the Asia Pacific University, foreign service department of De La Salle University, interest groups such as Cocofed, business associations such as the Makati Business Club and the Philippine Employeers Associations. Erap generally refused to participate in these forums usually giving the excuse of lack of time. In truth, however, the LAMMP campaign strategists believed that these forums were organized more to benefit the organizers than to shed genuine light on issues. In organizing campaign activities the Scheduling Team also saw these elitist activities as a waste of time.

The media reports coming out of of these events proved the strategists right. The reports were almost always critical of the candidates who participated in the forums. However, the criticisms were mainly focused not on substance but on extraneous things such as the candidates' physical characteristics and styles of delivery: Roco's nervous tic, his glib answers and tendency to use kilometric words to appear erudite; Erap's mumble, his stumbling over certain words, his pompadour hair style and bristly moustache; Lim's monotone and his Robocop stiffness; De Villa's scowl and small-town parochialism; Morato's dead-fish eyes and fastidious earnestness; Osmeña's big teeth and his provincial shallowness; De Venecia's droopy eyebrows and baggy eyes and his verbal diarrhea; Dumlao's ever dangling crucifix and cock-eyed economic theories; and Santiago's unique "Ilonggish" accent and her acid tongue—these seemed to be the only things college audiences could remember about the forums and what they talked about. There were hardly any analysis of issues and so-called panelists and commentators were more intent on preening before live audiences than focusing on substantive matters.

The idea of a debate would have been good if there were only two or three presidential candidates. But in a field of 11, even if not all of them showed up, too many debaters had very little time for honest interchange of ideas. The forums, then, turned out to be mechanisms for prepared recitations of what candidates will do, what they have done in the past, and why the audience should vote for them. In rare occasions, there were real sparks of debate on the campus. In general, however, most of the events were boring, superficial and an utter waste of the candidates' time and efforts.

One debate that could have been great, however, was the one where De Venecia and Erap were to meet one-on-one, *mano a mano*, without the benefit of seconds or the meddling of media elites eager to increase their popularity ratings. The thing started with a challenge by Speaker De Venecia to Erap to debate the economic situation in the country. A cocky De Venecia said that Erap could bring along his 30 advisers if he wanted to, he was ready to take them all on.

The challenge was debated by the Policy and Media Group in LAMMP. There were the usual dismissing views—De Venecia is desperate, his popularity rating is stuck in single digits, he needs a media event—why give him that event? We have more to lose in that debate. This election is going to be won in the villages, far from Metro Manila. Why waste Erap's time in Metro Manila?

De Venecia, however, will not drop the issue. He said Erap was just too chicken to meet him. He was being protected by his handlers who doubted his ability to engage in an intellectual discussion. Erap was not only *bobo* (stupid), he was a coward too.

In one of the rare moments in the campaign when we disagreed with the rational view, we wrote in a briefing memo that there was something to be gained from accepting De Venecia's challenge. JdV had issued the challenge to meet either at the Manila Overseas Press Club or the National Press Club. Why not accept the challenge but hold the debate in Plaza Miranda in Quiapo or Plaza Moriones in Tondo? De Venecia was the challenger—in any challenge, the person challenged has the right to choose venue (or weapons). We proposed to Erap—accept the challenge by De Venecia but tell him, Meet me in Plaza Miranda!

The following morning's headline was: ERAP TO JDV: SEE YOU IN PLAZA MIRANDA.

To political scientists who know their history, Plaza Miranda is the hallowed spot for debates. In fact, one only has to recall the late President Magsaysay's criterion for any government program to appreciate the meaning of the place. Magsaysay's ultimate test of any proposal was: "Can we defend this in Plaza Miranda?"

On Plaza Miranda, in front of the Quiapo Church that houses the miraculous image of the Black Nazarene, generations of Filipinos had listened to their leaders debate the great issues of the day. Quezon challenged Osmeña at a Plaza Miranda debate. The great Claro M. Recto challenged General Carlos P. Romulo to a presidential debate in Plaza Miranda but, unfortunately, that debate fizzled out because Romulo went to deliver his speech in another plaza instead. In the years after World War II, great rallies and countless *miting de avance* were held in the small square. They only stopped when a grenade thrown at a Nacionalista Party rally almost wiped out the whole senatorial slate of the party and injured prominent people like Senator Salonga and Mayor Ramon Bagatsing.

We got very excited about the prospect of a Plaza Miranda Great Debate and started researching in-depth Q & A (Question and Answer) briefing memos for it. Unfortunately, Speaker De Venecia ruined everything by raising issues about Erap's health and issued another challenge that he and Erap should undergo a treadmill test first to show if both were healthy enough to take on the job of president. Erap got peeved by this silly test and challenged De Venecia to a boxing bout instead. From then on, the issue was dropped and the Philippine public missed a great opportunity to see the two main challengers for the presidency take each other on in a real debate.

So, instead of enlightened discussions of issues, the 1998 election season featured a few TV debates and open presidential forums. Perhaps, it was just as well because public debates, especially those on television, are really not the best occasions to discuss intellectual issues. The media and academic elites hold the mistaken belief that presidential debates give the voters substantive information about the issues of the day. The truth is, TV as a medium does not encourage intellectual discourse. The bright images on the screen are just too distracting for a true exchange of ideas. As shown in the Nixon-Kennedy debates, the Clinton-Bush debates and even the vice presidential debates, TV favors the sound bite rather than sound reasoning, the witty quip to the reasoned discourse, the nice pleasant face to the brilliant idea. Who can forget the perfect squelch that killed the vice presidential ambitions of Dan Quayle: "I have known President Kennedy, Mr. Quayle and let me tell you, you are no Jack Kennedy!" Nasty, mean, a grab for the jugular. But absolutely devastating.

## The Erap Response to the Elites

Faced with the stubborn rejection of the elite, the Erap political strategists decided, from the very outset that the focus of the electoral campaign would be on the *masa*. The elites could be safely ignored since they made up only a tenth of the voting population. True, many members of the elite owned factories that employed many poorer workers and they might influence them not to vote for Erap. Others may control a number of "command votes" they could deliver to De Venecia, Lim, Roco or other candidates of the elite. It did not matter. Ignoring the elite was a risk worth taking.

The policy of ignoring the elite took the form of Erap's refusal to appear in televised debates or to discuss his party platform in campus symposia. Invitations by Makati business groups for Erap to explain his program of government to them were generally turned down. So were invitations by prestigious universities such as Ateneo, De la Salle and the University of the Philippines.

These refusals were met with derision. Accusations were aired that Erap was scared, that his minders were worried he would trip and make a mistake in answering questions. He was described as being a know nothing, someone weak in economics, an inarticulate clod who could not defend his program of government because he had no program of government. An especially mean columnist devoted column inches of diatribe on Erap as the "silent candidate." Another repeatedly called him a coward, which was the ultimate insult to this very macho man.

A few TV debates where Erap participated in confirmed the wisdom of the "ignore the elite" maneuver. After a well attended "debate" held at the Manila Mandarin Hotel, it became quite obvious that these occasions were aimed more at the entertainment of the so-called intellectual elites than genuine efforts to shed light on what the candidates stood for. Erap friend Congressman Joker Arroyo advised strongly against accepting any more debates. "These individuals are running for President of the Philippines," Joker said, "they should be treated with more respect. They should not be lined up like so many student debaters and made to perform, only to be asked silly questions like 'Define globalization.' They should refuse to be judged by third-rate journalists and alleged intellectuals."

It also became quite obvious from some of the invitations that one of the intentions of the debate organizers was to trip the candidates so that one major mistake could cost them the election. Some of the LAMMP strategists questioned why Erap should be exposed to this kind of risk. Manny Zamora, who chaired the Management Committee, was completely against participating in the debates.

"In the United States," observed Manny, "debates were a normal part of the campaign because the people expected them. Even there, however, the candidates who were ahead in the polls usually did not favor debates. Why should they? The debates only allowed lesser known candidates to gain media exposure while the leading candidates took the risk of making a mistake. We are way ahead of the game. Why should we expose our candidate to risks and help our opponents by letting them share the same stage with him?"

Manny and his brother Ronnie Zamora were fully conversant with the Kennedy-Nixon debates. They observed that the debates were most favorable to Kennedy because he was the young challenger, relatively unknown, and he was considered a lightweight because his record in the Senate was so skimpy. Nixon fell into the trap of debating with Kennedy on TV because of hubris—he was a combative debater in college, had a great deal more experience, and was very conversant with all the issues. What he did not count on was the merciless eye of the camera that caught Nixon's dark beard, his shifty dark eyes, his pointy nose and his quirky nervous movements. Next to Kennedy's youthful good looks, tousled hair, easy grin, and flat Boston accent, Nixon was dead meat.

Zamora brothers Manny and Ronnie had no doubt at all that Erap would do well in any televised debate. As a veteran movie actor, he had the professional touch and the natural feel for performing on the stage. He had the good looks and the easy charm that compared well with the others. He was quick with the quip, had perfect timing for the punchy comments, knew exactly when to come up with the perfect sound bite. The problem, however, was that the format of the televised debates provided very little time to each candidate for Erap to use all these advantages. With all eleven candidates present, each one was lucky to have three minutes within which to explain programs. Panelists were not of much help as they were more interested in looking and sounding cute than really finding out what the candidates thought of key issues facing the nation.

Erap's relationships with the intellectual and academic elites were better than those with the business and media elites. As already mentioned, many of these intellectuals had been with Erap for some time. They shared his love and identification with the poor, his nationalistic stand, his artistic inclinations and his belief in social justice. They appreciated his willingness to listen and openness to new ideas. They were grateful to him for providing the opportunity to translate some of their theories into action.

What, then, will be Erap's relationships with the business, media, intellectual and artistic elite of the country? In one of his thoughtful columns, Adrian Cristobal said that Erap's victory has shown that "the elite has been routed." In a not-so-gentle slap at the elite, Adrian wrote: "Somehow, one can't help feeling that when the defeated elites say that President Estrada must be supported for the sake of 'national unity,' they merely want to be 'united' with the winner on whom they did not place an iota of faith during the campaign. A blunt person would say, 'Who needs your support? I have the support of the people.'"

However, the advice of Adrian Cristobal to President Erap is also blunt: "A revolution fails not concretely but for being untrue to its intentions." If Erap does the right thing, Adrian said, "as he and his people see it, it won't matter very much if he does not succeed in all of them."

Having ignored the elites in his campaign, Erap now has to deal with them. As Adrian observes, "It isn't Estrada's image that needs refurbishing for the benefit of the business class and the elite, but the other way around. He has been a star and knows all about 'images.' His best adviser is Polonius: To thine own self be true."

# PART IV

## THE CENTENNIAL PRESIDENT

*Family celebration after Erap's electoral victory. L-R, Pat de Guzman, Eleanor Laquian, the President-elect, Raul de Guzman and Prod Laquian*

# Chapter 14

# The Erap Program of Government

When Raul de Guzman and his wife Pat first asked us to help in the Erap campaign, we accepted with great enthusiasm. We had grand romantic visions of late-night strategy sessions with Erap like the ones the Kennedy brothers were supposed to have had with their political advisers at Hyannis Port. We fantasized about long discussions with Erap at his Greenhills home where we would analyze the results of the latest public opinion polls or review the draft outline of a history-making policy speech. Our imaginations were inflamed by the excitement of a presidential quest. We said we would explore the possibility of going on sabbatical leave from UBC to write a book about the campaign—the perfect cover for our political activities.

We tested the political waters in the summer of 1996 as two *balikbayans* on holidays in Manila. Raul had invited us to join a Policy Studies Group he had been running for the past three years in the Office of the Vice President. The PSG had been meeting every Thursday afternoon at the OVP, on the second floor of the Philippine International Convention Center (PICC). It was composed of U.P. public administration professors, a number of retired civil servants, a couple of military types, some political operatives, and old OVP staff Erap inherited from former Vice President Salvador "Doy" Laurel when he assumed the second most powerful office in the land. The membership of the PSG expanded or contracted according to the tasks at hand. Sometimes, the group would meet at the U.P. College of Public Administration in Diliman, Quezon City but the usual routine was to hold the Thursday Club meetings at the PICC.

Ever the public administration professor, Raul had assigned to the PSG the drafting of an Erap program of government. We were amazed at what we thought was Raul's naiveté. Putting on our best hard-boiled political strategist stance, we stressed the importance of a campaign organization instead. We argued that what was needed was a well-oiled campaign that could kick the butt of the party in power by bringing Erap's message of *Erap para sa Mahirap* directly to the people. A theoretical program of government, to us, was not important for an Erap victory—popularity, political machinery and plenty of money were the keys to victory.

Like Raul, most Filipino intellectuals believe that elections should be won or lost on the basis of issues. What will an Erap government do compared to what a De Venecia administration promises to do? How realistically does each candidate diagnose the Philippine socio-economic situation and how logical is the program of government he or she proposes to deal with the country's problem? In other words, the enlightened voter, it is hoped, asks the question: what will a presidential candidate do, if elected, to make life better for the Filipino?

The first PSG meeting we attended crushed whatever fantasies we had that this group could serve as the Erap "think tank." A retired professor of public finance was invited by Raul to give a paper on taxation. We thought he would come up with policy statements on how an Erap presidency might improve Customs and internal revenue collections—a key policy concern for an incoming president. To our disappointment, the professor gave a boring lecture on principles of taxation and quoted detailed regulations on how to implement the law on the value-added tax. There were long irrelevant anecdotes about corruption at Customs and BIR but no suggestions on how to solve the problem. It was a wasted afternoon. The only thing that saved the meeting for us was the tasty *merienda* that Mai Reforma had thoughtfully ordered.

Subsequent PSG meetings confirmed our initial impression that we were wasting our time with these Thursday Club efforts to formulate a program of government. The format of the meetings was almost always the same: an invited guest speaker spoke endlessly and a free-for-all open forum followed, if there was any time left. The 20 or so PSG participants said whatever popped in their heads, there was no discipline and very little regard for time. Group members came completely unprepared for discussions, they rarely read the papers provided by the presenters. Detailed minutes of the meetings were meticulously prepared but no one raised any questions about these except, occasionally, someone would complain that his or her name had not been spelled right or was left out. A couple of participants loved to hear their own voices too much, they had the rare gift of talking a lot without actually saying anything. A lot of valuable time was wasted listening to reminiscences and anecdotes from retired officials who had nothing better to do.

Not wanting to appear uncooperative or arrogant but emboldened by our acquired Canadian sense of efficiency, belief in the wise use of time, openness and frankness, we told Raul that the PSG as set up, was inadequate to respond to Erap's need for policy advice. If he wanted a good program of government, more technically prepared professionals were needed. We suggested inviting a few friends with expertise in specific policy areas to join the PSG. However, some of these experts did not share our enthusiasm for the idea of Erap as president. A few self-absorbed intellectuals doubted that Erap had the capacity to run the country. Others were turned off by his alleged womanizing, drinking and other vices. Many said they were too busy to spend an afternoon a week even for a good cause. After a frustrating couple of months wrestling with an Erap program of government that summer, we returned to Canada promising Raul that we would think about what difference Erap would make in the future of the Philippines. However, our first brush with the realities of Philippine politics had dashed cold water on our initial enthusiasm.

The following summer of 1997, we returned to the Philippines better prepared. Like good academicians, we had brought Raul a number of books that we thought important for the campaign. First, we handed him a copy of Theodore H. White's *The Making of the President, 1960* (Atheneum, 1961) the classic story of how Kennedy's Camelot began. This, to us, is still one of the best accounts of a presidential campaign ever written. A rather slim volume, Joe McGinnis' *The Selling of the President* (Trident Press, 1968) was less literary but useful—it detailed the media strategies for Richard Nixon's 1968 presidential campaign.

Two books, hot off the press, we thought Raul should read, Dick Morris' *Behind the Oval Office: Winning the Presidency in the Nineties* (Random House, 1997) which was a fascinating account of how Clinton was re-elected, and Ed Rollins' *Bare Knuckles and Back Rooms: My Life in American Politics* (Broadway Books, 1996) which chronicled the Ronald Reagan 1984 campaign. We thought that these blood-and-guts books on modern campaigning were excellent guides for an Erap strategist like Raul.

For good measure, we also gave Raul David Halbertsam's *The Best and the Brightest* (Pan Books, 1974) and Richard Goodwin's *Remembering America: a Voice from the Sixties* (Harper and Rowe, 1988). We could not shake the idea that the Kennedy campaign was the right model for the Erap crusade. We felt the same kind of emotional rush, the belief in a great historical cause that we associated with the Kennedy Camelot years (we were both graduate students at Boston University, Harvard and MIT in the early 1960s). In 1998, we felt that an Erap win would be as earth-shaking as Kennedy's electoral victory then. We believed it would change the course of Philippine history if Erap was elected by the masses directly instead of winning because of elite coalitions and machinations by traditional politicians.

Getting back to harsh reality, we told Raul that Erap's weak *Partido ng Masang Pilipino* would not be enough to get him elected. Where would the money for the campaign come from? Who would be the prime movers in the campaign? What media strategy would be used to kick-butt the party in power? How can the showbiz friends of Erap help in the campaign? Is there a grand strategy for the whole effort? A patient Raul just listened to our ranting and raving, after which he said quietly that other people were looking after those things. Erap had assigned to him the job of formulating a program of government and he needed our help for that.

## The JEEP Platform Committee

A chance meeting at Erap's Greenhills home with JEEP President, Robert Aventajado, gave us the opportunity to participate in the policy discussions of the JEEP Platform Committee. On its own, JEEP had been running policy meetings at its headquarters on the $26^{th}$ floor of the Pacific Star Building, where one must leave an ID card with the security guard to enter, in Makati. We were very impressed with the JEEP Platform Committee when we attended its meetings for the first time.

The question raised by Erap critics much much later about the "30 Erap advisers" and what he would do in the midst of their disagreements was clearly brought home to us at the JEEP meeting. It was held in a plush conference room dominated by a huge picture of Erap wielding an Armalite rifle in his movie role of Tonyo in *Sa Kuko ng Agila*,(In the Eagle's Talons) an anti-US bases movie. The larger than life picture, shot 40 or 50 lbs. ago, heightened our sense of unreality about the whole room. There was also incongruity in discussing poverty and social justice concerns amidst such opulent surroundings.

The meeting brought together U.P. economics professors Benjamin Diokno, Gonzalo Jurado and Felipe Medalla; Makati business people Titoy Pardo, Art Alvendia and Abraham Co; World Bank economists Vic Paqueo, Orlando Sacay, Ned Santiago, and Ed Campos; and cause-oriented progressive "leftists" Horacio "Boy" Morales, Edicio "Father Ed" de la Torre, and Fely Villareal. To our surprise, the meeting was friendly, warm and very civilized—there was no open clash of ideologies among the group members although it was obvious from the discussions that individual perceptions of issues differed widely.

These were, indeed, strange bedfellows in an Erap campaign but they were typical of the intellectual lights attracted to the Erap flame. There were personal links, of course—the U.P. professors were friends of Robert who took economics at the state university. Boy was head honcho of the Beta Sigma fraternity and he dragged some members along who just happened to be with the World Bank. Fely and Ed had been together in "agitprop" (agitation-propaganda) activities with Central Luzon farmers. We had known most of the people in our long careers—the only strangers to us were the Makati business types. Still, we knew the great disdain of the Makati Business Club for Erap and it was great to actually see some of them in this camp.

The economists, both from U.P. and the World Bank gave a lot of credit to the Ramos government's economic program. This was not surprising because quite a number of them had been advisers to President Ramos before the De Venecia *trapos* took over. An initial program of government drafted by the group started with the following statement:

> After an extended period of political decline, economic stagnation and social deterioration due to the excesses of corruption and cronyism associated with the Marcos regime, the Philippines finally restored constitutional democracy, embarked on a process of structural reform in the economy and took cognizance of the crisis in the social fabric. The national awakening and reorientation began in 1986 under the leadership of President Aquino and is continuing under the able stewardship of President Ramos.

The positive tone of the proposed program of governance bothered us—if things were so great under Ramos, why were we pushing for Erap? However, the economists had the numbers—from zero growth, the economy was zipping along at 5 to 6% per year. Even the incidence of poverty, if the Ramos state of the nation speech was to be believed, had gone down from more than 40% to about 35.5% of all households. The Philippine economy, while not as great as Malaysia or Thailand, was not that bad. The economists thought that, at least, it was not as vulnerable to global or regional influences as other Asian economies precisely because it was still at a low level of development.

### The Philippine Situation

Our own evaluation of the Philippine situation was a great deal more dismal than the one portrayed by our economist friends from the World Bank. The agricultural sector, on which more than 50% of Filipinos depended for their livelihood, has a production rate of 3 metric tons per hectare,one of the lowest in Asia. The country has been importing 515 metric tons of rice annualy 720,000 metric tons of corn. Manufacturing was practically stagnant at 2% per year. Worse, the distribution of the fruits of production was very uneven—the richest 20% of Filipinos received 50% of the national income while the poorest 40% received only 17%. President Ramos could contest the accusation of the Catholic Bishop's Conference that the poor were becoming poorer and the rich richer in the Philippines with official statistics but both the World Bank and the Asian Development Bank evaluations of the economy did not share the government's optimism.

Unemployment in the Philippines was between 8 to 12% and under-employment was probably more than double that. Compared to other Asian countries, the Philippine social indicators were not good. The infant mortality rate was 45.8 per 1,000 live births compared to 13 in Singapore and 36 in Thailand. The Philippine population, growing at 2.3% per year, had the highest rate of growth in Asia—during the Aquino years, in fact, our per capita economic growth rate was actually negative because babies were born faster than the production of goods and services.

Only 68% of children who entered grade 1 finished grade 6. About 3.4 million families lacked adequate housing. The Philippines was known as the "kidnap capital of Asia," and *Fortune* magazine ranked it as the second most corrupt country in the region (next only to Indonesia). As Filipinos living abroad, we could discern all these problems with cold eyes. Surely, we thought, these assessments justified why Erap should be elected president of the Philippines.

The issue of "continuity" of the Ramos economic policies became the bone of contention among the potential Erap policy advisers. The World Bank and U.P. economists were full-square behind continuity—they batted for liberalization, deregulation, privatization and globalization. They argued strongly for the dismantling of tariffs, quotas, licensing arrangements and non-tariff barriers to trade. They wanted to reduce excessive regulations on investments and local and international trade. They proposed to dispose of "non-performing government assets" not only to raise revenue but to make governmental operations more efficient. They argued vehemently for the wisdom of following the market and removing all policies and programs that got in the way of economic competitiveness.

Most of our U.P. public administration and political science colleagues disagreed almost violently with these views. Leonor "Liling" Briones was of the view that the drastic cutback in social services demanded by a drastic 25% across-the-board cut in the government's budget imposed as a World Bank "conditionality" hurt the poor too deeply. She argued that a more selective cutback would have been less harmful to the poor. Romy Ocampo also deplored the reduction in social services, particularly in social housing. Danny Reyes disagreed with the government's policies on privatization—he felt that the sale of the country's "family jewels," while solving immediate problems of public finance, would come back to haunt the government later. Unfortunately, said Danny, this would probably happen during an Erap presidency.

In these policy debates, we found ourselves siding with the public administration realists and progressive "leftists" who did not quite agree with the economists' blind faith in the market. Having seen the devastating effects of World Bank-imposed structural adjustment policies in Africa and Latin America on the poor and the underprivileged, we could not be that sanguine about free markets and "the invisible hand." We argued strongly for "safety nets" and the need to ensure that the imperfections of the market should be dealt with to lessen the negative effects of liberal policies on the poor. We did not even start to consider yet the devastating effects of free market economic ideas on the environment, social justice, basic human rights, and the destruction of the commons.

We reserved our most vehement attacks on the Ramos government's unfortunate choice of imagery in the Philippine *bibingka* (rice cake) as the analogy for having a larger cake first before ensuring that each person's slice can be larger. To us, this sounded dangerously like "trickle down economics." Having lived in China for six years during the early Deng Xiaoping years, we were familiar with the argument that "It is all right to be rich, and for some people to be initially richer than others." However, the Philippines was not China and we felt that the rich in the Philippines had already pocketed too much of the country's wealth. As far as trickle down economics was concerned, we agreed with John Kenneth Galbraith's definition of it as "a sparrow following a horse and hoping to get some of its droppings."

## Erap's Priority Concerns

To help resolve some of the group's policy disputes, we arranged a meeting with Erap at the JEEP headquarters. Erap amazingly arrived on time. He walked around the room shaking hands and greeting old friends. He laughed at the Macho Tonyo picture on the wall and asked, "What is that doing there?" He was very relaxed, sat at the head of the table and, never one for small talk, said, "*O, papa'ano, mag-umpisa na tayo.*" (Okay, let's get started.)

We took turns expressing our views on what should be included in a program of government and Erap listened attentively. Everyone stuck to his or her three minutes, having been warned that Erap easily got bored with long lectures. Erap did not take notes and asked only a few questions. Then, he spelled out his policy concerns in "bullets" form snapping out the issues one by one.

First, he wanted the highest priority given to agriculture. He said that as a senator, he was accused of having authored only two bills: one on irrigation and another on protecting the carabao. He wanted these laws implemented in an Erap administration because they will help the farmers.

Second, Filipinos must have decent jobs.

Third, something must be done about prices. What good is a job if the basic necessities of life were too expensive?

Fourth, basic education must be improved. He wanted poor kids to have both a school feeding and a "brain feeding" program.

Fifth, health and sanitation must be raised to higher standards. He did not just want more hospitals—preventive health and programs for mothers and children were needed.

Sixth, the environment must be protected and conserved. The destruction of our forests and oceans as well as the pollution in big cities required urgent attention.

Seventh, social housing must be provided. Erap said that when he was Mayor of San Juan, he moved 1,800 squatter families to Taytay, Rizal, where they are happy now. He wanted a social housing program as successful as Taytay.

Eighth, peace and order must be restored. He said he would finish what he started with PACC to stop crime.

Ninth, graft and corruption will be reduced if not eradicated. Erap said that the most effective way to solve graft and corruption was to ensure that anyone found guilty would be prosecuted and jailed. Within the first 100 days of an Erap administration, he said, there will be a few good "samples" of grafters who will be jailed—then, the others might mend their ways.

Tenth, decentralization must be fully implemented. Erap said that as a former Mayor, he knew that local officials are capable of running their own governments. He will assume the position of Secretary of the Interior and Local Governments himself to make sure that decentralization will be achieved.

It was an impressive performance. In a few quick moments, Erap had stated what the country could look forward to in the event he was elected President of the Philippines. The most amazing part of it all was that he had expressed his vision of governance in highly personal terms. This was not a cold-eyed strategist figuring out how to win an election. This was a man with clear ideas of what he wanted to do and strong feelings about how he would go about doing it.

In laying out his policy concerns, Erap expressed the proposed programs in terms of a personal vision. The areas of governance he enumerated came from inside him, they were not intellectual pieces he was laying out to the group in a logical manner. The best parts of the presentation on his program of government were those that arose from his experience as Mayor of San Juan. He admitted that solving the problems of the Philippines would be a lot more complicated than dealing with San Juan but, basically, he believed that if the policy approaches were honest, transparent and not tainted with any corrupt motives, what worked in San Juan would work for the Philippines too.

After the discussions with Erap, it was decided that the PSG and the JEEP platform committee would divide the responsibility for preparing the Erap vision of government. The PSG looked after the social development sectors of the program: agriculture, education, health, civil service reform, judicial reform, infrastructure, peace and order, housing and urban development, and decentralization of authority to local governments. The JEEP committee, in turn, would prepare the sections on macro-economic development, public finance, the regulatory environment, industry and manufacturing, employment, poverty alleviation, environment, and financing the program.

Drafts of the various sections were prepared and circulated. In October 1997, a joint meeting of the PSG and the JEEP platform committee was held to consolidate all the reports into one document. By that time, the LAMMP coalition had been formed and a party platform was needed for the party convention.

Both the PSG and the JEEP were very concerned about the final LAMMP party platform to avoid a repeat of the convention of the *Partido ng Masang Pilipino* in 1997 when the party platform document was rushed and it turned out to be inadequate. It contained a mere listing of issues (1-35), a lot of ill-conceived cartoons and empty rhetorical phrases.

Sure enough, the LAMMP party platform turned out to be another near disaster.

The first complete draft of the program was put together by Gonz Jurado of the U.P. School of Economics. It had the nice balance between the substantive robustness and intellectual weight of the initial documents and the inspirational flourish of a propaganda tract needed for a party convention. However, enroute to the convention, the personality and other differences between the LAMMP Secretariat and JEEP muddled the situation. Somehow, the LAMMP Secretariat decided to write and print its own Program of Governance, basing its product on an eclectic picking of sections from the PSG submissions and its own. The printed Program of Governance circulated at the LAMMP Convention on 18 January, therefore, was *bakla* (hermaphroditic)—it was neither JEEP nor PSG and it lacked the coherence of the draft prepared by Jurado. Seeing this printed platform, we just consoled ourselves with our original belief that no one reads party platforms anyway and that they don't influence election outcomes.

If the official Erap Program of Government printed by LAMMP is not a good guide to what people can expect from an Erap presidency, it may be useful to indicate here our reading of what Erap will implement in the next six years. This is based on a number of discussions with him on the subject, listening to his speeches, and following him around the country in the three-month campaign period. These programs come from Erap's heart, they are the "lessons learned" from his more than three decades of experience as a public servant. They reflect his true perception of what the Philippines needs and how he would deal with those needs. They reflect what Erap himself has said in unguarded moments and are based on what we had observed when Erap takes action. In other words, the following programs are personalized actions that we believe Erap himself will do. They reflect what can be expected in an Erap presidency as set forth in the Vision of Governance we presented to him (see Appendix 1) as defined by the LAMMP party platform.

## Agriculture and Food Security

The top priority, in Erap's view, is food. Every Filipino is entitled to three square meals a day, no Filipino should have to go to bed hungry.

To Erap, one of the most serious mistakes of the Ramos administration was the neglect of agriculture. He attributed this to the desire of the government to become a NIC (newly industrializing country) like Korea, Singapore, Hong Kong and Taiwan; it placed all its eggs in the special economic zones basket. The economic rationale for this policy seemed to have been that if the Philippines produced enough high-tech stuff (say computer motherboards), it would earn enough foreign exchange that could be used to import rice and other food stuff. To Erap, this was the argument that resulted in serious rice shortage that the Philippines faces every year.

Erap vehemently disagreed with this policy. To him, the Philippines must have food security. In one argument, he asked—suppose we have money from exporting high tech goods but Vietnam or Thailand refuses to sell us any more rice because they need it themselves. How can we eat computer chips?

The Erap program of government, therefore, would expand agricultural and fisheries production. To Erap, this meant setting up more irrigation systems. He recalls a Cabinet meeting when he was still actively attending them when they were discussing the rice crisis. President Ramos asked Secretary Roberto Sebastian why rice yields in the Philippines were so low. He said Secretary Sebastian stated that there were three solutions to the rice shortage problem and they were "Irrigation, irrigation, and irrigation."

Erap vowed that under his administration, irrigated crop lands would be dramatically expanded. The emphasis would be on building shallow tube wells rather than large and complicated irrigation systems that require so much in terms of water pumping, construction and maintenance of irrigation canals, and systems management. Many irrigation systems in the past failed because of graft and corruption—contractors built shallow canals and supplied inferior pumps, collectors pocketed irrigation fees, people hired to maintain the canals did not do their jobs.

To Erap, placing the responsibility for irrigation systems on the shoulders of cooperatives and irrigation associations would increase efficiency and effectiveness as it would involve the people most benefited by irrigation—the farmers themselves. He believed that reducing the bureaucracy in charge of irrigation would help make the system more effective.

Erap wanted irrigation fees abolished. In addition, other farm inputs (better seeds, fertilizers, insecticides, pesticides) would be sold to farmers at a lower price because they will be imported tax-free. Post-harvest technologies such as better dryers for crops, rodent-proof warehouses, and food processing would be provided. Low interest loans would be extended to farmers in order to help them buy more inputs and avail of professional agricultural extension services.

Another bottleneck to agricultural development was lack of access to credit. Many small farmers could not improve their productive activities because they had to pay exorbitant interest to money lenders. Revitalization of farmers cooperatives and marketing associations would make money available to farmers on easy term loans. Rural banks and other financial institutions would be strengthened in an Erap presidency to serve the farmers better.

Research and development in agriculture has been neglected as academic institutions have had their budgets cut and the private sector has not been encouraged to look into higher value-added products based on agriculture. Under an Erap administration, the nation-wide system of state universities would be mobilized to carry out more R & D. At the same time, the private business sector would be provided with incentives to develop more and better products. Agriculture, as the key to Philippine development, should be given the highest priority in public funding. At the same time, the main thrust of agricultural development and productivity should be carried by the private sector to achieve efficiency and timely response to people's needs.

The Erap agricultural program, then, will implement policies and programs of agrarian reform. Past land reform programs have been emasculated by high officials who are, themselves, big landowners. The main intervention to implement land reform is to provide credit and technical assistance to farmer beneficiaries. In the past, many agrarian reform projects reverted to landlordism because land awardees found it too difficult and unprofitable to till a small piece of land without adequate logistical and backstopping support.

It was interesting that in presenting his agricultural program, Erap did not assume the role of the expert like De Venecia who gives the impression he thinks he knows everything. Erap had never farmed in his life although he did play the role of a tenant farmer in a number of movies. What Erap advocates to improve agriculture comes from his having listened to farmers and poor people. What impressed us most in the policy advisers' group was the extent to which he had personalized the situation and how consistent his "feel" for the situation was with the numbers crunched by the so-called experts.

## Jobs for the Masses

With an unemployment rate of more than 8% and an under-employment rate probably double that the Philippines faces a severe crisis in human resources development. The country has to send more than 8 million of its citizens abroad for them to earn a living. While the remittances of overseas Filipino workers (OFWs) help the economy a lot, it also creates many problems such as skills shortages in key areas, abandonment of families, and juvenile delinquency among neglected children. Besides, some Filipinos working abroad are subject to abuse, loss of dignity, and even physical harm and death.

To Erap, agriculture is still the best solution to joblessness as our labor-intensive methods readily absorb workers. Jobs are available not only in agricultural production but in food processing, marketing, transport, and exports. Self-employment is regarded by Erap as one of the best absorbers of human resources. In this regard, availability of credit to small scale entrepreneurs, especially those involved in the informal sector of the economy, is seen as a key solution to unemployment.

The private sector will be the main provider of jobs in an Erap presidency. While emergency employment may be made available through government job creation programs, these would be temporary and meant primarily to only tide people over during rough times. Focus will be on encouraging the private sector to invest more in productive activities, that will provide more employment.

To maximize employment opportunities, infrastructure projects will be launched, especially in depressed areas. These will include farm to market roads, irrigation systems, water, sewerage and drainage, dredging of rivers and lakes, maintenance of highways and roads, etc. As these infrastructures make possible further investments in private enterprises, the jobs created will add to further productivity.

An educated and skilled work force is essential for further Philippine productivity. Vocational and trade schools will be given high priority in an Erap administration. Modeled after the Don Bosco school system where students learn and earn through well-designed vocational programs, public schools programs will prepare the students with marketable skills. Scholarships, apprenticeships and work study programs will be expanded. Training and education in high technology fields, such as in computing and electronics, will be stressed in the school curricula.

A group of advisers on education had recommended to Erap the setting up of a Youth Service Corps that will give young people opportunities to earn while they learn. A special credit program will be made available to young people entering into business ventures. Tertiary education will be emphasized, especially in courses that are geared to higher production and more efficient management of private and public enterprises.

## Stable and Affordable Prices

Erap's concern for the poor is reflected in his views on stable and affordable prices. To Erap, efficient production is the key to economic stability. While he believes in the ability of the market to keep prices stable, Erap argues that governmental intervention is needed to keep prices affordable so that price fluctuations will not negatively affect the welfare of the poor.

An Erap administration will maintain an adequate stock of prime commodities such as rice and corn so that the price of these commodities does not get manipulated by speculators. Maintaining an assured price for these staples, in Erap's view, would encourage farmers to maintain production levels. If necessary, adequate grains would be imported to maintain buffer stocks. However, improvements in production technologies and management, in Erap's view, should be the main policy instrument in keeping prices stable.

One of the most serious problems in the Philippines, of course, is that the country imports practically every drop of the oil products it consumes. Erap believes in opening up the oil industry to competition to prevent the manipulation of oil prices by cartelized oil companies. Since the price of gasoline and other oil products greatly affects the prices of other commodities, an effective oil policy is important.

## Education and Skills Training

To a college drop-out like Erap, the importance of education in a person's career advancement is obvious. "Not everyone is as lucky as I am," he once said to us, "at least, I was able to do well in the movies. To most Filipinos, having an education is the main guarantee of a good job and a good life."

Erap is acutely aware that the poor are severely disadvantaged by our educational system. This is because the children of the poor do not get adequate preparation before they enter the formal school system.

"The children of the rich," argues Erap, "go to nursery at three or four, then go on to prep and finally, kindergarten. All before they are six years old. So, when they enter first grade, they already know how to read and write. Their vocabulary has been enriched by watching TV and having parents who talk to them and read to them before they go to bed."

How about the children of the poor? They enter grade one without any preparation. They go to school hungry and therefore find it difficult to concentrate. Worse, the teachers in public schools earn very little and are not properly motivated. Their minds are bothered by many problems—not enough money at home, too many deductions from their pay, corrupt principals asking for too many contributions. So, how can the children of the poor compete in this unequal system?

Erap observed that in the good old days, the graduates from public schools had the best chances of going on to college. Because entrance into the University of the Philippines was based solely on academic merit, such public school graduates dominated the student body. At present, observed Erap, only the children of the rich—the graduates of private exclusive schools, are the ones who can get into the U.P. Merit is still required as the main criterion for entrance into the state university. The difference, however, is that with the disadvantage faced by the children of the poor who can only afford to study in the public school system, they cannot compete on the basis of pure merit anymore.

To Erap, the improvement of the school system starts at the pre-school level. He wants to launch a school feeding and "brain feeding" program. In other words, the children of the poor should attend nursery, prep and kindergarten and they should be given nutritious meals as well as taught their lessons properly. This is going to be a very expensive program but Erap believes that with the support of teachers, parents and community leaders, it should be possible to do it.

The situation of teachers, of course, demands immediate attention. Erap is keenly aware that with their low salaries, teachers are forced to engage in other activities to augment their income. For example, many teachers pool their resources together to run school canteens. However, in order to earn enough, they usually serve junk food and easy to serve items. This has the double disadvantage to children that they do not only have poor teachers, they also receive poor nutrition. To Erap, therefore, increasing the salaries and benefits of teachers and improving their motivation should help in making the educational system more effective.

## Health and Sanitation

The higher education and literacy rates of Filipinos help in maintaining good health and sanitation because most parents and children are aware of the importance of hygiene and nutrition in keeping their health. Poverty, however, is still the main cause for poor health and sanitation. To Erap, improvement in basic services such as clean water, sanitary toilets, and efficient collection and disposal of waste are keys to better health.

Married to a physician and having both a sister and a brother who are medical doctors, Erap is a firm believer in a good health system. However, he is aware that hospitals and clinics are not the solution to proper health. He understands that health depends on more basic things—good food, awareness and knowledge of proper nutrition, good habits and hygiene, exercise, and preventive health programs are the important things. An Erap program of government, therefore, gives top priority to these items.

One of the sensitive areas Erap will have to face in his presidency is family health. During the political campaign, Erap steered clear of the subject of family planning because the Catholic Church is against it. When asked about this now, Erap is in favor of a family planning program. He feels that every couple has the right to decide whether they will have children or not, how many children they will have, and when they will have them.

"The relationship between a person and his God is a personal matter," argues Erap. "If a couple want to know about family planning, they have the right to have access to such information. If they want to postpone having a child through contraception, they should have the right to choose what method to use to do this. If their religion prohibits them from using artificial method, that is fine. But if they want to use other methods, they should have the right to do so."

As a firm believer in the sanctity of human life, Erap does not believe that abortion should be considered a family planning method. He believes that the health services should not offer abortion as a means of limiting population growth. In this, Erap is committed to the position of the United Nations that does not see abortion as an acceptable family planning method.

## Environment Protection and Conservation

With less than 15% of Philippine forests still standing and coastal areas and coral reefs almost completely devastated by pollution, an Erap administration has its job cut out for it in the field of environment. Slash and burn agriculturists have followed loggers in destroying our timber resources. Fishermen using dynamite and poison have depleted our fish and aquatic resources. In Philippine cities, once mighty rivers like the Pasig are little better than stagnant sewers. Air, water and soil pollution are way beyond international standards of what is acceptable and rare species of flora and fauna are in danger of extinction because of wanton killings and the destruction of native habitat.

An Erap administration's top priority will be the vigorous implementation of environmental laws and regulations. An environmental impact assessment will be required of any project that affects the environment no matter how small. Officials charged with implementing environmental rules and regulations will be provided adequate training. They will also be given the proper equipment to enable them to do their job.

Erap is aware that only direct people participation will be able to reverse our deteriorating environmental situation. Thus, he plans to take the leadership in protecting and conserving the environment. For example, one of the Erap "crusades" is to get every Filipino to plant at least ten trees per year. Students, the boy scouts, brownies and other concerned segments of society will be mobilized to accomplish this task.

The planning of human setttlements in the Philippines needs to be more fully integrated with economic and social development planning. For example, in an Erap presidency, transport modes in very large urban areas such as Metro Manila and Metro Cebu will stress public transit (preferably rail-based) to the private automobile. The ownership, operation and maintenance of luxury vehicles will cost a lot more because of heavier taxes and other charges. At the same time appropriate transit systems, such as the LRT and MRT will be opened to serve the public.

## Social Housing

An estimated 3.4 to 5.2 million Filipino households are in need of basic housing, depending on whether you include rural housing in the calculation of housing demand or not (see Appendix 2). Despite its best efforts, the Ramos government could not meet the housing needs of the bottom 36% of Filipino households who essentially cannot pay even the cheapest housing option (a unit costing not more than Pesos 185,000). The private sector can barely meet 10% of the housing need. The greatest bulk of the Philippine housing stock is built by the people themselves directly—usually in slums and squatter communities.

Under an Erap administration, the private sector will continue to play the major role in housing. This policy is based on the observation that when government agencies build the houses themselves, practically half of the funds devoted to housing disappear in kickbacks and commissions. Social housing will be managed by a private non-profit foundation. In this way, corruption can be eliminated and the resources devoted to housing will benefit the people themselves (see Appendix 2 for Proposed Erap Social Housing Program).

In an Erap government, housing will be pursued in the context of a total human settlements and environmental strategy. The location of housing sites will be geared to places of employment, recreation, shopping and community services. This would limit commuting which, as every resident of Metro Manila suffering from traffic jams knows, is the bane of urban life. The housing projects provided by developers, such as Manny Villar and others, are great because they are affordable to many families with modest incomes. However, what one saves in money, one pays for in time spent in traffic, in inhalation of polluted air, in the frustration and sense of helplessness about one's lack of control over time, and the frayed nerves from the daily combat with rude and undisciplined drivers.

Housing and urban development would be planned from a national perspective. In other words, the location of housing and urban development projects would be used as an active instrument to influence population distribution. Emphasis will be placed on fulfilling the housing and urban development needs in cities all over the country such as Davao, Cebu, General Santos, Cagayan de Oro and other population centers. This will partly be done by delegating the major responsibility over housing and urban development to local government units.

One of the major problems of the Ramos government's housing and urban development policies has been the proliferation of government agencies involved in housing. There are at least six agencies involved in housing finance, mortgages and home insurance. Several agencies are involved in direct housing provision when what is primarily needed is the formulation and implementation of policies that could easily be carried out by private developers and local governments.

Most important of all, an Erap program on housing and urban development will be based on the participation of the people themselves. Too many programs in the past had been imposed by government. In the true traditions of a populist president, Erap's housing program will certainly help the poor because it will be planned and managed with the full participation of urban and rural poor. The resources of the poor will also be mobilized in terms of sweat equity and financial resources. The operation and maintenance of the project will be carried out by organized housing beneficiaries.

## Peace and Order

Erap has said many times that it is not a badge of honor for the Philippines to be known as the "kidnap capital of Asia." As the former head of the Presidential Anti-Crime Commission, Erap personally wants to lead the campaign against crime. While at PACC, Erap said he found out that about 52% of crimes in Metro Manila involved police officers and military personnel. He has vowed to go after "hoodlums in uniform" and apply the full force of the law against lawless elements.

Based on his experience in San Juan, Erap said that the best way of curbing criminality is to improve the lives and working conditions of police officers. He is fond of citing the homily of farmers and police officers. In the case of farmers, he likes to say, they will usually sell a carabao or a piece of land to get their children through college. Policemen, however, have no land and no carabao—but they have a gun. So, they use this primary asset to improve their lives and that of their children. They either "lease out" the gun for a fee or use it themselves for committing crime. The solution, then, is to increase the salary and benefits of police officers, help them support their children, and provide them with incentives such as housing, uniforms, insurance policies and scholarships for their children. If these benefits and incentives are significant enough, every police officer would think twice before risking to lose them by doing something illegal.

Of course, Erap would put in many reforms in peace and order administration, not just increase salaries and benefits. For example, the National Police Academy will be strengthened and revitalized to make pre-service education more than just military training. Recruitment, selection and testing for would be police officers will be made more rigorous. Performance standards will be set for appointment, promotion and other personnel movements, which will be strictly based on merit. The improved salaries, benefits, and working conditions for police officers, says Erap, will attract the best people into the police forces.

Erap will decentralize police services to local governments as much as possible. National efforts in peace and order will be mainly devoted to augmenting and supplementing the efforts of local governments. The Philippine National Police will be streamlined as a tactical force designed to assist local police forces with policies, standards, skills training and technical assistance. Full authority and responsibility for peace and order will be devolved to local officials.

Erap believes strongly that Filipinos are inherently law abiding and he will involve communities, professionals, parents and the youth in community-based peace and order programs. He is aware that law enforcement is basically supplementary to self-discipline, family support and the enforcement of community rules and regulations. By taking this people-centered peace and order philosophy rather than a punitive one, Erap is hopeful that peace and security can be achieved in the country.

**Graft and Corruption**

Erap is extremely sensitive to the ranking of the Philipines as the second most corrupt country in Asia, next only to Indonesia. As a public servant for more than 30 years whose name has never been involved in any case of anomalies or graft and corruption, Erap is in a strong position to curb—if not completely eradicate—this scourge in our governmental system.

As in peace and order, Erap is convinced that improvement of salaries, benefits and working conditions of civil servants will help solve the problem of graft and corruption. Essentially, such benefits should be improved to the point where losing these will hurt. Such hurt should not be confined to economic and personal benefits—the condemnation and shame that the community heaps on corrupt officials should serve as a strong deterrent to graft and corruption.

To Erap, combating graft and corruption boils down to a willingness on his part and the judicial system to file charges, prosecute, sentence and punish grafters to the full extent of the law. He would not brook any interference from anyone, relative, friend or influential patron, in cases involving graft and corruption. Within the first 100 days of his administration, vows Erap, he would throw in jail "sample cases" of known corrupt officials. By thus showing his sincerity and earnestness, Erap hopes to discourage others from engaging in graft.

Much of the efforts in combating graft and corruption will involve systemic reform in the judiciary. One of the sincere regrets of Erap, who grew up in a respected and law-abiding family, is the demeaning and corrupting of the judicial system in the Philippines. Erap has promised to go against "hoodlums in robes" to clean up the judiciary. He hopes to strengthen the Philippine Judicial Academy to upgrade the knowledge and capabilities of justice officials. He will reorganize the court system so that regional courts of appeals would be set up, instead of bringing all appeal cases to Manila.

Thorough going reforms in the civil service will also serve to combat graft and corruption. Erap seeks to strengthen the Career Executive Service Organization (CESO) to allow its members to serve as role models and as a modernizing force in public administration. This new "mandarinate" of senior higher civil servants will lead the way in fighting against graft and corruption and improving the efficiency and effectiveness of the civil service.

**Decentralization**

From what we know of him, Erap is not a micro-manager who will insist that all key decisions be made in Malacanang. To begin with, Erap has proposed to "regionalize" the executive office by setting up Malacanangs in Mindanao, the Visayas and Luzon where he would spend more time in order to be closer to the people. Erap has also committed himself to fully implementing the local government code of 1991 in order to pinpoint authority and responsibility on local officials.

As a former Town Mayor, Erap has strong empathy for the lot of local officials. He has vowed to be his own Secretary of the Interior and Local Governments. He also believes in not just devolving powers to local units—he is committed to extending to local officials all the taxing powers and financial resources (including increased internal revenue allotments) that they need to run their governments effectively and well.

The key to decentralization, of course, is grassroots empowerment. Erap is a great believer in local initiatives and he sees the development of civil society in the Philippines as the foundation of our continued democratic way of life. The role of NGOs and community based organizations will probably de-politicize local affairs. As more and more local officials become more accountable and responsive to local and community demands, there will be less dependence on national resources and reduced reliance on the benefits from centralized authoritarian politics

**Into the Next Millennium**

What will the Philippines be like when Erap wakes up on Wednesday, 1 July 1998, as the newly inaugurated President of the Philippines? And how will he lead the country into the next millennium as the elected Centennial President of a country celebrating one hundred years of democratic aspirations and independent nationhood?

What can the Filipino people expect of their newly elected leader?

Erap, to begin with, will be facing the highest and greatest expectations of people, especially the hopeful masses, who have voted for him as their leader despite the strident warnings of the elite members of society that he would lead the country to disaster. At the same time, he would have only meager resources to depend on in facing up to problems and challenges because the Philippines, like other Asian countries, is still staggering against the ravages of the Asian economic contagion that has eroded the value of the peso, increased interest rates, created serious unemployment, reduced economic productivity, and discouraged potential investors from putting more money into productive enterprises.

Happily, of course, the magnitude of the Erap electoral victory gives him some elbow room. He and he alone among the country's leaders probably has the status and convincing powers to ask the people for sacrifice—to postpone their gratification for a while, to reduce their demands for public goods and services, and to have a bit more patience with the government to allow things to work out. Such a period will probably be brief—newspaper columnists have already signaled that the honeymoon period with Erap can last only about a hundred days—and then, if things don't improve significantly, the long knives will be drawn.

# Chapter 15

# The Next Six Years

No. 1 Arlegui, Manila, is about 20 kilometers away from No. 1 Polk Street, Greenhills as the crow flies. However, as residences go, this new address of the Ejercito-Estradas is very far from home. Call it the nesting instinct—but how do you turn a centuries-old institution into a home?

Loi Ejercito, the new First Lady, is grateful to Ming Ramos, the outgoing First Lady, for leaving her beautifully tended plants in Malacanang. Ming could have taken these with her to her home in Alabang but she had said that if it was Loi who would be moving in as the new First Lady, she would leave them behind as she knows they will be in good hands. With so many social and medical programs to attend to in her new life, the Doktora will probably find very little time for gardening. Still, it would be nice to have fully flowering plants at the new place.

Erap has indicated that, unlike former President Cory Aquino and President Fidel V. Ramos, he would live in Malacanang and not in the renovated presidential residence on Arlegui. The two former presidents had refused to live in Malacanang, electing to transform it into a museum with all the traces of the Marcos-Imelda conjugal dictatorship very much intact. Not one for too much symbolism, Erap is quite happy to let the past bury its dead and to get on with the business of running the country. In fact, even before he was proclaimed president, Erap had given indications that he would be willing to have former President Marcos buried at the *Libingan ng mga Bayani* (The Cemetery of Heroes). It would not be a state funeral, said Erap, but he felt that Marcos, on his record as a soldier and guerilla fighter alone, deserved the right to a burial plot in the heroes' cemetery. Marcos had made many mistakes in his life but Erap believed that he deserved a Christian burial.

The presidential palace, Malacanang, is a rambling series of buildings on the banks of the Pasig, the river that divides Manila into a northern and a southern district. It was originally a Spanish mansion that was expanded by Spanish

Governors General and American High Commissioners as the official residence of the Philippine head of state. Most Philippine presidents had lived in the main Palace building until Cory Aquino and President Ramos. After the Marcoses fled Malacanang on board an American helicopter that took them to Clark Air Force Base and then, by plane, to exile in Honolulu, rioting mobs sacked parts of the palace, destroying the huge paintings of Marcos as a muscular *Malakas* and Imelda as a beautiful *Maganda* and vandalizing many of the rooms. The palace has been run as a museum since 1986, with all the Marcos-era paraphernalia on display.

We had visited Malacanang a couple of weeks after the 1986 EDSA revolution, along with a long line of tourists and locals who wanted to see this museum and tribute to the excesses of the Marcos dictatorship. Like many other curious onlookers, we saw the legendary pairs of shoes neatly stacked on shelves upon shelves along the aisles leading to the First Lady's room. We went down to the basement where Imelda's fur coats were hung in air conditioned comfort, saw the gallon-sized bottles of perfume (Christian Dior, Paco Rabanne, Jean Patou), the stacks of monogrammed shirts still in their original cellophane wrappings from Bloomingdale's, the gift boxes of luxury items that Imelda loved to bestow upon her friends after those luxury trips abroad.

The Marcos master bedroom was the real shocker. Hovering over a huge semi-circular bed was a triangle of steel and colored glass. The superstitious Marcoses had believed in "the power of the triangle" that was supposed to concentrate the forces and powers of nature and focus them on whoever was beneath the triangle. There, in their splendid isolation, the First Couple had slept, secure in the thought that all the forces of the universe were being focused on them. To us, that monstrous triangle symbolized, more than any other element in the presidential palace, the fantastic lunacy that had taken hold of the Marcoses in their fading years.

Loi Ejercito had been warned that there are ghosts in Malacanang. Certainly, the first order of business for the new First Couple should probably be a gigantic exorcism. The windows of the Palace must be opened wide to take the bad air out and let the fresh breezes in. The cobwebs of the past must be brushed away from this palace that has been the seat of power in the Philippines for so many years. The process of healing, so spontaneously started by the new President-elect even before his formal proclamation should continue. This positive outlook must now blossom and grace Malacanang for the next six years.

And yet, the process will not be easy. May is the *balimbing* (star fruit) season and the Ejercitos will be gifted with baskets of them within the next couple of months. The early "*balimbings*" had arrived at their Polk Street residence even before the vote tabulations were finished. The star fruit is the best symbol of the Filipino politician. The fruit is succulently sour and inedibly tart when unripe. If you cut it cross-wise, it makes for many perfectly proportioned stars that can be used for garnishing a salad or a fish dish. It is the perfectly proportioned five sides that makes the balimbing very much like a politician—no matter how you look at it, you get the same face. This fruit goes way beyond *doble cara* (double-faced)—you can turn this "turncoat" around and around and it gives you the same perfect face.

On 12 May 1998, as soon as Erap's electoral victory was signaled by the exit polls, the ABS-CBN broadcasts and the Namfrel quick count tabulations, the *balimbings* started trekking to the Ejercito-Estrada residence in Greenhills.

There was the newspaper columnist who had previously written that the only way Erap would win the presidency was on the shoulders of the *mga masang tanga* (the stupid masses). Now, on the day after the elections, he was seated at the table with Erap saying how "fantastic" his victory had been and how it reflected the maturity and wisdom of the Philippine electorate. *Balimbing! Sipsip!* (Kiss ass.)

There was the well-coiffed beauty queen who had appeared on the campaign stage with candidate Fred Lim—she had been a Cory Aquino camp follower from way back and she used to condemn Erap as an immoral womanizer, gambler and associate of underworld figures. Now, she was there at the same table with Erap, rubbing her bare arms against his shoulders, leaning as close to him as possible to whisper an intimate secret, now and then rubbing her stockinged legs to his as if by accident. Erap later impishly confided to us, when we asked him what was going on, that the lovely lady wanted to be a member of Eraps' cabinet, probably as head of tourism. "*Sorry na lang siya,*" (Too bad for her) said Erap afterwards, "I already promised the post to another beauty queen."

And so it went. With victory's many fathers, at this moment, the Ejercito-Estrada home was overflowing with paternal claimants. The people who had really worked on the campaign could only smile, roll their eyes, and marvel at the nerve of the *balimbings*.

## The Transition Process

Six months before Erap's victory at the polls, the Policy Studies Group under Raul de Guzman's leadership had started the process of working out the transition between the administration of President Fidel V. Ramos and the incoming government of Erap Estrada. At that time, the exercise seemed rather presumptuous but the PSG was certain of victory and, as good public administration types, they believed in planning ahead. U.P. professors and various experts were recruited for the transition teams.

Attention was focused on what to do within the first 100 days, mid-way in Erap's term, and what to expect after six years (For an example of a Transition Team Report on Social Housing, see Appendix 2).

When it became clear that Erap had won the presidency, he designated Ronnie Zamora, who would be his Executive Secretary to head the transition teams and to work with Colonel Alexander Aguirre, Ramos' executive secretary at Malacanang, the details attendant to the smooth turnover of power. Detailed plans were prepared for key governmental functions such as revenue generation, agriculture, peace and order, decentralization and other affairs of state. Of course, the transition plans were closely linked to the individuals who would be tapped to implement those plans.

Erap had also created a Screening Committee to review all potential individuals who could be appointed to key posts in an Erap government. It was estimated that about 3,000 positions would have to be filled up eventually but the Presidential Cabinet was top priority. Since Erap wanted at least three nominations per post, that would mean reviewing about 9,000 resumes!

Still, tough as the task of selecting key officials in the Erap administration is, it might prove a lot easier than running the country. Erap, with such massive support from the masses of the Filipino people, had taken on the toughest performance of his life. How would he fare within the next six years? What kind of government can be expected from him? How will he face up to the challenges posed by a country just celebrating its 100th year of independence and entering into the next millennium? Will Erap, the popular movie actor turned public servant be equal to the task? Will he be able to do what he said he would do and bring the country into the 21st century?

**Forming the New Erap Team**

When Erap wakes up on 1 July 1998 after he has been inaugurated as the 13th President of the Philippines, some awesome realities will greet him in the morning.

He will be the President—the first choice of more than 10.7 million Filipinos, the first time in the country's history that so many people have entrusted their hopes and dreams unto the hands of one man. It will be a formidable responsibility—the people, especially the *masa* have such great expectations—but Erap has a comfortable relationship with destiny and he will probably slide with ease into the ebbs and tides of authority and power.

Erap's critics have promised a self-imposed honeymoon period of 100 days when they will be gentle with him. No one can count on this—already, some of the long knives have been unsheathed and a hundred days is too long for those who make their living casting barbs. And anyway, Erap needs constant feedback on some of his decisions to make sure that he is on the right path.

Attention will have to be immediately focused on the people Erap will appoint to help him govern the country. So far, his choices have met with general approval—some with great sighs of relief, a few with some secret trepidation. Here, the Erap pattern of decision making is in full play. As in the past, when faced with complex decisions, Erap generally breaks them up into elements and tackles the easy ones first. Practically the first person Erap invited to join him in the Cabinet was Secretary Domingo Siazon of Foreign Affairs. Siazon had the perfect combination of real talent, management efficiency, long experience, and an excellent track record. To top it all, there is the human element—Siazon and Erap had been high school classmates at Ateneo and there is that emotional bond so important to smooth interpersonal relationships.

The next appointment, that of Ronnie Zamora as Executive Secretary, was also easy and predictable. Ronnie has massive technical competence, great experience (he had worked in the same job under President Marcos before), he has the wide network needed for acting as the Little President, and he is well trusted by Erap. Some may say that Ronnie's appointment was, in some ways, a reward for the difficult tasks he had to do during the campaign. In the Erap official family, investments in the process that resulted in victory is important. In truth, Erap needs Ronnie in such a key position.

The choice of Vice President-elect Gloria Macapagal Arroyo as Secretary for the Department of Social Work and Development was an inspired one. Most people expected Erap to do a Cory (to Laurel) or a Ramos (to Erap). In fact, Erap had made jokes in the past that if Gloria was elected Vice President, he would appoint her to the PACC. The awarding of a real substantive position to someone with obvious talent and management capabilities was met with approval by many. To Erap, who is not really interested in the period beyond his six-year term, the most important thing is delivery and not consideration of whether the job would contribute to Gloria's ambition to become President or not.

Very interesting cases of how the trial balloon can be used to good effect were seen in the floating of the names of Estelito Mendoza for Secretary of Justice, Panfilo Lacson as head of PACC and Susy Pineda Mercado as Secretary of Health. The reactions to these trial balloons were very negative. The specter of Marcos-style cronyism was raised right away. The connections of Mendoza to Lucio Tan were questioned, the possible impact on the morale of people at PACC of a Lacson appointment was raised, and uneasiness of some top health officials with Mercado was expressed. Erap has not stubbornly stuck to his choices, expecting to get more information on the candidates from other people to help him make a decision. Erap has made it clear that he and he alone will make the final decision on all appointments and people have welcomed that as the way things should be. The Selection Committee recommends but the President decides.

The next item of business for the new President is funding—how much money would be left from the budget of President Ramos? What are the immediate items of expenditures that need to be met? Here, the appointment of Benjamin Diokno is most appropriate—as a former Undersecretary of the Budget, Ben knows the governmental accounts well and he had been in constant touch with his former colleagues in the Budget Office. Erap had called for austerity and sacrifice and there was a willingness on the part of the government to try to live within its means. It is the job of Diokno to help Erap allocate the public funds wisely so that every peso goes to its best use.

Always putting first things first, Erap had given the highest priority to food security in the new administration. Here, the steady hand of Senator Edong Angara would be needed. In the meantime, however, while the one-year ban for defeated candidates from holding appointive offices is observed, the main responsibility for this task will go to Horacio "Boy" Morales, who will become the person in charge of agrarian reform. With his strong commitment and concern for the welfare of the rural poor, Boy is the perfect choice for the job. During the campaign, Erap's critics had asked what Erap would do with the group of "leftists" who had helped him in the campaign. The appointment of Boy in agrarian reform is a fitting response to that concern—you put at the heart of your administration, the people whose hearts are in the right place. That is one reason why Karina Constantino-David is the right person to head the new President's anti-poverty program. That is why Fely Villareal, who wears her heart on her sleeve, is Undersecretary of Social Work and

Development, bringing with her the social development models they had formulated within JEEP.

In the matter of selecting people for his government, Erap has followed an important rule throughout his career—"do not change the people, keep them but change their attitude."

When he was elected Mayor of San Juan, people expected that Erap would come in with a broom and sweep the rascals out. Instead, he talked to incumbent officials one by one. If they have had no history of crime and corruption, he asked them to stay. He pointed out how important continuity was in government—how costly the disruption of services became when new people had to be broken in and trained for the job.

"Besides, people who are grateful to you for asking them to remain in their jobs perform much better," Erap had told the Selection Committee when he asked them to help him choose the right people. And he was right. Many of the people around Erap had been "inherited" from other offices. Some of them have been with him since San Juan, others used to be in his old Senate Office, some had worked with Vice President Doy Laurel. By giving them his trust, Erap's people had given him their utmost loyalty and their best skills and talents. These are now needed for Erap's greatest performance of all.

### Top Priority Issues

Having chosen his team, the new President has to give his full attention to the main issues facing the country. Erap had given his pledge to the people, the *masa*, the poor and the underprivileged, that he would make their welfare his top priority. The campaign has already indicated those key items: food, jobs, decent wages, affordable prices, health, education and basic services such as water, drainage, housing, transportation, sanitation and garbage collection and disposal. There are also the top priority items without which public services would be extremely difficult to deliver—peace and order and the curbing of graft and corruption.

*Food Security*. Ensuring food on the table will not be easy in the face of El Niño that has cut down rice and corn production because of the long drought and the La Niña that is expected to bring floods and erosion. The Erap administration will probably have no choice but to import rice, corn, and other products. The worst thing that a new administration can face is the rice *pila* (queue)—people get really upset when they have to line up to get their rice ration. It will be the height of irony if Erap, who has been elected into office to improve the lives of the poor, will preside over disgruntled masses lining up to get their quota of rice.

*Peace and Order.* Also of the highest priority will be peace and order. Erap cannot afford to have highly publicized cases of kidnapping for ransom, bank hold-ups, and drug-related killings within his term—certainly not within the first 100 days. Because of his record at PACC, people will be expecting a lot. If criminal elements and drug lords want to test his mettle, he has to be firm and resolute in going after them. Now that he is the President, there can be no excuses for failure.

Erap had said during the campaign that criminality can be contained by a strong and honest police force, a reliable judiciary, and full community cooperation. The working conditions of police forces will need special attention—salaries and benefits will have to be improved, morale will have to be quickly restored. Erap had indicated that the full force of the law will be applied to those who break the law. He will have to break a number of sensational cases to drive that point home.

*Graft and Corruption.* Curbing graft and corruption is of the utmost urgency because that has been the rot sapping the economy by diverting public funds into private pockets, discouraging foreign and domestic investments because of cronyism and favoritism, and delaying things because of complex procedures and red tape. Erap is expected to do something dramatic in this area. Perhaps, a "sample" of a notorious graft case being resolved. Pursuing the PEA-Amari deal to its conclusion would be a good example. It was fine to promise that Erap would wage war on "rogues in uniform" and "hoodlums in robes"—it would be much better to see some of those grafters as convicted felons.

*Jobs.* The business community seems to have been re-assured that an Erap presidency will be friendly to free enterprise, will respect the forces of the market, and will ensure enterprises that no groups will be favored in a level playing field. The Erap administration is convinced that a robust and productive private sector is the best creator of jobs. If necessary, an Erap administration may launch labor-intensive employment programs that can absorb idle labor temporarily. Certainly, the need to expand public works to build irrigation systems, farm to market roads, flood control and drainage systems, etc., might be able to generate emergency employment. However, in the long run, it would be jobs created by the private sector that will provide lasting benefits. This includes jobs in the informal sector which require rapid development of risk-taking entrepreneurial skills where profits rather than salaried income would be the main motivation.

*Manufacturing and Industry*. The Ramos administration had achieved dramatic results by encouraging foreign investments to come to the Philippines. The Erap priorities will be closer to home. Agriculture. Manufacturing. Local industries. To Erap, these are the areas requiring immediate attention. Instead of all the hype heaped on high-tech industries, knowledge-based complexes and "pole vaulting into the 21$^{st}$ century," greater attention will be given to ensure the food supply, expand manufacturing, and encourage investments in industry.

The special economic zones and the export processing zones will be encouraged but the main motivation will be not to become a tiger cub and compete with our Asian neighbors. These enclaves of development will be linked more to their immediate hinterlands. The prosperity they generate will be shared with the people living around them. Regional development plans will be formulated and implemented placing the special zones in the context of their economic and environmental hinterlands. In much the same way Erap's social policies have attempted to cross class barriers, the exclusivity of development zones will be breached to link them much more closely with their surrounding areas.

*Housing and Urban Devlopment*. Even as Erap gives top priority to agriculture and rural development, he will not be able to ignore the sad plight of the urban areas. Happily, Erap will be the beneficiary of the long-term infrastructure investments of the Cory and Ramos administrations. He will probably have the privilege of opening up the MRT and LRT expansions as well as the skyway and superhighways linking Manila to the other growth poles in Luzon. Efficient urban management will be needed to operate and maintain these expensive projects. If the Erap administration will only help ease the traffic problem, if dependable water supply and electricity can be provided, if floods will not destroy property and disrupt people's lives in the rainy season, and if the garbage of the city can be collected and disposed of, Erap can become the greatest President this country ever had.

Dramatic programs in social housing will have to be opened by the Erap government pursuant to his campaign promises that a significant dent will be made in the country's housing need of 3.7 million dwelling units. For beginners, water, toilets, drainage, foot paths and electricity must be made accessible to millions of squatters and slum dwellers that clog our cities. Resettlement of people to far-flung areas where they have no jobs, housing and basic services will have to stop. New high density housing will be provided as close as possible to where the people work. The private sector will be tapped as the main provider of housing, with the government providing financial assistance, setting policies and providing targets and performance standards.

*Education.* Individual and social advancement are dependent on education but, unfortunately, this area has been neglected by previous governments. Erap has expressed serious concern about the lack of preparedness of the children of the poor for formal education. He believes that a nation-wide pre-school program is needed to make sure that all children, poor and rich alike, will be adequately prepared, mentally and physically for entering the formal school system. The pre-school program will be a joint enterprise among parents, teachers, the community and the government. It will involve food supplementation for poor children in addition to mental learning and psychological guidance.

The salaries and benefits of teachers will have to be increased to enhance their motivation and make them better teachers. Considerable resources will be needed for this but there is no choice—the improvement of teachers' quality is the cornerstone of the new educational program envisioned by Erap.

*Health and Sanitation.* The community orientation of the Erap government will be seen in the linking of health with educational facilities. The main approach to health care in an Erap government will be preventive rather than curative. Primary health care programs will be pursued and the health of women and children will be given highest priority.

## Decentralization of Government Functions

A major structural change within the next six years that the Erap administration will carry out will be the decentralization of governmental functions, authority and power to provinces, cities, municipalities and *barangays*. Erap has indicated he will be his own Secretary of the Interior and Local Governments. As a former Mayor, he believes in entrusting governance to the unit that is closest to the people.

As soon as Erap's victory became clear, there were moves right away to convince him to re-centralize health and agriculture functions which had been devolved by the Local Government Code to local government units. The reason given was that the local governments were not able or willing to meet the salaries of health and agricultural officers. This move toward re-centralization will go against the mandate and spirit of the Local Government Code that Erap has sworn to uphold. The need is probably not to re-centralize but to set up a national fund that could be used to support local governments with insufficient resources to implement the decentralization program. Most local governments are now perfectly capable of meeting service demands with their own resources. Only those still with inadequate resources will be assisted by the central government until they are able to take on their full responsibilities.

To bring the government closer to the people, Erap promised to set up "regional Malacanangs" in Luzon, Visayas and Mindanao. Instead of expecting everyone to go to Manila, he plans to hold office for six months in Luzon, three months in Mindanao and three months in the Visayas. Regional Cabinets of responsible officials will also be appointed to help him in managing each region. In this way, issues of more immediate concern can be given attention right away. The decentralized national government structure will also enable it to respond to people's needs as quickly as possible.

## International Affairs

Unlike President Ramos, Erap said he would not take many trips to foreign countries. In foreign affairs, he will be assisted by Secretary Domingo Siazon, who has already agreed to extend his term.

Erap has indicated that he would like to make his first official foreign trip to China to get some ideas on how the country is able to feed its 1.2 billion inhabitants. He may also benefit from observing China's social development policies that combine incentives for greater economic productivity with the establishment of safety nets that ensure the welfare of the people. China's economic development program, with its emphasis on agriculture as the base and manufacturing and industry as the keys to development has been growing at more than 10% per year for the past decade. Insights into how this process works will be of great help to the Erap administration as it focuses on a people-centered development strategy very much like China's.

Sooner or later, Erap will have to visit the United States. In 1996, he already had a "getting to know you" visit with Vice President Al Gore and it would be an interesting reunion with Gore and to meet President Bill Clinton. The special relationships between the Philippines and the United States have gone through some rocky times but they have improved through the years as the Philippines has evolved into a free wheeling democracy. The Philippines, more than any other country in Asia, has the potential to achieve both economic growth and political development. To the United States, who sought to accomplish these by colonizing the Philippines a century ago, this would be the fulfillment of a dream and a vindication of its belief in the democratic system.

## The Last and Best Performance

Erap has always believed that "Somebody Up There" loves him and that the guiding hand of Destiny has intervened in his life to take him to where he is now. It has been a long unpredictable journey from his birthplace in Tondo, his childhood years in San Juan, his career in the movies, the political offices he has held, and his arrival in Malacanang. Throughout all these, Erap's main strength has been the fact that he has remained true to himself. He will need all his strength to maintain this in the coming six years.

Throughout his life, Erap has used three tests for any decision he has to make.

- Is it good for the greatest number of Filipinos?
- Is it honest?
- Will it bring honor to the Ejercito family name?

These are three simple tests that Erap brings to bear on any decision he has to make. If he is able to answer "yes" to every one of them, his decisions will be right. Within the next six years, there will be many occasions when Erap will have to use this three-way test on policy issues. If he remains true to himself, these three questions will help him in carrying out this last, and best, public performance of his life.

# APPENDICES

Note: The two documents that follow were written by the authors, in collaboration with the Policy Studies Group as their contribution to the Erap Estrada Program of Governance and the Presidential Transition Team policy and program proposals.

*The Greenhills Group before rushing off to another rally. (Seated L-R) Dr. Loi Ejercito, Mama Mary Ejercito, Marita Ejercito and Raul P. de Guzman. ( Standing L-R) Prod Laquian, Monette Ejercito, Dr. Pilarica Ejercito, Dolly Ejercito and Pat de Guzman*

# APPENDIX 1

# PROGRAM OF GOVERNANCE

The electoral victory of Joseph Ejercito "Erap" Estrada provides a historic opportunity to change the direction of our country's development. Good governance is needed to effect this change. Governance, in turn, depends on a number of fundamental concerns that will guide an Erap presidency: growth with equity, a sustainable environment, and grassroots empowerment. The benefits of economic and social development will be shared by social groups in all regions.

In recent years, the Philippines has missed two golden opportunities to achieve development through good governance. The Marcos regime could have introduced basic reforms but it became corrupted by the desire to perpetuate itself in power. The Aquino administration, launched by massive "people's power," could have achieved lasting changes but weak leadership prevented it from living up to its promise.

*It is now left to an Erap presidency to carry out the governance reforms that will enable the Philippines to achieve both economic development and participatory democracy.*

The administration of President Fidel V. Ramos has initiated reforms designed to achieve political stability, economic growth and democratic decision making. As the Philippines faces the next millennium, however, it is apparent that fundamental adjustments are needed to sustain the country's development.

Official government figures show that the gross national product of the Philippines grew from 1.5 per cent in 1992 to 6.8 in 1996. Dramatic as the rates of economic growth have been, their results have not been equitably shared by all. At present, the richest 20 per cent of Filipinos own 50 per cent of national income while the bottom 40 per cent own only 17 per cent. The richest 10 per cent of Filipino families have 19.5 times more income than the bottom 10 per cent. Contrary to what some economists are saying (that equity comes with growth),

World Bank and Asian Development Bank figures show that the income gap between the rich and the poor in the Philippines is actually widening.

Opening up the Philippine economy to the outside world has generated P490 billion in investment approvals. The frequent trips of President Ramos abroad are said to have attracted US$21 billion in investments from 36 countries. Such investments have exploited our natural resources and have taken advantage of our skilled but cheap labor. Fast track economic growth, however, has failed to protect and conserve our environment. Privatization schemes have sold off some of our key enterprises to foreign capitalists. As the country looks more and more to foreign capital to fuel its economic growth, it loses control over its destiny and risks losing its very patrimony.

Some of the programs of the Ramos administration deserve to be continued. While building upon the positive elements of the Ramos programs, however, an Erap presidency will give the highest priority to the attainment of a just and equitable society. Economic growth alone will not make our society sustainable if the poor are left to depend on what trickles down from the tables of the rich. Development will not be sustainable if people do not fully support and exercise ownership over the government's programs. Above all, Philippine society will not progress if there is no coherent program of governance that will provide efficient and effective public services to the people.

Good governance, in turn, can help achieve these policy goals through a program of efficient management, civil service reform, electoral changes, decentralization and grassroots empowerment. It should take into consideration cultural, environmental, social and economic factors that influence the orderly management of public affairs. The question of social equity and justice should be carefully considered as well.

**Justice For All**

In order to achieve sustained development, a Government led by Erap will be founded on the principle of justice for all. The Government will achieve political stability based, not on centralized control, but on the equitable sharing of the fruits of economic growth. *Si Erap ay maka-mahirap ngunit sa kanya, bawat isa ay mahalaga.* Under an Erap Government, all sectors of society will be empowered to enable everyone to participate in governance. The Filipino masses, who will elect Erap, deserve a chance for a better life.

*1. Assuring personal security and safety*

The most basic function of Government is to guarantee the personal security and safety of every citizen. It is not a badge of honor for the Philippines to be known as the kidnap capital of Asia. An Erap presidency will restore peace and order. Criminals will be hit with the full force of the law. The rule of law, based on due process and respect for the basic rights of persons, will be upheld. The Philippines cannot achieve social justice if criminal elements violate the rights of ordinary people and remain unpunished. We cannot call ourselves a just society until every man, woman and child can walk the streets or enjoy the comforts of home without fear.

In 30 years of public service, Erap has been a fearless foe of criminal gangs, drug lords, kidnappers, gamblers and hoodlums. As head of the PACC, he was a relentless crusader against crime, until political expediency denied him the opportunity to continue serving the people. As President, Erap will bring the full force of the law against those who terrorize ordinary people and flaunt the public order. This will be done while respecting the basic human rights of persons and adhering to due process of law.

*Under an Erap presidency, the five pillars of a true justice system will be strengthened.*

First, there will be a comprehensive reform of all police and protective services. Recent studies have shown that about 52 per cent of crimes in Metro Manila involved police and other law enforcement officers. In one year alone, crime statistics revealed that no less than 114 military and police officers were found guilty of crimes against persons and property. The involvement of military and police personnel in crime, while morally inexcusable, does not come as a surprise in the light of their working and living conditions. A survey of the backgrounds of police personnel revealed that more than a third of them lived in slum and squatter areas where they were in daily contact with criminal elements. Their low salaries and benefits, poor housing, and lack of economic security for their families make it extremely difficult for them to resist the temptations of criminal activity.

Specific measures to be pursued by an Erap presidency include the following:

- The Philippine National Police (PNP) will be reorganized as a national force with each member subject to a Code of Discipline similar to a military code of conduct. As security officers charged with the authority to use armed force, members of the PNP should be covered by military discipline, not civil service law.

- Local government units will have the authority to create their own police forces subject to national policies and standards of performance set by the PNP. The PNP will provide technical assistance, training and other means of support to strengthen local police forces.

- The salaries and benefits of individuals involved in police and protective services will be increased to a level commensurate with the risks involved. A housing program for policemen and other protective services personnel, a scholarship program for their children, a comprehensive insurance scheme, and other incentives will be provided to raise morale and create a higher sense of motivation among concerned personnel.

- Erring members of the police forces will be weeded out. The certainty of punishment for illegal and immoral conduct will be clearly established in conformity with due process and strict adherence to the law. At the same time, meritorious actions of exemplary individuals will be rewarded. The improved working conditions and benefits to police personnel will be available only to those who live up to the standards of a professional police force.

- Entry requirements and standards of performance of police and other protective services personnel will be raised. Appropriate educational attainment, physical health and a thorough background check on the moral character of all applicants to the police profession will be strictly imposed.

- Pre-service training for member of the police forces will be raised to the highest professional standards. The teaching staff, facilities and equipment of the Philippine National Police Academy will be upgraded, the curriculum will be thoroughly revised, and all necessary actions will be done to ensure that graduates of the academy will be proud to be members of a professional police force.

- The arms, communication systems, transport, crime laboratories and other requirements of good police work will be upgraded. This will effectively deal with the anomalous situation where the police forces often find themselves outgunned and outmaneuvered by criminal elements who have better firepower, communication, vehicles, and other facilities than the police.

- A concerted program of police reform will be vigorously pursued, to restore the public's confidence and trust in the police forces.

Second, the standards and processes of prosecution will be upgraded in order to achieve timely execution of justice. The 1987 Constitution, in its Bill of Rights, cited fair and speedy disposition of cases as the cornerstone of the administration of justice. At present, however, it usually takes more than five years for even simple cases to be resolved, giving proof to the maxim that justice delayed is justice denied. To change this situation, an Erap presidency will carry out the following actions:

- Amend judicial procedures related to the issuance of writs of preliminary injunction. Under existing procedures, there is no limit on how long the issuing court issuing the injunction can cause the writ to remain effective. During the time the injunction is in place, witnesses may disappear, documents may be tampered with, memories of witnesses may fail or people may get impatient and take the law unto their own hands.

- The Philippine Judicial Academy will be strengthened. Completion of continuing education courses at the academy will be used as a primary consideration in the promotion and other personnel movements of prosecution staff.

- Courses on proper investigation and prosecution methods will be taught and upgraded at the National Police Academy. At present, there has been a tendency to recruit police officers from the military where the emphasis is on the use of armed interventions and military tactics. Good police work requires an orientation based more on gathering and analysis of facts within a legal context while respecting the due process of law. The professionalization of police investigation and prosecution will be stressed in an Erap presidency.

- The policy that no prosecutor will be assigned to a place where he or she has resided for the past ten years will be strictly adhered to.

Third, the country's court system will be overhauled, through proper legislation and consultation with the Supreme Court. An honest and fair judicial system is the bulwark of democracy but, in recent years, the traditionally upright judicial system in the Philippines has been tarnished by delayed justice and outright corruption. An Erap presidency will carry out the following measures:

- Weed out corrupt judges, prosecutors and other court personnel and appoint and provide full support to those who uphold the fair and speedy administration of justice. In the Judiciary branch, especially, there must be certainty that all persons found guilty of violating the law will be speedily punished regardless of their position or influence. The appointment and promotion of judges should not be influenced by politicians. To this end, the Judicial and Bar Council should be abolished and the power to review appointments of judges and prosecutors should be returned to the Commission on Appointments.

- Reorganize the court system to make it more responsive to people's needs. At present, the Philippines is divided into 13 judicial regions but there is only one Court of Appeals in Manila. The appeals court should be decentralized so that branches will be set up in the Visayas and Mindanao saving litigants the time and expense for the proper dispensation of justice.

- Existing rules of procedure will be reviewed and amended, especially those related to issuance of injunctions, temporary restraining orders, warrants of arrests, investigative methods, presentation of evidence, and trial procedures. At present, unscrupulous lawyers take advantage of faulty rules and procedures to delay and hold back the resolution of cases.

- When judges are transferred to other courts, they will not be allowed to move and take their oaths of office until they have fully cleared their existing case loads.

In brief, a comprehensive judicial reform program will be pursued to get rid of corrupt personnel. New court facilities, improved salaries and benefits of court personnel, streamlining of processes and procedures, and establishment of precise and rigorous performance standards will be instituted. The main goal is to restore the people's faith in the country's court system.

Fourth, the penal system needs to be reformed in order to simplify the relationship between the commission of a crime and the meting of punishment. New legislation will be passed to ensure that all guilty parties would be brought to justice swiftly and expeditiously, without regard to the wealth, position, or family and political connection of people.

- The Philippine jail system will be reformed and reorganized to enable it to fulfill its main functions of not only punishing those who violate the law but also reform and retrain offenders to become useful members of society. At present, the conditions in the jails are so bad as to constitute violation of basic human rights. Jails often serve to harden first offenders and criminalize those who are sent behind bars. People fear being jailed not because of the loss of freedom but because of the beatings, rape, sodomy, and various violations of human dignity perpetuated by criminals and recidivists who rule them

- Jail officials, prison guards and other staff who abuse prisoners, engage in inhumane punishment and tortures, favor certain inmates, and otherwise profit from the misfortune of prisoners should be prosecuted and punished.

- An effective program of prisoner rehabilitation, training, counseling, and skills development will be vigorously pursued. A supportive parole system will be established in order to give those who are turning over a new leaf to pursue a better way of life. The training of parole officers, social workers and other support personnel will be strengthened to give them the necessary professional knowledge and skills.

Finally, the justice system must have the full support of the community in ensuring that those who commit injustice are identified, tried, punished and effectively dealt with. At present, the level of cynicism about the honesty of law enforcement officers is so high that people hesitate to report crime incidents. The families of kidnap victims choose to negotiate ransoms with criminals directly rather than take the matter to the police because of the suspicion that police officers themselves may be involved.

To restore the community's trust in the justice system and regain community support, an Erap presidency will do the following:

- A police community relations program will be instituted in neighborhoods faced with threats of criminal activities. With the help of trained community organizers, communities will be organized and leaders trained on ways of preventing and combating crime.

- Neighborhood watch, community *rondas*, and "eyes on the street" committees will be formed. Households will be encouraged to mark all their valuables to prevent sale of stolen items. House to house police campaigns will be conducted to encourage people to practice "burglar proofing" of their homes by using deadbolt locks, better lighting of their premises, refraining from leaving their homes unattended, and knowing the modus operandi of thieves and burglars in order to carry out actions that anticipate problems and dangers.

- Special programs for the youth will be organized, with athletic activities and other wholesome recreation providing an alternative to gang and other activities that may lead to delinquency. Trained police community relations officers will be assigned to youth work in order to mobilize young people in the fight against crime, drugs and other social ills.

- The whole community will be mobilized in the war against drugs, substance abuse and other vices that often lead to criminality. In particular, the office of the Public Assistance and Reaction Against Crime (PARAC) under the Department of the Interior and Local Governments will be strengthened in order to mobilize citizen action against these threats to public order.

- An effective witness protection program will be instituted in order to encourage people willing to testify against criminals to assist the police in prosecution.

*2. Eradicating graft and corruption*

Governmental losses to graft and corruption have been estimated to be as high as 20 per cent of budgetary expenditures. In 1997, therefore, more than P108 billion of governmental resources were lost to corruption. If these resources had been "saved," they would have been enough to support the country's social housing program or provide irrigation facilities to all the farms in the country.

Erap's program of governance will deal with graft and corruption through the following programs:

- Government agencies such as the Anti-Graft Commission, the National Bureau of Investigation, and others charged with combating graft and corruption will be revitalized. Cases of graft and corruption will be ac-

expeditiously dealt with and people found guilty will be punished to the fullest extent of the law.

- Each government agency will have a resident Ombudsman with powers to fight graft and corruption. Transparency in all transactions will be required and full accountability for transactions will be exacted.

- Salaries and benefits of civil servants will be raised to a level where loss of employment because of indictment on graft and corruption charges will be a significant loss. Such salaries and benefits, however, will be provided based on meritorious performance, as assessed through an objective and fair performance evaluation system.

- Special campaigns against graft and corruption will be waged in government agencies where conditions are conducive to corrupt practices. For example, special efforts will be focused on revenue collection agencies, regulatory agencies, and those dealing with valuable public resources.

*3. Enshrining the rule of law*

A just society functions on the assumption that actions are predictable because they are based on laws, customs and shared norms of conduct. World Bank studies identify "unpredictable changes in laws and policies" as one of the main deterrents to economic development (the others are high incidence of criminality, unreliable judicial systems, and graft and corruption).

A country cannot be progressive if individuals and institutions can shirk their obligations at will on the basis of privileged status or political power. A person's word of honor should be his or her bond as the majesty of the law upholds the binding nature of agreements. Until the rule of law is assured, local entrepreneurs and international business people will hesitate to invest in a country's development.

Under an Erap presidency, adherence to the rule of law will be pursued in the following ways:

- A comprehensive judicial reform, led by the Supreme Court and supported by the Executive Branch will be launched after Erap's inauguration as President. Respecting the autonomy of the Judiciary, this reform measure will deal with the appointment, promotion, transfer and job allocations of judges and other key officials. Processes and procedures to celerate the resolution of cases will be streamlined. The primary goal of the reform will be to restore the people's faith in the impartiality of the Judiciary and its capacity to achieve justice for all.

- A special task force will be organized to simplify and codify all governmental rules and regulations related to public transactions. In this way, the public and clients of the public service will know in advance what needs to be done, minimizing the chances for "special arrangements" that lead to graft and corruption.

- Each government agency, especially those carrying out functions conducive to corruption, will be required to prepare a simplified manual indicating procedures for public transactions. Such manuals will be made available to the public. Manual provisions will be regularly updated and the public will be encouraged to suggest ways of improving these.

- The Public Defender's Program will be strengthened in order to achieve the ideal that those who have less in life should have more in law. Young and idealistic recent law graduates will be supported to spend at least two years in this program to instill in them a sense of public service as they defend people who cannot afford to pay legal fees.

**Sustained Economic Growth**

Good governance rests on a robust economy which depends on adherence to certain macro-economic fundamentals. At the same time, economic growth can be sustained only if there is equity and justice, environmental concerns are addressed effectively, and there is community support for the country's program of governance.

*4. Ensuring food security*

Each day, Filipinos consume 22,000 metric tons of rice or 8.030 million tons per year. The country produces about 8.145 million metric tons but, with the requirements of a buffer stock of 1.980 million metric tons, it has to import 515,000 metric tons annually. In addition, the Philippines has to import about 720,000 metric tons of corn annually, half of which goes to animal feeds.

With more than 50 per cent of the Philippine population dependent on agriculture for its livelihood, an Erap presidency will give top priority to agricultural development in its economic program. It is ironic that while the Philippines is an international leader in agricultural innovations, the rice production rate in our country (3 metric tons per hectare) is one of the lowest in Asia.

Under an Erap presidency, food security will be assured through the following measures:

- A program to increase crop production, especially rice, will be immediately pursued. Per hectare productivity will be increased from 3 metric tons to 4 metric tons through a concerted effort involving provision of irrigation facilities, post-harvest technologies, use of better seed varieties, and expansion of hectarage devoted to rice crops. Studies at the University of the Philippines at Los Banos indicate that rice yields can be increased in irrigated farms by at least 10 cavans per hectare. By irrigating at least 200,000 hectares, the country will be able to increase productivity by at least 910,000 metric tons of rice.

- The Philippines currently has the technology to produce poultry, eggs, pork, beef, and other food items. However, costs of production are high, particularly because of the need to import corn for animal feed. At present, the country imports 455,000 metric tons of soybean meal as animal feed (using $107 million of valuable foreign exchange reserves). Since soybean can easily be grown locally, the food security program will consider soybean production as a high priority item.

- There will be a careful review of Philippine commitments under international agreements and protocols such as the Uruguay Round of GATT (now the World Trade Organization), the Asean Free Trade Area (AFTA), the Asia Pacific Economic Committee (APEC), and bilateral agreement with trading partners such as the United States, Canada and others. In particular, the Philippine sugar industry faces great competitive pressures as tariffs are gradually reduced and imports from neighboring countries become more attractive. The industry should launch massive productivity schemes in order to be competitive without relying on governmental protective measures. Under an Erap presidency, supports and subsidies to the sugar industry will be drastically reduced to challenge the industry to regain its competitive edge. The coconut industry stands to benefit from increased access to international markets but it is hampered by low productivity arising from aged trees, limited replanting, lack of fertilizers, poor drying methods and inefficient processing. The industry will be revitalized by the allocation of public resources to deal with these problems.

- The rationalization of the Comprehensive Agrarian Reform Program (CARP) will be pursued in order to encourage greater investments in agri-business and other innovative enterprises. In addition to acquisition and distribution of land, the program needs access to capital and technical assistance to improve productivity of land use. Innovative approaches such as contract growing, nucleus estates and an employees stock ownership program should be incorporated into a re-invigorated CARP initiative.

- Access to micro-credit schemes for agriculture-based enterprises would be widened. Such schemes will be especially offered to small and medium-scale enterprises owned and managed by the poor and the underprivileged.

- The rural credit system will be strengthened through the establishment of regional banks designed to serve smaller rural communities. Credit schemes will be linked with the organized efforts of rural producers such as women's cooperatives, NGO projects, community-based efforts and traditional lending systems based on individual's reputations and community support.

- The Philippines will take advantage of export opportunities, especially to resource-poor countries in East and South Asia where there is a high demand for non-traditional export products such as seaweeds, prawns, fish, mangoes, bananas and other tropical fruits and vegetables. Quality standards for such exports will be assured at the highest levels. Packaging and preservation processes will be vastly improved. Trade offices of the Philippine Foreign Service Corps will be mobilized to foster marketing of these products.

*5. Establishing macro-economic development policies*

Setting up the economic fundamentals for sustained productivity is a primary function of good governance. Programs for encouraging a higher level of personal and institutional savings, curtailing deficit financing, pursuing an export-led and investment-fueled economy, and prudent implementation of policies of liberalization, deregulation and privatization, will be the hallmarks of an Erap-led government.

- The level of personal and institutional savings in the Philippines, estimated at 15 per cent of Gross Domestic Product, is one of the lowest in Asia. To deal with this problem, campaigns will be waged to encourage Filipinos to buy local products instead of imported items. Bank interest rates on personal savings will be kept at high enough levels to encourage saving. A government-instituted austerity program will balance the budget and avoid deficit financing.

- Erap's macro-economic policies will harness the strengths of private enterprise and the free workings of the market within the framework of good governance. The efficiency, discipline, and cost-consciousness of private enterprise will be applied to the delivery of social services. Privatization of key public enterprises as well as joint public-private ventures will be pursued. At the same time, the welfare needs of the public, especially the poor and the underprivileged, will be safeguarded by social safety nets and other forms of compassionate action.

- While foreign investments in the Philippines will be encouraged, emphasis will be placed on attracting more Filipino entrepreneurs to invest in the country's development. In particular, Filipinos investing in small and medium-scale enterprises will be given incentives. Investments will be welcomed in such fields as agriculture, food and beverage industries, energy, telecommunications, basic housing and local construction.

- Liberalization policies under the Ramos administration have attracted foreign capital that has helped to accelerate economic growth. Influx of speculative capital, however, had de-stabilizing effects in the country's foreign exchange situation. Opening Philippine capital markets to foreign investments under Erap-led policies will be more selective. Specifically, foreign direct investments in longer term productive enterprises rather than on short-term speculative ventures will be given preference.

- The deregulation of a number of key industries, particularly those of a monopolistic nature such as energy, telecommunication, water and sanitation, and mass transport has had positive effects. Allowing market-driven competition rather than bureaucratic control to shape the economy has encouraged productive energies to flourish. An Erap-led Government will continue to pursue such policies. More than that, it will encourage managers of such industries to go public and open them up to mass small-scale investors.

- The privatization of public enterprises has increased government revenues, cut bureaucratic red tape, and made enterprises more efficient. The benefits of private enterprise (cost savings, proper pricing, competitive marketing, responsiveness to customer demands) have greatly energized the enterprises. While encouraging privatization, however, the Erap-led policies will ensure that Filipinos will always have management control. Enterprises that belong to the national patrimony and form part of our national cultural heritage should not be placed under the control of foreign enterprises.

- Privatization of public enterprises should never adversely affect services to the poor and the underprivileged. An Erap-led Government will ensure that such services as water, electricity, telecommunications, mass transport, health, education, postal services, protective services, and solid waste collection and disposal, even when privatized, will continue to provide services that are within the capacity to pay of the poor. Furthermore, privatization should not result in the summary dismissal or dislocation of employees of privatized firms.

*6. Providing industrial infrastructure*

It is a primary function of Government to provide industrial infrastructure to support productive activities in all economic sectors. Public investments in improving and maintaining power plants, water utilities, telecommunications, airports, ports, harbors, roads and other infrastructures are absolutely necessary for sustained economic growth. An Erap presidency will give high priority to infrastructures in the following way:

- Local government units will be empowered to engage in the establishment, financing, and management of infrastructures. They will be allowed to tap domestic and international capital markets to finance infrastructure investments under special central government guarantees. They will be encouraged to set up special authorities to manage such projects. Where appropriate, adjacent local units sharing common resources and having common needs will be permitted to set up joint enterprises to establish and run area-wide utilities and public services.

- Private enterprise will be encouraged to invest in infrastructures. They may avail of a range of financing schemes such as built-operate-transfer (BOT), build-operate-own (BOO) and other arrangements.

- Certain infrastructures will be deregulated so that domestic and foreign investors can participate in their installation, financing and management.

*7. Access to housing and basic services*

An Erap presidency adheres to the principle that housing is a basic human right and that it is the responsibility of good governance to make housing accessible to all people. At present, 82 per cent of all households in the Philippines finance the construction of their homes with their own resources, 12 per cent rely on the private business sector, and only 6 per cent avail of government resources. An estimated 25 million squatters are found in cities and towns nation-wide, 4.5 million (about 700,000 households), in Metro Manila alone.

The Ramos administration had promised the construction of 1.2 million houses within six years—to date, barely 763,000 of those have been constructed and the remaining houses are promised before the end of the President's current term. The biggest problem, of course, is that people cannot afford proper housing—even if the proportion of families living below the poverty line is reduced to 30 per cent, families earning less than P54,000 a year still find it difficult to find the money to pay for a basic house that costs more than P180,000.

Pursuant to its housing principles and commitment, an Erap presidency will carry out the following programs:

- *Provision of basic services.* Recognizing that an immediate problem faced by the poor is lack of access to water, toilets, electricity, drainage, fire fighting, and garbage collection and disposal, an Erap-led administration will carry out a vigorous "on-site basic services" program. The basic services program will make such services accessible to all low-income communities regardless of their tenure status.

- *Private sector housing.* Housing finance depends on the capacity to pay of households. The private business sector can cater to about 25 per cent of households who can afford to get a mortgage from commercial banks. Government agencies, through the National Home Mortgage Finance Corporation (and the financial support of the Government Service Insurance System, Social Security System, and the Home Development Mutual Fund or *Pag-ibig*) can meet the needs of another 28 per cent. However, since more than one-third of Filipino households live below the poverty line, they require public subsidies.

- *Social housing.* The private sector will be encouraged, as much as possible, to engage in social housing. Instead of government agencies like the National Housing Authority managing housing programs, they should leave the construction, management, and maintenance of housing projects to the private sector. The known efficiency, cost consciousness and responsiveness to client demand of private enterprise should be fully availed of in housing administration. The main role of Government in housing would be to make financial resources available, setting minimum performance standards, and monitoring developments to make sure that those standards are adhered to.

- *NGO provided housing.* The energies and capabilities of the private NGO sector would be mobilized through the establishment of a *Sariling Bahay Foundation* (SBF) which will be a non-profit entity designed to support NGO and community-based initiatives. This foundation will be capitalized by a one-time grant from the Government and by tax-free contributions from donors. The foundation will be allowed to manage socialized housing projects financed from World Bank and other international loans.

- *Joint housing program.* Through the SBF, joint housing programs between the private and the NGO sector will be established. The SBF will approach owners of factories and other employers to make land available near job sites where workers' housing will be constructed. Employees will benifit by having access to affordable housing that will not require them to commute long distances, employers will be assured of employee loyalty and profit from low rates of absenteeism or tardiness and the larger society will benefit from reduced pollution arising from daily commuting.

- *Local government provided housing.*Local government units will be encouraged to invest in housing. They may make public lands available where SBF can construct affordable housing. They will be allowed to tap domestic and international credit for housing projects. By decentralizing responsibility for housing to local governments, they can bevome more responsiva to local housing needs.

- *Rural housing.* A rural housing program will be supported by an Erap-led Government to provide basic shelter, clean water, sanitation, electricity and other amenities to rural households. A "village cluster" approach will be used to provide basic services in a cost-effective way.

Such cluster will have thier own schools, health clinics, and community or *barangay* halls. They will be located close to town service centers and local markets to assure thier financial viability and access to services.

- *Housing for police, teachers, and civil servants.* Special housing programs will be setup for specific group of civil servants such as teachers and members of the police and protective services. The social housing will supplement the rather low salaries and benefits of such groups. The housing program will be co-managed by professional organization of these special groups. Such housing will supported by public funds to the extent that the average expenditure for housing of each household will not exceed 20 percent of household income.

## Environment

### *8. Protecting and preserving the environment*

In pursuing economic development, the Philippines has despoiled its natural environment so that forests are almost all depleted, coral reefs have been destroyed and rich crop lands are threatened by conversion to urban uses. A number of disasters (Mt. Pinatubo, earthquakes, droughts) and human-caused calamities (Marcopper, illegal logging) have contributed to the destruction of our environment.

Metro Manila, Cebu, Davao and other urban centers suffer from air, water, and soil pollution. Rivers like the Pasig are biologically dead while others have been turned into rampaging torrents during the typhoon season because of deforestation, soil erosion and silting. In Metro Manila, the 10 million residents produce 5,400 metric tons of garbage a day, and more than 10 per cent of that end up in canals, rivers, and vacant lots. The metropolitan area has run out of garbage dumps as neighboring municipalities refuse to receive the city's garbage. The metropolis produces 140 million liters of sewage per day and almost all of this is pumped into Manila Bay and other bodies of water untreated. As a result, clams, oysters, and other seafoods caught in Manila Bay and environs are now a threat to public health.

To counter negative environmental trends, an Erap presidency will do the following:

- Environmental control laws will be vigorously implemented and polluting industries will be subjected to fines and closure. No large scale projects will be approved by the Government without a valid environmental impact assessment. Officials charged with executing environmental laws will be given adequate training to enable them to carry out their tasks effectively. They will be given the proper equipment and other resources to allow them to do their jobs properly.

- A nation-wide effort to re-green the country will be launched with the help of civic-minded individuals and groups such as the Boy and Girl Scouts, the Armed Forces, community associations, NGOs and others. Native fast-growing tree varieties and shrubs will be identified and propagated. Millions of hectares of greenbelts will be set up all over the country, composed of productive trees and shrubs. Under the re-greening program, a target will be set whereby every Filipino will be encouraged to plant at least ten trees per year for the next six years.

- A national "Four Rs" campaign targeted on young children will be carried out whereby they will be encouraged to reduce their consumption of energy and resources, re-use materials, recover useful items, and recycle waste. The campaign will be carried out in schools and through youth organizations and clubs.

*9. Maintaining the environmental integrity of ecozones*

The Philippines is divided into natural ecological zones formed in accordance with such features as river basins, topographical features, elevation levels or the flora and fauna found in specific places. Under an Erap presidency, the planning, development and conservation of such ecozones will maintain their physical and cultural integrity.

- Using geographic information systems, systematic mapping and other techniques, the extent of natural ecozones will be determined. The congruence between such zones and administrative-political boundaries will be analyzed. On the basis of the analysis, comprehensive development plans will be formulated and executed to pursue the development of ecozones in an integrated manner.

- The protection of ecological zones focused on watershed areas will receive the highest priority. It is especially important to protect green areas around large human settlements to assure that water sources can be sustained for rapidly expanding populations and economic development activities. Planning and management of ecozones, based on natural features, such as river basins, forest preserves, and the traditional habitat of distinct species will be carried out in an effective manner.

- Where ecozones encompass several political boundaries, planning and implementation will be carried out in a collaborative and participatory manner. It is even possible that ecozones will transcend national boundaries, as in the BIMP-EAGA growth triangle made up of Southern Mindanao, Northern Sulawesi, East Malaysia and parts of Brunei-Darusallam. In such cases, planning and development will be pursued in a trans-national manner in accordance with the ecological integrity of the zone.

- A National Land Use Strategy will be formulated and implemented that will provide clear guidelines on which parts of the national territory will be marked for development, what parts will be ecological zones and protected forest reserves, what parts will be left untouched to conserve certain rare flora and fauna and endangered species, and what policies and measures can be adopted to implement the strategy in a rational way. The national land use strategy will embody a human settlements strategy to guide infrastructure and economic investment decisions in various types of urban areas.

- An agricultural lands conservation scheme will be adopted to prevent the conversion of rich agricultural lands to urban and other uses that has the effect of reducing the country's food production capabilities. A national policy preventing urban sprawl around large metropolitan areas will be adopted and implemented. Wherever possible, intensive urban agriculture will be pursued, using technological advances and techniques for producing vegetables, poultry, fish, fruits and other perishable items as close to the urban centers as possible to reduce transport costs.

## Peace and Stability

### *10. Maintaining peace and security*

Peace and stability are the foundations of sustained economic growth. Previous experience has shown that these can be achieved not through military might but by negotiations and agreements based on full recognition of the rights and interests of adversaries. Under an Erap presidency, therefore, peace will be achieved through the institution of social justice and transparent and fair dealings with all parties concerned.

To achieve peace and stability, all regions of the Philippines should be assured an equal opportunity for development. In particular, the *Mindanao Development Program* will be implemented vigorously in order to develop the region's rich agricultural, manufacturing and industrial resources. The special ties of the region with Asian neighbors, exemplified in the East Asean Growth Triangle development scheme, will be fully supported by the Government. In the *Visayas,*

Specific actions to maintain peace include the following:

- The Armed Forces of the Philippines (AFP) will be modernized and shaped into a lean military force fully supported by a civilian-based reserve force. While the Armed Forces are expected to protect the country's sovereignty and territorial integrity, a major role of the AFP will involve civic action, pursuant to the principle that peace is not gained by military might but by service to the people.

- The Armed Forces will protect the country's natural resources. Particular attention will be given to maritime resources under the rubric of the United Nations Conference on the Law of the Seas.

- The Philippines is visited frequently by natural calamities such as typhoons, earthquakes, volcanic eruptions, floods and other disasters. The Armed Forces will implement a disaster preparedness program featuring early warning systems, quick and adequate response, and full mobilization of resources for saving human lives and property. Efforts of the Armed Forces will be complemented by a Civil Protection Program to deal with disasters and calamities such as industrial accidents, environmental problems and health emergencies. The program will build up an efficient communication system and a community mobilization plan that can be used during times of crises.

- As noted in the section on security and safety, the PNP and local government police forces will be fully mobilized to achieve peace in the country. In the same way that the Armed Forces will rely on civic action, the PNP and local police forces will mainly depend on linkages and cooperation with communities in maintenance of peace and order. Most important, sustained economic growth and social justice will be the foundations of peace in the country as insurgency and ideological problems occur mainly when people are discontented and marginalized.

## Key Governance Programs

Good governance depends on Justice, Economy, Environment and Peace but its effective implementation can be achieved through such programs as civil service reform, improvement of the electoral process, and decentralization. Governance can also be achieved through the efficient delivery of key programs such as education and health and nutrition.

### *11. Instituting civil service reform*

Recent international ratings give the Philippines the dubious distinction of having one of the most corrupt and inefficient public services in Asia. The Philippine civil service, at the national and local levels, is beset with problems like low pay, inadequate benefits, bureaucratic red tape, incompetence and petty graft and corruption. It is obvious that if the civil service remains at this level, it cannot serve as an instrument for effecting sustained development.

An Erap presidency will pursue a vigorous program of civil service reform in the following manner:

- Pre-service education and training for civil servants will be given high priority by expanding the number of schools of public administration in the whole country. In such schools, the formation of a new group of dedicated civil servants will be started from the very beginning.

- The Government will launch the formation of a new group of elite civil servants, similar to the classical Mandarins of China or the Higher Civil Service of France—people who will be selectively educated and trained to take the leadership role in the civil service. This group will form the core of the Career Executive Service Organization (CESO) which will be strengthened.

- An Erap presidency will begin with a comprehensive Reorganization Program designed to achieve efficiency and effectiveness in the functioning of the whole governmental machinery. A National Reorganization Commission will be established and given the mission of coming up with a streamlined program of structural and procedural reform to make the public service more efficient and effective within six months after the President's inauguration. The recommendations of the Commission will then be implemented in a timely and expeditious manner.

*12. Decentralization of government services*

The Local Government Code of 1991 formally decentralized key governmental functions to provinces, cities, municipalities and barangays. Despite this policy decision, however, the bulk of financial resources are still controlled by the central government through the Executive and the Legislative branches. The proportion of internal revenue allotments and grants-in-aid in local government budgets remains high. Furthermore, piece meal allocation of Countryside Development Funds ( "pork barrel" ) by senators and members of the House of Representatives to their pet projects means that local officials continue to act as mendicants seeking allocations from the center.

As the only candidate for President who has been a local government official, Erap is committed to the principle of decentralization. In this regard, Erap as President will concurrently act as the Secretary of the Department of the Interior and Local Governments to give more attention to the needs of local government units.

An Erap presidency, therefore, will maximize the devolution of powers to local units. More specifically, the decentralization program will be pursued in the following ways:

- In pursuance of the Local Government Code, detailed implementing orders will be formulated and adopted that would accomplish two sets of tasks: (a) the Executive Branch and various departments and agencies will formulate operational policies and performance standards that local governments will follow in their exercise of delegated powers; and (b) local governments will be given explicit authority and power to raise their own revenues through taxation, fines, fees and user charges, to appoint competent personnel, and to adopt and implement productive processes and procedures for carrying out their functions.

- Local government units will be explicitly given the power and authority to support infrastructures. To this end, LGUs will be empowered to float bonds and to borrow from domestic and international credit sources for financing such infrastructures. Projects in the areas of agriculture, social housing, roads, markets and others that have a potential for revenue generation would be emphasized by local governments.

- The development of local tourism will be encouraged as a key responsibility of local governments. In this regard, tourism projects that reflect the regional values, culture and tradition of specific areas will be given preference. Instead of establishing high-level tourism facilities that offer "sun, sex and sin," projects that allow tourists to learn more about the Filipino way of life, and those that conserve and protect our environment will be given preference.

- Decentralization of governmental functions to LGUs will work only so far as local government executives and personnel are educated and trained to manage and coordinate public affairs. To this end, pre-service and in-service education and training programs for local officials will be expanded. Institutions like the Local Government Academy, the Civil Service Commission and colleges and school of public administration will be encouraged to expand their educational and training programs in local governance. The DILG will institute a scholarship fund that local officials and staff can tap to enable them to pursue human resources development efforts.

*13. Instituting electoral reforms*

A truly just society is based on the will of the people and open, safe, competitive and honest elections are needed to make sure that the best leaders in the country are democratically chosen. Unfortunately, although elections have been held in the Philippines since the turn of the century, there have been too many cases of cheating, intimidation, vote buying nd even terrorism to influence electoral results. In recent years, the infamous use of *dagdag -bawas* methods has been added to the bag of electoral tricks. There are even fears that computerization of the election process will only result in high-tech cheating.

During the martial law years, the electoral process became a farce, with the dominant party getting almost all the votes. Although naked political power was cloaked by efforts at legitimacy, the people knew they were being duped. At present, there are indications that the will of the people is being threatened anew by seemingly legitimate efforts to change the Constitution to postpone the 1998 elections. The argument of continuity of development policies is being used to allow a significant number of officials to remain in their offices without elections.

In an Erap presidency, the sovereign will of the people to choose their leaders will be guaranteed by instituting electoral reforms. Erap, if elected President, pledges that there will be no efforts during his term to allow him to serve beyond the constitutionally mandated six years. During an Erap presidency, new legislation will be passed to ensure that elections are open, honest, safe and truly competitive. This will be done through the following mesures:

- Absolute guarantees that the independence of the Commission on Elections (Comelec), as the constitutional body charged with administering the election process will be ensured.

- Legislation prohibiting the use of government funds to directly or indirectly support the candidacy of any person will be enacted and fully implemented. Similar laws setting a limit on how much each candidate can spend on elections and prohibiting campaigning within 90 days before the election date will be strictly implemened.

- The voter registration process will be conducted in an efficient manner. Each electoral precinct will be precisely delimited in a map. No more than 200 voters will be included in each precinct. A complete, computerized and alphabetized list of all individuals legally entitled to vote in each precinct will be prepared and made known to the public.

- Legitimately recognized political parties will be given the opportunity to check the list of voters to make sure that the lists are complete, accurate and truly reflective of the situation in each precinct. The parties will be given adequate time to verify and check the lists before election day.

- The best and most appropriate technological means will be used to ensure that the voting process is clean, honest and not subject to tampering. All votes should be counted in the shortest possible time and the results should be announced as soon as possible.

- Each political party will be represented in organized activities conducted at every level to carry out the elections, from the precinct level to the top. Each party will be entitled to at least one election watcher per precinct to ensure that electoral procedures are strictly followed.

- Civic associations, NGOs, community-based groups and concerned citizens will be mobilized tc monitor the electoral process as an insurance against fraud. The electoral process will be open to international observers, the mass media and other concerned groups to ensure that complete transparency in the process is observed.

*14. Fostering grassroots empowerment*

Philippine-style democracy is based on the active participation of more than 70,000 non-governmental organizations (NGOs), people's organizations (POs), community-based organizations (CBOs), cause-oriented groups, women's associations, youth groups, and other entities that provide energy and vigor to the functioning of a vibrant Civil Society. An Erap presidency, founded as it is on the interests of the masses, will enter into an active partnership with such groups in executing its Governance program. It is not enough that representatives of such groups are included in the formal structures of governance. What is more important is the allocation of authority and resources to such groups in order to empower them to achieve their goals.

To foster grassroots empowerment, an Erap presidency will pursue the following programs:

- A Civil Society Trust Fund will be established, initially with public funds but, increasingly, with private donations from local and international sources. Resources of this fund will be made available to POs, NGOs, CBOs, and other groups that seek to pursue developmental, civic, cultural and equity-related activities. The policies governing the Fund and its management will be in the hands of the grassroots organizations themselves. The Fund's priorities, programs and operating procedures will be decided by duly elected representatives of the concerned groups.

- Recognizing the special role of women in the functioning of the family, as productive members of society and as managers of community affairs, a special Women's Development Program will be organized initially with the support of public funds but later on with private donations and self-generated resources. A special feature of this program will be the extension of micro-credit facilities to individual women or women's organizations to enable them to carry out specific projects, especially those of an employment-creation and income-generating nature.
- The Filipino youth will provide the future leaders of this country and their enthusiasm and innovative energies will be mobilized in an Erap program of Good Governance. Young people, through such institutions

as the *Sanggunian ng Kabataan* and *Sangguniang Barangay* will be made an integral part of local governance and community-based action. Scholarships, such as those offered by the *Erap sa Mahirap Foundation*, will be expanded to offer more educational opportunities to poor but deserving young men and women all over the country. A National Youth Services Corps will be organized to support activities related to such concerns as environmental protection and conservation, disaster preparedness and crisis management, skills development, and the enhancing of entrepreneurial skills.

- Community groups will be mobilized in a nation-wide program to combat drugs and substance abuse as this plague saps the energies of the people, especially the youth. A massive information, education and communication campaign will be launched to provide more information about the dangers of drugs, how parents can detect if their children are into drugs, various methods for curing drug addiction, and how young people can be "street proofed" against the enticements of drug pushers and peddlers. Community-based programs will work closely with police and other authorities to eradicate the drug trade. More important, the demand for drugs and dangerous substances can be curtailed by an educated, alert, and well-informed citizenry.

- A Civilian Crime Prevention Program will be established with Civilian Peace and Order Councils organized at community level. The program will work closely with police authorities in setting up such initiatives as community policing, *rondas*, civilian crime information networks, neighborhood watch schemes, assets identification programs, and other approaches for preventing crime.

**Sectoral Programs**

*15. Improving basic education*

The main competitive advantage of the Philippines in this era of globalization lies in its highly educated, literate and skilled citizenry. More than 93 per cent of Filipinos aged seven and above are literate and most Filipinos are multi-lingual and able to compete in an international setting because of their knowledge of English.

One of the frustrations related to the educational system, especially on the part of the youth, is that it fails to prepare youngsters for the job market. At present,

56.2 per cent of 72 million Filipinos are under 24 and many of these will be ready to join the labor force. However, inadequate education and lack of vocational training have rendered them unprepared. Experience in other countries has shown that the ranks of the educated unemployed often serve as a destabilizing factor as they may translate their frustrations into anti-social activities. Government's failure to live up to the expectations of the youth, therefore, may be costly to the society.

An Erap presidency will introduce the following reforms:

- Highest priority will be given to values formation among children below the age of six. To this end, the establishment of the Department of Basic Education is of the highest importance. Pre-school nursery and kindergarten facilities will be supported at the community level with the full participation of parents, teachers and community leaders. At this level, emphasis will be given to the formation of moral character, personal discipline, and civic conscience that are reflective of Filipino culture and basic values. With the integration of pre-school education with child-rearing in the home and the full cooperation between parents and teachers, a sound preparation for all children can be achieved prior to entering the formal school system.

- Many private non-profit primary schools have been playing a very important role in providing quality basic education. With the improvements in public education, especially the increasing of teachers' salaries, these schools are finding it extremely difficult to survive. A careful evaluation of such schools will be made to determine which ones are doing a good job. Schools passing such an evaluation will be provided with subsidies—a specified amount for each student enrolled in such schools.

- Pre-schools and primary schools, especially those in communities where many of the students come from poor families, will have a publicly supported school feeding program. Current studies have shown that many students are unable to absorb lessons learned at school because they are too hungry or malnourished, not because they do not have the intellectual capacity to learn or lack motivation. The program will also help to solve malnutrition among young children, which is very serious in certain areas.

- The issue of the medium of instruction will be resolved. For the first two years, subjects will be taught in the child's native tongue. Pilipino will be introduced in the third grade. English as a second language will be introduced in the fourth grade. In high school, intensive English classes will be offered as optional subjects to students planning to pursue a college level education. At the same time, specialized English schools will be set up, where students will have to pay additional tuition if they desire to take such courses.

- Since education is designed to help people become gainfully employed, vocational subjects will be introduced at the appropriate school levels. The Technical Education and Skills Development Authority (TESDA) will be allocated greater resources. At the proper time, students can decide whether they would like to take a vocational or an academic track. Fully equipped vocational schools will be set up and existing ones will be strengthened. To prepare students for employment in high technology fields, special skills like those involving the use of computers, will be emphasized. The job apprenticeship program of the government will be expanded in order to prepare more young people for the job market.

- An Erap Government will establish a National Youth Service Corps that will provide college students and recent graduates an opportunity to "earn while you learn" and to apply what they have learned in an actual job setting. For example, recent law graduates will be encouraged to join the Public Defenders program; medical graduates will volunteer to join the Rural Health Service; and recent commerce and business administration graduates will join rural cooperatives. The NYSC will provide basic remuneration and allowances for participants and will formulate programs to make sure that the youth will really learn something while participating in the program.

- Since college education is a privilege rather than a right, tertiary education institutions will impose the highest possible standards for entering college. This is especially true of the U.P. system and other state educational institutions which are heavily subsidized by the government.

- Private tertiary institutions, especially those that regard education as a business, will be required to conform with strictly set national standards regarding quality of teaching, provision of equipment and facilities, size of classes, tuition fees imposed, etc. Periodic testing of students by the Commission on Higher Education (CHEd) should be carried out to assess these institutions' conformance with standards. Their financial viability will be monitored to ensure that students get quality education in return for personal investments in human resource development.

*16. Supporting health and nutrition*

Filipinos, with an average life expectancy of 69.5 years, enjoy relatively good health. However, the infant mortality rate, at 45.8 per 1,000 live births is still considerably higher than other Asian countries. Child and maternal mortality and morbidity rates continue to be high. First and second degree malnutrition, especially in rural areas and communities of the urban poor also remain unacceptably high. Too many children and mothers still die from what are essentially preventable causes. It is obvious that many of these problems are caused by the lack of sanitation.

The Department of Health (DOH) indicates that about 70 per cent of the health problems in the country are not due to pathogenic agents—they are essentially caused by lack of hygiene, limited access to potable water, poor nutrition, and inadequate health education. In other words, paying attention to environmental aspects of health and a preventive rather than a curative approach to health care will accomplish more than a heavy emphasis on hospitals and clinics. The active participation of people through community organizations in a primary health care program, a massive vaccination and inoculation campaign, and better nutrition education serve as the basis for a healthier citizenry.

An Erap presidency will ensure better health through these measures:

- The decentralization of the health function to local government units will be fully implemented. In particular, more *barangay* health stations will be set up and trained midwives will be fielded. Rural health stations, headed by nurses will also be augmented. Special attention will be given to the 275 municipalities in the country that do not yet have a municipal health officer, the 20 priority poverty alleviation target areas, and the 35 provinces designated by DOH as needing particular interventions. By the year 2004, almost all Filipino families should be within a ten minute traveling distance of a health facility.

- The occupational health and safety program will be expanded. The program will give highest priority to the prevention of work related diseases such as asbestosis, silicosis, tuberculosis, and schistosomiasis. This program will help make the Philippines more competitive in the global economy by minimizing losses due to absences arising from illness.

*17. Strengthening science and technology*

At a time when technological development is revolutionizing the global economy the Philippines lacks a coherent technology policy aside from a relatively small effort to foster science education at the secondary school level. Public and private investments in research and development are woefully inadequate. Even the meager results of R & D efforts in universities are not developed in such a way where they can be translated into productive enterprises. Government science and technology policy does not provide incentives to private enterprise.

Under an Erap presidency, the Government will support the following programs:

- National centers of excellence in science and technology will be established and strengthened in institutions such as the University of the Philippines, the Technological University of the Philippines and selected private universities. Universities will be encouraged to set up Research and Development Units charged with the responsibility of identifying scientific breakthroughs and discoveries and facilitating their development into productive enterprises.

- Top quality science high schools, focused on science and technology, will be established in key regions of the country. Such high schools will provide scholarships to poor but deserving students to encourage them to pursue a career in science and technology. The high schools will be fully supported with adequate funds to enable them to attract excellent teachers, buy appropriate equipment such as computers and laboratory facilities, and conduct field experiments involving teachers and students.

In all these efforts, the Government's role in science and technology development will be mainly facilitative and supportive. It will assume a service role and provide the policy framework wherein R & D can be carried out by government institutions and private and non-governmental entities.

*18. Re-orienting the foreign service*

The Philippines plays a strong regional and international role in foreign affairs and the history of our diplomatic efforts in the United Nations and other world forums has attested to our record as a free nation. In recent years, however, the

Philippines is known more as a sick economy, a corrupt society, a kidnap capital and a nation of domestics. Although our Department of Foreign Affairs continues to play a key role in ASEAN, APEC, WTO, and other world bodies, the country finds it difficult to project a positive image.

A primary goal in an Erap vision of governance is to change the attitudes of Filipinos and, eventually, the world at large, about the nature of our country. This change of attitude cannot be accomplished by public relations gimmicks—we have to earn it by posting sustained economic growth, achieving political stability, and practicing participatory democracy. To accomplish these goals, the following measures have to be carried out:

- The Department of Foreign Affairs will be re-oriented toward functions directly related to achieving economic growth, fostering trade and commerce, and protecting all Filipino citizens living abroad in addition to the traditional functions of diplomacy, safeguarding national security, and harmonious inter-country relations. Recruitment to the foreign service, and pre-service and in-service training programs for diplomatic personnel will emphasize these new functions. According to ADB's Development Outlook 1997, about 4.2 million Filipinos work in 120 countries all over the world. They comprise more than 15 per cent of the country's 26 million labor force. These overseas contract workers deserve the full support of foreign service officials and staff as they are a major contributor to our country's progress.

- The foreign service will be reorganized into a leaner organization focused firmly on its service orientation. Filipino officials in embassies and consulates abroad should have a unified identity, instead of bureaucratically reporting to separate agencies such as the Department of Trade, Department of Labor, National Security Council, etc. With the advances in communication technology world-wide, it is now possible to have fewer diplomatic posts and still maintain the efficiency and effectiveness of foreign affairs activities.

- Foreign service staff will be composed of professionally trained and technically proficient individuals (economists, engineers, labor lawyers, social workers, counselors) rather than generalist diplomats. They will be recruited, appointed, and promoted according to merit rather than political patronage or family connections. Aside from fostering a commitment to performance of technical and professional functions, all foreign service staff will be imbued with a service orientation—protecting, guiding and assisting all Filipinos living abroad and responding to their immediate needs.

**Conclusion**

To sum up, this vision of governance is not a mere dream—it is a carefully formulated strategy for the development of the Philippines during an Erap presidency.

The vision is focused on achieving a just and equitable society. It is based on the belief that economic development, especially if it is based too much on reliance on foreign investments and international loans, will not achieve a high quality of life for the Filipinos. To achieve sustainable development, political stability must first be achieved not by reliance on the police powers of the state but by the direct involvement of all citizens, the rich as well as the poor, in the decision making processes leading to development. Without full commitment to common ideals and a sense of ownership of the development process on the part of the people, it will be extremely difficult to attain lasting progress.

Governance in the Philippines has for too long been the private preserve of traditional elites and their political allies. Leaders among business elites, the media, and intellectuals have imposed their values and points of view on the whole society. An Erap presidency heralds the opportunity to directly involve the Filipino people in the full process of governance. This participatory democracy will reign not just during the electoral process when the country's elites are forced to go to the masses to gain their votes, but in the day-to-day running of the country. It is in this way that an Erap presidency will deliver growth with equity and grassroots empowerment through good governance.

The poor and underprivileged people of the Philippines, the teeming masses, have placed their trust in Erap Estrada for him to take the leadership that will take them out of poverty and helplessness. This does not mean that accomplishing the goals of this program of governance requires violent upheaval against the rich and the privileged. Rather, it is more a call for empowerment—for the lot of the masses to be improved, until, empowered at last, they are able to take unto their hands, the scope and direction of their true destiny.

## APPENDIX 2

# PROPOSED ERAP SOCIAL HOUSING PROGRAM

Key principles of the Erap Housing program are:

- Highest priority is given to social housing to meet the needs of low-income people who cannot afford economic housing.
- Formulation and implementation of housing programs are based on people's participation and organized community support.
- No housing demolition without adequate alternative accommodation.
- The private sector will play the leading role in housing design, construction, estate management, and delivery of basic services.
- Adequate services to be provided aside from shelter (e.g., water, sanitation, drainage, electricity, garbage collection and disposal).

### The Housing Need

Housing affordability studies show that 64% of around 15 million Filipino households can pay P150,000 or more for a house while 36% (about 5.4 million families) cannot meet the costs of even the most basic housing option.

Capacity to pay for housing is estimated as follows:

| | |
|---|---|
| Households who can afford luxury housing (P4 million+) | 1% |
| Can pay for high-income housing (P1 million+) | 4% |
| Can pay for medium-priced housing (P375,000+) | 17% |
| Can pay for low-cost housing (P180,000+) | 38% |

| | |
|---|---|
| Can only afford subsidized housing (P150,000+) | 4% |
| Cannot afford basic housing option (Less than P150,000) | 36% |

Private developers have no problem meeting the demand of families who can afford luxury, high-income and medium-income housing. In recent years, some private entrepreneurs have also shown the financial viability of low-cost housing, tapping financial incentives under the Government's Unified Home Lending Program (UHLP).

It is the 36% of households who cannot afford even the most basic housing option (a house costing not more than P150,000) that offers the biggest challenge to the Erap administration. About 78% of these low-income households (4.2 million) are living in urban areas where they are concentrated in slum and squatter communities, 720,000 in Metro Manila alone. Others are concentrated in Metro Cebu, Davao, General Santos, Cagayan de Oro and other cities.

In general, people in rural areas can build their own houses with local materials and indigenous building techniques. However, rural housing deteriorates quite rapidly and does not stand up to typhoons and other calamities. Rural homes usually do not have access to clean water, sanitation, electricity and other basic services.

## The Ramos Administration Housing Program

The National Shelter Program (1993-1998) of the Ramos administration estimated the housing need of the Philippines at 3.7 million housing units. This projected need was made up of the following components:

| | |
|---|---|
| A. Housing backlog | 873 |
| Households doubling up | 444 |
| Replacement housing | 422 |
| Housing for homeless families | 7 |
| B. Future Housing Need | 2,853 |
| New dwelling units | 1,498 |
| Houses needing upgrading | 1,355 |
| **Total Housing Need (A + B)** | **3,726** |

The Ramos administration's housing program claimed it was focused on meeting the needs of households at the bottom 30% of the income structure. For the period 1993-98, the target was to assist 1.2 million households. As of the end of 1997, the Government had assisted 833,000 households. In general, the Ramos housing program has not been able to meet its targets or to assist the poorest of the poor.

The Ramos housing program has resettled more than 47,000 families to relocation sites far from the cities, where jobs and services were not available. As a result, many of the relocated families have filtered back to the city core. The community mortgage program served 50,000 families, roughly 53.9% of the targeted families. Direct housing provision was extended to 300,000 families and loans and other types of assistance were given to another 437,000 families through the Indirect Housing Provision program. Despite all these efforts, however, the number of homeless people, squatters and slum dwellers in the country has not been significantly reduced.

The Erap housing program seeks to remedy the shortcomings of the Ramos administration. At the same time, it re-emphasizes the need to focus attention on the housing needs of the masses. While the Ramos program states its commitment to meeting the housing needs of the poor, it has concentrated on building units that the poorest of the poor could not afford. Its actual housing delivery has not lived up to the promises of the program.

**Future Housing Targets**

Taking into consideration natural rates of population growth and household formation, migration to urban areas, the housing backlog, the need to replace dilapidated housing, and the need to upgrade the quality of the housing stock, the real social housing need by the start of the Erap administration will be 5.4 million housing units.

Focusing the administration's attention on the bottom 36% of households with incomes of less than P50,000 per year and who cannot afford to pay for a house costing more than P150,000, the social housing target in the Erap housing program is set at constructing 1.9 million units within six years.

To achieve this target, housing activities will take short-term (first 100 days), medium term (first three years) and longer-term (up to six years) perspectives.

## Plan of Action

### Actions During the First 100 Davs

1. Immediately stop all demolition, eviction and relocation activities involving squatters and slum dwellers until appropriate and acceptable alternative sites are found and prepared to receive them.

2. Conduct a quick review of activities of the Housing and Urban Development Coordinating Council (HUDCC), National Housing Authority (NHA), National Home Mortgage Finance Corporation (NHMFC), Home Insurance Guaranty Corporation (HIGC) and the Housing and Land Use Regulatory Board (HLURB) to determine new targets, resource availability and staff adequacy for pursuing the new housing program. (Review team to be headed by Professor Benjamin Carino, Dean of the U.P. School of Urban and Regional Planning. Report to be submitted to the Office of the President within 30 days).

3. Conduct a quick review of financing activities of the Home Development and Mutual Fund (HDMF) or Pag-ibig Fund, Social Security System (SSS) and the Government Service Insurance System (GSIS) to assess funding capabilities. Create a *National Provident Fund* by combining the functions, resources, personnel and activities of the GSIS, SSS and the HDMF. Initiate legislation to streamline these organizations and come up with a more efficient Provident Fund. (Review Team to be headed by Professor Norman Ramos of the U.P. Planning and Development Research Foundation, Inc., or PLANADES. Report to be submitted to the Office of the President within 30 days).

4. Formulate, adopt and implement by Executive Order reorganization plans to create a *Department of Housing and Urban Development* to replace the HUDCC. The proposed DHUD would be headed by a Secretary of Cabinet rank, assisted by two Undersecretaries, one for Housing Operations and another for Housing Finance. Appoint these key officials. (Executive Order creating DHUD to be prepared and signed immediately after Erap is inaugurated President].

5. Establish the *Sariling Bahay Foundation (SBF),* a private, non-profit, non-governmental organization that will formulate and execute housing and urban development projects for the 36% of the population who

cannot afford economic housing. Appoint a Chief Executive Officer and other staff for this foundation. (Articles of Incorporation and other documents creating the foundation to be signed within the first week after Erap's inauguration).

6. Launch a *Pabahay para sa Manggagawa* (Workers Housing Scheme) under the SBF by convincing factory owners and other entrepreneurs to set aside land for medium-rise apartments (up to five storeys) adjacent to factories. The SBF will construct such housing and sell it to factory workers and staff. Profits from this economic housing scheme will be used to cross-subsidize low-cost housing projects.(First pilot project to be signed and started within the first month of Erap's presidency).

7. Launch a *Pabahay sa Nayon* (Rural Housing) program that stresses provision of basic services such as water, sanitation, electricity and other services. This program will emphasize the use of indigenous building materials, traditional construction skills, and the full participation of people using the *bayanihan* approach (Executive Order implementing this program to be signed within the first month of an Erap presidency).

8. Conduct a quick inventory of public lands that may be available for social housing. (Task Force to be headed by the Director of the National Housing Authority. Report to be submitted within one month after Erap's inauguration).

9. Start formulation of a loan document for low-cost housing to be submitted to the World Bank and the Asian Development Bank. Housing under this loan will be managed by the SBF. The loan will be guaranteed by the Banko Sentral ng Pilipinas. Housing policies and standards used by the SBF will be set by a multi-sectoral board to be chaired by the Secretary of DHUD, with representatives from urban poor groups, DILG, LGUs and professional organizations. (Negotiations to be started with World Bank and ADB within the first two weeks of an Erap presidency).

10. Formulate and announce a new National Housing and Urban Development Plan (1998-2004) together with a detailed financing scheme to be launched within the first 100 days of an Erap Presidency.

11. Launch a massive drive to extend basic services such as clean water, sanitary toilets, roads and pathways, drainage, garbage collection and

disposal, health centers, preparatory and primary schools, electricity, and other basic services to existing slum and squatter areas in an expanded *Community Upgrading Program.* (First pilot projects to be carried out with LGUs and the NHA within the first month of an Erap presidency).

12. Inaugurate medium-density housing projects (up to five storeys) in existing slum and squatter areas, that would be complete with basic infrastructures and urban services and amenities. Such housing projects will serve people as close as possible to where they are actually residing rather than relocating them to other places (First pilot project to be launched within the first 100 days).

## Actions During the First Three Years

1. Encourage private developers to venture into low- and medium-cost housing by making Provident Fund resources available. Public infrastructures such as roads, drainage, sanitation and sewerage, electricity, gas, and other utilities will be provided to housing projects. Provide serviced lands to private developers.

2. The Erap administration will minimize graft and corruption in all aspects of housing construction and management so that developers and construction companies will be paid promptly without resorting to bribery and commissions. In this way, the real cost of housing to homeowners will be reduced by almost 50%.

3. Encourage LGUs to devote more resources to housing by making public land available, providing counterpart financial resources, guaranteeing domestic and foreign loans devoted to housing, and giving technical assistance and managerial help to local housing agencies.

4. Formulate and adopt a National Land Use Plan that will concentrate clustered urban functions in central places and integrate housing with economic activities, governmental services, trade and commerce, and recreation. By such functional and spatial integration, commuting which results in heavy traffic flows will be minimized. Such a plan will provide appropriate transportation, communication and service linkages among urban central places. Transport will emphasize mass rapid transit systems rather than private individual vehicles.

5. Provide incentives for the formulation, adoption and implementation of comprehensive strategic and master plans for urban settlements (cities and municipalities) in order to rationally provide for housing and basic urban services in such places.

6. Establish low- and medium-income housing as integral parts of industrial estates, export processing zones, high-tech parks, agribusiness complexes and new towns in order to encourage people to locate in these settlements rather than moving to very large cities.

7. Encourage universities as well as private developers to engage in research and development focused on new and improved building materials, more efficient construction processes, and modern technologies in the field of housing.

8. Encourage community groups, NGOs and civil society institutions to contribute financial, human and organizational resources for affordable housing. Each housing project should be fully supported by a community organization that will help manage the project and look after operations and maintenance.

9. Establish a *National Housing Bank* fully dedicated to providing resources for affordable housing.

## Activities up to the Sixth Year

1. Raise additional financing for low-cost housing through the Provident Fund, the National Housing Bank, domestic and international loans, local government bonds, and user charges and fees to provide more funds for affordable housing units.

2. Expand the activities of the *Sariling Bahay Foundation* into economic housing in order to increase the resources that may be used to cross-subsidize projects for the poorest of the poor. Explore the possibility of using international loans for housing.

3. Review the National Housing and Urban Development Plan to make sure that housing targets, processes and procedures are updated and made more relevant to urban development patterns.

4. Ensure that national housing targets are fulfilled, especially those that benefit the urban and rural poor.

5. Formulate, adopt and implement a comprehensive National Urban Development Strategy that will be composed of: (a) land use plans, zoning ordinances and other location-specific plans and regulations; (b) detailed local government plans, zoning codes, subdivision regulations and building standards; (c) processes and procedures for urban finance; and (d) detailed provisions for urban management.

6. Ensure that housing plans are fully integrated with plans for transportation and communication, traffic, power supply, water supply, sewerage and drainage, solid waste management, and flood control.

7. Fully integrate housing and urban development with environmental conservation and pollution control. Make sure that human settlements are sustainable by taking environmental considerations fully in urban planning and management.

8. Adopt and implement a continuing training and capacity-building program for LGUs to focus on such areas as: land use planning, environmental management, capital investment programming, fiscal management, infrastructure planning, basic services delivery, revenue enhancement and development planning.

9. More fully decentralize housing and urban development functions to LGUs to make them responsive to people's needs and enable them to assume more responsibilities.

10. Promote joint ventures between the private sector and LGUs in the field of urban development and housing, with special emphasis on delivery of basic services such as water, garbage collection and disposal, flood control and traffic management.

## Financing the Housing Program

1. Taking inflation into consideration which makes the lower limit of P150,000 per unit unrealistic, even at the modest cost of P200,000 per unit, the 1.9 million housing units needed during the Erap presidency

will cost about P380 billion. On the average, this will require expenditures of P63 billion a year.

2. With proper incentives from the Government, the private sector should be able to provide capital resources for about a third of the required funds.

3. Private family savings, harnessed through the Provident Fund, the National Housing Bank, the Sariling Bahay Foundation, the commercial banking sector and other financial institutions should be able to generate another third of the housing finance requirements.

4. The remaining third will be derived from domestic and international loans incurred by the housing finance institutions, local government units and developers. Such loans will be guaranteed by the central government and LGUs.

5. The paid-in capital of the National Housing Authority should be doubled to P5.6 billion to take into consideration the expanded housing needs. A larger proportion of the portfolios of the financial institutions belonging to the Provident Fund should also be devoted to social housing.

The added investments in housing will not only make affordable housing more accessible to Filipinos. Studies have shown that housing multiplier effects are roughly 16.6 times per unit of cost, in terms of demand increases for raw materials, labor, taxes and value-added elements. Housing also has salutary effects on people's health and the motivation of family members to strive harder and earn more. In this way, the housing program of the Erap administration, focused as it is on the welfare of the masses, will surely generate more than just economic progress—it will also contribute to a higher quality of life for all.

## Analysis of the Ramos Housing Program

According to the *Housing and Urban Development Coordinating Council* (HUDCC), the Ramos administration set the target of building 1.2 million houses between 1993-1998. For the period ending December 1997, the government claimed to have exceeded its target of 768,000 units within four years and actually built 833,000 units (108.5% accomplishment rate). The HUDCC report indicated the following:

| Major Programs | Target | Actual | Accomplishment |
|---|---|---|---|
| Resettlement | 116 | 47 | 40.4% |
| Community Mortgage | 92 | 50 | 53.9 |
| Direct Housing Provision | 267 | 300 | 112.5 |
| Indirect Housing Provision | 293 | 437 | 149.1 |
| **Total Households (1000)** | **768** | **833** | **108.5** |

An analysis of the Ramos administration's housing accomplishments reveals that the main programs do not really benefit the poorest of the poor. The main intervention that directly affects the lives of the poor is Resettlement which is meant to move poor families from dangerous areas (the banks of canals and rivers, along railroad lines, on dump sites or on flood prone areas) or to resettle families occupying land needed by government infrastructure projects.

In reality, despite laws specifying that squatter shanties should not be demolished until adequate and acceptable accommodations are provided, thousands of poor families are evicted from their abodes every year. Relocation sites are often too far from the city where the poor people work, they do not have adequate transportation linkages and they generally lack even the most basic services such as water, sanitation, electricity and garbage collection. Because of problems with resettlement, the urban poor were actually much better off by the fact that only 40.4% of targeted families were resettled under the program.

The Community Mortgage Program finances schemes whereby slum dwellers are allowed to buy the land they are occupying (provided landowners are willing to sell). Through an upgrading program, the government then extends water, sanitation, electricity and drainage services to the place. However, as seen in the government's report, only 53.9% of target households were benefited by this scheme.

The Direct Housing Loan Provision program assists families with regular incomes who can afford to borrow from government agencies to buy land or build a house. The program relies on the *Home Development and Mutual Fund or Pag-ibig,* and the *Unified Home Lending Program* (UHLP) for support.

Loans are at concessional rates, 9% for P180,000 or less; 12% for loans between P180,000 and P225,000 and 16% for loans between P225,000 and P375,000. In 1996, housing loan releases were temporarily stopped because of funding problems under the UHLP.

The Indirect Housing Provision program lends money to private developers who then construct affordable housing. Loans are obtained directly from the Pag-ibig Fund, the *National Home Mortgage Finance Corporation* (NHMFC), the *Government Service Insurance System* (GSIS) and the *Social Security System* (SSS). The *Home Insurance Guaranty Corporation* (HIGC) guarantees and gives credit insurance to mobilize private sector funds. Standards and regulations for housing are set and imposed by the *Housing and Land Use Regulatory Board* (HLURB).

**Housing Organizational Structure**

The legal mandate for housing in the Philippines is embodied in Republic Act 7279 or the *Urban Development and Housing Act of1992* which also provides the framework for housing policies and programs. The *Comprehensive and Integrated Shelter Financing Act of1994,* in turn, provides funding for the National Shelter Program.

The main body for coordinating urban development and housing is the *Housing and Urban Development Coordinating Council (HUDCC)* which was created by Executive Order 90 (1986). Executive Order 357 (1989) strengthened the authority of HUDCC to coordinate the activities of housing agencies in the country.

The sole government agency mandated to engage in shelter production focusing on the needs of the poor is the *National Housing Authority (NHA)* created by Presidential Decree No.757 in 1975. The NHA is a government-owned and controlled corporation under the administrative supervision of HUDCC. Under Republic Act 7279 (1992), NHA was tasked to provide technical and other forms of assistance to local government units (LGUs) in the implementation of their housing programs. In 1994, NHA was given authority to carry out Resettlement, Medium-Rise Public and Private Housing, Cost Recovery and Local Housing under the National Shelter Program. As of December 1996, the NHA had paid in capital of P2.8 billion.

Key housing agencies, aside from the NHA are the NHMFC, HIGC and the HLURB. Housing funds are mainly provided by the HDMF or Pag-ibig, the SSS and GSIS.

Aside from these key housing and financing agencies, other government agencies support the housing program. Foremost among these is the National Economic and Development Authority (NEDA), which formulated the Medium Term

Philippine Development Plan (1993-1998) which highlighted the role of housing in socio-economic development. The Department of Finance, in charge of fiscal policy, looks into the financing of housing and the multiplier effects of housing on governmental finance. The Department of Budget Management (DBM) allocates funds for housing and related services.

Important elements in housing and urban development are local government units (LGUs) which are mandated by the Local Government Code of 1991 to provide financial resources, including loans, for housing. Also important are metropolitan agencies like the Metro Manila Development Authority which also have authority for providing housing aside from having jurisdiction over garbage disposal and traffic management. The Department of the Interior and Local Governments, by its supervisory powers over LGUs encourages housing programs.

Because housing is directly linked with basic infrastructures, the Department of Public Works and Highways plays an important role in housing. Privatized agencies such as the Metropolitan Waterworks and Sewerage System, the Manila Electric Company and private garbage collection companies are also important elements in the governmental housing structure.

## Assessment of Housing Delivery System

The claims of the Ramos administration that it has surpassed its national housing targets notwithstanding, the housing program leaves a lot to be desired. The main shortcomings are: (a) shortage of funds for housing; (b) problems with resettlement schemes; (c) shortage of land for housing; (d) lack of basic urban services support; and (d) failure of local government units to provide housing;

## Shortage of Housing Funds

The National Shelter Plan estimates that the government needs P185 billion over five years to effectively deal with the Philippine housing problem. This huge amount is meant to address the housing needs of only 30% of Philippine households who do not have the money to pay for economic housing. So far, the government agencies are able to meet only 40% of the identified housing need. The government is especially unable to meet the needs of the poorest of the poor. The Ramos administration has set the target of financing 1.2 million housing units within the period 1993-1998.

The biggest sources of low-cost housing finance in the Philippines are the HDMF or Pag-ibig Fund, the GSIS and the SSS. Essentially, the GSIS and SSS use the funds that are not needed to pay the insurance and other benefits of public and private sector employees for housing. The Pag-ibig Fund is a provident fund that also relies on the savings contributions of individuals, matched by their employers. The Fund is mandated to (a) administer the provident fund contributions of member employees and employers; (b) utilize funds not required for provident fund benefits for housing loans to members; and (c) develop saving schemes to enable members to acquire housing.

The Pag-ibig Fund had total resources of P1.7 billion as of the end of 1997. Since its establishment 17 years ago, it has released $850 million in housing loans, equivalent to funding 356,412 housing units. The Fund has twice floated asset-backed bonds amounting to $96.1 million with a term of five years.

The GSIS had net income of P30 billion in 1997. Its accumulated assets amounted to P121 billion by the end of the same year.

In September 1997, the Multi-Window Lending System for financing housing was introduced. In the past, interest rates on housing loans were set at 9%, 12% and 16% based on the amount of the loan. Instead, interest rates would be based on the reference mark or benchmark of treasury bills, treasury notes or other financial issues. In the case of banks, they are allowed to impose a maximum spread of 4% above the actual rate used by funding agencies. In this way, housing loans may be obtained through many outlets including commercial banks and other financial institutions. To help Pag-ibig in its lending operations, the Development Bank of the Philippines borrowed P5 billion worth of Yen, which it released to the Fund to subsidize the interest differential between the market interest rates and the socialized housing loans obtained by low-income earners from Pag-ibig.

With the Asian currency crisis that also hit the Philippines, the peso's value dropped from P26 to US$1.00 to P40 to $1.00. Prime lending rates of commercial banks shot up as high as 36% although the *Bangko Sentral ng Pilipinas* (BSP) has urged a return to more "reasonable levels" of around 24%. To curb the inflationary tendencies of real estate loans, the BSP imposed a cap of 20% on loans of the commercial banking system for real-estate lending (such loans made up 12.6% of portfolios in March). To help social housing programs, the BSP gave "special favorable treatment" to low- and medium-cost housing by exempting housing loans not exceeding P3.5 million and housing loans guaranteed by the National Shelter Program from the 20% cap.

Despite the good intentions of the BSP, the gap between the high market-dictated interest rates and the administratively set fixed interest rates for low-cost housing is too wide to encourage the banking sector to go into lending for social housing. Even with the permission to add 4% over the agency-mandated rates, the loans are still not attractive.

A very serious problem among government finance agencies involved in housing is the high rate of non-payment or defaults. Most recipients of housing units managed by the NHA and other government agencies refuse to pay their arrears using such excuses as non-delivery of promised services (no water, no garbage collection, poor maintenance). Penalties for non-payment are low and not imposed. Housing agency officials can be bribed, they are subjected to pressures from politicians.

The guarantee by government agencies of loan payments has not been observed. Collection of insurance premiums from members of provident funds and insurance systems has been inefficient. Among the three main funding agencies, only the Pag-ibig Fund has been prompt in remitting their contributions to the housing fund—the GSIS and the SSS are very slow in doing this.

**Problems with Resettlement**

HUDCC estimates that there are 432,450 squatter households in Metro Manila. Of these, 15.4% (66,334) occupy dangerous areas; 23.0% (99,175) occupy government land; 21.8% (94,490) occupy private lands; and 39.8% (172,451) occupy land marked for infrastructure development. In accordance with Republic Act 7279 (Urban Development and Housing Act), a full 55.2% of squatter households (238,785) are marked for resettlement.

Families living in dangerous areas are mostly those who have built their shanties on esteros, river banks, and frequently flooded marshy areas. Most families needing relocation, however, are those occupying land needed for infrastructure development. These include: the MRT project along EDSA (especially the North Triangle area in Quezon City), the PEA reclamation project in Paranaque, the Pasig River rehabilitation project in Pasig, and the Global City project in Tagig.

As of the end of 1997, the Government had resettled 1,050 squatter families to Montalban Heights, 856 under the Pabahay 2000 site in Bulacan, and 427 agreed to return to their provinces of origin. Other relocation sites were in Sapang Palay in

San Jose del Monte, Bulacan. Other relocation sites are being developed in Barangay Tigbi, and in nearby Bitungol in Norzagaray, Bulacan.

Families relocated to Montalban are given 40 square meters of land and P10,000 worth of building materials. A pit privy is dug and provisions for water connections are made. Roads, sewerage and drainage are supposed to be provided as well. Two garbage trucks, an ambulance and a utility van were turned over to the local government unit to service the relocation site. Three temporary school buildings with five classrooms each and five permanent school buildings were in the process of construction.

The main problems encountered by the resettled families are not related to shelter or services—it is the fact that the relocation sites require more than two hours by bus and/or jeep to Manila where most of the squatter families earn a living. There are no jobs in the relocation site except for temporary construction work. As such, breadwinners in the family have to find temporary rental accommodation in Manila and visit their families only on weekends (transportation can take up more than 10% of daily earnings). Eventually, many of the resettled families return to the inner city or suburban squatter sites because it is impossible for them to exist in the resettlement site.

## Shortage of Land for Housing

An inventory of government land available for low-cost housing in 1995 yielded an estimate of 226,375 hectares. Only about 0.7% of these (1,752 ha) were found in the Metro Manila area. Most of the idle lands were in rural areas and some of the plots were squatted upon.

In many Philippine cities, total housing costs are usually distributed as follows: cost of land, 50%; cost of dwelling structure, 30%; cost of services, 15%; and cost of design and other services, 5%. With the high proportion of land costs, availability of land is a serious constraint to social housing. Government policies to release more land for housing, such as a tax on idle lands, have not worked. The exercise of the Constitutional right of eminent domain has also been ineffective because landowners can usually delay developments through litigation. Land baking policies are needed so that the government will be able to avail of land in accordance with planned development. Care must be taken to not dispose of valuable government lands and other assets through privatization schemes just to earn enough money.

## Lack of Basic Urban Services

Most Philippine cities suffer from lack of basic urban services. In Metro Manila, for example, only 60.2% of the population (6,495,000 million out of 10,787,000) are serviced by the Metropolitan Waterworks and Sewerage System. The MWSS is able to deliver only an average of 2,700 million liters daily through 824,419 water connections, with the result that many areas lack water, especially during the summer months.

Barely 20% of Metro Manila's land area is served by sewerage systems. Only 111,382 out of Metro Manila's 2.2 million households (about 0.5%) are served by the treatment plants of the MWSS sewer system. There are only two treatment plants, one serving the Tondo foreshore upgraded area in Dagat Dagatan and the other serving the upscale Ayala subdivision in Makati. The great majority of households (about 600,000 units) use individual or communal septic tanks. The problem, however, is that the 5 desludging units used to take away raw sewage from the tanks are only partly operational and the disposal site for sludge in Marilao, Bulacan, is now closed.

In slum and squatter areas, most families rely on illegal water connections or buy drinking water by the can. Toilet facilities are usually lacking, with one pit latrine shared by as many as 20 households. Along *esteros* or rivers, people just use "overhang" toilets or wrap their waste in paper and throw it in the water. Human and animal waste is also often thrown in with the garbage or is disposed of in empty lots.

## Failure of Local Governments to Provide Housing

Although the Local Government Code of 1991 authorizes local government units to build and operate housing projects, only a few LGUs include housing in their usual functions. The City of Manila has operated some housing projects and so has Metro Cebu. Most local units, however, believe that housing is a central government function and do not have housing activities.

The heavy reliance of LGUs on internal revenue allotments (IRAs) leaves relatively meager resources for housing. Theoretically, LGUs can borrow both domestically or from the international market for housing. However, most LGUs are hesitant to do this, preferring to rely on central government agencies to supply housing for their residents.

## ABOUT THE AUTHORS

Aprodicio "Prod" and Eleanor Laquian served as personal advisers to presidential candidate Joseph Ejercito "Erap" Estrada during the Philippine 1998 elections while on leave from the Institute of Asian Research at the University of British Columbia, Vancouver. They were appointed as National Campaign Officers for Public Policies and Issues by the *Laban ng Makabayang Masang Pilipino* (LAMMP), the political party that helped Estrada win the presidency. They also served in the LAMMP Policy-Media Caucus.

The Laquians have combined international management careers in the United Nations with research, teaching and writing that have taken them to more than 80 countries all over the world. They have written more than a dozen books between them, the latest one being the controversial *The Silent Debate: Asian Immigration and Racism in Canada* (1998).

Prod has a BA in public administration, *cum laude*, from the University of the Philippines, and a Ph.D. in political science from Massachusetts Institute of Technology in Cambridge. Eleanor has a BA in journalism from Maryknoll College (where she was editor-in-chief of the *Chi Rho* and the graduation yearbook) and a Master's in public administration from the University of the Philippines. At present, Prod is professor of community and regional planning at the University of British Columbia and Eleanor is manager for administration and programs, and editor at UBC's Institute of Asian Research, Canada.